Handbook of Dialogical Self Theory and Psychotherapy

In the *Handbook of Dialogical Self Theory and Psychotherapy: Bridging Psychotherapeutic and Cultural Traditions*, the editors bring together a wide variety of therapeutic approaches to demonstrate how Dialogical Self Theory functions as a bridging framework crossing boundaries between countries and cultures.

The basic message is to facilitate a theory-informed dialogue between different perspectives: cognitive therapy, psychoanalytic therapy, gestalt therapy, emotion-focused therapy, Eastern, Indian-American and transpersonal approaches. The chapters present the theoretical notions, qualitative methods and practical implications of the presented projects with attention to their common dialogical foundation.

With its bridging approach and interdisciplinary aims, the *Handbook of Dialogical Self Theory and Psychotherapy* will be essential reading for psychotherapists and counsellors in practice and training and for those who are interested in the common factors underlying a wide variety of psychotherapeutic schools and traditions.

Agnieszka Konopka holds a PhD in the psychology of emotions, is a practising coach and therapist and author of a contemplative art-therapy/coaching method 'Compositionwork'.

Hubert J. M. Hermans is an emeritus professor of psychology at the Radboud University, The Netherlands, and creator of Dialogical Self Theory.

Miguel M. Gonçalves is a professor at the School of Psychology, University of Minho, Portugal. His main interests are research and clinical practice in dialogical and narrative perspectives.

'This book provides a tour de force of the development of dialogical theory and its contribution to psychotherapy theory, practice and research. It enables the reader to connect different therapeutic traditions and schools in a theory-guided way like no book has done before. This work launches the application of the view that the self has many voices in dynamic interaction into new territory and provides a significant contribution to the study of the self in psychotherapy.'

– **Leslie S. Greenberg**, Distinguished Research Professor
Emeritus, York University, Canada

'Dialogical Self Theory spreads its wings in this finely-honed *Handbook*, as its potential for integration and catalytic creativity stimulates dialogue across a broad spectrum of therapeutic orientations. As food for thought, this is a rich banquet indeed, as its contributors open conceptual doors and explore the implications for therapeutic practice.'

– **Kenneth J. Gergen**, author of *Relational Being:*
Beyond Individual and Community

'"How do I silence the self-critical voices in my head?" "What can I do about my vulnerable side?" The idea that human beings consist of many different "selves" is integral to a diverse array of psychotherapy and counselling practices. This unique and much-needed collection of chapters looks at how therapists can work with the "dialogical self": helping clients to overcome internal conflicts and find more cooperative, dialogical and satisfying internal relationships. Written by leading international experts in the field, the chapters provide a wealth of guidance, illustrated throughout with vivid and compelling case studies and narratives. A very valuable resource for therapists of all orientations.'

– **Mick Cooper**, Professor of Counselling Psychology,
University of Roehampton, UK

Handbook of Dialogical Self Theory and Psychotherapy

Bridging Psychotherapeutic and Cultural Traditions

Edited by Agnieszka Konopka, Hubert J. M. Hermans and Miguel M. Gonçalves

Routledge
Taylor & Francis Group

LONDON AND NEW YORK

First published 2019
by Routledge
2 Park Square, Milton Park, Abingdon, Oxon OX14 4RN

and by Routledge
52 Vanderbilt Avenue, New York, NY 10017

Routledge is an imprint of the Taylor & Francis Group, an informa business

British Library Cataloguing-in-Publication Data
A catalogue record for this book is available from the British Library

Library of Congress Cataloging-in-Publication Data
A catalog record for this title has been requested

ISBN: 978-1-138-50367-0 (hbk)
ISBN: 978-1-138-50397-7 (pbk)
ISBN: 978-1-315-14569-3 (ebk)

Typeset in Times New Roman
by Swales & Willis Ltd, Exeter, Devon, UK

To John Rowan (1925–2018),
For his invaluable contribution to Dialogical Self Theory.

Contents

PART II
Methodological innovations

PART III
Bridging cultures

Contributors

Evrinomy Avdi is an associate professor in clinical psychology at the School of Psychology of the Aristotle University of Thessaloniki, Greece. She is also a clinical psychologist, psychodynamic psychotherapist and dramatherapist. She teaches, supervises and researches in the fields of clinical psychology and psychotherapy. Her research interests lie in using qualitative approaches to studying the process of psychotherapy as well as the experience of serious illness.

Wim van Beers is a clinical psychologist with a PhD in stress management. He worked as an internal consultant for Philips from 1982 to 1987. From 1989 to 2010 he worked for Schouten & Nelissen as a consultant, manager and director. In 2010 he started his own business in management consultancy, coaching and mediation. Since 2013 he has worked together with Agnieszka Konopka in their company Compositionwork and together they have written several publications on the contemplative art-therapy/coaching method 'Compositionwork'.

Cátia Braga is a researcher who has been collaborating with the University of Minho Innovative Moment's Research Team since 2011. She finished her PhD at the University of Minho in 2017. Her research interests lie in the area of change processes in psychotherapy, specifically in ambivalence and ambivalence resolution in psychotherapy, in the context of which she has published a number of scientific papers.

Giancarlo Dimaggio, MD, is a psychiatrist and psychotherapist and a founding member of the Center for Metacognitive Interpersonal Therapy, Rome Italy. He is the author of many books, including *Metacognitive Interpersonal Therapy for Personality Disorders* (Routledge, 2015) and *Psychotherapy of Personality Disorders* (Routledge, 2007). He has co-edited *The Dialogical Self in Psychotherapy* (with Hubert J. M. Hermans, Routledge, 2004) and is the author of around 160 scientific papers. His model, Metacognitive Interpersonal Therapy, has recently received empirical support both in individual and group formats

Robert Elliott, PhD, is a professor of counselling at the University of Strathclyde. He is co-author of *Learning Emotion-Focused Therapy* (American Psychological Association, 2004), and *Research Methods in Clinical Psychology* (Wiley, 2016), plus more than 150 journal articles and book chapters. He has received the Distinguished Research Career Award from the Society for Psychotherapy Research.

Eugenie Georgaca is an associate professor in clinical psychology at the School of Psychology, Aristotle University of Thessaloniki, Greece. She teaches, researches and publishes in the fields of clinical psychology, psychotherapy and mental health, especially qualitative methodology, community mental health and critical perspectives on psychopathology.

Miguel M. Gonçalves is a professor at the School of Psychology, University of Minho, Portugal and a practising psychotherapist. His main research interests focus on the narrative and dialogical change processes in psychotherapy.

Dr Jay A. Hamm, PsyD, is a clinical psychologist practising in a community mental health setting in Indianapolis, IN, where his practice is focused on metacognitive psychotherapy for persons diagnosed with schizophrenia. Dr Hamm is active in the training of graduate psychology students and interdisciplinary mental health staff in recovery-oriented approaches to mental health services. He is author of over 30 peer-reviewed papers and two book chapters concerned with psychosis, metacognition and recovery approaches to psychotherapy.

Hubert J. M. Hermans is an emeritus professor at Radboud University, the Netherlands, and creator of Dialogical Self Theory. He is president of the International Society for Dialogical Science. His interest is focused on the self in relation to dialogue and democracy. For his scientific merits, he was awarded the decoration of Knight in the Order of the Netherlands Lion in 2002.

Agnieszka Konopka holds a PhD in the psychology of emotions, has a private practice focused on expatriates in transition, developed a contemplative, dialogical art-therapy method called 'Compositionwork' and trains practitioners internationally. She is an associate director at Portland Institute for Loss and Transition, co-founder of the International Institute for the Dialogical Self, and co-author of *Dialogical Self Theory: Positioning and Counter-Positioning in Globalizing Society* (with Hubert J. M. Hermans, Cambridge University Press, 2010).

Bethany L. Leonhardt, Psy D, HSPP is a clinical psychologist working in a first-episode psychosis community mental health centre in Indianapolis, IN. Her research and clinical work centre on recovery in serious mental illness and recovery-oriented, metacognitive approaches to psychotherapy with individuals with psychosis, with an emphasis on first episode psychosis. She is the author of over 45 peer-reviewed articles.

John T. Lysaker is chair and professor of philosophy at Emory University. His work spans philosophical psychology, the philosophy of art and ethics. Recent books include *After Emerson* (Indiana University Press, 2017) and *Philosophy, Writing, and the Character of Thought* (Chicago University Press, 2018). Along with Paul Lysaker, he is also the co-author of *Schizophrenia and the Fate of the Self* (Oxford University Press, 2008).

Paul H. Lysaker is a clinical psychologist at the Roudebush VA Medical Center and a professor of clinical psychology at the Indiana University School of Medicine. He has been involved in the formal study of recovery from psychosis for over 25 years and is the author of over 380 peer-reviewed publications. He is the author of a forthcoming volume from Routlege on individual psychotherapy for adults with serious mental illness.

Donald McCown, PhD, is an associate professor of health, co-director of the Center for Contemplative Studies and program director of the Graduate Certificate in Applied Mindfulness at West Chester University. He is primary author of *Teaching Mindfulness: A Practical Guide for Clinicians and Educators* (Springer, 2010) and primary editor of *Resources for Teaching Mindfulness: An International Handbook* (Springer, 2016).

Carina Magalhães has a master's degree in clinical and health psychology from the University of Coimbra. She has been practising clinical psychology since 2009, currently as a psychotherapist at the Psychology Association of the University of Minho, Portugal. She is also a member of the research team working on processes of change in psychotherapy at the University of Minho, Portugal.

Barbara Mainguy, MA, is a creative arts psychotherapist, affiliated with Wabanaki Health and Wellness, in Bangor, Maine, a centre for urban and commuter indigenous people from Maine and Eastern Canada. Her degrees are from the University of Toronto and Concordia University, Montreal. She is also affiliated with the School of Social Work at the University of Maine in Orono and is the education director for the Coyote Institute. She is the co-author of *Remapping Your Mind: the Neuroscience of Self-Transformation Through Story* (Simon & Schuster, 2015).

Michelle H. Mamberg, PhD, is an associate professor of psychology at Bridgewater State University, studied clinical psychology at Clark University, then became a mindfulness-based stress reduction instructor (Center for Mindfulness/UMMS). Her research interests include the dialogical and discursive constitution of self.

Claudio Martínez, PhD, is a full professor at the Faculty of Psychology, Universidad Diego Portales, Chile and director of the Center of Studies on Clinical Psychology and Psychotherapy. He is also an associate researcher of the Millenium Institute for research in Depression and Personality and clinical supervisor at the Psychiatric Institute in Santiago de Chile. He has worked in a private practice as a psychodynamic psychotherapist for over 30 years. His research interests are psychotherapy process, mentalizing in psychotherapy, subjective experiences related to suicide and other mental health problems.

Lewis Mehl-Madrona, MD, PhD, DFAPA, is an associate professor of family medicine at the University of New England, working at their Bangor Campus, where he is a faculty physician in the family medicine residency of Eastern Maine Medical Center. He is also assistant clinical professor of psychiatry at the University of Vermont. He comes from Lakota and Cherokee ancestry and is committed to bringing North American indigenous knowledge to mainstream health care. He is the executive director of the Coyote Institute in Orono, Maine, whose mission is to support indigenous health care.

Masayoshi Morioka, PhD, is a professor at Ritsumeikan University, Japan. His main field is the dialogical and narrative approach to psychotherapy and common essence in therapeutic conversations. He has published his research in a number of papers and books, including *Utsushi: Rinshō no Shigaku/Transition, Reflection, and Projection: Poetics in Clinical Practice* (Misuzushobo, 2005) and *Jungian and Dialogical Self Perspectives* (with R. A. Jones, Palgrave Macmillan, 2011).

Robert A. Neimeyer, PhD, is a professor of psychology at the University of Memphis, where he maintains an active clinical practice. He also directs the Portland Institute for Loss and Transition. He has published 30 books, including the Routledge series Techniques of Grief Therapy, and serves as editor of the journal *Death Studies*. He is the author of nearly 500 articles and book chapters and a frequent workshop presenter. He is currently working to advance a more adequate theory of grieving as a meaning-making process.

João Tiago Oliveira has an MSc in clinical psychology and is a PhD student of the doctoral program in applied psychology at the School of Psychology of University of Minho, Portugal. His PhD studies focus on ambivalence in psychotherapy and feedback interventions. He is also a therapist at the Clinical and Health Psychology Unit of the School of Psychology at the University of Minho, Portugal.

Paolo Ottavi is a clinical psychologist and CBT therapist, MIT (metacognitive interpersonal therapy) therapist, mindfulness teacher and EMDR practitioner. His primary field of interest is the psychotherapy of personality disorders and psychosis. He created the Metacognitive Interpersonal Mindfulness-Based Training (MIMBT) for patients with personality disorders and the Metacognition-Oriented Social Skills Training (MOSST) for patients with schizophrenia.

Raffaele Popolo is psychiatrist, psychotherapist, co-founding member of the Center for Metacognitive Interpersonal Therapy and a trainer at the Società Italiana di Terapia Comportamentale e Cognitiva (SITCC). He is interested in the therapeutic process of the treatment of psychoses and personality disorders. He is the author of six books and numerous articles.

António P. Ribeiro is a post-doctoral researcher at the School of Psychology, University of Minho, Portugal. His main research interest focuses on ambivalence in psychotherapy. Over the past years he has conducted research in ambivalence, studying this process from a narrative-dialogical perspective in different therapeutic models.

Catarina Rosa is a postdoctoral fellow at the University of Aveiro, integrated member of the Center for Health Technology and Services Research (CINTESIS) and collaborative member of the Psychology Research Center (CIPsi), University of Minho, Portugal. Her research interests, emerging from her clinical practice are self-system organization strategies that underlie psychological functionality, relations between therapeutic alliance and therapeutic outcome and the development of intervention strategies to reduce rumination.

John Rowan, PhD., is the author of some 20 books, including *Ordinary Ecstasy: The Dialectics of Humanistic Psychology* (Routledge, 2015), *The Future of Training in Psychotherapy and Counselling* (Routledge, 2005), *The Transpersonal: Spirituality in Psychotherapy and Counselling* (Routledge, 1993), *Personification: Using the Dialogical Self in Psychotherapy and Counselling* (Routledge, 2010) and *The Plural Self: Multiplicity in Everyday Life* (co-edited with Mick Cooper, Sage, 1999). He has led presentations and workshops in 25 countries.

Giampaolo Salvatore is a co-founding member of the Center for Metacognitive Interpersonal Therapy and a trainer at the School of Psychotherapy 'Humanitas' in Rome. He has written papers about the psychotherapeutic process and the pathology and treatment of schizophrenia and personality disorders, and in particular about persons with paranoid features.

Joana R. Silva, PhD, is a clinical psychologist and an assistant professor at the Department of Psychology and Education, Portucalense University, Portugal. In the last few years she has been developing her post-doctoral studies in psychotherapy process research into the Innovative Moments research program at the Psychology Research Center of the School of Psychology, University of Minho, Portugal. She has authored several articles and chapters on attachment, developmental psychopathology and more recently on psychotherapy process research.

Frank-M. Staemmler, PhD, has worked as a psychologist, gestalt therapist and teacher since 1976. He has written numerous articles, book chapters and many books, among them *Empathy in Psychotherapy* (Springer, 2011). He was editor of the *International Gestalt Journal* from 2001 to 2006.

William B. Stiles is an emeritus professor of psychology at Miami University, Oxford, USA, and adjunct professor of psychology at Appalachian State University, Boone, USA. He has been president of the Society for Psychotherapy Research and of Division 29 of the American Psychological Association and has served as editor of the journals *Psychotherapy Research* and *Person-Centered and Experiential Psychotherapies*. He has published more than 300 journal articles and book chapters, most dealing with psychotherapy, verbal interaction, and research methods.

Alemka Tomicic, PhD, is a researcher on clinical psychology and psychotherapy and an associate professor at the Faculty of Psychology, Universidad Diego Portales, Chile. She co-directs the Center of Studies on Clinical Psychology and

Psychotherapy and is associate researcher of the Millennium Institute for Research in Depression and Personality. Her research interests are psychotherapy effectiveness, psychotherapeutic interactions, subjective experiences related to psychological problems and social and cultural determinants of health.

William J. Whelton is a professor of counselling psychology at the University of Alberta, Canada, where he has taught emotion-focused therapy, relational Gestalt therapy and the history of psychology. His interest in the self has involved studying the dialectical-constructivist model of the construction of meaning. He has done research on self-criticism and self-compassion and their roles in psychotherapy.

Acknowledgements

We thank Robert Neimeyer for his thoughtful remarks, Jeannette Maingot for her careful language advice, Wim van Beers for his supportive feedback, Joanne Forshaw for her support and encouraging advice and Charlotte Taylor for her considerate editorial assistance.

1   Introduction

Miguel M. Gonçalves, Agnieszka Konopka, and
Hubert J. M. Hermans

The contemporary literature on psychotherapy research and practice is immense, raising the relevant question, "What is the added value of another Handbook?" Or putting it more specifically, what is the value of Dialogical Self Theory (DST) to psychotherapy theory, research and practice?

We would like to start by emphasizing two central findings from psychotherapy research that are – after several decades and thousands of studies – becoming relatively consensual (Lambert, 2013): psychotherapy is effective and relational aspects are central in the outcomes. The majority of meta-analyses conducted since the pioneering work of Smith and Glass (1977) support the idea that psychotherapy is an effective practice, and that it compares favorably in its efficacy with the majority of medical interventions (Wampold & Imel, 2015). Of course, there is a great deal of variability in outcome as a function of diagnosis (e.g. Cuijpers et al., 2013; Kliem, Kröger, & Kosfelder, 2010); as well other relevant variables (mainly those related to the clients, Bohart & Wade, 2013; and therapists, Baldwin & Imel, 2013), but as a whole psychotherapy works. Why and how it works is of course a matter of dispute, and the long debate continues on whether it is the specific factors (e.g. therapeutic techniques), or the common factors (e.g. relational factors) that are more relevant to change (Tolin, 2014; Wampold & Imel, 2015). Independent of these positions, advocates on both sides of the dispute agree that relational factors (see also Staemmler, Chapter 3 this volume) are central to psychotherapeutic outcomes. They may be conceived as central in themselves, as a form of "re-moralizing" the client (Frank & Frank, 1993), or even as a corrective relational experience (Castonguay & Hill, 2012). Or they may be primarily conceived as facilitators to implement the strategies or techniques (i.e. specific factors) of change that lead to good outcomes (see for instance how traditional cognitive therapy sees the relation between alliance and outcome, as in Beck, Rush, Shaw, & Emery, 1979). Independently of the preferable positions of theorists, meta-analytic findings suggest that relational factors have a medium, but robust effect on the outcome. For instance, the correlation between therapeutic alliance and outcome is 0.28 (Flückiger, Del Re, Wampold, Symonds, & Horvath, 2012), empathy is 0.31 (Elliott, Bohart, Watson, & Greenberg, 2011), and goal consensus is 0.34 (Tryon & Winograd, 2011), just to give some examples of relational conditions (Norcross, 2002).

So, taking these two ideas into consideration (i.e. psychotherapy is efficacious and relational factors are central to change), and coming back to the question posed at the outset, what has DST to offer to the field? DST emerged from the field of personality psychology and the study of the self (Hermans & Kempen, 1993) and suggested that the self might be better conceived not as a single entity with a true core but as a multifaceted structure, constituted by a diversity of positions that could be endowed with a voice and encouraged to narrate their own stories. The self had already been conceived as multifaceted by different theorists (e.g. Higgins, 1989; Markus & Nurius, 1986), but this was the first time that a theory of the self proposed that what we feel as our *self* was an intricate and dynamic result of our internal dialogues, resulting from our multiple positions (termed *I*-positions). Thus, inside the self we find multiple *I*-positions, which, when voiced, are able to become narrators, creating different perspectives on reality (see Rowan, Chapter 6 this volume).

Moreover, DST suggests that the relations inside our selves and their dynamics (e.g. agreement, disagreement, coalition) are similar to what takes place in interpersonal relations (Konopka, Hermans, & Gonçalves, Chapter 2 this volume). This allowed DST to expand its borders to other domains, such as development processes (Bertau, Gonçalves, & Raggatt, 2012), the cultural realm (Chaudhary, 2012; Van Meijl, 2012), and even the political domain (Hermans, 2018). Self and culture are different units of analysis, but the processes involved in each unit are similar from a DST perspective. For instance, the clash of two different cultural or political perspectives is not very different in terms of its dynamics from what we can observe inside the self between a self-critical position and a criticized one. To make sense of these dynamics, DST assumes the existence of internal *I*-positions (I as worried person), external *I*-positions (my mother in me), and even collective ones (I as Polish person) (Krotofil, 2013). To be clear, *I*-positions are not to be understood as explicit, merely cognitive or verbal positions as they may also be implicit and emerging from the body, standing at the edge of awareness (see Konopka & van Beers, Chapter 13 this volume). To sum up, the repertoire of relevant positions, as well their dynamic processes are of high relevance to understanding the self's stability and change. Some *I*-positions are more central, others are more peripheral; some are more cognitive, others more emotional or somatic; some are hierarchically higher (and thus implicating a lot of different, but related *I*-positions), others are more narrow in their impact, and so on. Importantly, in the dynamic of *I*-positions some are able to stand above the ordinary flux of communication and operate as meta-positions, facilitating the articulation of conflicts or mediating difficulties of understanding in the relationship between different *I*-positions (see also the concept of meaning bridge, Stiles, Chapter 5 this volume). These meta-positions are able to organize the interaction, much as an external mediator is able to do in interpersonal conversations. One important therapeutic task, from the perspective of DST, is the forming of meta-positions, and this is closely related with decentering processes (Dimaggio, Hermans, & Lysaker, 2010), a central therapeutic process emphasized in more recent cognitive-behavioral theories such as acceptance and commitment therapy (Hayes, Strosahl, & Wilson, 1999), metacognitive therapy (Wells & Simons, 2009) or mindfulness approaches (Germer, Siegel, & Fulton, 2016; see also Mamberg & McCown, Chapter 16 this volume).

From its origins psychotherapy has been dealing with the problem of multiplicity, at least since Freud's conception of the psychological apparatus divided into the id, ego, and superego. Other models of therapy, despite conceptualizing the self differently, still have had to deal with inner divisions and conflicts. As a further evolution of traditional psychodynamic therapy, object relations theories (Kernberg, 1994) look at the self as largely the result of earlier relationships. Humanistic models (Rogers, 1966) focus their attention on inner incongruence between the "self" as conceived and experienced, or on conflicts between the self and an internal critic (see Whelton and Elliott, Chapter 4 this volume) that may reflect outer conflicts between caregivers and the client. And cognitive therapists focus on tensions between dysfunctional thoughts and more adaptive ones. Furthermore, as elaborated by schema therapy (Young, Klosko, & Weishaar, 2003) but also clearly present in original cognitive formulations (Beck et al., 1979), these dysfunctional thoughts are viewed as dependent on schemas with their own developmental story, with a considerable impact of earlier experiences. These examples illustrate how the recognition of relational foundations to our clients' suffering characterizes a broad range of psychotherapeutic models.

Not only the self but also therapeutic relationship can be understood in DST terms as a dynamic relation between internal and external positions. A therapist can act as an external *I*-position in the domain of the client's self. Not only the physical, direct presence of the other but also the mental presence of the other can have an influence on the self (Neimeyer & Konopka, Chapter 8 this volume). Moreover an empathic therapist as an external *I*-position optimally functions as an external promoter position, which can initiate the development of an internal promoter position, in essence becoming an internal voice that encourages the client's ongoing development. Such a position, in turn, can act as a promoter position helping to accept and allow a variety of other *I*-positions as well as stimulate openness towards one's emotions and needs, ultimately facilitating self-direction and self-change.

Thus, as we suggested above, psychotherapy could be seen as primarily a relational practice, as the majority of issues that the psychotherapist needs to address are explicitly or at least implicitly relational in themselves. Our original question therefore can be restated as "How does DST conceptualize the self and relationships in innovative ways that serve as a *bridging theory* spanning a diversity of psychotherapeutic theories, each with its own language and practices" (Hermans & Gieser, 2012; Whelton & Elliott, Chapter 4 this volume). Moreover, DST has the ability to shed light on our conceptualization of relational processes at both an intra- and inter-individual level. For instance, several dialogical researchers (Lysaker & Lysaker, 2002) have studied major dialogical dysfunctions that clients may suffer, beyond their formal diagnoses (see Dimaggio, Ottavi, Popolo, & Salvatore, Chapter 10 this volume; Lysaker, Hamm,

Leonhardt, & Lysaker, Chapter 7 this volume). In clinical practice, we often observe situations in which some *I*-positions are dominating others, leaving them "un-voiced," reducing the complexity of the self and turning it more rigid in its adjustment to a variety of situations. If in very different situations a voice that states "you are useless" dominates the self, we may expect that suffering would be intense and that other dominated and silenced voices are kept in the background, unable to assert themselves (see also the Assimilation Model for a similar conceptualization, Stiles et al., 1990). On the other hand, if there is a high diversity of *I*-positions, but the articulation (i.e. the dialogue) between them is reduced, we may have what Lysaker and Lysaker (2002) termed a cacophonous self. A therapist interviewing a client with the first dysfunction – i.e. a highly dominant position excluding alternative others – may feel that the same old story (Angus et al., 2017) keeps repeating itself, while a therapist interviewing a client with the second dysfunction – i.e. cacophonous self – could feel completely at a loss, unable to grasp the meaning that the client is attempting to convey. In this last case, the narratives told may be fragmented and interrupted, as if it were voiced by different narrators (i.e. different *I*-positions) in a fragmented dialogue. Or even worse, as it often occurs in clinical practice, we may have a hard time accessing narratives of life, and the only thing that we can hear is a fragmented speech (or in other instances a very abstract discourse devoid of vitality).

Obviously, dialogical dysfunction is only one possible domain of concern for DST theorists, as its understanding could be highly important for practitioners dealing with these difficulties. Many other similar domains could be the focus of DST theorists and researchers.

We further propose that DST can be useful at the level of research, especially of a process or process-outcome variety. By providing a rich theoretical map of intrapersonal and interpersonal processes, DST facilitates the understanding of self stability and self change, as well how therapists can foster or hinder change. This Handbook contains several examples of tools supporting a highly dynamic psychotherapy processes (see Georgaca & Avdi, Chapter 11; Gonçalves et al., Chapter 9; Martínez & Tomicic, Chapter 12). We are just beginning this journey, but the development of these and other creative and rigorous tools promises to boost our understanding of the processes involved in therapeutic change.

This Handbook addresses these issues from multiple perspectives (e.g. psychodynamic, constructivist, humanistic), targeting such diverse topics as ambivalence (Gonçalves et al., Chapter 9), grief (Neimeyer & Konopka, Chapter 8), personality disorders (Dimaggio et al., Chapter 10), psychosis (Lysaker et al., Chapter 7), and non-clinical populations (Staemmler, Chapter 3). The bridging nature of DST is further reflected by its potential for crossing cultural boundaries as exemplified by contributions from Native-American culture (Mehl-Madrona & Mainguy, Chapter 15) and from Japanese culture (Morioka, Chapter 14). We hope that it may open a path, not to a new "school" of psychotherapy, but to a new bridge between theories of psychotherapy, contributing to the development of a dialogically informed theory, research, and practice. Finally, honoring our multiple selves, we intended from the outset that this Handbook would be a truly international project, involving therapists from different backgrounds and cultures.

This Handbook is organized in three parts. Part I addresses theoretical extensions that are especially relevant for clinical practice; Part II deals with methodological innovations of therapeutic practices, and Part III demonstrates how DST crosses the boundaries of different cultures.

References

Angus, L. E., Boritz, T., Bryntwick, E., Carpenter, N., Macaulay, C., & Khattra, J. (2017). The Narrative-Emotion Process Coding System 2.0: A multi-methodological approach to identifying and assessing narrative-emotion process markers in psychotherapy. *Psychotherapy Research, 27*(3), 253–269.

Baldwin, S. A., & Imel, Z. E. (2013). Therapist effects: Findings and methods. In M. Lambert (Ed.), *Bergin and Garfield's handbook of psychotherapy and behavior change* (6th ed., pp. 258–297). Hoboken, NJ: John Wiley & Sons.

Beck, A. T., Rush, A. J., Shaw, B. F., & Emery, G. (Eds.) (1979). *Cognitive therapy of depression*. New York: Guilford Press.

Bertau, M.-C., Gonçalves, M. M., & Raggatt, P. (2012). *Dialogic formations: Investigations into the origins and development of the dialogical self*. Charlotte, NC: Information Age Publishing.

Bohart, A. C., & Wade, A. G. (2013). The client in psychotherapy. In *Bergin and Garfield's handbook of psychotherapy and behavior change* (6th ed., pp. 219–257). Hoboken, NJ: John Wiley & Sons.

Castonguay, L. G., & Hill, C. E. (Eds.). (2012). *Transformation in psychotherapy: Corrective experiences across cognitive behavioral, humanistic, and psychodynamic approaches*. Washington, DC: American Psychological Association.

Chaudhary, N. (2012). Negotiating with autonomy and relatedness: Dialogical processes in everyday lives of Indians. In H. J. M. Hermans & T. Gieser (Eds.), *Handbook of dialogical self theory* (pp. 169–184). Cambridge, UK: Cambridge University Press.

Cuijpers, P., Sijbrandij, M., Koole, S. L., Andersson, G., Beekman, A. T., & Reynolds, C. F. (2013). The efficacy of psychotherapy and pharmacotherapy in treating depressive and anxiety disorders: A meta-analysis of direct comparisons. *World Psychiatry, 12*(2), 137–148.

Dimaggio, G., Hermans, H. J. M., & Lysaker, P. H. (2010). Health and adaptation in a multiple self. *Theory & Psychology, 20*, 379–399.

Elliott, R., Bohart, A. C., Watson, J. C., & Greenberg, L. S. (2011). Empathy. *Psychotherapy, 48*(1), 43–49.

Flückiger, C., Del Re, A. C., Wampold, B. E., Symonds, D., & Horvath, A. O. (2012). How central is the alliance in psychotherapy? A multilevel longitudinal meta-analysis. *Journal of Counseling Psychology, 59*(1), 10–17.

Frank, J. D., & Frank, J. B. (1993). *Persuasion and healing: A comparative study of psychotherapy*. Baltimore, MD: Johns Hopkins University Press.

Germer, C., Siegel, R. D., & Fulton, P. R. (Eds.). (2016). *Mindfulness and psychotherapy*. New York: Guilford Press.

Hayes, S. C., Strosahl, K. D., & Wilson, K. G. (1999). *Acceptance and commitment therapy: An experiential approach to behavior change*. New York: Guilford Press.

Hermans, H. J. M. (2018). *Society in the self: A theory of identity in democracy.* New York: Oxford University Press.

Hermans, H. J. M., & Gieser, T. (2012). Introductory chapter: History, main tenets, and core concepts of dialogical self theory. In H. J. M. Hermans & T. Gieser (Eds.), *Handbook of dialogical self theory* (pp. 1–22). Cambridge, UK: Cambridge University Press.

Hermans, H. J. M., & Kempen, H. J. G. (1993). *The dialogical self: Meaning as movement.* San Diego, CA: Academic Press.

Higgins, E. T. (1989). Self-discrepancy theory: What patterns of self-beliefs cause people to suffer? *Advances in Experimental Social Psychology, 22,* 93–136.

Kernberg, O. F. (1994). *Internal world and external reality: Object relations theory applied.* Lanham, MD: Jason Aronson.

Kliem, S., Kröger, C., & Kosfelder, J. (2010). Dialectical behavior therapy for borderline personality disorder: A meta-analysis using mixed-effects modeling. *Journal of Consulting and Clinical Psychology, 78*(6), 936–951.

Krotofil, J. M. (2013). Religion, migration, and the dialogical self: New application of the personal position repertoire method. *Journal of Constructivist Psychology, 26,* 90–103.

Lambert, M. J. (Ed.). (2013). *Bergin and Garfield's handbook of psychotherapy and behavior change* (6th ed.). Hoboken, NJ: John Wiley & Sons.

Lysaker, P. H., & Lysaker, J. T. (2002). Narrative structure in psychosis schizophrenia and disruptions in the dialogical self. *Theory & Psychology, 12*(2), 207–220.

Markus, H., & Nurius, P. (1986). Possible selves. *American Psychologist, 41*(9), 954.

Norcross, J. C. (Ed.). (2002). *Psychotherapy relationships that work: Therapist contributions and responsiveness to patients.* New York: Oxford University Press.

Rogers, C. R. (1966). *Client-centered therapy.* Washington, DC: American Psychological Association.

Smith, M. L., & Glass, G. V. (1977). Meta-analysis of psychotherapy outcome studies. *American Psychologist, 32*(9), 752–761.

Stiles, W. B., Elliott, R., Llewelyn, S. P., Firth-Cozens, J. A., Margison, F. R., Shapiro, D. A., & Hardy, G. (1990). Assimilation of problematic experiences by clients in psychotherapy. *Psychotherapy, 27*(3), 411–420.

Tolin, D. F. (2014). Beating a dead dodo bird: Looking at signal vs. noise in cognitive-behavioral therapy for anxiety disorders. *Clinical Psychology: Science and Practice, 21*(4), 351–362.

Tryon, G. S., & Winograd, G. (2011). Goal consensus and collaboration. *Psychotherapy, 48*(1), 50–57.

Van Meijl, T. (2012). Multiculturalism, multiple identifications and the dialogical self: Shifting paradigms of personhood in socialcultural anthrolology. In H. J. M. Hermans &. T. Gieser (Eds.), *Handbook of dialogical self theory* (pp. 98–114). Cambridge, UK: Cambridge University Press.

Wampold, B. E., & Imel, Z. E. (2015). *The great psychotherapy debate: The evidence for what makes psychotherapy work.* New York: Routledge.

Wells, A., & Simons, M. (2009). *Metacognitive therapy.* Hoboken, NJ: John Wiley & Sons.

Young, J. E., Klosko, J. S., & Weishaar, M. E. (2003). *Schema therapy: A practitioner's guide.* New York: Guilford Press.

Part I
Theoretical extensions

2 The dialogical self as a landscape of mind populated by a society of *I*-positions

Agnieszka Konopka, Hubert J. M. Hermans, and Miguel M. Gonçalves

The dialogical self has been described as a landscape of mind inhabited by a multiplicity of *I*-positions (Hermans, 2001). *I*-positions are understood as characters or parts of the self that are distinguishable and often divergent or even contradictory. *I*-positions represent a society of mind in which, like in regular society, a variety of positions enter into dialogical interactions with each other. There are many possible relations between *I*-positions, from self-love and self-compassion to self-conflicts and self-devaluation, as there are many forms of self-organization, with authoritarian or democratic forms of organization as particularly significant ones. *I*-positions are more or less powerful in the organization of the self and in different degrees influence the whole community of the self. The metaphor of landscape of mind reflects the spatial, multidimensional character of the self, picturing its depth and breadth, as well as the potential accessibility of the different areas in one's inner world.

In the context of these two metaphors, i.e. society of mind and landscape of mind, change in therapy can be seen as a reorganization of this society, directed towards a more free, dialogical, and democratic community of mind. It can be seen as a change of the mind's landscape from a frozen or limited space to a more open and lively process. These reorganizations can be characterized as an increase of dialogicality and freedom as opposed to living in a limited, isolated space of one's self, called an *I*-prison. The above developments are facilitated by the therapeutic relation, a dialogical space emerging between client and therapist, which creates a fertile and facilitating environment for the therapeutic process as a whole.

Positioning, counter-positioning, and repositioning

In Dialogical Self Theory (DST), the *self* is *multiple*. A person potentially has many facets (*I*-positions) from which he or she can face the other, himself, or herself. Positioning is *placing* oneself to the other or to oneself. "*I*-position is a spatial-relational act" (Hermans, 2018, p. xvii). When a person positions herself, there are always other positions involved – explicitly or implicitly – which function as counter-positions (Hermans & Hermans-Konopka, 2010). I can position myself toward a part of myself, or even towards my own emotion, towards an imagined other in myself or towards a real other. I may reach out to an imagined other in my mind or take a distance; I am critical towards myself or I am accepting myself and embracing my weaknesses. This is not only about the place I take in the "space" but also *how* I take it.

It is important to note that an *I*-position is not a trait or a thing. It is a dynamic process of positioning, counter-positioning, and repositioning. It is not an abstract, cognitive act but rather an embodied relational act that takes place within the self and between selves. A person can potentially relate to the same issue, problem, or aspect of himself from one position or from a variety of different positions and in this way create the opportunity to perceive a problem from more than one perspective. This can also be a source of ambivalence. According to Ribeiro et al. (2014) ambivalence that appears in psychotherapy can be seen as a cyclical movement between two opposing parts of the self *(I*-positions): the part that favors change and another one that opposes change.

Internal versus external positions

We distinguish between *internal* and *external I-positions*. Internal positions are aspects of one's self, like e.g. "I as competent," "I as artist," while external positions are voices of others, e.g. "my critical mother" or even metaphorical voices of imagined or imaginary figures, like "my idealized lover" or "my spirit." I can position myself not only in my internal positions, but I can also take the (external) position of my critical mother or accepting friend towards myself. This can have very different consequences. For instance, positioning myself as a competent person (activating this internal position) is very different from speaking to myself with my mother's critical voice (and probably feeling it as my own voice).

While the voices of significant others in the self have the potential to create problems when they are critical or destructive, the activation of supporting external positions may have advantages for the self. Working with external positions in therapy allows relating to people that are actually present in one's real life or even deceased ones. Including the voices of deceased ones creates an opportunity to work on relations with unresolved problems and even to reestablish a new bond (one of the purposes of grief therapy; Neimeyer, 2012). Moreover, introducing external *I*-positions enables working on unfinished business with significant others as well as activating growth promoting resources related to others, including imagined or fantasy figures.

Contextual nature and bandwidth of *I*-positions

Positions have a *contextual character* (Hermans, 2001), which means that in different relations different positions are coming to the fore and in different degrees. People are different versions of themselves in different relations. In one relation a person can easily position herself as playful while in another relation as controlled or anxious. Probably the most dialogical and therapeutic relations are those in which one is able to show also those faces that are usually covered and hidden so that one can feel accepted with these difficult or rejected aspects of one's self. When two or more people are involved in a good dialogue, they feel the emergence of a common space in which they feel respected as dialogical partners and feel the freedom to express their views and experiences. The "*bandwidth*" of such a space is broad and a diversity of positions can receive a voice (Hermans & Gieser, 2012). An effective therapeutic relationship allows a broad bandwidth of positions, creating a relational space that can hold and allow a variety of voices to be acknowledged, heard, and involved in a dialogue.

I-position is a *flexible* concept allowing the broadening of the bandwidth of one's repertoire of personal resources. Every form emerging in the landscape that has some personal or social significance can potentially become an I-position by being voiced. In this way it can be further explored, encountered, and enter into dialogical relations with other positions. Just as I-positions in their most known forms like "I as a man" or "I as mother" can be a part of the society that inhabits the landscape of mind, so can positions that emerge from direct embodied experience like e.g. "forest in my belly" or a "mosaic in my head" be treated as I-positions, giving them voice, and initiating dialogue with them, exploring their unique qualities and history. A dark feeling in the belly that one of our clients calls an "ugly frozen frog" can become an I-position and tell its own story. It enters into a dialogue and after being heard, it can become relaxed and melting. Important different aspects of a dream can be personified, placed on two chairs, and invited to enter into a dialogue. A character from a favorite story can be invited as an I-position and enter into a dialogue with an internal position of the client; for example, I as anxious. Moreover, as Rowan (2009) suggests, work with I-positions allows working on many levels, including the transpersonal, when positions as God, Buddha or soul can receive a place in a client's landscape and sometimes make his or her wisdom and resilience accessible.

Society of mind

> The judge who sits over the murderer and looks into his face, and at one moment recognizes all the emotions and potentialities of the murderer in his own soul and hears the murderer's voice as his own, is at the next moment one and indivisible as the judge, and scuttles back into the shell of his cultivated self and does his duty and condemns the murderer to death.
>
> (Hesse, 1963, p. 71)

I-positions are not collections of unrelated parts or processes, but rather interact with each other in a way similar to how people relate in society, a group, or a family. The quality of their relations determines the functioning and organization of the self. I-positions, like members of a society, can entertain a variety of relations, such as conflicts, wars, or cooperation. Some positions can create coalitions and support each other. For example, the position of "I as spiritual" can create a coalition with "I as professional" so that a deep meaningful ideal or spiritual value is realized via professional work. In some cases, transforming a conflict into a coalition can become an important therapeutic task. Such processes can be supported by introducing a *third position* that can encompass and integrate two different or even conflicting positions (Hermans & Hermans-Konopka, 2010). An example of use of a third position can be "I as an artist," which integrates "I as enjoyer of life," and "I as a hard-working professional."

Personal and social positions

Another relevant distinction can be made between personal and social positions. *Personal positions* are expressions of personal preferences, needs, and character-istics, e.g. "I as dreamer," "I as anxious." *Social positions* are those that are more defined by social and cultural rules. They can be, for example, "I as manager," "I as mother," "I as therapist." Such distinctions may be relevant in therapy when we need to differentiate between personal and social aspects that play a role in the self, as well as between personal voices and voices of others that are active in one's self.

The combination of personal and social positions reveals how a person is giving form to the role he or she is playing in society. Saying that somebody is a "teacher" is giving only superficial information about the way this person is doing her job. We know more when somebody is defining herself as an "inspiring teacher," or as a "teacher with a sense of humor," or as a "supportive teacher." Typically, social positions, such as teacher, mother, professional, employer or employee, and other roles defined by social expectations and prescriptions, receive their characteristic expression by their coalition with one or more personal positions.

From a psychotherapeutic perspective, a fit or misfit between personal and social positions is particularly salient. When a catholic priest falls in love with a woman, his personal position of "being in love," and certainly its public expression, contradicts the public expectations of his social environment. When the priest feels increasingly alienated from his celibate status, and perhaps from his position of being a priest as a whole, there emerges an irreconcilable conflict between his social and personal positions that may end in his exit from the Church. Thus, there can be situations in which a misfit between social and personal positions exists or emerges to such a degree that they may induce important turning points in people's lives. Exploration of the extent of fit or misfit allows therapist and client to explore conflicts between one's societal position and personal inclinations.

Promoter positions and their role in the self

From a DST perspective, *promoter positions* play a central role in the organiza-tion of the society of mind (Hermans, 2006; Valsiner, 2004). They act as supporters and facilitators for the development of the self. Promoters are those positions that operate as innovators, imply a considerable openness towards the future, and have the capacity of organizing and producing a diverse range of more specialized positions. They give a sense of direction to the self and in this way provide a "compass function" (Hermans, Konopka, Oosterwegel, & Zomer, 2017). There can be many different promoter positions, both internal as well as external ones. External promoters are those people who help us to embrace a variety of sides of ourselves, often including those that were neglected or marginalized. Internal promoters are those aspects of the self that help to integrate a variety of different *I*-positions and add to the sense of a meaningful direction in life, for example, I as compassionate or I as creative. A promoter position stimulates a more complete sense of the self, which, as in a Tibetan mandala, requires allowing not only the positive and strong aspects of ourselves, but also the dark ones, which in DST terms, are called shadow *I*-positions. Promoter positions are often sources of development and healing, which people may not be aware of. They may need to be discovered and cultivated in psychotherapy. A psychotherapist optimally acts as an external promoter position in the self of a client, who stimulates the development of other internal and external promoters. For example, an empathic attitude towards a client can lead to the development of self-empathy and self-compassion. The therapist can also stimulate a client to discover and develop relations with other external and internal positions that have promoter functions.

Landscape of mind

> One always sooner or later, comes upon a city which is an image of one's inner cities. Fez is an image of my inner self. This may explain my fascination for it.
>
> (Nin, 2014, p. 74)

Landscape of mind (Hermans, 2001) is a metaphor that pictures the self as a spatially organized multiplicity of *I*-positions involved in mutual interchange. Some *I*-positions can be more central, visible and accessible, while others are hidden or not accessible at all. Positions are dynamic processes of positioning in the space of the extended self, including distance, centrality, and movement. The self can be seen as a spatial dynamic whole in which *I*-positions are composed and recomposed in the mind space. The spatial metaphor invites thinking about processes that are happening in the self in a simultaneous rather than a sequential way. It helps to understand interconnections between aspects of the mind landscape and allows seeing them in a broader context.

Horizontal versus vertical movements in the self

As Guttenplan (2000) argues, the advantage of the landscape metaphor is that it allows not only horizontal but also vertical investigation of the mind. On exploring the landscape of mind at first you can see the surface of the self, analogous to a map with its seas and continents. In order to understand why it looks this way, you may need to gain insight into the layers that lie under the surface, enter the underground that forms the shape of the terrain. If you move further in this "geological adventure," "you may discover how the whole land-scape is supported on the deepest layers, on the tectonic plates of the bedrock" (Guttenplan, 2000, p. 2). *I*-positions are not only horizontally (e.g. opposed to each other), but also vertically organized, and the positions on the surface can be influenced by deeper, not immediately accessible, positions that may be, for example, sources of resistance that need to be addressed in psychotherapy.

Landscape of mind offers a *metaphorical language* for capturing the richness of personal experience, as expressed in images of a volcano, a sea, a swamp, heaven, or hell as well as an imaginary flora and fauna. These metaphors allow transcending the linear and logical language and relate to the dimensions of the self that go beyond the verbal, or as Huxley (2014) portrays it, they reach the antipodes of mind that are outside the system of conceptual thought.

Otherness in the self

The geographical metaphors also express the essential otherness of the mind's continents, and the relative autonomy of their inhabitants (Huxley, 1956), which in DST is not seen as a sign of dysfunction but an expression of dialogicality and differences within the self. *I*-positions may significantly differ from each other and have their relatively autonomous perspectives. Self-otherness points to a state when we can experience "elements of our own being as mysterious, enigmatic and transcendent to our 'self,' just as we can experience the being of another person" (Hermans & Hermans-Konopka, 2010). Like a landscape, the self can have its mysteries, hidden treasures, or even unknown exotic lands. *Self-otherness* (Cooper & Hermans, 2007; Hermans & Hermans-Konopka, 2010) acknowledges difference and diversity in the self, including those aspects that are felt as strange, not known, or even "not mine." Self-otherness can also be an outcome of internalization. Parts of the self-landscape that originally belong to somebody else became internalized (Hermans, 2001), or in terms of psycho-analytic or Gestalt theory, introjected (Perls, Hefferline, & Goodman, 1951).

Dialogical self in psychotherapy

For psychotherapy it is imperative to acknowledge that spatially located *I*-positions are *living dynamic processes rather than entities*. Let's think about a natural landscape as part of a living process. Seasons are changing and the atmosphere of the landscape is changing dynamically from day to day or even from moment to moment. Sometimes it is nostalgic and foggy, at other times the sun brings such optimistic and sparkling energy that you feel its light as joy in your heart. This landscape is varied and alive. Imagine another landscape, an industrial terrain with many buildings that have been designed and located a hundred years ago. Over time it has not changed very much but become older and more desolate. Sometimes it feels oppressive to be inside the building and one may want to escape. It is a limited space and one has no view outside its walls. One lives in an *I*-prison.

The first described landscape is a living, changing process. It is characterized by naturalness and spontaneity. Positions that appear in this landscape are dynamic processes that come and go. They interact with each other and the landscape is open. The second landscape is fabricated and not flexible and can be called a landscape of artificial structure. It lacks freshness and openness and its space is limited and enclosed. It serves as a metaphor for an *I*-prison in the form of a reified self, centered around a fixed and rigid concept (e.g., I am not worthy). It is defined by a rigid and dominant narrative, rather than based on the interactive experiential process in which a variety of different positions can emerge and dissolve.

Therapeutic change from the perspective of the dialogical self can be seen as moving from a limited inner space (*I*-prison) towards a living, open, and varied landscape of mind. It is a movement from a frozen landscape to a fluid one, from a self as a reified thing to a self as a living process (Mamberg & Bassarear, 2015), from identifying with a rigid narrative towards one that is open to new experiences (Gonçalves & Ribeiro, 2012). It can also be described as a movement from a totalitarian state dominated by one powerful *I*-position, a self structure dominated by rigid non-evolving monologues or cacophony (Lysaker & Lysaker, 2002) to a more dialogical and democratic organization of the self (Hermans, 2018; Hermans et al., 2017).

This change represents a movement from a limited experiential space that, as in in schizophrenia, can be experienced as barren, desolated, and emotionally dead (Lysaker & Lysaker, 2002) to a more varied space marked by a greater emotional richness. Such greater emotional range can be described according to Hermans as a "health promoting emodiversity" (Hermans, 2018) that is characterized by more differentiation *within* the domains of both positive emotions and negative emotions, where also negative emotions, including their differentiations, receive their place and value.

Landscape, or "landscaping" as a process, is defined by flexible movement of *I*-positions. In Morioka's terms: "Psychotherapy is conducted to facilitate the reconstruction of the client's repertoire of *I*-positions such that the client is able to move flexibly between positions" (Morioka, 2008, p. 82). Flexible movement in the landscape of mind implies accessibility to varied aspects of this landscape and is a feature of mental health. From this perspective, *I*-positions need to be seen and treated as dynamic processes, not as traits or self-concepts. *I*-positions, for example, "I as depressed," "I as hurt," "I as in grief," can be fixed and reified in one's mind when approached as fixed concepts. Such positions can be frightening if people believe in their solidity, or if people believe that they exist as entities with which one identifies.

In the process of therapy, positions can be experienced as embodied felt experience that can become more fluid and changeable. For many clients it may be liberating and empowering to experience dominant *I*-positions and negative emotions as transient processes that come and go. This can be stimulated by moment-to-moment embodied attention as, for example, introduced in mindfulness-based practices (Mamberg & Bassarear, 2015) or in Gendlin's (2003) focusing-based interventions, or even in analogical listening (Neimeyer & Thompson, 2014). Difficult positions and emotions are like a stream that people are afraid of and block off, so it becomes more ingrained and more frightening, more pressing, or just frozen. But the water can flow and go only if it is allowed to come and go and if one can hear the subtle voice of the stream that in some cases whispers about new meanings and indicates where it needs to flow.

Society of mind: towards a more dialogical, democratic society

When the society of mind is in a state of war or when relations between its members become hostile, voices become rigid and monological (Lysaker & Lysaker, 2002). Or, when one member dominates the whole organization and creates a totalitarian state (Hermans et al., 2017), such situations become seriously limiting for one's development and threatening for one's well-being.

According to Lysaker and Lysaker (2002), loss of dialogical capacities in the society of mind can be observed in schizophrenia:

> With only the barest dialogical opportunities available, a self might arise that is defined by a radically limited number of inflexible self-positions [...] These self-positions may be expressed as brief monologues or entrenched positions whose relations and relative standing do not change.
>
> (p. 212)

According to those authors, psychological disturbances are a function of diminished dialogues with others and between *I*-positions that support a sense of self. When previously constructive dialogues among multiple internal and external *I*-positions have weakened or failed, the self is experienced as similarly reduced. The dialogue can be interrupted in three different ways (Lysaker & Lysaker, 2002); namely in a barren, monological, or cacophonous mode.

In the barren mode, dialogue disappears when varied *I*-positions are not expressed or when they are absent. What follows is a barren state, one in which persons experience themselves as distant observers, not engaged in their lives, experiencing themselves as blank or empty.

In the monological mode, dialogue disappears if one or a few *I*-positions assume a lot of power in the self and dominate most other ones. In this process, a single and reappearing *I*-position evolves, but it lacks interaction with other internal and external *I*-positions.

In the cacophonous mode, dialogue would disappear because different *I*-positions were expressed without relation to one another. Such persons would be overwhelmed by the chaotic appearance of a multiplicity of affectively varied *I*-positions interacting without any organization.

Thus, a loss of sense of self reflects a diminished capacity to bring both internal and external *I*-positions into dialogue. In Lysaker and Lysaker's (2002) view, that sense of self recovers when dialogue within the self and between the self and others is reestablished.

It is worthwhile to note that relations between *I*-positions can take different problematic forms. Parts that are hostile towards each other are sources of emotional pain and can block adaptive actions (Elliot, Watson, Goldman, & Greenberg, 2015). Rigid self-criticism, an example of a conflictive relation between parts of the self (Whelton & Greenberg, 2004), is one of the relevant issues to be addressed and reworked in psychotherapy. According to Whelton and Greenberg (2004), the goal of such work is to create "a sense of harmony and peace developed through an emotional shift that allows for a shift in perception and meaning on both sides" (p. 115).

Positions differ in power and in some cases the society of mind can be organized by dominant *I*-positions silencing other *I*-positions. Some clients in therapy habitually act from such dominant positions, not being aware of the whole spectrum of possible other positions. Such self-organization is limiting and impoverishing, since most of the positions are silenced and do not receive a possibility to express their voices and needs. Self as a totalitarian state is full of tensions, and there is an unrealized potential of suppressed positions.

Facilitation of dialogical relations between the members of the society of mind as well as moving from the totalitarian organization of the self towards a more democratic one, where all members are respected, acknowledged, and heard, can be an important therapeutic aim. This also includes members that are "unusual," "weird," or "strange," or are a minority in the society of mind and are treated as shadow members that are rejected or exiled.

Some relations between positions need to be transformed in a dialogue in order that "problematic members" would be able to give a constructive contribution to the inner society. Carefully chosen forms of inner dialogue may also address issues of unfinished business (Perls et al., 1951) and help to deal with problematic voices of significant others.

Dialogical space

Morioka (2015) suggests that space is an important factor in therapy: "The transitional psychic space between *me* and *mine* is the basis of the subject's experience. It is the container that accepts the movement of meaning in the ongoing here-and-now situation" (p. 83). Space between *I*-positions has been described in the context of Japanese culture as "*ma*" (Morioka, 2015). *Ma* is described as space between one thing and another or between one moment and another moment. It can be a distance of (one part of) the self towards (another part of) the self. As Morioka (2015) argues, facilitating space between two different *I*-positions is an important aspect of therapeutic process:

> According to the dialogical self perspective, the client's narratives are concerned with dialogue between the characters in his or her story. When self-narratives are created gradually in the therapeutic process, a significant

> distance will appear between the different voices of the self. Change in psychotherapy includes a process of distancing oneself from oneself.
>
> (p. 91)

This space gives freedom to "answer" instead of automatically "react." Stepping back from a dominant position and creating an experiential space between "I" and a particular position can be a liberating factor. Such space is the basis for dialogical relations within the self. A dialogical relation requires differentiation between two spatial positions. Without this space, a dialogue is not possible. One of the most important issues in psychotherapy is differentiating and creating space between dominant social or cultural voices and one's personal positions, so that a person can respond from his own standpoint and strengthen his or her "response-ability." Response-ability, understood as an ability to give one's own answer, is empowering and provides a basis for being an agent and a subject rather than an object in relationships of social power.

Taking a meta-position

Another form of creating space is taking a meta-position. According to Dimaggio (2012) a meta-position is a specific part of the metacognitive system. He emphasizes the role of the meta-position in psychotherapy arguing that, "psychotherapy is about forming meta-positions able to reflect upon the more crystallized aspects of the self and provides new solutions to problems" (p. 358). A meta-position, as presented by Hermans and Hermans-Konopka (2010), permits a certain distance toward the other positions.

> It provides an overarching view so that several positions can be seen simultaneously, and their mutual relationships become visible [...] It also facilitates the creation of a dialogical space [...] in which positions and counter-positions engage in dialogical relationships and gives a broader basis for decision making and for finding one's direction in life.
>
> (p. 147)

Facilitating a meta-position in the process of psychotherapy supports the development of the transitional space and helps to see the landscape of mind from a broader, relatively free, perspective.

Externalization

Externalization can be seen as creating "space between." Its role in psychotherapeutic change has been presented by White and Epston (1990) in the context of narrative therapy. According to them, "externalizing" helps people to "objectify and sometimes personify the problems" (p. 38). During the process of externalization, a problematic experience becomes "a separate entity and thus external to the person or relationship," which helps to create a situation of dialogue rather than monologue about a problem (p. 38). In the process of externalization, client and problem are put in contrast; they become separated and get their own identities, which helps to create and explore the relationship between them. From the perspective of DST, a problem can be potentially personified and treated as an *I*-position in a dialogical space and considered from a meta-position.

Externalization stimulates an optimal working distance, as in the task of clearing space as introduced in the practice of focusing (Gendlin, 2003). According to Leijssen (1998), it allows the healing power of the observing I. It enlarges one's space of freedom towards what is observed and supports one's agency toward problematic or oppressive experiences. In a method based on DST, "Compositionwork" (Konopka & van Beers, 2014), externalization receives a nonverbal spatial form, in which personal experiences are symbolized (by the client) in a concrete composition of stones in sand. In the form of stones, *I*-positions are placed "out there" in front of the client, which creates an optimal condition for taking the broader perspective of a meta-position.

Positioning and emotions

The role of emotions in therapy has been explored in many schools of psychotherapy and described by leading authors in the field (Freud, 1963; Greenberg, 2002; Perls & Andreas, 1969; Rogers, 1951). There is a great body of knowledge regarding this subject. Psychoanalysis highlights the role of neglected affect; client-centered therapy emphasizes the connection between therapeutic change and a full experience of feelings in awareness. In Gestalt therapy, emotions and their expression are seen as critical to change and fear of undesired emotions is considered to be a source of many problems (Perls et al., 1951). Special emphasis on emotions as factors of change has been presented in emotion-focused therapy by Leslie Greenberg and colleagues (Greenberg, 2002; Greenberg & Watson, 2006). DST acknowledges, as Greenberg (2002) holds, that emotions are foundational in the construction of the self and a key determinant of self-organization.

In this chapter we will not address the broad subject of emotions but will look at the relation between the self and emotion from the perspective of DST. Seeing this relation from the angle of positioning and multiplicity can help to explore its complexity and dynamism. From a dialogical perspective, the self and emotions are described as interconnected in a bi-directional dynamic relationship that can potentially be dialogical (Hermans & Hermans-Konopka, 2010). Emotions necessarily involve the whole sense of self in a complex way. They may position the self towards others, for instance "I as angry" or "I as anxious," and towards one's self in the form of self-criticism or self-loathing. Emotions can be described as ways of positioning. At the same time, the self is an agentic factor that can influence or change emotions by taking a position towards an emotion. The relation a person has with his or her emotions can be seen as a complex process of positioning. In the process of positioning oneself towards one's emotions, two basic aspects can be distinguished: spatial and qualitative. This concerns *where* one stands in the landscape of the mind towards his or her emotions and *how* one stands and moves from or towards them. The spatial aspect of positioning refers to the distance one takes towards emotions: is one coinciding with one's anger or looking at it from a distance, or maybe pushing it away? How great is the distance? Is it still a living creative field or is there no experiential connection with the emotion?

Creating some distance and dis-identifying from a dominant emotion can be an important step in increasing a person's agency and ability to use emotions as sources of information but not as sources of absolute truth. The value of this kind of dis-identification is strongly appreciated in contemplative traditions, also including mindfulness-based practices. The process of dis-identification can take the form of taking some distance towards an emotion, taking a meta-position, externalizing, appreciating space in Gendlin's task of clearing space, or in the form of a more profound shift in the sense of self. The last one is typical of systematic contemplative training (Hayward, 1999), where the sense of self becomes reallocated more in one's "background awareness" than in the content of the emotional experience. In terms of DST, this can be called "de-positioning" (Hermans-Konopka, 2012). However, especially in the case of people who overregulate emotions, stimulating a more immersed experience can be an adequate and necessary way to access and intensify emotions. In these cases, entering emotions in an embodied way, positioning one's self in them, to knowing them from within or to being transformed by them can be an important task in therapy (Hermans & Hermans-Konopka, 2010). Both ways of dealing with emotions (depositioning and immersed positioning) are relevant in different contexts. It is rather the ability to move in a flexible way between immersed and detached ways of relating with one's emotions than the preference for one of them.

Developing dialogical relations with emotions can be one of the major goals of psychotherapy, since only if a person can allow an emotion, acknowledge its message, and provide an answer to it, can he or she use it as important information. Dialogical relations with one's emotions enhance the use of the adaptive potential of emotions by openly receiving their message and allowing them to be supportive for one's adaptive actions. Emotions show what is personally important to the self. People who silence their potentially adaptive emotions are likely to be dominated by voices of others since they cannot recognize their own needs.

Dialogical relation as a fundament of therapy

The quality and strength of the therapeutic collaboration is reliably and significantly associated with positive therapy outcomes (Ribeiro, Ribeiro, Gonçalves, Horvath, & Stiles, 2013). A dialogical relation seems to be the carrier and the basis for a growth-promoting therapeutic process. Decades of research indicate that the provision of therapy is an interpersonal process in which one of the main curative components is the nature of the therapeutic relationship (Wampold & Imel, 2015). DST points to the fact that interpersonal processes cannot be seen separately from the intrapersonal ones. The dialogical space in a therapeutic relation encompasses a multiplicity of *I-*

positions that can be engaged in both internal and external dialogues. From this perspective, the therapeutic relationship is a dynamic, multiple, complex organization of *I*-positions emerging from the dialogue between therapist and client. Optimally, such relation needs to be characterized by "good dialogue," which according to Hermans and Hermans-Konopka (2010) has the following features: it is innovative, allows a broad bandwidth of *I*-positions, has tolerance for misunderstanding, creates a dialogical space, recognizes power differences between *I*-positions and recognizes their differences and alterity, and profits from moments of silence. In such dialogue, the presence of the therapist creates a holding environment for the process of therapy to unfold (Neimeyer, 2012). For a healing dialogue to evolve, such presence needs to be connected with emphatic engagement and attunement (Elliot, Bohart, Watson, & Greenberg, 2011; Neimeyer, 2012) as well as acceptance of the client's experiences. As Staemmler (2011) notes, "A therapeutic relation without empathy is hardly conceivable. How could therapists respond to their client's mental situations if they were not, to a certain extent, able to enter into their subjective worlds?" (p. 4). Particularly, empathy and acceptance also need to be directed towards the client's shadow positions that are not fully expressed and are at risk of being held back in contact with the therapist.

References

Cooper, M., & Hermans, H. J. M. (2007). Honoring self-otherness: Alterity and the intrapersonal. In L. Sima & J. Valsiner (Eds.), *Otherness in question: Labyrinths of the self* (pp. 305–315). Greenwich, CT: Information Age Publishing.

Dimaggio, G. (2012) Dialogically oriented therapies and the role of poor metacognition in personality disorders. In H. J. M. Hermans & T. Gieser (Eds.), *Handbook of dialogical self theory* (pp. 356–372). Cambridge, UK: Cambridge University Press.

Elliott, R., Bohart, A. C., Watson, J. C., & Greenberg, L. S. (2011). Empathy. *Psychotherapy, 48*(1), 43–49.

Elliott, R., Watson, J. C., Goldman, R. N., & Greenberg, L. S. (2004). *Learning emotion-focused therapy: The process-experiential approach to change.* Washington, DC: American Psychological Association.

Freud, A. (1963). The concept of developmental lines. *The Psychoanalytic Study of the Child, 18*, 245–265.

Gendlin, E. T. (2003). *Focusing.* London: Rider.

Gonçalves, M. M., & Ribeiro, A. P. (2012). Narrative processes of innovation and stability within the dialogical self. In H. J. M. Hermans & T. Gieser (Eds.), *Handbook of dialogical self theory* (pp. 301–318). Cambridge, UK: Cambridge University Press.

Greenberg, L. S. (2002). *Emotion-focused therapy: Coaching clients to work through their feelings.* Washington, DC: American Psychological Association.

Greenberg, L. S., & Watson, J. C. (2006). *Emotion-focused therapy for depression.* Washington, DC: American Psychological Association.

Guttenplan, S. D. (2000). *Mind's landscape: An introduction to the philosophy of mind.* Malden, MA: Blackwell.

Hayward, J. (1999) A rDzog-chen Buddhist interpretation of the sense of self. In S. Gallagher & J. Shear (Eds.), *Models of the self* (vol. 5, no. 2, pp. 379–394) Exeter: Imprint Academic.

Hermans, H. J. M. (2001). The dialogical self: Toward a theory of personal and cultural positioning. *Culture & Psychology, 7*, 243–281.

Hermans, H. J. M. (2006). The self as a theater of voices: Disorganization and reorganization of a position repertoire. *Journal of Constructivist Psychology, 19*(2), 147–169.

Hermans, H. J. M. (2018). *Society in the self: A theory of identity in democracy.* New York: Oxford University Press.

Hermans, H. J. M., & Gieser, T. (Eds.). (2012). *Handbook of dialogical self theory.* Cambridge, UK: Cambridge University Press.

Hermans, H. J. M., & Hermans-Konopka, A. (2010). *Dialogical self theory: Positioning and counter-positioning in a globalizing society.* Cambridge, UK: Cambridge University Press.

Hermans, H. J. M., Konopka, A., Oosterwegel, A., & Zomer, P. (2017). Fields of tension in a boundary-crossing world: Towards a democratic organization of the self. *Integrative Psychological and Behavioral Sciences, 51*, 505–535.

Hermans-Konopka, A. (2012). The depositioning of the I: Emotional coaching in the context of transcendental awareness. In H. J. M. Hermans & T. Gieser (Eds.), *Handbook on dialogical self theory* (pp. 423–438). Cambridge, UK: Cambridge University Press.

Hesse, H. (1963). *Steppenwolf.* New York: *Modern Library.*

Huxley, A. (1956). *Heaven and hell.* London: Chatto & Windus.

Huxley, A. (2014). *The doors of perception & heaven and hell.* Toronto, ON: New Canadian Library.

Konopka, A., & van Beers, W. (2014). Composition work: A method for self-investigation. *Journal of Constructivist Psychology, 27*(3), 194–210.

Leijssen, M. (1998). Focusing microprocesses. In L. S. Greenberg, J. C. Watson, & G. O. Lietaer (Eds.), *Handbook of experiential psychotherapy* (pp. 121–154). New York: Guilford Press.

Lysaker, P. H., & Lysaker, J. T. (2002). Narrative structure in psychosis schizophrenia and disruptions in the dialogical self. *Theory & Psychology, 12*(2), 207–220.

Mamberg, M. H., & Bassarear, T. (2015). From reified self to being mindful: A dialogical analysis of the MBSR voice. *International Journal for Dialogical Science, 9*(1), 11–37.

Morioka, M. (2008). Voices of the self in the therapeutic chronotope: Utushi and ma. *International Journal for Dialogical Science, 3*(1), 93–108.

Morioka, M. (2015). How to create ma—the living pause—in the landscape of the mind: The wisdom of the NOH theater. *International Journal for Dialogical Science, 9*(1), 81–95.

Neimeyer, R. A. (2012). *Techniques of grief therapy: Creative practices for counseling the bereaved.* New York: Routledge.

Neimeyer, R. A., & Thompson, B. E. (2014). Meaning making and the art of grief therapy. In B. E. Thompson & R. A. Neimeyer (Eds.), *Grief and the expressive arts: Practices for creating meaning* (pp. 3–13). New York: Routledge.

Nin, A. (2014). *The early diary of Anais Nin, Vol. 2 (1920–1923).* Boston, MA: Houghton Mifflin Harcourt.

Perls, F. S., & Andreas, S. (1969). *Gestalt therapy verbatim.* Lafayette, CA: Real People Press.

Perls, F. S., Hefferline, G., & Goodman, P. (1951). *Gestalt therapy.* New York: Souvenir Press.

Ribeiro, A. P., Ribeiro, E., Loura, J., Gonçalves, M. M., Stiles, W. B., Horvath, A. O., & Sousa, I. (2014). Therapeutic collaboration and resistance: Describing the nature and quality of the therapeutic relationship within ambivalence events using the therapeutic collaboration coding system. *Psychotherapy Research, 24*(3), 346–359.

Ribeiro, E., Ribeiro, A. P., Gonçalves, M. M., Horvath, A. O., & Stiles, W. B. (2013). How collaboration in therapy becomes therapeutic: The therapeutic collaboration coding system. *Psychology and Psychotherapy: Theory, Research and Practice, 86*(3), 294–314.

Rogers, C. R. (1951). *Client-centered counseling.* London: Constable.

Rowan, J. (2009). *Personification: Using the dialogical self in psychotherapy and counselling.* London: Routledge.

Staemmler, F. M. (2011). *Empathy in psychotherapy: How therapists and clients understand each other.* London: Springer.

Valsiner, J. (2004, July). The promoter sign: Developmental transformation within the structure of dialogical self. In Symposium (Hubert Hermans, Convener) Developmental aspects of the dialogical self. ISSBD, Gent.

Wampold, B. E., & Imel, Z. E. (2015). *The great psychotherapy debate: The evidence for what makes psychotherapy work.* London: Routledge.

Whelton, W. J., & Greenberg, L. S. (2004). From discord to dialogue: Internal voices and the reorganization of the self in process-experiential therapy. In H. J. M. Hermans & G. Dimaggio (Eds.), *The dialogical self in psychotherapy: An Introduction* (pp. 108–123). London: Routledge.

White, M., & Epston, D. (1990). *Narrative means to therapeutic ends.* New York and London: W. W. Norton & Company.

3 Gestalt therapy, Dialogical Self Theory, and the "empty chair"

Frank-M. Staemmler

If for classical psychoanalysis the couch was the outstanding symbol, the "empty chair" was the prominent icon for classical Gestalt therapy, by which it became both famous and infamous in the 1960s and early 1970s. Frederick S. Perls had borrowed the various techniques that he implemented by the use of a chair from Jacob Moreno (1964; see also Zerka Moreno, 1965). Perls, however, did not base his application of these techniques on Moreno's theory; he worked with them without linking them to any particular theoretical background.

Subsequent generations of gestalt therapists imitated Perls' technical approach; to a large degree, they did not even acknowledge their psychodramatical origin. So the way in which Gestalt therapy became established, was, on the one hand, very much equated with empty chair work, and, on the other hand, the frequent use of furniture for technical purposes took place without much theoretical grounding. I find both aspects regrettable.

The disregard of Moreno's socially oriented concepts meshed well with the individualistic bias, into which Perls (1969) relapsed in the last years of his life: "I do my thing, you do your thing ... And if by chance we find each other, it's beautiful. If not, it can't be helped" (p. 4). With this bias, however, Perls deviated pretty much from the notions he had previously developed in collaboration with Paul Goodman, a social critic and anarchist philosopher. In the book *Gestalt Therapy: Excitement and Growth in the Human Personality* (Perls, Hefferline,[1] & Goodman 1951) the two of them had put forward ideas that defy any individualistic interpretation; one of the most basic and salient ones reads like this: "It is the contact that is the simplest and first reality" (p. 227).

Another quote, which – even more clearly than the one above – illustrates the influence George Herbert Mead had on Paul Goodman and also demonstrates one of the similarities that can be found in the tradition of Gestalt therapy as well as in the one of Dialogical Self Theory (subsequently abbreviated as DST – see Hermans & Hermans-Konopka, 2010; Hermans, Kempen, & van Loon, 1992): "Social relations ... are original in any human field, long prior to one's recognizing oneself as an idiosyncratic person ... Personality is a structure created out of such early interpersonal relationships" (Perls et al., 1951, p. 320).

This statement can easily be traced back to one of Mead's most perceptive observations:

The self is something which has a development; it is not initially there, at birth, but arises in the process of social experience and activity, that is, develops in the given individual as a result of his relations to that process as a whole and to other individuals within that process.

(Mead, 1934/1963, p. 135)

It is obvious that when Perls and Goodman worked together, they drew on Mead's insights when they formulated their basic theory, as did Hubert Hermans (who also referred to compatible writings, for instance by William James (1890) and Michail Bakhtin (1984, 1986), among others, when he asserted that "the self can only be truly dialogical when the other person is seen as not purely outside, but simultaneously part of the self and even constitutive of it" (Hermans, 2011, p. 654).

Although my heart beats for Gestalt therapy, I have to admit that Hermans' theorizing has functioned as a bridge for me that linked fundamental propositions such as the one by Mead with my understanding of the efficacy of the therapeutic techniques that Perls used in an individualistic fashion. Only after I thoroughly delved into DST, the connections between the anthropological, social-psychological, and practical therapeutic realms became clear to me (see Staemmler, 2015) and made it possible for me to work with "empty chairs" in a non-individualistic, relational manner. In what follows I will try and explain my current point of view.

Participatory appropriation: contact first

To better understand the relevant connections it may be helpful to characterize in more detail the developmental psychological processes that Lev Vygotsky (1978, 1981) called "interiorization." This term does *not* describe a *linear* activity,[2] by which something that has first taken place outside of the person is then transformed into something psychic without modification – "one-to-one," so to speak. Rather, we are dealing with a process of *creative, "participatory appropriation* ... [that] is a process of becoming, rather than acquisition" (Rogoff, 1995, p. 142, original italics),[3] as a result of which the properties the child develops find their personal form:

> An individual participating in ... communication is already involved in a process beyond the individual level. Benefiting from shared thinking thus does not involve *taking* something from an external model. Instead, in the process of participation in social activity, the individual already functions with the shared understanding. The individual's later use of this shared understanding is not the same as what was constructed jointly; it is an appropriation of the *shared* activity ... that reflects the individual's understanding of ... the activity.
>
> (Rogoff, 1990, p. 195, original italics)[4]

First, the joint activity consists of a shared attentiveness and goes along with the kind of "inter-subjectivity ... whereby infants begin to manifest co-awareness of things in the environment, engaging in systematic bouts of joint attention with others" (Rochat, 2010, p. 177). Interactions are also the critical dimension, when it comes to the question, what is essentially appropriated: With respect to the view of developmental psychology I propose here, it is decisive that the process of appropriation does not primarily refer to the behavior of individual others, to their personal features, or to the contents of the messages they communicate. Processes of internalization like these do, of course, also exist (*later* in development). But on the fundamental level we have to acknowledge that first of all "it is the *interactive experience* that is internalized, not 'objects'" (Stern, 2010, p. 144, italics added)[5]; it is the appropriation of a "*dual* being" (Merleau-Ponty, 1962, p. 345): the duality of self *and* other. What gets owned is what first has been *shared*, not what belongs to the individual other only. Therefore Barbara Rogoff speaks of "the process of appropriation from shared activity, in contrast to the process of internalization of external activity" (1990, p. 195). And she concludes: "Hence, participation is itself the process of appropriation" (1995, p. 151).

This observation is crucial since it underlines that *contact* – or, as we may prefer to say today, relationality – is the primary reality, to which the highest priority must be attributed. Consequently, both "external" and "internal positions," as they are referred to in DST,[6] are *secondary* phenomena that are preceded (both temporally and systematically) by *shared* activities. So relatedness is the *conditio sine qua non* of individuality. Hence from the very beginning and for the rest of the lifespan, all sorts of individual psychological processes carry a dialogical quality; the self is, once and for all, provided with a dialogical "format": To develop a self is to make the relatedness with others and the interaction with them one's own project and, thereby, to constitute oneself. "Mental activity which is initially distributed or shared between individuals is later actively reconstructed on the internal plane" (Fernyhough, 2008, p. 228).

A self, then, is the sum of its appropriated shared activities that manifest as external and internal positions – plus its ongoing participation in interactions with others by which internal positions and outside positions relate to each other; hence the self is relational and permanently engaged in dialogues with others (external and outside) and with itself (internal positions). This is why in Gestalt therapy we "call the 'self' the system of contacts at any moment" (Perls et al., 1951, p. 235).

In other words, "*to be* means *to communicate*" (Bakhtin, 1984, p. 287, original italics), and that is not only the case with outside or external positions, the latter of which Stern (1985, pp. 111ff.) calls "evoked" others, but also with one's internal positions. A human being is not only a *self in relation* to other persons – a notion that Brent Slife (2004) has named "*weak* relationality" – but also a "*relational being*" (see Gergen, 2009) in the sense of what Slife calls "*strong* relationality." Relatedness is not only influencing the self, once it is constituted, it is constitutive of the self in the first place. Therefore Heidegger (1962) can maintain: "Dasein's Being-in-the-world is essentially constituted by Being-with ... Being-with is an existential characteristic of Dasein even when factically no Other is present-at-hand or perceived" (p. 156).

The Gestalt therapist supports the client to explore and clarify these psychological processes by assuming what Hermans calls an (outside) "promoter position" for the client. If the client wants to work on his relationship to another person, the therapist introduces the "fantasy conversation technique" (including an *I*-position and an external position). In a similar vein, for therapeutic ends the "technique of soliloquy" may be used to help a client externalize and enact a self-talk that is taking place between two (or more) of her or his internal positions (each of them assigned to a respective chair), by having her or him clearly *identify* (and maybe name) her or his relevant positions, *externalize* and locate them in different places (e.g. chairs) in the room, and then *enact* them and have them *respond* to each other in turn.

Multiple relatedness and the plurality of the self

The subsequent train of thought builds on what I have said above and begins with a statement that is both very significant and may seem trivial at first sight: As a rule of thumb, from birth on human beings do not interact with *one* other person only, but with *several*. Usually, this starts with the fact that infants do not only engage in contacts with their mothers but also with their fathers and other caregivers as well as with siblings, grandparents, further relatives, etc. Moreover, the number of attachment figures increases as children get older: "We do not live in a world of *one* other human being, but in the world of human *beings* ... Part of the human condition is the plural" (Schmid, 2002, p. 86, original italics).

As Daniel Stern (1985, p. 97) has demonstrated with his concept of "Representations of Interactions that have been Generalized (RIGs)," already in the first months of life it is relevant (and hence not trivial at all) for the development of the dialogical self that "each of the many different self-regulating other relationships with the same person will have its own distinctive RIG. And when different RIGs are activated, the infant re-experiences different forms or ways of being with a self-regulating other" (p. 110f.).

One may also state: Since any respective RIG has originated from an interaction with a certain other person, it always includes an implicit reference to the interaction with exactly *this* person. The particular interactive experience manifests itself in a self-experience, one might – admittedly a little laboriously – denote as the "self-that-I-am-in-dialogue-with-*this*-person." Thus the self, as it actualizes itself in a given situation, is connected in this way with the experience of what it is like to interact with *this* person. Any RIG, therefore, includes a memory of another person, who is then called the "evoked companion" by Stern. And there are many.

This brings about a number of consequences, among them the fact that any experience of the self is connected with a more or less implicit memory of one (or several) other person(s). In principle, a self without reference to (one or several) other(s) is impossible, even though this reference can, of course, be more or less conscious; in addition, it may be superimposed, transformed, or obscured by subsequent psychic processes. As a result, the clarification of blurry references can count as a common element in all forms of psychotherapy.

The fact that interactions with *different* others contribute to varying kinds of self-experiences is only *one* constellation that results in the plurality of the self. In addition, significantly diverse interactive experiences with the *same* partner *in unlike situations*, during which the partner actualizes a *certain* one of his many possible *I*-positions, lead to a particular RIG and, hence, to a special experience of the "self-that-I-am-in-contact-with-this-person-in-*this*-situation." In sum, *various* forms of self-experience will emerge; the self becomes *plural*: "How you are when you affect me is already affected by me, and not by me as I usually am, but by me as I occur with you" (Gendlin, 1997, p. 30); in DST terms we are dealing with a certain *I*-position that forms in a particular joint situation.

As quoted before, Gestalt therapy theory defined the self according to the above-mentioned principle as "the system of contacts at any moment" (Perls et al., 1951, p. 235). And Perls and his coworkers immediately added: "As such, the self is flexibly various" (ibid.). Within their interactions with various others as well as within different interactions with the same others, human beings form diverse ways of self-experience. So it can be seen as a matter of course that strong relationality inescapably must lead to the plurality of the self: Relational beings necessarily are plural beings.

To put it simply: I am a different self, when I am participating in a dialogue with Peter or Paula, and I am a different self, depending on whether I am engaged in a loving or in a controversial dialogue with Paula. In the words of George Herbert Mead (1934/1963):

> We carry on a whole series of different relationships to different people ... There are all sorts of different selves answering to all sorts of different social reactions. It is the social process itself that is responsible for the appearance of the self; it is not there as a self apart from this type of experience.
>
> (p. 142)

This means that a "multiple personality, as an abnormal phenomenon, seems to be the pathological side of a healthy functioning dialogical self" (Hermans & Dimaggio, 2004, p. 3; see also Rowan & Cooper, 1999).

However, between the many positions or "voices" that take part in the dialogue of a plural self, there are not only relationships of mutual supplementation, support, and harmony. Contradictions, inconsistencies, and incongruences abound and are – to individually differing degrees – quite tolerable to the extent to which the various selves or part-selves ("internal positions" in DST) engage in a dialogical exchange with each other in spite of their differences, instead of trying to dominate, marginalize, or ignore each other. Human beings desire to be understood, not only by others, but also by themselves (see Staemmler, 2012a).

Metaphorically speaking, one can conceive of the dialogical self as a "society of mind" (see Hermans, 2002, 2005) with diverse and various positions, coalitions, and contradictions that have to find a way of living together without falling into fragments on the one extreme or being subjected to confluence or totalitarian egalitarianism on the other extreme. This task can be mastered if *all* positions are provided with equal rights of existence and dialogical participation, so that they can engage in a psychic discourse, which is following the ethics of *inclusion.*[7] What Perls et al. (1951) say about the contact between different people is equally true for the contact between different *I*-positions:

> One person and another are confluent when there is no appreciation of a boundary between them, *when there is no discrimination of the points of difference or otherness that distinguish them* ... When persons are in contact, not in confluence, they not only respect their own and the other's opinions, tastes, and responsibilities, but actively welcome the animation and excitement that come with the airing of disagreements. Confluence makes for routine and stagnation, contact for excitement and growth.
>
> (pp. 118ff., original italics)

Accepting and cherishing alterity, otherness, and differences is an essential prerequisite for this attitude (see Buber, 1957, 1965; Cooper & Hermans, 2007; Lévinas, 1969, 1999). Therefore, "in therapeutic applications of dialogical psychology, different, often conflicting, voices are encouraged to be spoken/listened to and brought into open dialogue with each other" (Adams, 2010, p. 343). The aim of this process is not primarily the establishment of unity, consensus, or harmony among the various positions; first of all the aim is the dialogue itself, since

> for the word (and, consequently, for a human being) there is nothing more terrible than a *lack of response* ... Being heard as such is already a dialogic relation. The word wants to be heard, understood, responded to, and again to respond to the response, and so forth *ad infinitum.*
>
> (Bakhtin, 1986, p. 127, original italics)

In order to be heard and to be responded to, the various voices of the psyche often need support. It is part of the therapist's task to provide the client with this help. The discourse ethics, as they have been outlined by Habermas (1993) with respect to societal communication, can also serve for the therapist's orientation in dealing with her or his clients' various *I*-positions, since it has developed criteria that – with certain qualifications – can also be applied to the psychic processes of the individual. – I have added some bracketed extensions to the subsequent quote:

> Anyone [any *I*-position] ... may take part in discourse ... Anyone [any *I*-position] may render any assertion [by any other *I*-position] problematic ... Anyone [any *I*-position] may introduce any assertion into the discourse ... Anyone [any *I*-position] may express his/her opinions, wishes and needs ... No speaker [no *I*-position] may be prevented by constraint within or outside the discourse from making use of his/her rights established in [the previous sentences].
>
> (Alexy, 1990, pp. 166f.)

What is good in society, is good in the society of mind as well. What on an interpersonal level shows up as *ethics*, can be seen as standards for psychological *health* on the individual level. Just as political groups in a society do not need to agree or even like each other, different positions in the society of mind do not have to live in perfect harmony; discrepancies and frictions can have their places.

"An 'inner society of voices' ... does not, in essence, differ from the communications in the outside world" (Hermans, 2003, 94). In order to live together well, divergent positions need to accept each others' existence and respective rights and, moreover, must be ready to engage in a continuous dialogue. So in my view, it is part of the task of psychotherapists to promote their clients' recovery and/or growth by supporting the standards of discourse ethics in the way in which the clients converse with themselves: "'Good' psychological plurality seems to be about a dialogical relationship and openness between the different positions that someone has" (Cooper, in Cooper, Mearns, Stiles, Warner, & Elliott, 2004; p. 178; see also Cooper, 2003).

Self as process

If we conceive of the self as dialogical and plural, the consequence has to be: The self cannot be a thing such as a computer or a cardiac pacemaker, some "ghost in the machine" (Ryle, 1949, pp. 15f.), or some kind of homunculus, which would exist somewhere in the so-called "inside" of a person (in a "Cartesian theater") and would pull the strings from there. "A person is a fluid process, not a fixed and static entity; a flowing river of change, not a block of solid material; a continually changing constellation of potentialities, not a fixed quantity of traits" (Rogers, 1961, p. 122). Even if people – including psychologists – frequently tend to imagine processes as things, it would be erroneous to reify the self: "There are no homunculi," Carl Rogers (1959, p. 196) stated, and neuroscientific research concedes this point to him: "One should, indeed, be skeptical of a homunculus-like knower, endowed with full knowledge and located in a single and circumscribed part of the brain. It makes no sense physiologically. All the available evidence suggests that nothing like it exists" (Damasio, 1999, p. 190). Just as the procedural character of the self prohibits any reification, its plurality renders it difficult to speak of a homogeneous or even "true" self. The plurality of the self makes it most unlikely that – maybe except for paranoid, fanatic, or otherwise very unusual psychological conditions – only one single *I*-position captures the entire foreground of a person's awareness for a longer period of time, whereas all others remain in the background. As I have quoted Perls et al. (1951, p. 235) before, from a Gestalt therapy vantage point the self is a dynamic and fluctuating pattern of its contacts at any given moment; although (actual, remembered, or fantasized) interpersonal contacts play a predominant role in self-formation, other contacts such as the one with gravity, oxygen, food, etc. are also relevant.[8]

Although the self is fluid, it also has continuity. It configures itself at any point in time from the *I*-positions that it actualizes, but this does not mean that it has to be fragmented, as some critics of a procedural and plural self-concept fearfully assume. This fear is based on a limited understanding of the self's plurality, which means that there are almost always *several* contacts activated in a given situation along with their respective *I*-positions. Whereas some contacts vanish and are replaced with new ones as the situation changes, there are also still some other contacts that are maintained from one situation to the next. Accordingly, some *I*-positions recede into the background of awareness, whereas others may stay in the foreground, in case they are also useful in response to the new situation. Thereby the situational selves are connected to each other over time, even if they differ from each other to a more or less large degree (see Staemmler, 2015, pp. 25ff.).

Moreover, *I*-positions must not be reified, too; they are neither global agencies (as, for instance, in Freud's structural model) nor "sub-personalities" with necessarily lasting essence. They can change with time, disappear entirely, or emerge newly under the conditions of novel situations and contacts. "It is commonly said that each of our relationships 'brings out' different traits in us, as if all possible traits were already in us, waiting only to be 'brought out'. But actually you affect me" (Gendlin, 1997, p. 30), and under this impression I sometimes create a new position, a personal response that I newly invent and with which I surprise myself, as it were.

By implication, the various positions that constitute a respective self at a given situation can relate to each other in different ways. They can exist side by side without referring to each other, they can complement and support each other, they can question, challenge, or sabotage each other. Their coherence is not a must; it is also variable. The degree, however, to which a certain person can tolerate inconsistencies among *I*-positions and situational selves, can be more or less high depending on the personal tolerance for ambiguity and situational conditions (see Frenkel-Brunswik, 1949; Whelton & Greenberg, 2004).

Last but not least, I would like to point out another implication that results from what I have said before: Gestalt therapy's egalitarian understanding of the positions that form a society of mind implies that *in principle* there is no prefigured hierarchy that would attribute a general dominance or an "overarching view" (Hermans, 2003, p. 123) to any one of them over all others; according to my therapeutic experience, *any* position has the potential to become a meta-position that "creates a certain distance toward the other positions" (ibid.) for a certain amount of time, and any meta-position can turn into an ordinary *I*-position again.

A clinical vignette

My client, who was a therapist herself and who I will call "Eileen," was difficult for me to work with for a long time, although I liked her and felt strong compassion [the therapist as an external promoter position] both for the chronic disease from which she suffered and for her shame about the disease [a self-critical position of the client], because of which she excluded herself from many social activities. At the time of the session described in what follows, the therapy centered on the way she tried to cope with these conditions.

What I found demanding was a behavior she displayed again and again in our sessions: Although, on the one hand, Eileen hauntingly conveyed to me how desperate she felt and how urgently she needed help, on the other hand, she would not acknowledge any responsibility for her withdrawn way of living and shameful experience [two versions of her dependent, helpless *I*-position]; she constantly blamed her terrible fate, objected to any suggestions I made and criticized any feedback I gave her as unfounded or off target [her self-critical position directed at the outside world]. My attempts at understanding our interaction as a form of projective identification (see Staemmler, 1993) were met by her with a lack of comprehension. She also rejected my proposals to engage in some chair work to explore her self-depreciative soliloquy and/or to establish a self-compassionate, internal promoter position (see Staemmler, 2012b).

I felt thwarted, and even though I told her about my frustrating experience in a friendly manner, I was left without resonance [my *I*-position as a failure was activated]. In my experience, our conversation remained awkward and without any flow. After having consulted my supervisor [an external promoter position], I decided to discuss this general pattern with her at the beginning of our next session [i.e. I mobilized my internal promoter position].

To my great surprise, Eileen immediately appeared interested in my reflections and engaged in a very constructive and clarifying conversation with me [her cooperative *I*-position]; she also seriously considered my remarks without showing any signs of mortification or shame. Moreover, she confirmed my impression of the infertile pattern in our previous sessions [a self-reflexive meta-position]. She said she had experienced our conversations as some kind of "fight." While she had been aware of opposing my efforts, she also had had a sense of doing the wrong things all the time and even of *being* basically wrong [from the meta-position she referred to her self-critical *I*-position].

It occurred to her that this resembled a feeling she used to experience again and again as a child and an adolescent towards her mother for whom she never seemed to do things in the right way [a critical external position]. She had repeatedly promised to her to improve in order to maintain the connection with her, but had never had an idea what exactly she should do to satisfy her mother's expectations [her dependent, helpless *I*-position]. As a result she had formed the persevering self-image of being fundamentally "difficult" and "wrong" [her self-critical *I*-position].

I suggested that this self-image was not a fact, but an *introject* she had generated as a result of the interactions with her mother; so the originally outside mother-position had turned into an external *I*-position that frequently "talked" to her with a shaming and denigrating voice.[9] Given the impression that I did not have to be very careful with my words, I called my client's introject "crap" [I took a friendly-critical promoter position in support of her self-reflexive meta-position]. With my choice of drastic words, I intended to shatter her belief in the veridical character of, and her submissive stance towards, her self-critical position. When she heard me say this, her face brightened up very obviously.

I also told her that I saw both some parallels and some differences between her situation with her mother and her situation with me: In contrast to how she remembered her mother [a critical external position], I had not left her uninformed about what she could do, but had made precise suggestions how to proceed [acting as an external promoter position towards her] that she, however, had not picked up. She agreed and described how she nevertheless had felt left alone. My suggestions had taken her into a feeling of solitude; she had experienced me at a distance – giving her advice without being personally palpable for her, as if I had told her: "Since it is your problem, you need to do your work by yourself, and I will just watch you working without getting involved as a person myself" [from the perspective of her dependent, helpless *I*-position she had experienced me as a cold and distant external position].

So it turned out that my proposals of two-chair work had enhanced this experience, since to her they had suggested a scene in which she was confronted with herself [her self-critical *I*-position as well as her dependent, helpless *I*-position], thereby losing sight of me, her therapist [as an external promoter position], and feeling left alone [helpless] with her internal struggle. In other words, given the resonance with the external position of the mother, from her perspective my choice of technique resembled a critical position and as such failed as a promoter position.

In contrast, during the phases of our "fights," she had felt a *connection* between us; it had been a fight between herself and *another* person. As unpleasant as they were, these fights provided her with the feeling of being in touch with me [her *I*-position "I as being connected"]: Whenever I responded to her avoidances, she had the impression that I was *directly* responding to her [her therapist in the position of relating to her]. So from her perspective, we stayed in close exchange with each other, since our respective contributions succeeded each other closely, and their contents were tightly related to each other.

I asked her how our current conversation felt for her: Did she feel connected or left alone? Her response was unequivocal: connected [her *I*-position "I as being connected"]. She said that for her this was so, since I talked *with* her directly, showed my commitment [her therapist in the position of relating to her and supporting] so that she had a sense of the two of us being active *together* [her position, "I as being connected" expanding into "I as being part of a We"].

The next day Eileen sent me a letter:

> I have been surprised about how I felt after our session. This feeling of happiness that emerges from a sense of easiness and connection was unknown to me before. I guess I have never felt happy like this before. It is not a "loud" feeling; I do not need to express it emphatically. It is mine, but I want to share it. Telling you about it, helps me experiencing it again.

For me as a therapist this episode was most salutary. It taught me in an impressive way that the therapeutic work on the relationship between my clients' different *I*-positions needs to be supplemented with the parallel work on the relationship between my clients and myself. As the notion of strong relationality highlights, human relatedness means, first of all, relatedness between people, which leads in a second developmental step to the dialogical relatedness of a person to herself. In adult life the one can never be separated from the other.

Concluding note

Carl Rogers (1961) once remarked: "It seems to me that at bottom each person is asking, Who am I, *really*? How can I get in touch with this real self, underlying all my surface behavior? How can I become myself?" (p. 108, original italics). He was certainly right in that many people are engaged in this sort of soliloquy, asking themselves these questions and trying hard to find their answers. Probably Rogers was one of them, too. And whenever such questions are put and the respective answers sought, they are informed by the prevailing culture and *zeitgeist*.

Against the backdrop of my conception of strong relationality and the dialogicality of the self, my questions and answers are different from Rogers' and his time. The presumption that there would be something like a "real self," that one could find and from then on would not have to search for anymore, because once and for all one would have become oneself, does not have much validity for me anymore. In a similar vein, the notions of depth psychology that conceived of a "true" self that was to be found somewhere "under" the surface by excavating it in an archaeological manner, appear obsolete to me today.

It is my impression that contemporary people living under the current post-modern conditions need support not to hope for any certainty from some more or less definite truths about the world and about themselves, but to look for ways to get along with the flow of the external world as well as with the fluidity of their own selves. This is a demanding task that can only be mastered with a fair amount of tolerance for uncertainties and inconsistencies as well as with an open-mindedness for the idea of inclusion – both with respect to other human beings as to one's own society of mind.

It is my hope that I have been able to explain, how the non-individualistic tenets of Gestalt therapy can be infused with the differentiated concepts of DST in order to clarify the links between the anthropological, psychological, and practically clinical realms including the techniques that use chairs, which only together can form a holistic approach to psychotherapy.

Notes

1 Ralph Hefferline only played a marginal role in terms of theory development.
2 A linear process in this sense is sometimes denoted with the term "introjection."
3 The similar term used in traditional Gestalt therapy theory to describe this phenomenon is "creative adjustment" (Perls et al., 1951).
4 This is obviously not a simple process of accommodation in the sense of Piaget.
5 Below I will return to Stern's (1985, pp. 110ff.) related concepts, the "RIGs" and the "evoked companion."

6 The meaning of these terms is explicated in Chapter 1 of this volume by Gonçalves, Konopka, and Hermans, as well as by Raggatt (2012).

7 The notion of an "integration" of diverging positions into a "leading culture" is not compatible with this norm, neither on a societal level nor on an individual level.

8 Rosa (2016, pp. 331ff.) has subdivided human relations with the world into three categories or "axis": the "horizontal" (relations with other human beings), the "diagonal" (relations to material things), and the "vertical" (religious or similar relations to nature in general, to God, to the universe etc.) In this chapter I focus on the first axis.

9 At this point in time, I remembered Perls et al.'s (1951) observation that "to eliminate introjects . . . the problem is not . . . to accept and integrate dissociated parts of yourself. Rather, it is to become aware of what is not truly yours, to acquire a selective and critical attitude toward what is offered you" (pp. 190f).

References

Adams, M. (2010). Losing one's voice: Dialogical psychology of the unspeakable. *Theory & Psychology, 20*(3), 342–361.

Alexy, R. (1990). A theory of practical discourse. In S. Benhabib & F. Dallmayr (Eds.), *The communicative ethics controversy* (pp. 151–190). Cambridge, MA: MIT Press.

Bakhtin, M. M. (1984). *Problems of Dostoevsky's poetics*. Minneapolis, MN: University of Minnesota Press.

Bakhtin, M. M. (1986). *Speech genres and other late essays*. C. Emerson & M. Holquist (Eds.), Austin, TX: University of Texas Press.

Buber, M. (1957). Distance and relation. *Psychiatry: Journal for the Study of Interpersonal Processes, 20*(2), 97–113.

Buber, M. (1965). *The knowledge of man: A philosophy of the interhuman*. New York: Harper Torchbooks.

Cooper, M. (2003). "I-I" and "I-Me": Transposing Buber's interpersonal attitudes to the intrapersonal plane. *Journal of Constructivist Psychology, 16*(1), 131–153.

Cooper, M., & Hermans, H. (2007). Honoring self-otherness: Alterity and the intrapersonal. In L. M. Simao & J. Valsiner (Eds.), *Otherness in question: Labyrinths of the self* (pp. 305–315). Charlotte, NC: IAP.

Cooper, M., Mearns, D., Stiles, W. B., Warner, M., & Elliott, R. (2004). Developing self-pluralistic perspectives within the person-centered and experiential approaches: A round-table dialogue. *Person-Centered & Experiential Psychotherapies, 3*(3), 176–191.

Damasio, A. R. (1999). *The feeling of what happens: Body and emotion in the making of consciousness*. London: Heinemann.

Fernyhough, C. (2008). Getting Vygotskian about theory of mind: Mediation, dialogue, and the development of social understanding. *Developmental Review, 28*(2), 225–262.

Frenkel-Brunswik, E. (1949). Intolerance of ambiguity as an emotional and perceptual personality variable. *Journal of Personality, 18*(1), 108–143.

Gendlin, E. T. (1997). *A process model*. Chicago, IL: Chicago University Press.

Gergen, K. J. (2009). *Relational being: Beyond self and community*. New York: Oxford University Press.

Habermas, J. (1993). *Justification and application: Remarks on discourse ethics*. Cambridge, MA: MIT Press.

Heidegger, M. (1962). *Being and time*. San Francisco, CA: Harper.

Hermans, H. J. M. (2002). The dialogical self as a society of mind. *Theory & Psychology, 12*(2), 147–160.

Hermans, H. J. M. (2003). The construction and reconstruction of a dialogical self. *Journal of Constructivist Psychology, 16*, 89–130.

Hermans, H. J. M. (2005). Self as a society: The dynamics of interchange and power. In M. W. Baldwin (Ed.), *Interpersonal cognition* (pp. 388–414). New York and London: Guilford Press.

Hermans, H. J. M. (2011). The dialogical self: A process of positioning in space and time. In S. Gallagher (Ed.), *The Oxford handbook of the self* (pp. 654–680). Oxford & New York: Oxford University Press.

Hermans, H. J. M., & Dimaggio, G. (2004). The dialogical self in psychotherapy: Introduction. In H. J. M. Hermans & G. Dimaggio (Eds.), *The dialogical self in psychotherapy* (pp. 1–10). New York: Brunner-Routledge.

Hermans, H. J. M., & Hermans-Konopka, A. (2010). *Dialogical self theory: Positioning and counter-positioning in a globalizing society.* Cambridge: Cambridge University Press.

Hermans, H. J. M., Kempen, H. J. G., & van Loon, R. J. P. (1992). The dialogical self: Beyond individualism and rationalism. *American Psychologist, 47*(1), 23–33.

James, W. (1890). *The principles of psychology* (Vol. 1). New York: Holt.

Lévinas, E. (1969). *Totality and infinity: An essay on exteriority.* Pittsburgh, PA: Duquesne University Press.

Lévinas, E. (1999). *Alterity and transcendence.* New York: Columbia University Press.

Mead, G. H. (1934/1963). *Mind, self and society: From the standpoint of a social behaviorist.* C. W. Morris (Ed.). Chicago, IL: University of Chicago Press.

Merleau-Ponty, M. (1962). *Phenomenology of perception.* London: Routledge & Kegan Paul.

Moreno, J. L. (1964). *Psychodrama* (Vol. 1, 3rd ed. with new introduction). Beacon, NY: Beacon House.

Moreno, Z. T. (1965). Psychodramatic rules, techniques and adjunctive methods. *Group Psychotherapy, 18*(1–2), 73–86.

Perls, F. S. (1969). *Gestalt therapy verbatim.* Moab, UT: Real People Press.

Perls, F. S., Hefferline, R. F., & Goodman, P. (1951). *Gestalt therapy: Excitement and growth in the human personality.* New York: The Julian Press.

Raggatt, P. T. F. (2012). Positioning in the dialogical self: Recent advances in theory construction. In H. J. M. Hermans & T. Gieser (Eds.), *Handbook of dialogical self theory* (pp. 29–45). Cambridge: Cambridge University Press.

Rochat, P. (2010). Me and mine in early development. In T. Fuchs, H. C. Sattel, & P. Henningsen (Eds.), *The embodied self: Dimensions, coherence and disorders* (pp. 175–181). Stuttgart: Schattauer.

Rogers, C. R. (1959). A theory of therapy, personality, and interpersonal relationships, as developed in the client-centered framework. In S. Koch (Ed.), *Psychology: A study of a science – Vol. 3: Formulations of the person and the social context* (pp. 184–256). New York: McGraw-Hill.

Rogers, C. R. (1961). *On becoming a person: A therapist's view of psychotherapy.* Boston, MA: Houghton Mifflin.

Rogers, C. R. (1965). A humanistic conception of man. In R. E. Farson (Ed.), *Science and human affairs* (pp. 18–31). Palo Alto, CA: Science and Behavior Books.

Rogoff, B. (1990). *Apprenticeship in thinking: Cognitive development in social context.* New York and Oxford: Oxford University Press.

Rogoff, B. (1995). Observing sociocultural activity on three planes: Participatory appropriation, guided participation, and apprenticeship. In J. V. Wertsch, P. del Río, & A.

Alvarez (Eds.), *Sociocultural studies of mind* (pp. 139–164). Cambridge, UK: Cambridge University Press.

Rosa, H. (2016). *Resonanz: Eine Soziologie der Weltbeziehung.* Berlin: Suhrkamp.

Rowan, J., & Cooper, M. (Eds.) (1999). *The plural self: Multiplicity in everyday life.* London: Sage.

Ryle, G. (1949). *The concept of mind.* New York: Hutchinson.

Schmid, P. F. (2002). Anspruch und Antwort: Personzentrierte Psychotherapie als Begegnung von Person zu Person. In W. W. Keil & G. Stumm (Eds.), *Die vielen Gesichter der Personzentrierten Psychotherapie* (pp. 75–105). Wien & New York: Springer.

Slife, B. D. (2004). Taking practice seriously: Toward a relational ontology. *Journal of Theoretical and Philosophical Psychology, 24*(2), 157–178.

Staemmler, F.-M. (1993). Projective identification in gestalt therapy with severely impaired clients. *British Gestalt Journal, 2*(2), 104–110.

Staemmler, F.-M. (2012a). *Empathy in psychotherapy: How therapists and clients understand each other.* New York: Springer Publishing.

Staemmler, F.-M. (2012b). Self-esteem, compassion and self-compassion: From individualism to connectedness. *British Gestalt Journal, 21*(2), 19–28.

Staemmler, F.-M. (2015). *Das dialogische Selbst: Postmodernes Menschenbild und psychotherapeutische Praxis* [*The dialogical self: Postmodern image of man and psychotherapeutic practice*]. Stuttgart: Schattauer.

Stern, D. N. (1985). *The interpersonal world of the infant: A view from psychoanalysis and developmental psychology.* New York: Basic Books.

Stern, D. N. (2010). *Forms of vitality: Exploring dynamic experience in psychology, the arts, psychotherapy and development.* Oxford & New York: Oxford University Press.

Vygotsky, L. S. (1978). *Mind in society: The development of higher psychological processes.* M. Cole, V. John-Steiner, S. Scribner, & E. Souberman (Eds.), Cambridge, MA and London: Harvard University Press.

Vygotsky, L. S. (1981). The genesis of higher mental functions. In J. V. Wertsch (Ed.), *The concept of activity in Soviet psychology* (pp. 144–188). New York: Sharpe.

Whelton, W. J., & Greenberg, L. S. (2004). From discord to dialogue: Internal voices and the reorganization of the self in process-experiential therapy. In H. J. M. Hermans & G. Dimaggio (Eds.), *The dialogical self in psychotherapy* (pp. 108–123). New York: Brunner-Routledge.

4 Emotion-focused therapy

Embodied dialogue between parts of the self

William J. Whelton and Robert Elliott

One of the reasons the self draws such extensive research and commentary across disciplines is because of its complexity. In this chapter we address one reason for this tension between how simple and basic the self can *appear* to be and how difficult and elusive it is. In our experience, *most of the time*, our sense of self is unitary. We feel that we are one unified person, with a familiar body, coherent and accessible memories and feelings, and a sense of familiar self-labels and identity rooted in these memories, with familiar habits, likes and aversions, and with core stories we tell ourselves to make the passage of time seem coherent and meaningful. And it is true that in some basic ways a healthy self is experienced as unitary. After all, we have but one body, gradually aging over time and perhaps fraying a bit at the edges, but still of a piece and ours.

Nevertheless, this semblance of unity is the hard-won product of many complex, underlying emotion processes that through conflict, cooperation, and synthesis work to build or construct our sense of self. And at these underlying levels, beneath the surface tension of relative unity, there can be enormous discord, turbulence, fragmentation, and dissociation, accompanied by emotional pain and at times relief, with parts of the self engaged in substantial conflict or even at war with each other (Greenberg & Pascual-Leone, 2001).

In this chapter we will describe the model of self used in emotion-focused therapy (EFT), a model that is explicitly constructivist and dialogical in ways that correspond closely, if not exactly, with Dialogical Self Theory (DST). We will describe the crucial elements of the model, highlighting one element that differentiates it from many similar models: its strongly situating many key aspects of the self in the flesh, that is, in bodily, felt emotion processes. This model derives partly from focusing (Cornell & McGavin, 2008; Gendlin, 1981) but largely from a close analysis of what happens in effective psychotherapy. The latter half of the chapter will give a case example with some examples of how dialogues between parts of the self form effective clinical interventions in EFT.

Dialogical Self Theory

Hermans (1996) and several collaborators (e.g., Hermans & Kempen, 1993; Hermans, Kempen, & Van Loon, 1992) developed Dialogical Self Theory

(DST). This "bridging" theory posits that the self is fundamentally multi-voiced and dialogical, that is, that different aspects of the self have and voice different values, views, attitudes, and priorities and that these need to be negotiated and re-negotiated continually through dialogue. DST is a narrative view of the self as multi-voiced, distributed, and de-centralized. Narrative in this sense is understood not only to represent the dramatic arc of a story over time but also the drama of voices, contradictions, and conflicts occurring simultaneously in space. A range of *I*-positions (voices) can be spatially plotted in relation to one another in the landscape of the mind. These *I*-positions occur not only "within" a traditional Cartesian self (which is illusory), but are both internal and external; that is, the dynamic process of the self and its *I*-positions can occur both internally and in an immediate social environment that is also viewed as belonging to the self (Hermans & Hermans-Konopka, 2010). These dialogues and these voices and their utterances may be personal, social, and cultural events, so that the boundary of the self in this view is very permeable both flowing into and receiving from the social and cultural worlds. At any given time some voices are heard, others are silent, some are powerful, others are squelched and marginalized (Hermans & Gieser, 2012).

These insights foreshadow this chapter, because EFT deals in splits within the self and, as we shall explore at some length, the prototypical dialogue that EFT attempts to resolve is that of the oppressive inner tyrant, which at times acts as an inner critic while at other times (or even at the same time) seeks to control the self through alternating between relentless driving forward and heartlessly blocking or interrupting the self.

The classic split that EFT identifies within the modern self is that of the inner voice of self-criticism or self-condemnation, berating and controlling the self in a sometimes annihilating and terrifying manner. So far, this voice has been found to be central to depression (Greenberg & Watson, 2006), substance misuse (Gilbert, 2014), eating difficulties (Brennan, Emmerling, & Whelton, 2015), social anxiety (Elliott & Shahar, 2017), general anxiety (Timulak & McElvaney, 2018), and borderline or fragile processes (Elliott, Watson, Goldman, & Greenberg, 2004) however, these are only the client populations that have been systematically examined to date.

Emotion-focused therapy

EFT emerged in a multi-vocal way out of the humanistic-experiential psychotherapy tradition (cf. Elliott, Watson, Greenberg, Timulak, & Freire, 2013) integrating the Rogerian therapeutic conditions (Rogers, 1959) with the idea of bodily lived experience from focusing (Gendlin, 1981) and Gestalt therapy ideas about in-session experiments (Perls, Hefferline, & Goodman, 1951), all within an affective science framework (Greenberg, Rice, & Elliott, 1993). Building on the conversation among these elements, extensive empirical research has helped to specify the processes through which people change in psychotherapy (Greenberg & Safran, 1987). The EFT view that emerges from all this posits that the self has many parts and many voices within a complex and variably organized framework, and that the fundamental "glue" that binds these self-organizations is emotion. This "multivocality" of emotions and emotion processes is a basic element of our human heritage. A very frequent goal of EFT is to heal, strengthen, and unify the self by a reorganization of these parts and voices.

Emotion-focused theory of the self

Specifically, the model of self in EFT is based on two underlying theoretical frameworks. Within this model the self is seen as a self-organizing system that is constructed without any homunculus or central executive. The most essential feature of the self is that it is an ongoing, ever-changing process as opposed to a fixed or enduring substance. Emotion is seen as the core organizing process in the construction of the self.

The first framework is that of *affective science*. The broad field of affective science has been growing steadily for over 30 years, especially the neuroscience of emotion (e.g. Davidson, 2000). Emotion is generally understood now to be an evolutionary inheritance that triggers and guides adaptive action (Frijda, 1986) and is generally a rapid, automatic, and global system that differs in many ways from the slow, deliberative processes of higher cognition. It has been shown, for example, that emotional signals generating action are most adaptive if they are able to bypass intermediate cognitive systems when necessary (LeDoux, 1996). Emotional processes usually interact considerably with cognitive processes forming a unique contribution and proving indispensable to effective perception, judgment, and decision-making (e.g. Damasio, 1999). Emotion can perhaps best be understood as a form of information processing that prompts the self to know what really matters to it in its environment and that organizes the self to act in response to that centrally meaningful information (Frijda, 1986; Greenberg, 2010). Since what is most meaningful to people is almost always social information, emotion is also vital to human communication as well as to action.

But emotions are not just basic physiological and neuropsychological hardware. Emotional experience is what gives life color and meaning and these experiences become deeply emotionally anchored in memory. Lived experiences from childhood contribute to the formation of emotion schemes, including emotion self-schemes, which are automatically generated self-organizations formed around learned perceptual, somatic, affective, cognitive, motivational/behavioral aspects of self-experience in common situations in an individual's life. Emotion self-schemes are constructed from the impact of learning and experience on inborn emotional structures; when these have become rigid or stuck ("maladaptive") they form the target of several EFT interventions. What helps to transform painful, maladaptive emotion self-schemes is usually an emotional deepening process in which the person accesses the healthy, resilient, and adaptive power of expansive or assertive emotions (Fredrickson, 2001; Pascual-Leone & Greenberg, 2007).

The second theoretical framework is *dynamic systems* more generally, and *dialectical constructivism* in particular. Dynamic systems theory (e.g., Mahoney, 1991; Thelen & Smith, 1994) posits that given the dynamic interaction of countless variables across subsystems in an organizing system, stable patterns ("attractor states") emerge out of apparent chaos. These are not fixed structures but are continually synthesized in the moment such that a new emergent order can be created if a certain threshold of change in the underlying variables is attained. The agency and identity that are core to being a self are built up over time from a sense of ownership of the complex array of self-states that have been organized into a narrative identity.

Dialectical constructivism provides a more specific dynamic systems account for understanding self processes in EFT (Greenberg & Pascual-Leone, 2001; Pascual-Leone, 1987) and obviously has many parallels to DST (e.g. Hermans, 1996). In this view the self is constructed from moment to moment by the complex interplay between two basic processes, which form an essential, continuous dialectic. On the one hand, there are the bottom-up processes, which start from elements that are physiological and neurochemical, and organize these elements at greater levels of complexity, to finally emerge through repeated higher-level syntheses into bodily felt emotional experience. On the other hand, and in constant interaction with bodily experience, are top-down, culturally based processes of interpretation, symbolism in language, cognitive categorization, and storytelling. People constantly work, and even struggle deeply, to make sense of their experience through the stories and narratives they tell themselves and that have been developing all their lives.

The dialectical constructivist model tells EFT therapists never to lose sight of the actual bodily and experiential roots of self-organizations. Some social constructionists tend to view everything related to the self as the product of language and story, but EFT, following its humanistic traditions, has always argued that interpretations entirely rooted in family and culture can prove to be in deep conflict with a person's authentic, lived, bodily experience.

In this model, to live wisely is to live with a deep immersion at both poles of the dialectic: It is to live in and with the tension, holding a keen sensitivity to bodily experiences and complex feeling states and also to reflect deeply, with all of one's capacity for thought, on the meaning of one's daily experiences. The path to a healthy, wise and meaningful way of life requires the continual integration of both head and heart in this endless, constructive process.

A process and dialogical view of self

This is a modular view of the self and of its possibilities for change and growth that is deeply and inherently multi-vocal and dialogical. It is the basis for the ways in which EFT operationalizes and builds dialogues between parts of the self within therapy. According to the EFT model of self, there exist many voices within each person, every voice ready to speak, given conditions conducive to utterance. Similarly, in the narrative, multi-voiced model of DST, every voice that speaks expresses an *I*-position, but some *I*-positions remain silent, not yet having attained a voice. In EFT, each voice is tied to an actual or potential self-organization, characterized by one or more emotional states. Some of these self-organizations are habitual, they are strong and frequently actualized, and have become very effective attractor states within a person's repertoire. Others appear only infrequently and may generate struggle and anxiety, seeming hesitant and awkward when they show a glimpse of themselves at all. With sufficient support and practice they might gain a stronger foundation and be more frequently synthesized in the moment. Together they form the set of possible selves (a "parliament of selves"), within which in each particular moment a given self-organization will emerge ("vote") when the necessary pre-conditions are present.

A basic principle of these self-organizations and the voices they express is that whereas they can work in unison, they are also frequently at odds, existing in conflict and sometimes intense opposition to each other. In the face of the multiple conflicting demands that life presents, the multi-vocal self does not naturally live in any kind of unity and harmony; rather, unity and a deep inner integrity can only emerge from protracted awareness and dialogue, and is very often the result of intense emotional processing. Many internal voices express criticism of the self and attempt to stifle, block, interrupt, or disrupt self-expression or self-assertion. These self-attacks are often based in a fear of the self's desires and actions that is rooted in childhood adversity and a frantic quest for safety. Some voices (*I*-positions) are squelched and marginalized. Other self-organizations are actuated but entirely out of awareness.

It is apparent that power and the quest for dominance and control is as much a part of this inner world as it is part of the interpersonal world. In DST terms, there are many different possible relations between *I*-positions and the internal world reflects the same concern for power and dominance as one would find in the external social world (Hermans & Hermans-Konopka, 2010). Strong and dominant voices attempt to silence, oppress, and marginalize other aspects of the self. When clients arrive at therapy organized into self-states expressing cynicism, resignation, passivity, and shame one element of these defeated postures is an expression of relative powerlessness not only in the external domain but in the internal as well. Maladaptive self-states that are attacking, denigrating, and controlling the self are often very powerful and dominant. However, what is maladaptive in an adult, typically began as a necessity, a means of safety and survival for a child trapped in circumstances in which their options and cognitive capacity for understanding were constrained.

The process view of the self is rooted in humanistic principles of freedom and choice. The therapeutic focus in EFT is on change, growth, and new possibilities. The self is not viewed as reified, but as operating within a number of constraints, and as a system capable of generating novelty. The therapist in EFT focuses a lot in the early stages on awareness because many self-organizations have never been fully attended to and explored. Deep feelings of hurt and pain have often been avoided, hidden, or disguised. EFT has described emotions as primary, secondary, or instrumental; for example, a secondary emotion (typically an emotional reaction to another more basic, but difficult to face emotion) such as anger can keep a deeper feeling of grief or sadness hidden and buried. As mentioned, dominant self-organizations that are largely negative and self-destructive can marginalize and negate other, growth-oriented possible self-organizations such as hope, pride, joy, and constructive anger. These possible selves may surface weakly if at all in the beginning because they have had very little support and opportunity to develop and grow, but they hold the seed to transformation and change. Research has shown that the pathway out of negative emotions such as shame and debilitating anxiety is often through mobilizing a powerful anger into a forceful and assertive voice (Pascual-Leone & Greenberg, 2007; Timulak & Elliott, 2003). A cornerstone of EFT and similar therapies is to provide clients with the necessary support to give adequate and sustained voice to parts of themselves and possible self-organizations that have been silenced (Elliott & Greenberg, 1997; Stiles, 1999), as the following case example illustrates.

Case example: using EFT to treat clinical depression

Jamie is a composite of several clients; we will highlight key moments from his therapy to illustrate some of the principal ways in which EFT works dialogically with different types of splits or conflicts. A core feature of many of these interventions is that the client is asked to represent the different parts of self in different chairs (thus in DST terms literalizing the metaphor of *I*-positions). The client is asked to speak in turn from each part or position of the self and in particular to dialogue between them, which helps to separate and amplify the different parts. Communication and dialogue emerges from dramatic contact between positions. The voices of parts of the self not only create verbal meaning: clients while in a given chair attend to their bodies and to inner emotional referents in order to symbolize accurately a real inner process.

Jamie is a 44-year-old unemployed lawyer. He has been married to Ashley, a pediatrician, for 14 years, and they have two daughters. He worked as an associate for 12 years at a major law firm but he was let go in a downsizing two years earlier. While he was a prudent and thorough lawyer who tended to win cases he was told he was "sub-optimal" at recruiting new business to the firm. The only work he has found since then has been occasional, part-time, contract work in the legal field. Jamie has been moderately depressed for over a year. For a period he had also suffered from addiction to pills and alcohol but he has been attending a 12-step group for the past three months and it has been under control.

Jamie was the youngest of three sons. His mother was warm and affectionate, but she was dominated and overshadowed by his father who was a very severe, demanding and critical man. While he pushed and bullied all his sons he was hardest on Jamie. Jamie's father, a businessman who ran a small and quite successful trucking company, has always been macho and is a devoted sports fan. He worked in a determined way at producing very masculine, athletic, and aggressive sons. The two older boys, though still criticized for any deficiency, excelled at hockey and football, and generally managed to adopt the stance their father preferred. Jamie made some half-hearted efforts to do so, but liked to write poetry in high school, excelled at fine arts, especially painting, was not at all aggressive, and was neither particularly interested in, nor good at sports though he did join the swim team in high school. While his father joked about his being a sissy for doing so, he also attended all the competitions, freely offering unsolicited advice about Jamie's performance, and had a "melt-down" when Jamie at age 15 unilaterally quit the team. His father, while usually trying to frame his comments as humor, regularly called him a wimp and a loser. Jamie has grown into a profoundly self-critical man. Furthermore, this self-critical organization is embedded within a broader self-interruptive split, by which Jamie numbs himself and shuts himself down, a pattern that is also found in complex trauma (Paivio & Pascual-Leone, 2010). Together, the self-interruption and the self-critical splits are what make him depressed.

Self-interruptive splits in EFT

With moderately to severely depressed clients, access to feelings is partially or completely shut down or blocked by a self-interrupting part of the self, a protective *I*-position. As a result, deeper self-critical processes can't be worked with initially, until the self-interruption is addressed. Self-interruptive splits typically involve a part of the self blocking the expression of specific feelings, thoughts, or actions (Greenberg et al., 1993). At an even deeper level, however, the very awareness of emotion and experience can be suppressed or impeded. To the client this can feel like a "numbing out," or like a feeling of blankness and emptiness.

The process of exploring and resolving a self-interruptive split is done in the form of a two-chair dialogue, with the therapist encouraging the client to speak or act from the interrupting part of the self. Chairs are placed opposite each other and the client moves back and forth between them with the active facilitation of the therapist. Self-interruptions often work implicitly or even physically without words, so the therapist often begins by saying, "Show me how you keep her from feeling [e.g. angry], what you say or do to her." The client begins by enacting how they are blocking the self by openly expressing their implicit commands, or even getting up and demonstrating the bodily process of the self-interruption, such as choking or pushing down the other part. If the enactment begins with a physical action, the therapist then helps the client to put their fears and motivations into words. The overall process generally evolves into a spoken dialogue between the two parts, with the goal of resolving the conflict by understanding and working through the interruption. This process helps the client open up access to work on their deeper self-critical split.

Jamie's self-interruption split work

Jamie was in the sixth session and starting to explore feelings related to his marriage when he became aware that he had gone blank, and felt flat and empty inside. The therapist explored this with him and concluded that a process of self-interruption had begun, perhaps because they had begun to approach what was for him a highly sensitive topic: his marriage. She explained the two-chair intervention for self-interruption to Jamie; he consented to work in this way; they set up the chairs and began:

THERAPIST (T): So come over to this chair. In this chair you will be the part of Jamie that is blocking or interrupting his feelings, leaving him feeling barren and empty inside. Look at Jamie sitting over here in this chair. He was starting to discuss his worries and fears about his marriage and he suddenly went blank. Talk as the part of Jamie that is interrupting him and leaving him feeling so empty and blank.

SELF-INTERRUPTOR (SI): This feels very strange . . . and weird . . . I don't know what to say.

T: Do you mean, that this feels like a weird thing to do, or that your head feels weird right now?

SI: My head feels weird.

T: Yeah, that's a thing that can happen in this. It's part of the shutting down/interrupting process. Is it OK to work with that, how you do that? (SI: Yeah, OK) Try to focus on capturing the perspective of the part of Jamie that is shutting him down. What seems so unsafe? Talk to Jamie over here.

SI: Well Jamie, I was pretty confused when you started to talk in a very personal way about Ashley and your relationship. You know that that is a very painful area for you, a topic that can go down some very embarrassing roads. I'm not really sure how I am making you go numb, but I hate when you open up so much about very painful things and I do wish you would shut up about that stuff.

T: (gently) So this is very sensitive territory, maybe a little embarrassing, and it sounds like you are very concerned for Jamie, you want him to be safe . . . is that it? You're afraid about exposing something delicate?

SI: Yes, that's it . . . that word "exposure," that's right on the money . . . why expose issues that will only make you feel like crap . . . Don't do that. Keep some secrets. Sometimes going numb makes a lot of sense.

T: So come over here. (Client switches chairs.) In this chair you are Jamie, being told to keep quiet about painful things. Go inside. What is happening in here (gesturing toward the throat and chest area)? Are you still feeling numb and blank? What's it like to be told to keep a lid on delicate and painful feelings?

JAMIE (J): I still feel mostly numb inside, but there is something else happening now too, around the edges. It's like a feeling of tears, like a big lump filled with tears. It's like I have to work to keep myself from crying.

T: I invite you not to struggle to hold back the tears. Let them come.

J: No, I can't cry. I'm not going to be able to let go or cry. The numbness is too strong. [Note: It's useful to hear that this is not really a report of an experiential fact but rather the voice of the interrupting part saying, "Don't cry! I'm not going to let you let go."]

T: There's so much sadness and the tears in there but you're holding them back. Come over here then. (Client switches chairs.) I want you now to be this large numbness that is shutting down Jamie's sadness and tears. Speak for the numbness. What does the numbness want to say?

SI: You need me, Jamie. You need numbness. You know you do. To feel this is like a death. You know what this is all about and you know how much pain is locked in there. When you think about this you have terrible thoughts, even of harming yourself. You want the world to swallow you up so that you can just disappear. I don't want you to expose this, I'm trying to help you stop that. With all due respect, you don't know this woman (the therapist) or what she would think. I'm trying to help you here, Jamie. I'm on your side.

T: OK, switch. (Client switches chairs.) (With a very gentle and prizing voice:) There is just something dreadful, so dreadful that it's . . . it's really hard to say. (30-sec. pause) There is so much pain there, it's soaked in shame. And the tears want to come so badly.

J: (Sits silently, for 30 secs.; his face starts to look more and more sad; then he bends over and begins to sob, ever more forcefully)

T: (Gently:) That's it, let it go. Let the tears come. Let them pour out. It just hurts so much. There's so much pain locked up in there. (When there is an opportunity she hands him a box of tissues)

J: (After several minutes of crying and then wiping his face:) I sometimes wonder if he was right . . . about what a pitiful loser I am. He predicted I would be a failure. What's killing me right now . . . (30-sec. pause) . . . is that for months I haven't been able to have sex. Usually I can't even get it up, but even if I do I barely begin and I lose my erection. My wife brought me home some pills but the thought of taking them . . . (he begins to sob again) . . . it makes me feel sick, it just makes me feel like shit . . . I mean, fuck, I'm not an old man. What kind of loser can't have sex?

T: (with gentle compassion) Having sex has been very difficult for you and it leaves you feeling awful about yourself. And there is so much pain and such an overwhelming sense of shame that goes with not performing. It's like, "Wow, here's one more way I'm not living up to my expectations for myself as a man." And it leaves you wanting to shrink and hide and numb out . . . it sounds like you're so alone and isolated in it? You shut down at the thought of talking about it.

After this, they spent two sessions exploring the difficulties that Jamie had been having with sex and the profound and corrosive shame about it that led to the self-interruption. The emotion of shame and the desire to hide dominated one of the core self-organizations toward which Jamie has been strongly pulled, especially since his depression has deepened. As illustrated, it is often necessary to work through the self-interruption split that protects the deeper harshly self-critical process in order to fully access and begin to work with it. This self-interruption is the basis for the anhedonia and the pervasive numbing that are common characteristics of clinical depression. This self-organization, which is both strongly self-interruptive and harshly self-critical, is one in which the self feels small, crushed, and unworthy, leaving it wanting to hide away, out of sight.

Two-chair work for self-critical conflict splits in EFT

Self-criticism, a key component of perfectionism, can be understood as an enduring personality process or self-organization rendering one vulnerable to a number of psychological difficulties, including depression, substance abuse, eating difficulties, relational difficulties, anger and aggression, and many other forms of psychological distress (Blatt, 2004; Zuroff, Mongrain, & Santor, 2004). Research has shown that being highly self-critical is rooted in painful or traumatic childhood developmental experiences with both peers and parents (e.g. Kopala-Sibley & Zuroff, 2014; Mongrain, 1998). Self-criticism when mild can be self-corrective and adaptive but when harsh can be merciless and annihilating (Gilbert, Clarke, Hempel, Miles, & Irons, 2004) as in the case example of Jamie.

As with self-interruption, EFT intervenes in self-criticism by creating a dialogue between two parts of the self: an inner "critic" and another part of self that is the target of the criticism (the "experiencer" or "experiencing self"). The conceptualization here is compatible with DST, in which critical and attacking *I*-positions from the social environment can be brought into the internal "society of mind" where the attack is transformed and intensified. A re-positioning of these voices is required for a transformation toward greater balance and health (Hermans & Gieser, 2012). As the target of habitual attacks, the experiencing self often has felt pressured, helpless, defensive, or even wounded. This process is normally a tacit, private, internal conversation, with fuzzy boundaries between aspects of the split, but the two-chair intervention within EFT brings the conflict alive by making it a dramatic, external dialogue between these two parts of the self. Each part is separated and clearly demarcated from the other: While seated in either chair the client is to speak only for that one voice, that one designated part of the self. The central idea is to externalize and dramatize these internal voices in order to work toward a resolution of the conflict based on a constructive dialogue between aspects of the self. By creating a dramatic dialogue the voices are not disembodied but take on deeper texture and meaning through bodily gestures, vocal tones, facial expressions, and other indications of both emotion and of the power differential. Emotion schemes are vividly activated by enacting the angry self-attack and contempt of the critical self-organization and the sinking and shrinking of the injured, shame-ridden experiencer self-organization. These then activate episodic memories, often from childhood mistreatment.

Working through Jamie's self-critical split

In the ninth session of Jamie's therapy, this self-criticism came sharply into focus when Jamie referred to himself as a "loser" for not being able to properly support his family. This is what EFT calls a marker of a self-critical split. We will look at parts of this two-chair work, after the chairs have been set up and it has begun:

THERAPIST (T): (speaking to the critic:) So continue criticizing Jamie. What is he doing wrong? How does he not measure up?

CRITIC (C): It's not that you're doing something wrong; you're not doing anything at all. You're useless. Thank God you're married to someone who can support her family. If you didn't have her you'd all be homeless.

T: OK, keep going. Let's not talk about Ashley now. Focus on Jamie and be as specific as possible. What is wrong with him?

C: In a nutshell, you're a loser. You're not a man. A man can support his family. You can't even keep a job. You didn't even have the balls to go out and scrape up some business for your firm so that you could keep your job. You're nothing. You're empty space.

T: OK, change. Come over here. (Client switches chairs.) I want you to take a moment now and let those words sink in. He says you're a loser, that you can't keep a job and take care of your family. (Gently:) What's it like to hear that?

EXPERIENCING SELF (ES): (45-sec. pause, then he speaks in a soft, resigned voice:) He's right. He's completely right. I agree with him. I've been a disaster at taking care of my family.

This collapsed experiencing self is very common in depression and involves the experiencing self largely agreeing and identifying with the critic; in fact, it can be argued that this *is* what depression is. This collapse leaves the experiencing self initially unable to achieve separation and differentiation from the critic. In some clients, especially those badly abused as children, the self might have been so flattened for so long that quite a bit of preliminary work building it up is required, using empathic affirmation and focusing. This was not the case with Jamie who, despite his intense self-criticism, had a fairly robust, but hidden, self. In such cases a little bit of coaching can be effective:

T: OK Jamie, I'm hearing your agreement with the critic. But is there some part of you, however small, that disagrees with the critic? Is there some part of you that wants to speak back against this criticism?

ES: (Looking at therapist:) Yes, there is. This critic just doesn't get how hard I've tried.

T: Ok. Don't tell me about it. Look at the critic and tell him, talk to him.

ES: (Looking at the critic:) You have no idea. You think I was goofing off at the law firm? I was trying my guts out. It was a fucking nightmare.

At this point we have clear separation between the two parts. While the process and goal of two-chair work is not to have an argument or debate, it is necessary that there is a critic who is berating the self and a distinct self who is both the object of the criticism, and a subject who reacts to it. As the last talk turn suggests, at this point the client tends to complain and make excuses, but as the criticism becomes more painful and more pointed they will access deeper emotions in response to it. A very important part of the process of transformation in successful two-chair interventions, and one that resonates deeply with DST's focus on power relationships between *I-*

positions, is a change in the power distribution in the parts of the self. In a very self-critical person, the critic is ferocious and strongly dominant. Ironically, what the critic possesses is the self's own power that has become alienated and turned against it in a destructive manner. The process of effective two-chair work entails a shift in power and dominance so that the experiencing self, as it re-owns a greater sense of its agency, recovers a sense of its autonomy and control, with a parallel reduction in the power and voice of the critic. The following gives some sense of the beginning of this emotional re-organization:

c: It's hard to believe that Ashley can even tolerate you. You're so weak and ineffectual. You lost your job. It's even worse really. You lost your career. You were getting well established at a great firm, you'd been there years, and then they decided they could live without you. They weighed you in the balance and they decided you had no value, you gave them nothing.

t: OK, change. What's that like to hear? You gave them nothing.

es: It's terrible ... It really hurts. It's not true. I gave them a lot over the years. I gave the best of myself. You're a liar. They were bastards to me at that firm. I worked hard. It was the situation that was intolerable.

t: Change back.

c: (in a mocking tone:) Yeah, I'm the liar. Where's your job then? You're a loser. They weren't bastards to you. They saw what they needed and then they saw you and they did the arithmetic. Your father was right. There's nothing to you. You're a failure.

t: Say that again.

c: You're a failure.

t: Change. Jamie, take a moment and hear those words.

es: (saying nothing for a long time, head hanging very low; then a deep shudder runs through his body). I feel so small ... like a tiny little ball. (Tears are starting to run down his face.)

t: So small ... so tiny ... and that leaves you feeling what? Is it like sadness, a sad feeling?

es: (Now starting to sob:) Not exactly. I just feel empty. Just empty and crushed. Like what am I even? This ... this thing just won't ever leave me alone. There's just no escaping this thing with its terrible words. They tear at me. That word "failure." That fucking word. I've heard it all my life. It's like a dagger cutting into my heart. It hurts me so badly.

t: That sounds so incredibly painful ... the words ripping into you, into the very core of you (he starts to sob more loudly)... Let the tears come, Jamie, let them flow freely ... these words are like knives cutting into your heart and soul ... especially that one awful word, that's what hurts the most. (Pauses, then gently:) What do you need, Jamie? What do you need from him?

es: (After a couple of minutes – first of crying, then slowly calming into a silence – then speaking very slowly and softly:) Go away. I wish you would just disappear. I need you to stop tormenting me.

t: Yes. Just leave me alone.

ES: Do you have any idea how much you hurt me? Stop it. Leave me alone. It just makes me question who or what I am or whether I deserve anything. Am I really such a loser? (Silence) Then after that I begin to feel such emptiness in the face of the barrage.

T: Stay with that emptiness for a while. Even if it's a bit uncomfortable, be in the emptiness. What is it like? Describe it.

ES: Well it's really quiet, eerily so. And very dark. (Long silence) I can't see anything, but I feel like something is rumbling, like I'm in a cave and some large force is coming toward me. Like I don't know, maybe lava. It's odd but it's a bit scary but not overly so.

T: OK, get in touch with that large force, let yourself feel it. What happens?

ES: It's lifting me up, like a surge of water in the rapids. That feels a bit scary, like it might completely swamp me.

T: Just sit in that surge for a minute. Let it flow around you. What happens in you?

ES: Part of me wants to cry . . . and part of me wants to just scream.

T: Stick with the scream . . . feel the scream . . . Is it surging up inside?

ES: Yes.

T: See if you can give it words.

ES: (In a very small, tentative voice while looking at the therapist:) Uh . . . Fuck off?

T: Great! Say that to the critic sitting there. But say it with more volume.

ES: (a little more loudly) Fuck off!

T: More. Let him have it.

ES: I want you to FUCK OFF! Back up off of me and shut up. (Starting now to lean forward, point at the critic, and speak in a forceful, angry voice:) I am so furious with you. I am so fed up with you. You're nothing but a useless albatross around my neck. I am a good husband and a competent lawyer and it sickens me to keep hearing you say the opposite.

This two-chair intervention continued in a very powerful manner in this session and was repeated in various forms in later sessions. The overall effect was a transformation of a maladaptive emotion scheme of shame through accessing and promoting a strong tacit assertive anger that had been buried. This resulted in a stronger, more cohesive self. The critic softened considerably over a long slow process leaving Jamie feeling much more unified and self-accepting. The critic was very deeply rooted in Jamie's experience of a hostile, demanding father who pushed relentlessly for him to be someone other than who he was. Even Jamie's choice of the law as a profession, one generally viewed as more bellicose and competitive than most, was at least partly due to his effort to appear strong and masculine, to not be a failure. In later sessions the two-chair intervention was supplemented by the empty-chair intervention in which suppressed and unfinished emotional responses were fully expressed to imaginative representations of both his parents, particularly his father. This took several sessions as his harsh and emotionally abusive father took up a great deal of psychological space in Jamie's emotional life. The great burden of sorrow and grief carried by Jamie was tied to the loss of the support that he had so deeply wanted and never received from his father. His representation of his father was transformed by a growing awareness that much of the criticism and pressure was rooted in his father's own inadequacies, shame, and failure. Over the course of therapy, dominant self-organizations of shame-inducing self-criticism gave way to rising emotional awareness, self-assertion, and peacefulness as his depression began to lift.

Conclusion: dialogue with DST

In working on this chapter, we read quite a bit of DST. In closing, we now attempt to stand back from the details of EFT chair work with conflicting parts of self in order to reflect on what we see as the similarities and differences between DST and EFT. Here are some of our observations:

DST through the lens of EFT: common ground

Clearly, DST and EFT share much in common: Both understand the self not as a fixed or unitary entity, but as a process involving multiple aspects. These theories share an interest in understanding both internal relationships between multiple aspects of self (*I*-positions) and external relationships with important others, and also understand that there are many overlaps and parallels between internal self–self relationships and external self–other relationships. Furthermore, many DST concepts have parallels in EFT, making it possible to translate between DST and EFT; see Table 4.1 for examples of EFT translations of key DST concepts.

Compared to DST, EFT has been strongly shaped by its primary focus on clinical populations

We suspect that many of the apparent differences between DST and EFT have evolved out of EFT's focus on understanding and helping clinically distressed populations. Incremental change within the theory has emerged largely from a bottom-up process of analyzing the psychotherapeutic process in real casework. For example, working with depressed clients has given rise to EFT's elaborate description of self-critical and self-interruptive processes and two-chair dialogues. DST has commonly focused more on nonclinical populations, which has led to a greater emphasis on concepts such as promoter positions and a broad, general interest in the structure and function of the self.

EFT is more concrete and messy ("funky") than DST

We continue to be impressed by DST's development and its flexibility as a broad explanatory framework and a "bridging theory." Fundamentally, as we see it, DST relies on a topological or geometric model of self as of a "landscape of mind inhabited by a multiplicity of *I*-positions" (Hermans, 2001). There is of course a long history of topological models in psychology, including Freud's (1923) tripartite model of the mind and Lewin's (1943) field theory. Such models are appealing in their elegance, which in part derives from their highly abstract character, allowing them to be applied to a wide range of phenomena.

In contrast, going back to the earliest writings on EFT tasks (Rice & Greenberg, 1984), EFT has always been more interested in concrete mini-theories and the pragmatics of effective interventions in therapy as opposed to more ambitious theories (see also Greenberg, 1984). Thus, for example, it is more interested in building a model of the self as it unfolds and evolves through two-chair work on self-interruptive and self-critical conflict splits (Greenberg, 1984). In keeping with this, as EFT emotion theory has evolved, we have come to see parts of the self not as points on a map of possible self-positions, but rather as organized

Table 4.1 Definitions and EFT translations of key DST concepts

DST concept	EFT translation
Dialogue: The opposite of monologue; characterized by listening to different voices (internal or external) with genuine curiosity and empathy	• External: A relationship characterized by empathic attunement, communication of genuine empathic prizing, and task collaboration • Internal (two-chair work): an interaction between two parts of self characterized by separation and contact, and moving toward deepening and emotional transformation
I-position: An aspect of self; an internal (or even external) voice that is owned as part of one's self. Emerges dynamically in response to the external or internal situation. Distinct from other *I*-positions but provides a sense of coherence and continuity	Part of self; organized around an emotion-based self-scheme
Meta-position: A higher-level *I*-position that allows mindful self-reflection on other *I*-positions	Meaning perspective (a self-reflective mode of emotion processing)
Centering movements: processes that bring greater integration or coherence in the self; opposite of decentering	Integration or resolution (a stage of task resolution) in which the person experiences relief, reduction of conflict, and forward movement
Depositioning: Direct, receptive, non-categorizing awareness of self and situation that transcends boundaries or *I*-positions	Attending (a mode of emotion processing) to an unclear feeling
Promoter position: This position organizes and gives direction to other *I*-positions. It provides self-compassion and self-support	Self-support or self-compassion (positive treatment of self)

Note: DST sources include Hermans and Gieser (2012) and Hermans and Hermans-Konopka (2010).

around key emotion schemes. Emotion schemes are messy self-organizing processes, held together by particular explicit or implicit emotions and made up of memories or perceptions, immediate bodily experiences, linguistic or iconic symbolizations, and motives or actions. In EFT, self organizations are united and recognizable by characteristic emotional states. Critical parts are primarily recognized by their self-directed anger and contempt. Experiencing self parts may be, at different times, organized around rebellious anger (at the beginning of the chair work), despair/numbness (when they have collapsed), or protective anger or self-compassion (as the person moves toward resolution). This means that different self organizations are themselves made up of multiple related emotion schemes, a further level of experiential complexity.

All of this makes EFT seem rather messy and sometimes even chaotic as the therapist struggles to keep up with the client's constantly shifting experiences and aspects of self. In general, it is fair to say that EFT is "funky" (Kurt Renders, quoted in Geelen, 2013). In contrast, DST can at times seem fairly abstract and even bloodless, as if body and emotions were being avoided. Being highly abstract is probably necessary for a good bridging theory, which must have broad-based appeal and applicability. On the other hand, focusing on emotions as they appear and change over the course of psychotherapy is going to be very messy (e.g. Pascual-Leone, 2009). We are aware that *I*-positions, like emotion schemes, are technically described as embodied (Hermans, 2001) and that DST writings (e.g. Hermans & Hermans-Konopka, 2010) have also addressed emotions; however, our point here is that EFT, rooted in the desire to understand how to help people grow and change in therapy, focuses on the embodied nature of emotion schemes and emotion in general to a much greater extent, pointing to possibilities for further productive dialogue between DST and EFT.

References

Blatt, S. J. (2004). *Experiences of depression: Theoretical, clinical, & research perspectives.* Washington, DC: American Psychological Association.

Brennan, M., Emmerling, M. E., & Whelton, W. J. (2015). Emotion-focused group therapy: Addressing self-criticism in the treatment of eating disorders. *Counselling and Psychotherapy Research, 15,* 67–75.

Cornell, A. W., & McGavin, B. (2008). Inner relationship focusing. *The Folio: A Journal for Focusing and Experiential Therapy, 21*(1), 21–33.

Damasio, A. R. (1999). *The feeling of what happens.* New York: Harcourt-Brace.

Davidson, R. J. (2000). Affective style, psychopathology, and resilience: Brain mechanisms and plasticity. *American Psychologist, 55,* 1196–1214.

Elliott, R., & Greenberg, L. S. (1997). Multiple voices in PE therapy: Dialogues between aspects of the self. *Journal of Psychotherapy Integration, 7,* 225–239.

Elliott, R., & Shahar, B. (2017). Emotion-focused therapy for social anxiety. *Person-Centered and Experiential Psychotherapies, 16*(2), 140–158. doi: 10.1080/14779757.2017.1330701

Elliott, R., Watson, J. C., Goldman, R. N., & Greenberg, L. S. (2004). *Learning emotion-focused therapy: The process-experiential approach to change.* Washington, DC: American Psychological Association.

Elliott, R., Watson, J. C., Greenberg, L. S., Timulak, L., & Freire, E. (2013). Research on humanistic-experiential psychotherapies. In M. J. Lambert (Ed.), *Bergin & Garfield's handbook of psychotherapy and behavior change* (6th ed., pp. 495–538). New York: Wiley.

Fredrickson, B. L. (2001). The role of positive emotions in positive psychology: The broaden-and-build theory of positive emotions. *American Psychologist, 56*, 218–226.

Freud, S. (1923). The ego and the id. In J. Strachey (Ed.) *The standard edition of the complete psychological works of Sigmund Freud* (Vol. 19, pp. 1–66). London: Hogarth Press.

Frijda, N. H. (1986). *The emotions*. Cambridge, UK: Cambridge University Press.

Geelen, E. (2013). "EFT is funky": Een interview met Juliette Becking en Kurt Renders. *Tijdschrift Cliëntgerichte Psychotherapie, 51*, 62–66.

Gendlin, E. T. (1981). *Focusing* (2nd ed.). New York: Bantam Books

Gilbert, P., Clarke, M., Hempel, S., Miles, J. N., & Irons, C. (2004). Criticizing and reassuring oneself: An exploration of forms, styles, and reasons in female students. *British Journal of Clinical Psychology, 43*, 31–50.

Gilbert, S. E. (2014). Using mindful self-compassion to improve self-criticism, self-soothing, cravings, and relapse in substance abusers in an intensive outpatient program (Doctoral dissertation). University of Tennessee, Knoxville. Retrieved from Trace.Tennessee.Edu. (utk_graddiss/3128).

Greenberg, L. S. (1984). A task analysis of intrapersonal conflict resolution. In L. Rice & L. S. Greenberg (Eds.), *Patterns of change* (pp. 67–123). New York: Guilford Press.

Greenberg, L. S. (2010). *Emotion-focused therapy*. Washington, DC: American Psychological Association.

Greenberg, L. S., & Pascual-Leone, J. (2001). A dialectical constructivist view of the creation of personal meaning. *Journal of Constructivist Psychology, 14*, 165–186.

Greenberg, L. S., Rice, L. N., & Elliott, R. (1993). *Facilitating emotional change: The moment by moment process*. New York: Guilford Press.

Greenberg, L. S., & Safran, J. D. (1987). *Emotion in psychotherapy: Affect, cognition, and the process of change*. New York: Guilford Press.

Greenberg, L. S., & Watson, J. C. (2006). *Emotion-focused therapy for depression*. Washington, DC: American Psychological Association.

Hermans, H. J. M. (1996). Opposites in a dialogical self: Constructs as characters. *Journal of Constructivist Psychology, 9*, 1–26.

Hermans, H. J. M. (2001). The dialogical self: Toward a theory of personal and cultural positioning. *Culture & Psychology, 7*, 243–281. doi: 10.1177/1354067X0173001

Hermans, H. J. M., & Gieser, T. (Eds.) (2012). *Handbook of dialogical self theory*. Cambridge, UK: Cambridge University Press.

Hermans, H. J. M., & Hermans-Konopka, A. (2010). *Dialogical self theory: Positioning and counter-positioning in a globalizing society*. Cambridge, UK: Cambridge University Press.

Hermans, H. J. M., & Kempen, H. J. G. (1993). *The dialogical self: Meaning as movement*. New York: Academic Press.

Hermans, H. J. M., Kempen, H. J. G., & Van Loon, R. (1992). The dialogical self: Beyond individualism and rationalism. *American Psychologist, 47*, 23–33.

Kopala-Sibley, D. C., & Zuroff, D. C. (2014). The developmental origins of personality factors from the self-definitional and relatedness domains: A review of theory and research. *Review of General Psychology, 18*, 137–155.

LeDoux, J. (1996). *The emotional brain: The mysterious underpinnings of emotional life*. New York: Touchstone.

Lewin, K. (1943). Defining the field at a given time. *Psychological Review, 50*, 292–310.

Mahoney, M. (1991). *Human change processes*. New York: Basic Books.

Mongrain, M. (1998). Parental representations and support-seeking behaviors related to dependency and self-criticism. *Journal of Personality, 66*, 151–173.

Paivio, S., & Pascual-Leone, A. (2010). *Emotion-focused therapy for complex trauma: An integrative approach.* Washington, DC: American Psychological Association.

Pascual-Leone, A. (2009). Dynamic emotional processing in experiential therapy: Two steps forward, one step back. *Journal of Consulting and Clinical Psychology, 77*, 113–126.

Pascual-Leone, A., & Greenberg, L. S. (2007). Emotional processing in experiential therapy: Why "the only way out is through." *Journal of Consulting and Clinical Psychology, 75*, 875–887.

Pascual-Leone, J. (1987). Organismic processes for neo-Piagetian theories: A dialectical causal account of cognitive development. *International Journal of Psychology, 22*, 531–570.

Perls, F. S., Hefferline, R., & Goodman, P. (1951). *Gestalt therapy: Excitement and growth in the human personality.* New York: Julian Press.

Rice, L. N., & Greenberg, L. S. (1984). *Patterns of change: Intensive analysis of psychotherapy process.* New York: Guilford.

Rogers, C. R. (1959). A theory of therapy, personality, and interpersonal relationships as developed in the client-centered framework. In S. Koch (Ed.), *Psychology: The study of a science* (Vol. 3, pp. 185–256). New York: McGraw-Hill.

Stiles, W. B. (1999). Signs and voices in psychotherapy. *Psychotherapy Research, 9*, 1–21.

Thelen, E., & Smith, L. B. (1994). *A dynamic systems approach to the development of cognition and action.* Cambridge, MA: Massachusetts Institute of Technology Press.

Timulak, L., & Elliott, R. (2003). Empowerment events in process-experiential psychotherapy of depression: A qualitative analysis. *Psychotherapy Research, 13*, 443–460.

Timulak, L., & McElvaney, J. (2018). *Transforming generalized anxiety: An emotion-focused approach.* New York: Routledge.

Zuroff, D. C., Mongrain, M., & Santor, D. C. (2004). Conceptualizing and measuring personality vulnerability to depression: Revisiting issues raised by Coyne and Whiffen (1995). *Psychological Bulletin, 130*, 489–511.

5 Assimilation of problematic voices and the historicity of signs

How culture enters psychotherapy

William B. Stiles

This chapter considers how words and other signs absorb their meaning from the experience and cultural context of people who have used them, a property called *historicity*. Through the historicity of the signs they use, therapists' and clients' cultural backgrounds shape clients' understanding of and solutions to their problems. The account is framed in terms of the assimilation model (Stiles, 2011; Stiles et al., 1990).

The assimilation model

According to the assimilation model (Stiles, 2011; Stiles et al., 1990), people's experiences leave traces that can be reactivated by new experiences that are similar in some way. Experiences involve actions and intentions as well as perceptions, thoughts, and feelings. So when the traces are reactivated, they too encompass actions and intentions. That is, they can act and speak. To emphasize the active, agentic nature of experiential traces, assimilation theorists and researchers often refer to them as *voices* (Honos-Webb & Stiles, 1998; Stiles, 1997). The reference can be understood as metaphorical, but it has observable manifestations: Different internal voices often speak with distinguishable voice qualities (Osatuke, Gray, et al., 2004; Osatuke, Humphreys et al., 2005; Stiles, 1999).

With time and experience, traces of people's experience tend to become linked with traces of other experiences by a process we call assimilation. This linking can occur through physical similarity or contiguity of the experiences; however, much of the assimilation is mediated by semiotic *meaning bridges* – words, stories, and other constructions that link the experiences – as described later in this chapter. In this way, the voices of experience become resources that can be addressed by events. Because they are addressed by events that are related, they are reactivated and tend to emerge at times when they may be useful. For most people, most experiences are unproblematic and can be assimilated smoothly. Mutually accessible experiences are thereby aggregated by a *community of voices* in which each member is a resource that can be called upon when it is needed. For example, voices of cooking experiences emerge in the kitchen; voices of teaching experiences emerge in the classroom.

Some experiences are problematic, however, because they are traumatic, incompatible with the person's usual self, or otherwise distressing or unacceptable.

Problematic experiences leave traces too, and the voices of the problematic experiences also try to respond when they are addressed. However, they cannot be smoothly assimilated because they evoke powerful negative affect when they begin to emerge. As a consequence they tend to be excluded from the community of voices to varying degrees, remaining suppressed, avoided, or distorted (Stiles, Osatuke, Glick, & Mackay, 2004). In therapy, meaning bridges are often built first between the therapist and the client's problematic voices. These interpersonal semiotic links can then be used as intrapersonal bridges among the client's own internal voices.

The assimilation model also describes how a client's problematic voices can be integrated (assimilated) during successful psychotherapy, turning them into resources. Assimilation tends to follows a systematic developmental progression summarized in the eight-stage *assimilation of problematic experiences sequence* as the meaning bridges evolve (Stiles, 2002, 2011; Stiles et al., 1991): (0) warded-off/dissociated, (1) unwanted thoughts/active avoidance, (2) vague awareness/emergence, (3) problem statement/clarification, (4) understanding/insight), (5) application/working through, (6) resourcefulness/problem solution, and (7) integration/mastery.

This semiotic and developmental account has been supported and elaborated in intensive case studies involving a variety of types of psychotherapy (e.g. Basto, Pinheiro, Stiles, Rijo, & Salgado, 2017; Brinegar, Salvi, Stiles, & Greenberg, 2006; Caro Gabalda, Pérez Ruiz, & Llorens Aguilar, 2014; Caro Gabalda & Stiles, 2013, in press; Caro Gabalda, Stiles, & Pérez Ruiz, 2016; Honos-Webb, Stiles, & Greenberg, 2003; Leiman & Stiles, 2001; Mendes et al., 2016; Osatuke, Glick et al., 2005; Ribeiro et al., 2016; Stiles et al., 2006; see also a summary of earlier work in Stiles, 2002). Studies have also shown that good therapeutic outcomes are statistically associated with assimilation progress, whereas poor outcomes are associated with little or no progress (Basto, Stiles, Rijo, & Salgado, 2018; Detert, Llewelyn, Hardy, Barkham, & Stiles, 2006).

Bridges to Dialogical Self Theory

As pointed out by Konopka (2017, personal communication), there are many possible theoretical links between the assimilation model and Dialogical Self Theory (DST). Voices could be, in DST language, additionally called *I*-positions (Hermans, 2002). Building meaning bridges between voices to enlarge a community of voices could be described in DST terms as changing relations between *I*-positions or within the society of mind (Hermans, 2002). Developing close relations between *I*-positions is, in a DST perspective, stimulating centering or centripetal movements in the self (Hermans & Hermans-Konopka, 2010), whereas disconnected or avoided experiences may be related to the decentering or centrifugal voices in the self. Building meaning bridges has some similarity to the concept of developing meta-positions.

Centering movements like assimilation have been described from the DST perspective as movements towards a greater integration and order, working in the direction of coherence and unity. They restore the organization of the self when an existing order has been challenged. Decentering movements are those movements in the self that create disintegration, disrupt or undermine an existing order and integration, although these movements also have the potential to innovate the organization of the self (Hermans & Hermans-Konopka, 2010).

Presumably assimilation theory and DST overlap because both seek to describe and explain the same underlying reality. Attempts to conceptualize should tend to converge as new observations suggest adjustments in the tenets and concepts (Stiles, 2009). However, caution is warranted, as terms are not precisely translatable across theories (Leiman & Stiles, 2002). For example, the concept of *I*-position carries meanings that are not included in the assimilation model concept of voice.

> The theoretical advantage of the notion of *I*-position is that it brings unity and continuity in the self, while preserving its multiplicity. The I is continuous over time: in the process of appropriation and rejection, it is one and the same I who is doing this.
>
> (Hermans & Hermans-Konopka, 2010, p. 139)

In the assimilation model, people's (variable) sense of unity and continuity of the self is not built into a concept but requires explanation. It is posited to reflect the degree of smooth mutual access between voices, mediated by meaning bridges (Stiles, 2011).

Within scientific theories like the assimilation model and DST, terms and expressions should mean the same thing to everybody, and the meanings should remain stable across time, except for explicit modifications in light of new observations (Stiles, 2006, 2017). Psychological theories don't fully achieve such consistency and stability, of course, but they are important goals, and deviations risk problems in logic and understanding. This is why theorists must be careful and explicit about defining their terms and why numbers are so appealing to scientists. More than most other words, numbers tend to mean the same thing across people and time (Stiles, 2006, 2009).

Signs and meanings

The concept of meaning bridge in the assimilation model rests on a concept of *sign* that draws on the work of Bakhtin (1984, 1986), Voloshinov (1929/1986), and Leiman (1992, 2011): A sign, such as a word or an image, or a system of signs, such as a sentence, a narrative, a theory, or a picture, has two aspects, a physical, observable aspect and an experiential, epistemologically private aspect. First, it has a concrete presence in the world, such as marks on a page or a screen or vibrations in the air. Second, it refers to people's experience of events in the world or in their minds (Stiles, 1997, 2011).

The second, experiential aspect of a sign is the sign's meaning. The meaning includes the experience of the author who produces the sign and the experience of the addressee or others who perceive the sign. That is, in this theory, meanings are experiential and epistemologically private.

In contrast to scientific theories, social conversations and psychotherapy do not require that meanings remain consistent and stable. This is fortunate, as word meanings normally vary across people, and they change and grow constantly. Psychotherapy makes use of these changes, as addressed in the rest of this chapter.

A sign's meanings to an author and an addressee are never exactly the same; we never understand each other perfectly. Further, signs have a different meaning each time they are used. People's experience changes from moment to moment, so any word that refers to it changes meaning at the same time. The word *sign*, for example, means something at least slightly different to you and to me now than it did at the beginning of this chapter.

Even the shared meanings of simple common words can change substantially across time. For example, since I began school in the 1950s, English gender pronouns have shifted meaning. A sentence like, "A therapist should pay attention to everything his client says" could refer to either a male or a female therapist. Now it is understood by most Western professionals as either referring to only male therapists or insensitive to issues of sexist language. In either case, the meaning – the experience of the addressees – is different. Technology has shifted many meanings. For example, people still dial phone numbers even though more than a generation has passed since telephones had the round, rotary dials from which the verb was derived, and that in turn had been derived from the round clock dials that measured the day (*dies* in Latin).

In this fluid view of meaning, dictionaries can be considered as historical summaries of meanings that words have had. They can be useful guides to understanding the experiences that people who use them are trying share. But they should not be considered as an authoritative source of stable or immutable properties of words.

Meaning bridges

Signs mediate communication; they offer a way for people to share their experiences with each other and across space and time. As you read this chapter, you are sharing experiences that I had when I wrote this at my home in North Carolina, probably years ago. To the degree that my words' meanings are similar to you as they were to me, you understand me, and the text of this chapter is a meaning bridge.

People generally, and therapists and clients particularly, work hard to ensure that the words they say convey the meanings they intend, and they work hard to understand the meanings that others intend. To the degree they succeed, the sign or system of signs is a meaning bridge between them. Meaning bridges are thus a semiotic glue that binds people's experiences together.

According to assimilation theory, meaning bridges serve the same function intrapersonally as interpersonally. That is, the same semiotic glue can bind experiences together whether author and addressee are different people or different voices within the same person.

Meaning bridges make experiences smoothly accessible within and between people. People can move from one experience to the other using shared signs or systems of signs. Meaning bridges take a variety of forms: Names can make things similar. The term *tree* links diverse experiences of tall, woody plants, both within and between people. Terms like *car parts* or *deterministic theories* can make even more disparate objects or experiences similar. Narratives can link characters and scenes to each other by plot and chronology. Scientific theories link disparate observations; for example, the theory that the earth is round pulls together observations that ships disappear over the horizon, that the sun and moon rise and set each day, and that you can go either east or west to get from New York to Beijing.

Semiotic meaning bridges also underlie the process of aggregating experiences, and in this capacity, they are the mechanism of assimilation. By bringing two experiences together in awareness – reactivating their traces at the same time – a meaning bridge produces a new, aggregate experience, involving elements of both (see Stiles, 2011). Any experience that involves recognition, familiarity, or perceived similarity illustrates this process. Traces of aggregate experiences yield aggregate voices. For example, smoother access can be facilitated by giving experiences a common label ("I can see that this was another self-defeating moment") or making them part of a story ("my father hit me when he was drunk because of his own demons, not because I was despicable"), bringing even unpleasant experiences into the community of voices.

Historicity

Although signs continually change meaning, the old meanings are not lost. On the contrary, signs accumulate these meanings; each use adds another layer. This property of accumulating meanings is called the *historicity* of signs.

To understand how signs accumulate meanings, consider: To the extent you understand what I mean in this chapter, you are sharing some of my experience. If and when you use some of these words or expressions later, their meaning (your experience of these words as author) will incorporate a little of the experience I shared with you. Then, to the extent that your addressees understand your meaning, they will therefore share a bit of my experience along with yours through your words or expressions.

Further, I was not the first person to use these words and expressions. My understanding of signs owes a great deal to discussions with Mikael Leiman (1992, 2011), whose understanding drew on reading work on semiotics by Bakhtin (1984, 1986), Voloshinov (1929/1986), and Vygotsky (1978). Thus, as you read, you are sharing Leiman's, Bakhtin's, Voloshinov's, and Vygotsky's experience as well as mine. When you mention it later, your addressees will also share a bit of their experience. And of course the history does not end there. Every lecture and discussion and conversation draws on and shares the experience of the generations who have previously used the expressions; their experience is embedded in the signs. As Bakhtin (1986) put it, "the word ... is bottomless" (p. 127). DST was also inspired by the work of Bakhtin, among others (Hermans & Hermans-Konopka, 2010).

Theoretically, historicity underlies how words come to have the meanings they have for us. We learned the meanings from others when they shared their experience with us. Subsequently we use those words to share similar experiences with others. In this way, historicity accounts for the stability of language. Most words have so much experience already invested in them that speakers of the language use them similarly. This is why dictionaries work.

Nevertheless, new terms and expressions and new uses for old ones enter the language continually. As people use words to share new experiences, old words are used in new ways and contexts, as illustrated in the earlier examples of gender pronouns and the verb *dial*. Mass media – books, newspapers, radio, television, and the Internet – speed up and broaden the sharing. Words and phrases from pundits, politicians, and popular songs make their way into everyday conversations and psychotherapeutic dialogue, as people find uses for them in sharing their own experience.

Although the meanings of words, expressions, and stories are constructed from others' experience, the voice of any one of the previous users is likely to be extremely faint, diluted to homeopathic levels by the many other voices whose experience is also shared by the word. Even expressions attributed to well-known figures share not only the experience of the attributed source but also the experience of those who have repeated, commented, interpreted, or recommended the expression. Likewise scientific concepts and theories, which should be experienced similarly by everybody, share the (hopefully similar) experiences of researchers, textbook writers, the teachers, students, and others who have studied or used them, as well as that of the originators.

The concept of historicity describes what is available to authors and addressees. However, nothing in the concept of historicity requires that what the signs mean is accurate, honest, or complete. Authors make their own choices about what experiences they share, and addressees can determine what they accept.

Penumbras of meaning

The theory suggests that sign meanings can be retained and shared even though they are not fully conscious. People's experience of signs seems to extend beyond what they are fully aware of in the moment. Sometimes the layers of meaning can be unpacked. For example, etymologies can make implicit historical meanings explicit (see e.g. Elliott's (2006) analysis of the term *insight*), yielding a sense of recognition. Attending to an expression, as when a therapist repeats a client phrase, can lead more layers to emerge.

When people listen to their own words, they may hear the voices of people who have used those words previously along with their own voices. In a sense, writing or speaking, even to oneself, can be a dialogue with forebears. Likewise, an addressee may become aware of meanings that were subliminal to the author.

The possibility of understanding more than the speaker is obvious in the case of words and stories that are recited (e.g. dramatic productions), but theoretically it is characteristic of all sign-mediated communication. Conversely, some communications are intentionally off-record; hints, for example, or manipulations, intended to be recognized by their addressees but not as having been intended, apprehended as if the ideas were the addressee's own (Stiles, 1986).

Therapists are familiar with subliminal meanings, and indeed, it is appreciating these that allow the therapist to reflect and interpret the client's experience deeply enough to be helpful, to re-state or reframe their clients' expressions so that they realize more fully what they were saying, making explicit what was implicit. In general, people say more than they know. As Hattersley (1976/1991) said about a conversation with author John Braine: "I remember him explaining to me the true message and real moral of *Room at the Top* and discovering how much better was the novel I had read than the one he had written" (p. 120).

Meaning seems to survive translation. Much of the original depth of meaning is lost when an utterance is recast in a different language, of course, but something is preserved. Much depends on the intermediation of the translator or of those who develop mechanical translation systems. The historicity of the terms in the translation may mislead. But in principle, this is much like translations across media: writing represents a translation from spoken language; electronic reproduction is a translation from the original sound. In some cases translations may even improve communication, making some subliminal meanings more explicit in the translation than in the original.

Words as tools

Language and other signs are tools for sharing experience. In using semiotic tools, authors are not restricted to dictionary meanings or standard grammar but can use any available semiotic resources. There is plenty of scope in the means of delivery to convey even very subtle aspects of an author's experience. Paralinguistic features, for example, include intonation, tonal contours, emphasis, pauses or the absence of pauses, loudness variations, length of syllables, laughter and other vocal noises, and nonverbal accompaniments to speech can convey meaning (Edwards & Lampert, 1993). Authors can use neologisms, slang, metaphors, gestures, facial expressions, pictures, drawing material, or sand trays. All of these are semiotic, and all can accumulate meanings.

Success in the task depends partly on the authors' and the addressees' cleverness, resourcefulness, creativity, and persistence, but also on what is in the toolbox. Through the process of historicity, semiotic tools have been shaped by generations of previous users to deal with their needs. We can imagine that interpersonal and psychological problems were salient among those needs. In consequence, words, expressions, theories, and stories are well adapted for addressing such problems.

The semiotic tools available to therapists and clients include theories and lore – the formal professional work of theorists and researchers and well as other therapists and former clients whose experience went into building theories of therapy. Their thoughtful experience is embedded in the terms, formulations, and interpretations that therapists use as they practice. These tools include formal treatment protocols, which share the experience of successful therapists and theorists. Scientific writing about individual psychology and psychopathology share the experience of scientists. Perhaps less authoritatively, aphorisms, folk wisdom, and common knowledge about human relations and human feelings share the voices of forebears, having been passed through many people, accumulating their experience as they pass. Comments by supervisors and colleagues and tones of voice and postures learned from watching successful therapists are available, bringing those voices into the consulting room.

Sharing experience is a two-sided exercise. In building meaning bridges, authors on both sides of the dialogue must contend with uptake by their addressees. Authors select and modify their semiotic tools to fit their addressees. Professionals use different terms with other professionals than with lay people. Words have different meanings in conversations with intimates than with strangers. Talking with children requires different semiotic tools than talking with adults. And idiosyncratic meanings develop within relationships, particularly psychotherapy, as people find ways to refer to complex or subtle personal experiences. Thus, signs are shaped by the addressee as well as by the author. As Voloshinov (1929/1986) put it,

> A word is a two-sided act. It is determined equally by whose word it is and for whom it is meant . . . A word is a bridge thrown between myself and another. If one end of the bridge depends on me, then the other depends on my addressee.
>
> (p. 86)

Finding an internal meaning bridge between a problematic experience and the self is also a two-sided act. That is, to be a meaning bridge, the signs must be acceptable from the perspective of the problematic voice as well as from the perspective of the self (Stiles et al., 2004).

Culture enters psychotherapy through signs

Culture is ubiquitous. It is there in every word. Words and other signs bring representatives of the culture into the room. The words, expressions, stories, and theories that are available to clients and therapists were also the tools that forebears – professional and nonprofessional – have used to build internal meaning bridges, to name, confront, and overcome their personal and interpersonal problems. To put this another way, voices of the culture speak to and through clients and therapists as they speak to each other, bringing cultural experience concerning interpersonal and intrapersonal relationships to bear on the client's current problems.

Historicity theory helps explain why intercultural therapeutic dyads may have problems. Clients and therapists with different traditions and perhaps different native languages are relatively likely to miss or misconstrue some of the meaning of what is said and what is done. It will be harder to bring as much of the meaning into awareness. Both author and addressee have to work harder to be understood and to understand. Accurate communication and building meaning bridges may take more time.

On the other hand, modern communication, travel, and immigration have expanded opportunities for acquiring meaning. Increasingly, therapists and clients are exposed to other cultures in mass media, restaurants, and on urban streets. Popular representations of anthropology and history expose people to semiotic representations of experience in diverse cultures, even if the representations are not completely accurate. Targeted cultural education affects not only those exposed directly, but all those with whom those who are exposed interact. In this way people can absorb the experience not only of people living now but of their forebears as well. Not perfectly, of course, but in part and in flavor.

Examples of historicity in psychotherapy

I offer two commented case examples to illustrate how historicity works, drawn from assimilation case studies. Both were studied following the four-step assimilation analysis procedure used in most assimilation case study research (Stiles & Angus, 2001): (a) familiarization and indexing, (b) identifying and choosing themes, (c) extracting passages representing a chosen theme, and (d) describing the process of assimilation. The fourth step may include coding according to the assimilation of problematic experiences sequence and/or quali- tative analysis of the issues selected for scrutiny, such as the nature of the signs used in meaning bridges between therapist and client and among the client's internal voices.

Debbie's rejecting voice

Debbie was a 29-year-old mother of two who sought treatment for depression at Guys Hospital in London, England, where she was considered to have borderline characteristics. She was seen for 16 sessions of cognitive analytic therapy (CAT) as part of the Guys Borderline Project (Ryle, 1997; Ryle & Kerr, 2002). She was considered a successful case.

In Debbie's opening statement, she described an encounter with her estranged husband, which had occurred three months previously and that, she felt, had greatly intensified her depression.

> He sort of, he came over the last occasion
> and basically said that
> he'd never wanted to know me the whole time he'd been with me.
> Which –
> That was the last.
> You know, after I'd,
> I'd had ten years of torture anyway,

living with someone in that condition.
And then –
And that was like the final.
There was nothing else to say, and
I sort of went down from there.
I'd been depressed leading up to that,
but not that bad.
And then, once that had been said,
I just, I just stopped, basically.
The next day I couldn't,
I couldn't take the kid to school.
I just, I couldn't get out of bed.
And my mum came down and stayed for a week,
and I basically didn't do a thing.
I sat on the couch for a week.

Following this episode, Debbie said, she could not stand to see her husband because it reminded her of this rejection. She said she had lost control and physically attacked him the last time he had shown up unannounced.

It emerged that Debbie had a long-standing pattern of occasional angry outbursts, apparently triggered by signs of rejection. In therapy, there were some brief intrusions of defiant, angry content, spoken in a distinctive voice, louder, more rapidly, in a lower register, likewise triggered by discussions of times she had been rejected (Stiles, 1999). Debbie's outbursts were mainly verbal; the physical attack on her husband was unusual and extreme. After the outbursts, which she described as uncontrolled, she said she would feel horrible about herself. Most of the time Debbie was docile and unassertive.

A distinctive part of the CAT approach is a written formulation of the client's relevant strengths and problems, usually given in session 4. Among other things, the therapist suggested that Debbie's outbursts seemed to involve flipping from a meek reject*ed* role into the complementary reject*ing* role. Such reciprocal role procedures involving alternation between positions and counter-positions are discussed in the CAT literature (Leiman, 1997; Ryle, 1997; Ryle & Kerr, 2002), and incorporated in DST (Hermans & Hermans-Konopka, 2010).

Debbie took this formulation on board and worked with it. The following passage, from the middle of session 8, illustrates her progress in building a meaning bridge between the rejected and rejecting voices. The passage was part of a discussion of a telephone call in which Debbie had told her husband how irresponsible she thought he had been for failing to show up to take their children on a promised outing. From her description, the conversation seemed to have been a forceful expression by her rejecting voice. However, she was less impulsive than in previous episodes, and she did not feel so horrible and rejected afterwards. As she explained,

Even with that, sort of that rejecting now,
    when I said yesterday on the phone –

I knew that I would feel rejected after I'd said it.
Because ...
he'll ...
He'll reject me
because I'm not going along with what he says.
    And I'm not being nice.
    And I'm not being, you know ...
So I did feel like that a little bit
But then I thought,
No.
I did the right thing.
I can't start feeling bad
because I'm saying what I think's right.

The term "rejecting" in the first line of this excerpt was a reference to the therapist's formulation. Debbie's explanation can be understood as an account of her progress in assimilating – gaining smoother access to – her rejecting voice. That is, the rejecting voice was becoming a resource for assertion rather than a disruptive and unwelcome intrusion. The smoother access was manifested as somewhat greater moderation and control in employing it and in less anguish and remorse afterwards, though it was still not fully under control. By the end of the 16-session therapy, she was still more comfortable and facile with her new assertiveness (Stiles, 1999).

The formulation of reciprocal rejected and rejecting voices was thus part of a meaning bridge Debbie built to her disconnected rejecting voice. The therapist brought this formulation into the treatment, having drawn directly on CAT theory. We could say the voice of Ryle (1997) and other CAT authors spoke to Debbie through the therapist. Beyond that, the formulation built on the experience of the many previous users of the term *reject*, which entered the English from Old French and Latin, carrying the experience of those cultures. It also drew on the contrast of English -ed and -ing verb forms and hence on the centuries of experience that have honed that linguistic device.

Richard's use of avatar software

Culture enters therapy through nonverbal signs as well as verbal ones. Richard (pseudonym) was a 14-year-old boy with (high-functioning) autistic spectrum disorder (ASD), who was seen for anxiety and disruptive behavior in a clinical trial of what we called avatar software in school counseling (van Rijn, Chryssafidou, Falconer, & Stiles, submitted). The therapeutic focus in Richard's counseling was on his distressing experience of being different, "mocked" and excluded by his peers, which he attributed to his ASD.

Using the avatar software, clients can digitally create visual representations of their inner worlds and life situations on a computer monitor. The action is set in a rural, somewhat medieval landscape containing hills, fields, a forest, a river, and a castle. Androgynous avatars can be created to represent self or others and assigned names, emotions, and expressions. A variety of props, such as bridges, walls, roadblocks, and treasure chests can be added and given labels.

In his first encounter with the software, Richard created a scene within the walls of the castle, which he described as a "secure base," and populated it with avatars representing himself and his peers and milestone props labeled with recent accomplishments. A campfire prop labeled "happiness," confirmed this as a reference to an inner refuge where he felt safe. Later Richard chose a sunlit forest glade in the digital landscape and added a section of wall prop, which he labeled "cannot get past it" with a treasure chest on one side labeled "normal" (later expanded to four treasure chests) and an avatar named "fitting in" on the other side with a "crying and stressed" emoticon, a posture of "stressing/ regretting/OMG [oh, my God!]," and an inner voice saying, "I can see it but I cannot achieve it" (see Figure 5.1). This representation of his core problematic experience of being different seemed more poignant and powerful than his verbal characterizations at the time.

Theoretically, the images were powerful tools for Richard because they carried cultural voices that trace at least to medieval forebears. These images have been used continuously over the intervening thousand or so years, not least in modern video games. As Richard used the images to share his experience with the

Figure 5.1 Treasure chests labeled "normal"; wall labeled "cannot get past it"; avatar named "fitting in" on the other side of the wall with a "crying and stressed" emoticon, a posture of "stressing/regretting/OMG," and an inner voice saying, "I can see it but I cannot achieve it."

counselor, he could see them too. Theoretically the metaphorical visual representations, like an apt choice of words, made his experience more salient or clear to his own other inner voices, suggesting deeper meanings, drawing on the images' cultural history.

Discussion: therapist as representative of the culture

Through the historicity of the words and other signs they use, therapists' and clients' cultural backgrounds shape the meaning bridges and hence clients' understanding of and solutions to their problems. Just using words or other signs puts people in contact with the forebears and can be therapeutic, as illustrated in the expressive writing paradigm (Pennebaker & Beall, 1986; Sloan & Marx, 2004). But having a therapist in the room helps too, as a cultural representative who can help bring appropriate forebears' experience to bear on the psychological problem at hand. The job is easier if the therapist is conversant with the client's culture.

Therapists try to find the right words for interventions (Stiles, 2017), framing the client's problems in ways that fit for the client while bringing to bear professional and other cultural resources, pointing toward solutions that worked for others who have expressed their problems in similar terms.

Professional psychological knowledge is central, of course, but broad understanding of the human condition is also useful. Authors reaching back to Freud and Jung have emphasized the value of knowledge of art and literature for understanding otherwise mysterious intrusions into client's experience. Jungian archetypes (Jung, 1981) are more understandable if we understand "racial memory" as "cultural memory" and suppose that the encoding is not in the DNA but in the historicity of language and imagery.

Theoretically, cultural voices enter all human interaction, not just psychotherapy, though the historicity of signs. But perhaps an understanding of the mechanism can suggest ways to use signs more effectively in therapy.

Historicity from a DST perspective

The account of historicity in this chapter was offered from the perspective of the assimilation model, but the assimilation model is arguably a member of the dialogical self family of theories. The account is, I think, largely compatible with DST and perhaps offers some tentative elaborations with respect to the role of signs, sign meanings, and meaning bridges in dialogue and psychological change. For example, the meaning bridge that Debbie built to her disconnected rejecting voice could be seen in DST as her developing a connection between two opposite *I*-positions. The assimilation account elaborates this by describing a semiotic mechanism for how this connection was built, involving deep meanings of the verb *reject*.

One of this chapter's important conclusions was that the meaning of words and stories is composed, in part, of the experience of the forebears who used them previously. As a result, any speaking or writing brings the experience of those forebears into the room, drawing on it to address present concerns. From a DST perspective (Hermans, 2002) this could be described as an intermingling of internal *I*-positions with external ones. DST suggests such voices express the mental presence of the significant others in the self, and internal dialogue can often be understood as a dialogue with a significant other in the extended domain of the self. The concept of historicity extends this, suggesting that even distant, unknown forebears may contribute a bit to the dialogue. There may be a large society of mind involved in some interactions, as when therapists bring to bear an accumulation of skills and theories passed to them by teachers, supervisors, colleagues, authors, and others, all in making a particular intervention.

DST might say that bringing cultural experience to bear though language and imagery is a manifestation of cultural *I*-positions. For example, Richard's use of a castle to represent a secure base and a treasure chest to represent a valued personal goal might be considered as expressions by cultural *I*-positions (Hermans & Hermans-Konopka, 2010). In such interactions, the therapist or counselor, as a cultural representative, can initiate a dialogue with a variety of external, cultural *I*-positions, which are an accessible part of the extended domain of the self.

References

Bakhtin, M. M. (1984). *Problems of Dostoevsky's poetics*. C. Emerson Ed. & Trans. Manchester, UK: Manchester University Press.

Bakhtin, M. M. (1986). *Speech genres and other late essays*. Austin, TX: University of Texas Press.

Basto, I., Pinheiro, P., Stiles, W. B., Rijo, D., & Salgado, J. (2017). Symptom intensity and emotion valence during the process of assimilation of a problematic experience: A quantitative study of a good outcome case in CBT. *Psychotherapy Research, 27*, 437–449. doi: 10.1080/10503307.2015.1119325

Basto, I., Stiles, W. B., Rijo, D., & Salgado, J. (2018). Does assimilation of problematic experiences predict a decrease in symptom intensity? *Clinical Psychology and Psychotherapy, 25*, 76–84. doi: 10.1002/cpp.2130

Brinegar, M. G., Salvi, L. M., Stiles, W. B., & Greenberg, L. S. (2006). Building a meaning bridge: Therapeutic progress from problem formulation to understanding. *Journal of Counseling Psychology, 53*, 165–180.

Caro Gabalda, I., Pérez Ruiz, S., & Llorens Aguilar, S. (2014). Therapeutic activities and the assimilation model: A preliminary exploratory study on the insight stage. *Counselling Psychology Quarterly, 27*, 217–240.

Caro Gabalda, I., & Stiles, W. B. (2013). Irregular assimilation progress: Reasons for setbacks in the context of linguistic therapy of evaluation. *Psychotherapy Research, 23*, 35–53. doi: 10.1080/10503307.2012.721938

Caro Gabalda, I., & Stiles, W. B. (in press). Therapist activities preceding therapy setbacks in a poor-outcome case. *Counselling Psychology Quarterly*. doi: 10.1080/ 09515070.2017.1355295

Caro Gabalda, I., Stiles, W. B., & Pérez Ruiz, S. (2016). Therapist activities preceding setbacks in the assimilation process. *Psychotherapy Research, 26*, 653–664. doi: 10.1080/ 10503307.2015.1104422

Detert, N. B., Llewelyn, S., Hardy, G. E., Barkham, M., & Stiles, W. B. (2006). Assimilation in good-and poor-outcome cases of very brief psychotherapy for mild depression: An initial comparison. *Psychotherapy Research, 16*, 4, 393–407. doi: 10.1080/10503300500294728

Edwards, J. A., & Lampert, M. D. (Eds.) (1993). *Talking data: Transcription and coding in discourse research*. Hillsdale, NJ: Lawrence Erlbaum.

Elliott, R. (2006). Decoding insight talk: Discourse analyses of insight in ordinary language and in psychotherapy. In L. G. Castonguay & C. E. Hill (Eds.), *Insight in psychotherapy* (pp. 167–185). Washington DC: APA.

Hattersley, R. (1991). *Goodbye to Yorkshire*. London: Pan Books. (Originally published 1976.)

Hermans, H. J. M. (2002). The dialogical self as a society of mind: Introduction. *Theory & Psychology* (*Special Issue on the Dialogical Self*), *12*, 147–160.

Hermans, H. J. M., & Hermans-Konopka, A. (2010). *Dialogical self theory: Positioning and counter-positioning in a globalizing society*. Cambridge, UK: Cambridge University Press.

Honos-Webb, L., & Stiles, W. B. (1998). Reformulation of assimilation analysis in terms of voices. *Psychotherapy, 35*, 23–33.

Honos-Webb, L., Stiles, W. B., & Greenberg, L. S. (2003). A method of rating assimilation in psychotherapy based on markers of change. *Journal of Counseling Psychology, 50*, 189–198.

Jung, C. G. (1981). *The archetypes and the collective unconscious (collected works of C. G. Jung Vol. 9, Part 1)*. R. F. C. Hull (Trans.). Princeton, NJ: Princeton University Press.

Leiman, M. (1992). The concept of sign in the work of Vygotsky, Winnicott and Bakhtin: Further integration of object relations theory and activity theory. *British Journal of Medical Psychology, 65*, 209–221.

Leiman, M. (1997). Procedures as dialogical sequences: A revised version of the fundamental concept in cognitive analytic therapy. *British Journal of Medical Psychology, 70*, 193–207.

Leiman, M. (2011). Michael Bakhtin's contribution to psychotherapy research. *Culture & Psychology, 17*, 441–461.

Leiman, M., & Stiles, W. B. (2001). Dialogical sequence analysis and the zone of proximal development as conceptual enhancements to the assimilation model: The case of Jan revisited. *Psychotherapy Research, 11*, 311–330. doi: 10.1080/713663986

Leiman, M., & Stiles, W. B. (2002). Integration of theory: Methodological issues. In I. Säfvestad-Nolan & P. Nolan (Eds.), *Object relations and integrative psychotherapy: Tradition and innovation in theory and practice* (pp. 68–79). London: Whurr.

Mendes, I., Gomes, P., Rosa, C., Salgado, J., Basto, I., Caro Gabalda, I., & Stiles, W. B. (2016). Setbacks in the process of assimilation of problematic experiences in two cases of emotion-focused therapy for depression. *Psychotherapy Research, 26*, 638–652. doi: 10.1080/10503307.2015.1136443

Osatuke, K., Glick, M. J., Stiles, W. B., Greenberg, L. S., Shapiro, D. A., & Barkham, M. (2005). Temporal patterns of improvement in client-centred therapy and cognitive-behaviour therapy. *Counselling Psychology Quarterly, 18*, 95–108. doi: 10.1080/09515070500136900

Osatuke, K., Gray, M. A., Glick, M. J., Stiles, W. B., & Barkham, M. (2004). Hearing voices: Methodological issues in measuring internal multiplicity. In H. H. Hermans & G. Dimaggio (Eds.), *The dialogical self in psychotherapy* (pp. 237–254). New York: Brunner-Routledge.

Osatuke, K., Humphreys, C. L., Glick, M. J., Graff-Reed, R. L., Mack, L. M., & Stiles, W. B. (2005). Vocal manifestations of internal multiplicity: Mary's voices. *Psychology and Psychotherapy: Theory, Research and Practice, 75*, 21–44.

Pennebaker, J. W., & Beall, S. K. (1986). Confronting a traumatic event: Toward an understanding of inhibition and disease. *Journal of Abnormal Psychology, 95*, 274–281. doi: 10.1037/0021-843x.95.3.274

Ribeiro, E., Cunha, C., Teixeira, A. S., Stiles, W. B., Pires, N., Santos, B., . . . Salgado, J. (2016). Therapeutic collaboration and the assimilation of problematic experiences in emotion-focused therapy for depression: Comparison of two cases. *Psychotherapy Research, 26,* 665–680. doi: 10.1080/10503307.2016.1208853

Ryle, A. (1997). *Cognitive analytic therapy and borderline personality disorder: The model and the method.* Chichester, UK: Wiley.

Ryle, A., & Kerr, I. B. (2002). *Introducing cognitive analytic therapy: Principles and practice.* Chichester, UK: John Wiley.

Sloan, D. M., & Marx, B. P. (2004). Taking pen to hand: Evaluating theories underlying the written disclosure paradigm. *Clinical Psychology: Science and Practice, 11,* 121–137.

Stiles, W. B. (1986). Levels of intended meaning of utterances. *British Journal of Clinical Psychology, 25,* 213–222.

Stiles, W. B. (1997). Signs and voices: Joining a conversation in progress. *British Journal of Medical Psychology, 70,* 169–176.

Stiles, W. B. (1999). *Signs, voices, meaning bridges, and shared experience: How talking helps.* Visiting Scholar Series No. 10 (ISSN 1173–9940). Palmerston North, New Zealand: School of Psychology, Massey University.

Stiles, W. B. (2002). Assimilation of problematic experiences. In J. C. Norcross (Ed.), *Psychotherapy relationships that work: Therapist contributions and responsiveness to patients* (pp. 357–365). New York: Oxford University Press.

Stiles, W. B. (2006). Numbers can be enriching. *New Ideas in Psychology, 24,* 252–262.

Stiles, W. B. (2009). Logical operations in theory-building case studies. *Pragmatic Case Studies in Psychotherapy, 5,* 3, 9–22. doi: 10.14713/pcsp.v5i3.973

Stiles, W. B. (2011). Coming to terms. *Psychotherapy Research, 21,* 367–384. doi: 10.1080/10503307.2011.582186

Stiles, W. B. (2017). Finding the right words: Symbolizing experience in practice and theory. *Person-Centered and Experiential Psychotherapies, 16,* 1–13. doi: 10.1080/14779757.2017.1298048

Stiles, W. B., & Angus, L. (2001). Qualitative research on clients' assimilation of problematic experiences in psychotherapy. In J. Frommer & D. L. Rennie (Eds.), *Qualitative psychotherapy research: Methods and methodology* (pp. 112–127). Lengerich, Germany: Pabst Science.

Stiles, W. B., Elliott, R., Llewelyn, S. P., Firth-Cozens, J. A., Margison, F. R., Shapiro, D. A., & Hardy, G. (1990). Assimilation of problematic experiences by clients in psychotherapy. *Psychotherapy, 27,* 411–420.

Stiles, W. B., Leiman, M., Shapiro, D. A., Hardy, G. E., Barkham, M., Detert, N. B., & Llewelyn, S. P. (2006). What does the first exchange tell? Dialogical sequence analysis and assimilation in very brief therapy. *Psychotherapy Research, 16,* 408–421.

Stiles, W. B., Morrison, L. A., Haw, S. K., Harper, H., Shapiro, D. A., & Firth-Cozens, J. (1991). Longitudinal study of assimilation in exploratory psychotherapy. *Psychotherapy, 28,* 195–206.

Stiles, W. B., Osatuke, K., Glick, M. J., & Mackay, H. C. (2004). Encounters between internal voices generate emotion: An elaboration of the assimilation model. In H. H. Hermans & G. Dimaggio (Eds.), *The dialogical self in psychotherapy* (pp. 91–107). New York: Brunner-Routledge.

van Rijn, B., Chryssafidou, E., Falconer, C. J., & Stiles, W. B. (submitted). *Digital images as meaning bridges: Case study of assimilation using avatar software in counseling with a 14-year-old boy.* Manuscript submitted for publication.

Voloshinov, V. N. (1986). *Marxism and the philosophy of language*. L. Matejka & I. R. Titunik, Trans. Cambridge, MA: Harvard University Press. (Original work published 1929.)

Vygotsky, L. S. (1978). *Mind in society: The development of higher psychological processes*. M. Cole, V. John-Steiner, S. Scribner, & E. Souberman (Eds.). Cambridge, MA: Harvard University Press.

6 *I*-positions and the unconscious

John Rowan

The notion of the dialogical self considers the self as 'a dynamic multiplicity of relatively *autonomous I*-positions in the landscape of the mind' (Hermans, 2001, p. 174, emphasis added). These *I*-positions offer a way of talking that neatly sidesteps the problem of reification inherent in such older concepts such as archetypes, complexes, subpersonalities, ego states and parts. *I*-positions come and go with the situation, and are not regarded as solid, continuous entities. It also gets over the problem of making a space for such concepts as soul, spirit or God/Goddess, which are clearly not sub anything, nor are they ego states or parts of the person. Some clients, and some therapists, make use of such ideas, and in most theories they are hard to handle. But they can be *I*-positions.

Carnivalisation

And this results in the carnivalisation of psychology and the carnivalisation of psychotherapy. Carnivalisation is the practice of turning things upside down, or inside out, or a radical questioning of accepted ideas and theories.

The idea comes from Mikhail Bakhtin (1984), who says:

> Carnival is a pageant without footlights and without a division into performers and spectators. In carnival everyone is an active participant, everyone communes in the carnival act. Carnival is not contemplated and, strictly speaking, not even performed; its participants *live* in it, they live by its laws as long as those laws are in effect; that is, they live a *carnivalistic life*. Because carnivalistic life is life drawn out of its *usual* rut, it is to some extent 'life turned inside out', 'the reverse side of the world'.

> (pp. 122–123)

This gives us a freedom that is quite endless, where we can see the individual person as an ever-shifting group of people, each of whom may have their own motives, their own assumptions, their own rules and customs. This means that the old ego gets dethroned, and is no longer regarded as the ruler, the monarch, the president even. In fact we now do not need the ego to be in place at all. Bakhtin (1984) tells us that:

The primary carnivalistic act is the *mock crowning and subsequent decrowning of the carnival king*. This ritual is encountered in one form or another in all festivities of the carnival type: in the most elaborately worked out forms – the saturnalia, the European carnival and festival of fools (in the latter, mock priests, bishops or popes, depending on the rank of the church, were chosen in place of a king); in a less elaborated form, all other festivities of this type, right down to festival banquets with their election of short-lived kings and queens of the festival.

(p. 124)

In psychotherapy, this corresponds to the dethroning of the mature ego. Instead, we have a multitude of *I*-positions, which can take up a variety of roles.

To make this clearer we can mention carnivalistic literature, such as Francois Rabelais with his *Gargantua and Pantagruel*, Lawrence Sterne with his *Tristram Shandy*, Miguel de Cervantes Saavedra with his *Don Quixote de la Mancha (The Ingenious Hidalgo)*, Lewis Carroll, with his *Alice in Wonderland* and *Alice Through the Looking-Glass*, James Joyce with his *Ulysses* and Finnegans *Wake*, Kenneth Patchen and *his Journal of Albion Moonlight* and so on.

This is of course a radically new way of seeing the person, and seeing ourselves as therapists. Instead of being a solid reliable therapist or counsellor or coach, operating out of a mature ego, we now become dancers, actors, clowns, able to meet the client in whatever *I*-position he or she presents. If we really want to understand what this means, the YouTube video 'Topsy Turvy Day' (2014) gives a very clear illustration in pictorial form.

Promoter position and the carnivalistic turn

The usual idea of the promoter position is usually positive. For example, here is a typical quote:

Imagined figures as well as actual figures may function as promoter positions. Some people return, particularly in a period of stress or pain, to an image or picture of a deceased family member or a friend for support and advice. People with a religious or spiritual background often consult the picture, image, or statue of a buddha, Christ, or holy person, and many people have daily dialogical contact with an image of God, whom they approach as the ultimate promoter position.

(Hermans and Hermans-Konopka, 2010, p. 234)

However, if we take a carnivalistic position, we can expand this repertoire considerably. We can open the door to the rebel, the trickster, the hermit, the clown, the vampire, the warrior, the destroyer and so forth. Caroline Myss (2003) has presented us with a pack of 80 Archetype Cards, which includes those just mentioned and many others. She agrees with Jung that these emerge from the collective unconscious, and points out that each and every one of them has a positive and a negative, a light and a dark side. In their combination of light and dark sides, such positions provide avenues to turn an existing self-organisation upside-down. This represents a considerable expansion of the notion of the promoter position, and I think forms a genuine extension of the whole idea of the promoter position.

Having now seen what carnivalisation means, we can go on to examine the idea of the unconscious from this point of view.

The unconscious

Hence of all the possible names for the multiple locations within the person, '*I*-positions' is the most flexible, and the least liable to lead to problems in practice. This means that in therapy we can escape from the tyranny of just one unconscious mind, which can be so complex and difficult to consult that we can seldom be sure of what it says or what it wants. It may seem unnecessary to contest the concept of the unconscious, but many different voices nowadays are urging us to do just this (Chiari and Nuzzo, 2010; van Deurzen, 2010; Wilber, 1997). Perhaps the concept of the unconscious, like so many of the older ideas in psychotherapy, is not needed now that we have more adequate and interesting theories.

Instead of a therapist saying, 'Consciously you say it is OK for me to go on holiday for six weeks, but at an unconscious level you may resent or fear it', it is more natural (in the sense of being closer to everyday speech) and more accurate to say,

> From your immediate *I*-position you may say that it is OK for me to go on holiday for six weeks, but you may have another *I*-position (perhaps an adolescent) who resents it and may be very angry, or another *I*-position (perhaps a child) who feels neglected and set aside and undervalued, or another *I*-position (perhaps an infant) who feels abandoned and unsafe. Let's explore that a bit.

It may be worth saying here that therapists who use everyday speech in this way often find it easier to relate to the client in the room. One of the advantages of doing it this second way is that we can actually talk directly from one *I*-position to another, and get a reply back again. The one who resents the long holiday may be a teenager who can be interrogated; the one who feels neglected may be a child who can be talked with, and the one who feels abandoned may be an infant, who 'by some miracle' can also talk back. By encouraging the client to take up these *I*-positions, we can find out more about what is going on within the client. And this puts us as therapists in a position to do something to change the situation. We can reason with the teenager; we can empathise with the child, we can attend to the needs of the infant and get to the bottom of the screaming and apparent craziness.

It is often forgotten that the Freudian unconscious is not a single entity. The *Dictionary of Kleinian Thought* (Hinshelwood, 1989) says this: 'The unconscious is structured like a small society. That is to say, it is a mesh of relationships between objects. An unconscious phantasy is a state of activity of one of these "internal" object-relations' (p. 451). This psychoanalytic idea of internal objects was elaborated by Melanie Klein: '[T]he internal world is a full arena of varied objects in various degrees of synthesis and separateness in different contexts and at different times' (p. 71). This is not so different from our view, except that of course the idea of having a conversation with one of these internal objects was never even considered by the analysts, never mind acted upon.

Resistance

One of the functions of the unconscious is resistance. In psychoanalysis this is regarded as part of the negative transference. Our more precise idea is to say that an *I*-position resists whatever it may take against: thus, for example, if the therapist says something true or valid, and the client denies this, or will not engage with it, we simply say that an *I*-position has a different view. It may then be possible to ask this *I*-position what the problem is, and get an answer. It is resistance that can make it hard for us to explore and deal with our shadow material. This is a very common and very useful idea, as has been pointed out by various writers now. How do we deal with it in the dialogical self model? The first thing is to identify the resistance. This can be done very gradually and tactfully if necessary: 'Do you ever feel that there is a voice within you which is saying just the opposite to your conscious intentions?' or 'Do you ever get the sense that some part of you wants nothing to do with your plan or your program?' or 'Is there a part of you who does not want to be here right now?' In doing this work, of course, we must always respect the client's belief system and way of seeing things. Having identified the resistance – for example as a saboteur, or a perfectionist, or a procrastinator – the next step is to put it in a chair, or on a cushion, or in some other convenient location. For example, if it just takes the form of a wall, we could just visualise the wall in the middle of the floor.

The next step is to visualise the resistance. Encourage the client to bring some picture, image or vision to mind that puts the resistance into some concrete form. This may need some shaping to make it easier to handle: for example, if the client says it is a fog, encourage him or her to visualise it as a particularly deep and dark fog, almost solid in its thickness. Once the client is visualising the resistance, ask him or her to speak to it. There is no need to put words into the client's mouth – just wait until the client produces something. What the client says to the resistance does not matter very much. It is the dialogue itself that is the important factor. Don't let the client talk about the resistance – he or she must talk directly to it, as if it were some kind of person. Keep on encouraging the client to talk until it seems clear that some reply is needed. Then ask the client to change places, positioned in such a way that it is easy to talk back to the space where the client was sitting.

Now the client is the resistance. Help the client to take a moment or two to really get into role. Often the voice changes at this point, as William Stiles (Stiles et al., 2004, p. 240) has pointed out. Answer the requests or accusations or whatever the client has been saying. This is the crucial point, and the interaction can be quite intense. Encourage the resistance to talk more. At an appropriate moment, it is often a good idea for the therapist to talk to the resistance direct, finding out what role it is taking in relation to the client – what it thinks it is doing. Much can emerge from this kind of dialogue.

Transference

It is worth pointing out that if we have the concept of the dialogical self we do not need to preserve or use the concepts of transference or countertransference. Some 20 years ago David Smith (1991) was demonstrating that there was actually no theoretical justification for the concept of transference, using a very careful examination of the classic documents in psychoanalysis, and we can now see that if we have *I*-positions we do not need transference. Instead of saying 'Perhaps your strong reaction to me is really directed at your father', we might say instead 'Perhaps you could express these strong feelings to this empty chair, and see who appears there'. If this worked, a dialogue could then ensue, which would reveal the material needing to be dealt with here.

This leads, of course, to the further question – what is the dialogical view of transference? It is simply that one *I*-position has latched on to some incorrect definition of who the therapist is, taking the therapist to be someone else. We can then ask which *I*-position takes this view, and perhaps start to find out which *I*-position it is, and how it took up that false identification. This is very straightforward, and does not require any very complex idea to explain it.

The same applies to projection, a very common function of the unconscious, in most accounts. With Dialogical Self Theory (DST), we can simply say that a dominant *I*-position insists on misidentifying the person being observed, and question that *I*-position about its assumptions and its needs.

I call the process of using *I*-positions 'personification' – in other words, we are effectively turning the entity, whatever it may be, into a person for the purposes of dialogue. There are basically three forms of personification in the world of therapy, counselling and coaching.

Chair work

Out of the theory of the dialogical self has come the notion of *I*-positions, as we have just pointed out. Yet it seems curious to me that so little of the research involving *I*-positions has featured the practice of letting the *I*-positions talk to each other. Of course, there have been some examples, such as can be found in Verhofstadt's (2003) psychodramatic application of DST, my own contribution in the *Handbook of Dialogical Self Theory* (Hermans and Gieser, 2012) and West-wood's idea of therapeutic enactment (Westwood et al., 2003). What I want to do now is to show how useful it can be to use *I*-positions in this way. In other words, I want to add to what has been done in the existing literature, and relate it to other work in the field. I argue that one of the main advantages of the dialogical self approach in psychotherapy is that it offers, in the concept of *I*-positions, a more effective way of approaching the multiplicity within the person than any previous method. As is well known from a great deal of previous work (Rowan, 1990), many different schools of psychotherapy have embraced such multiplicity and found ways of working with it. The most common of these ways is to use chair work – that is to say, by personifying a character that has emerged during the course of therapy, and talking directly to it, and then talking back as the character itself. In the concept of *I*-positions we have a way of approaching chair work that is less loaded with unnecessary assumptions than any previous approach. It is compatible with all the existing approaches, such as Gestalt therapy, transactional analysis, persona therapy, psychosynthesis, psychodrama, schema therapy, experiential process therapy, transformational chair work, voice dialogue, narrative therapy and so forth, and offers them, for the first time, a really adequate vocabulary. The dangers of reification, such a temptation in many of these other schools, are virtually eliminated. The possibility is also opened up of working in a productive way with the transpersonal, as we shall see in due course.

Empty-chair work

This is the basic idea, pioneered by Jacob Moreno originally (Moreno et al., 2000) and popularised by Fritz Perls (1969), of asking the client to imagine that the object of his or her affections or enmity or questioning is sitting on an empty chair. The client then first of all describes and talks to the character involved, and then moves over into the other chair and enters into and speaks for that character. In recent years this has been formalised by the Integral Institute as the 3-2-1 method: first we describe the character in the third person (he or she is like this or that), then in the second person (addressing the person as 'you'), and finally in the first person (turning the person into an 'I'). Fritz Perls was the great master of this method, and showed that we could put into the empty chair such things as 'the number plate in your dream', 'your smirk', 'the dream you did not have' and so forth. This is the classic way of bringing people who are hard to reach into the room, such as your mother, your dead father or your aborted fetus. The more recent work has been well written up by Goldman (2002).

Two-chair work

In this version we identify two (often incompatible) parts of the client, and put each one on to a separate chair. The client is then encouraged to speak for each of the parts in turn, and may then be encouraged to engage in a dialogue between the two parts: perhaps they may want to convince the other part that they are more necessary or more valid than that other part. Robert Elliott and others in the group led by Les Greenberg has done much research on this technique in recent years (Greenberg et al., 1998). This is important because it is only in recent years that there has been the present emphasis on research and evidence, and of course the dialogical self school has been responsible for some of this big surge. More examples are to be found in the work of Victor Bogart (2007).

Multiple-chair work

This is particularly often used by the voice dialogue school, who may use up to ten or more chairs to personify different parts of the person (Stone and Winkelman, 1985). Again they may speak individually or engage in dialogues with other 'persons' on the other chairs. The idea has been taken up by Kellogg (2004) in recent years, and more research is now on the way. It has been used very creatively in the last few years by Genpo Roshi in his Big Mind workshops, a transpersonal approach. He introduces characters such as the controller, the sceptic, the vulnerable child, the damaged self, the seeking mind – and then the non-seeking mind, big mind, big heart and so forth, and invites people to enter such states for short periods, and speak from that position. In this way ordinary people can be introduced to some extraordinary ways of seeing the world. The whole process can be carnivalised.

This is therefore a very flexible idea, which can take a number of forms. In recent years I have been urging that it is now possible, using the idea of I-positions, to have dialogues with one's soul or even one's spirit (Rowan, 2010). This idea was pioneered by Moreno again, who sometimes asked a protagonist to stand on a chair and be God. But it was refined and developed further by the psychosynthesis practitioners, particularly Molly Young Brown (1993). I have found, for example, that if a client needs advice on making a choice, I can invite him or her to choose a helpful figure of some kind and dialogue with it. In DST, these are called 'promoter positions', (Hermans and Hermans-Konopka, 2010), although I now prefer to call them 'helper positions'. Such helpers may include the goddess Kali, the god Shiva, the Dalai Lama, the wise person, the god Krishna, the inner teacher, the soul, the angel Gabriel, Saint Joan of Arc, Saint John of the Cross or any local pagan god or goddess – there is no end to the choices here. This is the carnivalisation of the promoter positions.

Reification

There are two main reasons why the nomenclature of I-positions is superior to any of those just mentioned: one is that it is less liable to reification. When we succumb to the temptation of reification we make the inner selves too strong, too solid, too long lasting – we tend to think of them as permanent or at least semi-permanent, living for weeks, months or years within the person. Reification is of course rampant in the psychological sciences, with various authorities bandying about personages like the oral type, the masochistic position, the macho man, the inner child, the femme fatale and so forth. With I-positions there is none of this. It is quite clear and explicit that they can come and go with great frequency at times, and are 'of the moment' rather than 'of the essence'. This is a great advantage, because reification is rife throughout the psychotherapeutic literature, as we have pointed out, and any method or approach that avoids this is to be welcomed.

The other great advantage of *I*-positions is that there is no suggestion with them of subordination, of them being lesser in some way than the whole person. This makes it possible to think of the soul, of the spirit – even of God – becoming an *I*-position. All we mean by this is that we can, in therapy, put the soul (for example) on the empty chair, visualise it, talk to it, and then take up that position on the chair and talk back as the soul. If we do not like the word 'soul' there are plenty of synonyms, such as the higher self, the *antaratman*, the inner teacher, the *daimon* and so forth. And some of these make it clear that the soul may be seen as something outside that can inspire us, or something inside that we can enter into and be. If we accept the idea of the transpersonal – and there is now a vast research literature on this, usefully summarised in the book by Andrew Shorrock (2008) – this is particularly valuable in transpersonal therapy. This is important because of the way in which the transpersonal is ignored in much of the psychological literature and in psychotherapy and counselling and coaching. But if we want to do justice to the whole person (and most psychotherapeutic approaches give at least lip service to such an ideal) it is not valid to omit all mention of the soul and the spirit. These may well be concepts or *I*-positions that are important to our clients and hence considered real from within their experienced lifeworld. We certainly do not want to omit or ignore anything that is meaningful to the client.

It is obvious that the notion of an *I*-position makes all these moves more transparent and less worrying conceptually. It is important not to regard this as merely a technique (or set of techniques) that are useful in therapy, but to realise that it is a very free and flexible way of construing or understanding what people are really like. John Beahrs (1982) put it very well when he said:

> When is it useful or not useful to look upon an individual as a single unit, as a 'Cohesive Self'? When is it useful or not useful to look upon anyone as being constituted of many parts, each with an identity of its own? When is it useful to see ourselves as part of a greater whole? I use the term 'useful' rather than 'true' since all are true – simultaneously and at all times.
>
> (pp. 4–5)

This last statement is helpful, I think, to all those who want to work with the dialogical self. They will continually be faced by critics who question the whole idea that the person can be multiple. To realise that this can be true, yet not the whole truth, is an important step forward. Since I have criticised some of the dialogical self researchers for not using these techniques in their work very much, it behoves me to give an example myself. This has to do with the difficulty of working with extreme emotions. Here is the example:

Case example: the murderess

This was a 60-year-old woman who had been married for 40 years. At the age of 22 she had given birth to a baby with birth defects. A medical decision was made to let the baby die after a few days. The baby was named and given a religious burial. The woman had never visited the grave, and felt guilty as a murderess. This crime weighed on her conscience so that she came into therapy.

All this took some time to emerge, by which time we had built up a trusting therapeutic relationship. It now seemed that we were ready to tackle this major issue. I put out a cushion on the floor in front of her, and suggested to the client that her baby was sitting on the cushion, and by some miracle could talk back if she addressed it. It took some time before she had the confidence to ask it to forgive her.

I asked her then to sit on the other cushion and be the baby and answer back. After a lot of tears and hesitation the baby answered that forgiveness was not on. The mother was guilty and should suffer. 'How could you do that to me?' The baby was adamant. The client cried a great deal.

It took some time before we dared to approach the matter again. In the meantime the client had investigated further and talked it over with me, and it did seem clear that she had actually had no part in the decision apart from assenting to the doctors' suggestions.

We returned to the cushion and the baby, and tried again to negotiate. But the baby was still not convinced, and accused my client of collusion and evasion of responsibility. She was still guilty. More tears ensued.

After a few more weeks we came back to the baby again, and this time there appeared to have been a shift. The baby was still uneasy about being too ready to make allowances and did not understand the concept of compassion. But there was a grudging assent to the idea that it was not all the mother's fault.

After another gap, we tried again, and this time the baby was much easier about the matter, showing much more understanding and placing the blame in a much more diffused way on the whole surrounding cast of characters. My client felt forgiven and absolved from blame. I was very moved by this process.

Soon after that she visited the little grave and cleared away the debris that had collected on it and decorated it with flowers. She reported crying a great deal, but said that those were healing tears.

With later clients too, I found that it was possible to put an aborted fetus on a cushion and find out its attitude, often coming to a positive resolution with the woman involved.

Here we have a good example of the case put forward by the dialogical self school:

> As we argued earlier, the self is characterized by oppositions, ambivalences, and ambiguities, in which a broad variety of positions play their part, not only those that are foregrounded as presentations to the outside world but also those that are backgrounded as 'shadow positions' (Hermans, 2001), 'exiles' (Schwartz, 1995) or 'disowned selves' (Stone and Winkelman, 1989) in the darker spaces of the self.
>
> (Hermans and Hermans-Konopka, 2010, p. 178)

I give this example to illustrate the point that dialogical work can lead us into some very deep areas, and may suggest ways of working that are theoretically quite unusual. It can also be used in group work, as has been well described by Sewell et al. (1998).

You can see at once that the concept of the unconscious is not needed here, because the idea of *I*-positions is more effective, as well as being simpler.

The transpersonal

The transpersonal is a vast realm for psychotherapy, counselling and coaching, and it has been emerging as a really important aspect of the therapeutic engagement over the past 30 years or more. I focus on it because it is all too common in our psychological work to leave out the element of spirituality, which has been well written about recently by David Mattison (2008) for example. If we want to do justice to the whole person it is not valid to leave out such important components as the soul or the spirit. The term 'transpersonal' is superior to the term 'spirituality' for the reasons succinctly stated by Roberto Assagioli. He described the transpersonal as

> a term introduced above all by Maslow and by those of his school to refer to what is commonly called spiritual. Scientifically speaking, it is a better word; it is more precise and, in a certain sense, neutral in that it points to that which is beyond or above ordinary personality. Furthermore it avoids confusion with many things which are now called spiritual but which are actually pseudo-spiritual or parapsychological.
>
> (Assagioli, 1991, p. 16)

The clearest and most useful map of the transpersonal, in my opinion, has been given to us by Ken Wilber (2000). He says that we are all on a path of psychospiritual development, whether we know it or not and whether we like it or not. And this process has three main phases. First, there is the prepersonal – the whole realm of childhood development when we see ourselves as part of a family rather than as a separate and distinct personality. Second, there is the personal – the vast realm of role playing in society, where we grow up believing that we have to defend and enhance our self-image, which is very much like a mask. We learn about rationality, and science and determinism. This process ends up with a mature ego, as psychology generally describes it, capable of self-defence and self-enhancement in very effective ways. Third, there is the transpersonal – the later realm where we first of all shake off the shackles of the self-image and discover authenticity, then later perhaps admit that we are spiritual beings capable of enjoying symbols and images and archetypes and exploring altered states of consciousness and opening ourselves up to inspiration and joy, and then later perhaps again shake off all that and open up to the total freedom of the One, the All or the None, where we no longer need concrete representations of the divine. This is all very well described in the relevant literature.

There is no suggestion in Wilber's writings that we should all go to the transpersonal, and indeed it seems that to go very far along this path is rare and difficult. The path to the mature ego is easy, because society is right behind us, encouraging us to be a better and better role player. In fact, it very often takes a crisis, perhaps quite painful, to get us to leave the familiarity of the personal – what has sometimes been called the 'consensus trance'. When we do, it is very often along the lines of – 'I have spent 30 years building up my social self, and learnt very well how to play my roles for the benefit of other people, but what about me? Who am I really, behind all the roles?' And at that point we may get into counselling or psychotherapy, or even take a course to become a therapist, as many people have done in recent years. In fact, therapy is of great help to put us on the road to the transpersonal, because it enables us to deal with our shadow material. The shadow is a concept introduced by Jung (1951) originally, but it is vitally necessary for us to understand it if we are to move on into the transpersonal realm without self-deception. The shadow comprises all those aspects of us that we either reject or do not understand or do not even know about, although its effects are very often obvious to others. To go on into the transpersonal without dealing with the shadow is asking for trouble, and Wilber (2006, p. 126) is very clear about this.

As suggested earlier in this chapter the implications here run very deep. The concept of the unconscious historically emerged from the discovery of persons within the person. It grew and developed from the middle of the eighteenth century until today, as has been shown in great detail. But if it was invented to account for the evident multiplicity within the person, it is not needed now that we have the improved theory of the dialogical self, which states that this multiplicity is not something odd or strange, which needs special explanation to handle, but rather something natural and basic to what human beings are. All this highly complicated and unusual apparatus (Freud's system of the unconscious and so forth) can go into the fire. The many arguments and reported researches in books like Hermans and Dimaggio (2004) bring alive the theory in extremely convincing ways, and we do not need to shrink from applying the lessons in a radical way.

Discussion

Working with the dialogical self in this way is, I believe, the wave of the future. It arises very naturally out of the work with clients and coachees. It was exciting, for example, to pick up a recent book by Robert Neimeyer (2009) on constructivist psychotherapy, and find in the very first chapter a case vignette where a woman was encouraged to put her dead father in a chair and have dialogue with him, with good results. It was enthralling to discover the work of Scott Kellogg (2004) who actually calls his approach 'transformational chair work' and uses the idea as to the manner born. It has been very encouraging to see how Les Greenberg and his colleagues (1998) have been conducting serious research on empty-chair work and two-chair work, as for example in the chapter by Barry Wolfe and Patti Sigl on experiential psychotherapy of the anxiety disorders, or by Robert Elliott, Kenneth Davis and Emil Slatick on process-experiential therapy for post-traumatic stress difficulties, in the same volume.

But it is important to go back to the basic breakthrough being canvassed here. It is that when we work with human beings, what we are actually doing in all cases is to facilitate the processes of positioning, repositioning and counter-positioning, which enable us as therapists to address the self in highly dynamic and non-reifying ways. By working in this way we enable new configurations of the self to open up. And it is interesting to note that, in the person-centred school, which many of us have regarded as very simple and basic, the concept of 'configurations of self' is now part of the basic theory being taught (Mearns and Thorne, 2000). The dialogical self is not a sport, an exception, a peripheral thing, but part of a broad movement towards a new vision of the person, which is more and more popular in the therapeutic world of today. And we discover that an *I*-position is a real self, not a self-image imposed on us by other people.

Much of the important work has been put together in my own book, *Personification: Using the Dialogical Self in Counselling and Psychotherapy* (Rowan, 2010), which goes very thoroughly into the historical use of these ideas by virtually all the great names in the field of psychotherapy. It also goes into the question of how we can believe at one and the same time in the unity of the self and the multiplicity of the self: both of these are vitally necessary. It does seem to me that this is the way to go if we are to do justice to what human beings are, and how to conduct therapy with them. And now we can add the concept of carnivalisation to the mix.

References

Assagioli, R. (1991). *Transpersonal Development*. London: Crucible.

Bakhtin, M (1984). *Problems of Dostoevsky's Poetics*. Minneapolis, MN: University of Minnesota Press.

Beahrs, J. O. (1982). *Unity and Multiplicity*. New York: Brunner/Mazel.

Bogart, V. (2007). *Explore the Undiscovered You*. Walnut Creek, CA: Baskin.

Brown, M. Y. (1993). *Growing Whole*. Center City, PA: Hazelden.

Chiari, G. and Nuzzo, M. L. (2010). *Constructivist Psychotherapy*. Hove, UK: Routledge.

Elliott, R., Davis, K. L. and Slatick, E. (1998). Process-experiential therapy for posttraumatic stress difficulties. In L. S. Greenberg, J. C. Watson and G. Lietaer (Eds.), *Handbook of Experiential Psychotherapy*. New York: Guilford Press.

Goldman, R. N. (2002). The empty-chair dialogue for unfinished business. In J. C. Watson, R. N. Goldman and M. S. Warner (Eds.), *Client-Centered and Experiential Psychotherapy in the 21st Century*. Llangarron, UK: PCCS Books.

Greenberg, L. S., Watson, J. C. and Lietaer, G. (Eds.) (1998). *Handbook of Experiential Psychotherapy*. New York: Guilford Press.

Hermans, H. J. M. (2001). The dialogical self: Towards a theory of personal and cultural positioning. *Culture and Psychology*, 7, 243–282.

Hermans, H. J. M. and Dimaggio, G. (Eds.). (2004). *The Dialogical Self in Psychotherapy*. London: Brunner-Routledge.

Hermans, H. J. M. and Gieser, T. (2012). *Handbook of Dialogical Self Theory*. Cambridge, UK: Cambridge University Press.

Hermans, H. J. M. and Hermans-Konopka, A. (2010). *Dialogical Self Theory: Positioning and Counter-Positioning in a Globalizing Society*. Cambridge, UK: Cambridge University Press.

Hinshelwood, R. D. (1989). *A Dictionary of Kleinian Thought*. London: Free Association Books.

Jung, C. G. (1951). '*The Shadow' Collected Works of C. G. Jung* (Vol. 8). London: Routledge.

Kellogg, S. H. (2004). Dialogical encounters: Contemporary perspectives on 'chairwork' in psychotherapy. *Psychotherapy: Research, Theory, Practice, Training*, 41, 310–320.

Mattison, D. R. (2008). *Exploring the Spiritual: Paths for Counsellors and Psychotherapists*. Abingdon, UK: Routledge.

Mearns, D. and Thorne, B. (2000). *Person-Centred Therapy Today*. London: Sage.

Moreno, Z., Blomkvist, L. D. and Rützel, T. (2000). *Psychodrama, Surplus Reality and the Art of Healing*. London: Routledge.

Myss, C. (2003). *Archetype Cards*. Carlsbad, CA: Hay House.

Neimeyer, R. A. (2009). *Constructivist Psychotherapy*. Hove, UK: Routledge.

Perls, F. S. (1969). *Gestalt Therapy Verbatim*. Moab, UT: Real People Press.

Rowan, J. (1990). *Subpersonalities: The People Inside Us*. London: Routledge.

Rowan, J. (2010). *Personification: Using the Dialogical Self in Counselling and Psychotherapy*. Hove, UK: Routledge.

Schwartz, R. (1995). *Internal Family Systems Therapy*. New York: Guilford Press.

Sewell, K. W., Baldwin, C. L. and Moes, A. J. (1998). The multiple self awareness group. *Journal of Constructivist Psychology*, 11, 59–78.

Shorrock, A (2008). *The Transpersonal in Psychology, Psychotherapy and Counseling*. Basingstoke, UK: Palgrave Macmillan.

Smith, D. L. (1991). *Hidden Conversations*. London: Routledge.

Stiles, W. B., Osatuke, K., Glick, M. J. and Mackay, H. (2004). Encounters between internal voices generate emotion: An elaboration of the assimilation model. In H. J. M. Hermans and G. Dimaggio (Eds.), *The Dialogical Self in Psychotherapy*. London: Brunner-Routledge.

Stone, H. and Winkelman, S. (1989). *Embracing Our Selves*. Marina del Ray, CA: Devorss & Co.

"Topsy Turvy Day" (2014). YouTube video. www.youtube.com/watch?v=emmpnBDM0R8.

van Deurzen, E. (2010). *Everyday Mysteries* (2nd ed.). Hove, UK: Routledge.

Verhofstadt-Deneve, L. M. F. (2003). The psychodramatical 'social atom method': Dialogical self in dialogical action. *Journal of Constructivist Psychology*, 16, 183–212.

Westwood, M. J., Keats, P. A. and Wilensky, P. (2003). Therapeutic enactment: Integrating the individual and group counseling models for change. *Journal for Specialists in Group Work*, 28, 122–138.

Wilber, K. (1997). *The Eye of Spirit*. Boston, MA: Shambhala.

Wilber, K. (2000). *Integral Psychology*. Boston, MA: Shambhala.

Wilber, K. (2006). *Integral Spirituality*. Boston, MA: Integral Books.

Wolfe, B. E. and Sigl, P. (1998). Experiential psychotherapy of the anxiety disorders. In L. S. Greenberg, J. C. Watson and G. Lietaer (Eds.), *Handbook of Experiential Psychotherapy*. New York: Guilford Press.

7 Disturbances in the dialogical self in psychosis

Contributions from the study of metacognitive disturbances

Paul H. Lysaker, Jay A. Hamm, Bethany L. Leonhardt, and John T. Lysaker

Although the etiology and course of schizophrenia spectrum disorders remain widely debated, it is beyond dispute that these conditions interrupt the lives of people experiencing them. Whether these conditions are attributed to alterations in basic brain function (Andreasen, 1984; Andreasen et al., 1998) or aspects of social and political injustice (van Os, 2004; Selten et al., 2013; Firmin et al., 2016) they involve marked changes in the life trajectories of persons as they struggle to find security and meaning in a world of contingency. The hopes, dreams, roles, and plans of people identified as having these conditions lose coherence and direction, with some feeling as if their orientation in the world has been irretrievably compromised. As identified in a meta-synthesis of qualitative studies of the experience of psychosis, these changes lead to the loss of a previously held cohesive and coherent sense of self (McCarthy-Jones et al., 2013).

Over the last decade this has led to calls for the need to systematically characterize and study the vicissitudes of first person experience in schizophrenia (Lysaker & Lysaker, 2008; Lysaker et al., in press). As Barham (1993) noted over two decades ago, we have to be able to understand persons diagnosed with mental disorders as "as an active participant in social life" in order "to identify more adequately where he fails as a social agent" (p. 78). Moreover, a sense of first-person experience is even more necessary in order to broaden an understanding of schizophrenia to include the other side of disability: recovery. Failing to consider the first-person aspects of schizophrenia risks objectifying persons with this condition and obscuring the capacities that might enable them to interpret and respond to challenges and ultimately become well. Certainly, it seems impossible to develop psychosocial and other non-pharmacological treatments such as psychotherapies that assist with recovery from serious mental illness without a meaningful account of the experiences of those human beings who live with these mental health conditions.

Of note, understanding first-person experience in schizophrenia requires more than a description of anomalous experience or abstract existential dilemmas. Unlike a rash that might affect a patch of skin, the symptoms associated with schizophrenia reverberate across a life and deeply impact sense of self and agency. Kean's (2009) descriptions of her experience of schizophrenia make this apparent:

> What lies behind the symptoms is a tormented self, a highly personal experience unchangeable and irreplaceable by any physical treatment ... a sense that I had lost myself, a constant feeling that my self no longer belonged to me ... it is purely a distorted state of being.
>
> (p. 1)

An adequate grasp of the first-person dimensions of schizophrenia thus requires an account of the interplay and impact of immediate experience, personal interpretations of life events, sense of identity, and shifting emotional states that often involve considerable anguish and pain (Andreasen et al., 2003; Hamm et al., 2015).

In this chapter, we will describe and update a model drawn from Dialogical Self Theory (DST), which originally sought to describe and capture the complexities of first-person experience in schizophrenia (Lysaker & Lysaker, 2008). We will first detail that model's theoretical roots, its original application to the first-person dimensions of schizophrenia, including alterations in sense of self and agency and its treatment implications. We will then describe the limitations of this model, which include an inability to describe alterations in self-experience in a sufficiently nuanced manner. We next present recent research on a related field of study that further focuses on a facet of this model: the capacity to think complexly about self and others, or metacognition. We will discuss the implications of that work for the further development of a more comprehensive account of severe mental illness and more effective forms of psychotherapy.

It is important to note two points about the terminology used in this chapter. First, we will use the construct of schizophrenia to describe the mental health condition in question. As we acknowledge above, this term is also not without controversy. Many suggest this term is stigmatizing and question its scientific basis. We thus use the word schizophrenia with caution. We are more comfortable with this term than others, however, given its roots in ancient Greek for the splitting or shattering of the mind, which we see as an apt explanation for the fragmentation of associations that often occurs in those diagnosed with these conditions. Second, when describing people in treatment with the condition we will use the word "patient." We realize this is also a controversial term that may offend some people. Many have experienced the mental health care they received as stigmatizing and marginalizing. Others object that the word patient positions the sufferer in a passive stance and does not capture the idea that wellness requires an active role in the face of suffering. As a result, terms such as service users, clients, consumers, and even psychiatric survivors have been used to replace patient. We chose to use "patient" given its roots in the Latin and Greek words meaning "to suffer," recognizing that people with these conditions do indeed suffer but not to imply passivity is needed for wellness.

A dialogical model of schizophrenia

Theoretical basis

Our dialogical model of schizophrenia was first published in 2001 (Lysaker & Lysaker, 2001) and culminated in a lengthy discussion published in 2008 (Lysaker & Lysaker, 2008). In this work, we took the position that dialogism, as a theory of self-experience could be seen to emerge from diverse roots including the seminal philosophical texts of Kierkeegard (1949/1980), Nietzsche (1886/1966), and Dewey (1922/1988). We also believed this view was influenced by work outside of philosophy including the novels and short stories of Dostoyevky as illuminated by Bakhtin's critical analysis (1929/1985) and contemporary social, cognitive, personality, and developmental psychological research (Hermans, 1996; Hermans & Gieser, 2011; Gonçalves & Ribeiro, 2012; Hermans & Hermans-Konopka, 2010). We understood a dialogical view of the self to suggest that human beings: (i) do not have direct, intuitive access to their selves, but (ii) sense themselves in a variety of self-world interactions. Moreover, (iii) there is no singular, stable, core self to sense, and thus (iv) sense of self is always dynamic, multifaceted, and occasionally conflictual.

Instead, self-awareness arises through dialogues among the many facets of the self as they animate and receded through self-world interactions. The self is thus best described as an interanimating constellation of elements. Self-experience gains its richness from the number and depth of different elements, *I*-positions, which arise in and enable one another to coherently respond to ongoing life experiences as persons pursue their own unique goals in life.

"Sense of self" in our original dialogical model of schizophrenia was accordingly a contextualized, *manifold* disclosure revealed in various pursuits, experiences, and explicit moments of self-regard. We use the term "manifold" because the self was not one of these elements. As knower and known, the self is a multipositional, dynamic, interanimating system, which is situated in fluidly changing ecological, political, social, and historical contexts. Thus, this dialogical view of self-experience explicitly departed from both ego-centered, or Cartesian conceptions of the self, as well as accounts that dissolve the self into larger patterns of social order.

Disturbances in the self as disturbances in dialogue

The initial application of the dialogical model of the self to first-person experience in schizophrenia came in the response to the question of what it means when persons with this condition report a compromised sense of self. Specifically, when persons with schizophrenia report, as they have in clinical and qualitative work (Lysaker & Lysaker, 2010) that their previous sense of self had been altered or diminished, what were they experiencing? Further, when people recover and a previously held sense of self returns, how should we account for that?

In response, we proposed that this alteration in sense of self was a function of diminished, ongoing dialogues with others and between *I*-positions that support sense of self (Lysaker & Lysaker, 2010). We posited that previously operative dialogues among multiple aspects of the self and between the self and others had weakened or ceased. As a result, the self was experienced as similarly diminished or receding. Thus, a loss of sense of self did not reflect the actual destruction of a self but a diminished capacity to bring self-facets, hereafter referred to as *I*-positions, and self-world interactions into dialogue. As a corollary, we proposed that sense of self would recover as dialogue within the self and between the self and others was rekindled.

We next proposed that dialogue could be interrupted in three different ways (Lysaker & Lysaker, 2002, 2004, 2008). In the first type of disturbance, which we labeled the barren mode, dialogue could falter when different *I*-positions were not expressed. What resulted was a barren state, one in which persons experience themselves as being more or less blank or even empty. In this state, persons would most likely find themselves as a spectator distantly watching their own lives, witnessing the events that befall them, always observing rather than participating in their lives.

In a second type of disturbance, labeled the monological mode, we suggested that dialogue could collapse if one *I*-position dominated and ordered most experience (e.g. "self-in-danger" or "self-as-powerful"). In contrast to the barren state in which nothing rises to the fore, here single and recurring *I*-positions arose but without meaningful interaction with other *I*-positions and self-world interactions. In the midst of a monologue persons might experience themselves in particular ways (e.g. persecuted or possessing special qualities) but those ideas would be unresponsive to the environment.

In a third type of disturbance, labeled the cacophonous mode, dialogue would cease because multiple *I*-positions were expressed without reference to one another or without any attention to context. Such persons would experience neither emptiness nor the tyranny of a monologue. Instead, they would be overwhelmed by the manifest appearance of multiple aspects of their selves and lives. There might be considerable and varied affect, unlike the first two modes, but also chaos. Using the metaphor of actors on the stage, in the cacophonous mode the self would seem like a group of actors all speaking at once without any organization. The monological mode would involve one actor repeating the same material, and the barren mode would have a stage with actors who never spoke.

Linking a loss of sense of self with alterations in agency

In the next stage of development, we suggested that persons with barren, monological, and cacophonous modes not only would experience a sense of self reduced in richness and diversity but also diminished agency. Unable to effectively situate themselves in evolving situations, many of which animate multiple *I*-positions, such persons, we posited, would struggle to plan and enact life projects, thus leaving them with the sense that they were no longer vital presences in their own lives (Lysaker & Lysaker, 2005; Lysaker et al., 2006). In other words, as dialogue recedes and any of the three non-dialogical modes emerge the basis for the felt experience of agency would be imperiled. For example, an impoverished set of connections between *I*-positions could prohibit the formation of the perspective needed and afforded by dialogue to (a) make explicit evaluations of our own effectiveness, and (b) to sustain an implicit and ongoing sense of our effectiveness.

Agency and sense of self would be further compromised, we argued, as dialogical disturbances undermined the intersubjective webs that sustain these two core features of human identity. People do not decide solely for themselves whether they are managing things but do so in dialogue with others as is expressly one of the central concerns in Dialogical Self-Theory (Hermans & Hermans, 2010). With a barren, monological, or cacophonous state, however, intersubjectivity would be expected to be potentially overwhelming as they elicit any number of different *I*-positions (Lysaker & Lysaker, 2005, 2008). Specifically, dialogical compromise could make it difficult to integrate the different *I*-positions stimulated by encounters with others. And this, in turn, could lead to the experience of abandonment and social alienation, which might intensify feelings of diminished agency and leave sense of self unrecognized and thus all the more fragile.

Application to psychotherapy

Turning to treatment we finally posited that this model had a number of far reaching implications for mental health services and especially for psychotherapy. If sense of self and agency were compromised by the collapse of dialogue then perhaps psychotherapy could be uniquely useful as a means to reignite dialogue. Perhaps psychotherapy could offer a means of entering into a dialogue with patients in order to promote the restoration of dialogue. But how should therapists enter and nurture a conversation with someone for whom dialogues have largely ceased and for whom intersubjectivity is threatening?

In response, we proposed each of these modes of dialogical compromise present with different challenges for the re-establishment of dialogue, each of which requires different responses (Lysaker & Lysaker, 2011). First, the silence of the barren patient may provoke anxiety on the part of the therapist. Therapists may therefore, foremost need to resist the temptation to fill in a void by filling the silence with their own questions. Therapists should instead tolerate the emptiness and instead listen to what is there. By contrast, therapists facing patients in the monological model likely need to resist the temptation to silence the dominant voice by either arguing with patients or aggressively introducing other points of view. Here therapists may need to better manage their own anger, which can be provoked by the assault of the monologue and instead be willing again to think carefully about the patient's experience of the monologue itself. Facing patients in the cacophonous mode therapists may experience their own sense of confusion and disorientation, or at least difficulties connecting their own thoughts while listening to the many thoughts of the patient. Here therapists may need to focus on whatever fragments of experience are present and not try to connect them quickly into larger ideas.

Regarding technique, with the barren narrative the therapist may need to focus more on the relationship and the account of the moment shared by patient and therapist. With the patient in the monological mode, the therapist may need to empathize with the self as tyrannized by the monologue and employ more cognitively oriented interventions to examine the bases of the dominant *I*-position that rigidly control the monologue. In the cacophony, while not bringing order to chaos the therapist may do best to mirror briefly fragments of self as they emerge and spend more time mirroring what emerges.

Summary and limitations

As a whole, our original dialogical model offered a sense of potential compromises in first person-experience, which could account for and match self-reports of the profound interruptions that occur in the lives of persons with schizophrenia. By locating sense of self within the interanimating play of *I*-positions, an opportunity was offered for understanding how persons might experience a waning sense of agency. We could, for example, appreciate how with reduced dialogicality, persons could become observers of a diminished life as opposed to active protagonists in a tale of unfolding possibility. Further, in contrast to some phenomenological accounts that clearly present a seamless process of creeping dysfunction prior to and throughout chronic illness (Nelson et al., 2014), this model allowed for the possibility of an intact agency and self-experience prior to illness. It also allowed that these disturbances in self-experience involve ongoing interactions between the self and the world, each integral to the dynamic and irreducible constellation that characterize human being-in-the-world. More importantly, unlike some phenomenological accounts (Parnas et al., 2008), the dialogical model was consistent with a robust body of qualitative and quantitative research, allowing for full and meaningful recovery from schizophrenia (Leonhardt et al., 2017).

As we have detailed elsewhere (Lysaker et al., 2018), however, a lingering limitation of this work concerned the subjective processes that might be implicated in a reduction in dialogical capacity. In several places, we suggested (Lysaker & Lysaker, 2008) that dialogue was enabled by shifting hierarchies of *I*-positions and that perhaps compromise occurred when there were alterations in hierarchies. However, this claim remained too vague to drive future research. For example, we were unable to specify the basic nature of these hierarchies and to articulate what psychological processes support and/or interfere with them. Moreover, we came to believe that the language of "dialogue" connotes conversations among speakers, which is misleading when the issues concerns pre-reflectively operative events. (Lysaker, 2006) We also ran up against the uncertain ontological status of *I*-positions (Lysaker, 2017; Lysaker et al., in press). It was clear that they were not sub-personas, and it made no sense to suggest that they were smaller singular selves. It was suggested that they exist in dialogue with other *I*-positions, but this metaphor was confusing to us because it called to mind conversations among speakers, which does not adequately describe core embodied experience that plays an immense role in any person's sense of self.

Accordingly, in trying to restore dialogue in psychotherapy, the amorphous nature of something like "dialogical capacity" became a stumbling block. What was it, and what did it address? We believe we need to answer such questions if we are to understand how a conversation in a consulting room could lead to richer self-experience, increased senses of agency, and less threatening, more meaningful interactions between persons.

We think that research on metacognition over the last decade may allow us to make progress at some of these points. To elucidate this, we will first present research on metacognition and then discuss its application.

Metacognition and the dialogical self

The integrated model of metacognition

Most simply, metacognition refers to a thought about other thoughts (Flavell, 1979) in a manner similar to how the term meta-position from DST refers to thoughts about other *I*-positions. Through multiple studies across various disciplines such as educational, cognitive, developmental, and abnormal psychology a broader model of metacognition has emerged, however, which we refer to as the integrated model. In the integrated model, metacognition is a spectrum of activities that, at one end, involve awareness of specific thoughts, feelings, or wishes, while, at the other end, integrate those discrete experiences into a larger complex sense of oneself and others (Lysaker & Dimaggio, 2014). These different ends of the spectrum are further conceptualized as informing one another, as any larger sense of self or other must incorporate elements of experience, and the meaning of any experience is partially determined on the basis of a larger sense of self and others.

In this model, metacognitive processes are integral to a person's sense of self, others, and worldly situations. When functioning well, metacognitive processes help us recognize and distinguish specific mental experiences. In particular, they help us perceive how mental experiences change or remain continuous, and allow us to richly compare and contrast mental experiences with each other and with the demands of the world. Metacognition also helps us see how our mental experiences are nested in the flow of concrete situations, and how those concrete situations fit or fail to fit into larger narratives concerning our lives and the lives of others. Metacognitive processes are consequently a basis for deciding how to respond to psychosocial stressors and how to participate meaningfully in and across communities.

From the integrative point of view, metacognitive processes have at least three characteristics. First, they occur and evolve intersubjectively. Just as Dialogical Self Theory refers to the intrinsic link between internal and external positions, metacognition requires that selected states and experiences are given meaning and expressed in ways that can be shared and acknowledged between people, in real or imagined interactions (Cortina & Liotti, 2010; Tomasello et al., 2005). Second, metacognitive processes are multidimensional and may be distinguished from one another on the basis of foci. As noted by Semerari et al. (2003), reflection about the self can be distinguished from reflections about others, one's larger community and ultimately from mastery (i.e. the ability to use one's understanding of self and others to respond to social and psychological challenges). Third, persons may vary from one another such that persons with lesser metacognitive capacities may have less complex and integrated senses of self and others. Importantly, this is not to say that persons with lesser metacognitive capacity have less experience of the self or others, but instead that they have experiences of self and others that are less integrated or more fragmented. This is consistent with Hermans and Hermans' (2010) assertions that meta-positions offer an overarching or distal view, which allows for individual experiences to be integrated within a larger picture and consequently without such structures the world and self are reduced to fewer dimensions.

Measuring metacognition

One of the first efforts to operationalize the construct of metacognition as applied to how persons form an evolving but lasting sense of self and others was the Metacognition Assessment Scale (MAS; Semerari et al., 2003). The MAS offered several advances in the study of metacognition including differentiating metacognitive activity according to focus and also describing processes that allow for more than momentary awareness of self and others. Lysaker, Carcione et al. (2005) adapted this instrument, transforming it into an ordinal scale that framed the different metacognitive processes identified by Semerari et al. (2003).

This new scale, the Metacognition Assessment Scale Abbreviated (MAS-A) retained the original three scales of the MAS: self-reflectivity (S), understanding other's minds (O), and mastery (M). It also included decentration (D), previous a subscale of O as its own scale. The MAS-A though made several significant changes to the instrument. Primarily, whereas the original MAS was intended to allow a trained observer to code the number of times a metacognitive function was used or not used within psychotherapy transcripts, the MAS-A is intended to allow a trained observer to rate overall metacognitive capacity, as a continuous variable on the basis of a structured interview that elicits personal narratives, or a therapy session.

Research on metacognition in schizophrenia

Research has suggested the MAS-A has adequate psychometric properties (Lysaker & Dimaggio, 2014) and assesses mental processes that are distinct from social cognition (Lysaker, Gumley et al., 2013; Hasson-Ohayon et al., 2015) as well as metacognitive beliefs (Popolo et al., 2017). To date, research has revealed that persons experiencing first-episode psychosis and prolonged schizophrenia have significant reductions in metacognitive capacities. Specifically, they experience disruptions in more elemental levels of metacognitive capacity than persons with prolonged non-psychiatric medical conditions or substance abuse disorders (Lysaker, Leonhardt et al., 2014; Lysaker, Vohs et al., 2014; Vohs, Lysaker et al., 2014), minor anxiety and affective disorders (WeiMing et al., 2015), and community members without mental health conditions (Hasson-Ohayon et al., 2015; Popolo et al., 2017). Lesser though significant reductions in metacognitive capacities have also been noted in first-episode and prolonged depression (Ladegaard et al., 2014), borderline personality disorder (Lysaker et al., 2017), post-traumatic stress disorder (Lysaker, Dimaggio et al., 2015), and bipolar disorder (Popolo et al., 2017). Disruptions in more basic levels of metacognition have been linked to reduced functional competence (Lysaker, McCormick et al., 2011), subjective recovery (Kukla et al., 2013), poorer therapeutic alliance in cognitive therapy (Davis et al., 2011), less ability to reject stigma (Nabors et al., 2014), a more sedentary life style (Snethen et al., 2014), anhedonia in the absence of depression (Buck et al., 2014), reduced clinical insight (Lysaker, Carcione et al., 2005), and lower levels of intrinsic motivation (Luther et al., 2016b) regardless of symptom severity. Earlier disruptions in metacognitive capacity have been also found to predict future levels of work performance (Lysaker et al., 2010), negative symptoms (Hamm et al., 2012; Lysaker et al., 2015; McLeod et al., 2014), and intrinsic motivation in schizophrenia (Luther et al., 2016a) regardless of baseline functioning. Across these studies metacognitive disturbances are not reducible to symptom exacerbation but as noted seem more likely to be a risk factor for relapse rather than a cause. Recent meta-analysis (Arnon-Ribenfeld et al., in press) affirmed that reductions in metacognitive capacities are linked with symptomatic and psychosocial functioning in people diagnosed with schizophrenia. Finally, results from both case studies and open trials suggest that participation in psychotherapy can lead to improvements in metacognitive capacity as reflected in increased scores over time on the MAS-A (e.g. Bargenquast & Schweitzer, 2014; de Jong et al., 2016; Hamm & Firmin, 2016; Leonhardt et al., 2016; Lysaker & Klion, 2017).

The dialogical model of schizophrenia in the light of metacognitive research

Returning to the limitations of our dialogical model of schizophrenia we would propose that this body of research on metacognition offers some crucial insights. For one, it may be that dialogue does not falter primarily because of an inability to shift between hierarchies of *I*-positions, and more because of a loss of access to diverse aspects of being resulting from metacognitive compromise. Persons who experience decrements in some of the most basic metacognitive functions would struggle to form ideas about their own mind and may be unable to see their own affective and cognitive states changing over time. They may indeed be vulnerable to experiences in which their internal *I*-positions, given the lack of metacognitive abilities, become externalized and external positions could become easily internalized, by the same token, resulting in an even more fragmented sense of self. They would also be less able to form complex ideas about contradictory or unrelated aspects of the self and hence opportunities for inter-animation among different *I*-positions would be reduced.

At a more specific level, this also helps us understand how growth in metacognitive capacity could pave the way for the recovery of dialogue. First, with metacognitive growth, greater opportunities should arise for the experience of self as differentiated and situated. With greater levels of self-reflectivity we would expect increasing acknowledgment of diversity among one's feelings, desires, beliefs, and commitments alongside and within an increasingly diverse field of narrative episodes or situations. With growth in a decentered awareness of others and one's community, we expect persons could increasingly acknowl-edge the presence of others whose lives follow their own diverse courses. This should allow for a growing awareness of how one's own life is intertwined with as well as separate from others. Ultimately for persons for whom dialogue has been compromised, the growth of metacognitive capacity would allow for the kinds of relationships in which dialogue could flourish again, one where depen-dence and independence, similarity and difference, agreement and disagreement co-exist and allow for mutuality.

Thus, consistent with the original model we do not posit a self that is somehow changed, made opaque, or lost in schizophrenia. Persons with schizo-phrenia still undergo their fate and interpret it. However, we would expect persons with greater metacognitive capacity to have greater opportunities to engage in more complex forms of meaning-making that allow for contradiction and complementarity within the self, others, and their inter-relationships within larger communities. Metacognitive research does not suggest that with greater metacognitive capacity an increasingly unified, simple self is discovered. Instead, the self, its relations, and the situatedness of the self and its relations should become more complex and varied, in a manner that could allow more flexible adjustments to changing circumstances. In this way, a person with higher levels of metacognition might in fact be expected to encounter a self that is at once more familiar but more complex, possibly even opaque at points. But that opacity could be recognized for what it is, for example, unusual preferences, difficulties with certain family members, or anxiety-producing social situations. Without sufficient metacognition, such opacities lose their specificity and often collapse into broader and blunter anxieties and interpretations.

As noted above, to discuss larger senses of self that sustain coherence, scholars studying the dialogical self have proposed the idea of a meta-position (Dimaggio et al., 2003; Hermans & Hermans, 2010). While *I*-positions in DST reflect distinct elements of the self that can be conceptualized as interacting in metaphorical space, meta-positions refer in essence to reflectively generated *I*-positions that help organize the interplay of other *I*-positions. Considering the integrative model of metacognition, it would seem that those meta-positions that provide a larger sense of self within narrative contexts (Dimaggio et al., 2003), cannot be generated until persons are capable of integrating information about the self and others at relatively higher levels. In fact, the highest levels of the metacognitive capacities referred to as self-reflectivity and awareness of the other involves such integration specifically both within and across narrative contexts. Thus, metacognitive function could be seen as a necessary, but not sufficient, condition for meta-positions to arise. Thus, one potential way to integrate work on metacognition with larger work on meta-positions would be to suggest that metacognition describes the set of activities that allow for access to the kinds of self-awareness out of which meta-positions could emerge and evolve. In this sense metacognitive capacities are necessary though not necessarily sufficient for the formation of meta-positions. This certainly points to the important possibility of assessing both metacognitive capacities and the existence and strength of meta-positions within a range of clinical and community groups to better under-stand their relationship. It also raises the empirical question of whether relatively strong and more diverse meta-positions might also recursively strengthen more elemental metacognitive functions creating a system in which embodied experi-ence and the larger ideas humans have of themselves interact in a complex system that cannot be distilled into modules.

Finally, this research also offers insight into how treatment might help promote dialogical capacity in patients with schizophrenia or other conditions. In fact, it may be, as suggested above, that psychotherapy facilitates the kinds of dialogues that sustain health by providing intersubjective contexts from which to offer interventions that stimulate integration and the emergence of a more coherent and integrated sense of selves, similar again to what other scholars call meta-positions. In this model, psychotherapeutic intervention supports an integrative process that allows for multiplicity and inter-animation.

Conclusions

In this chapter we have reviewed our original dialogical theory of schizophrenia. In order to deepen that original model at certain key points, we have attempted to incorporate research from the integrated model of metacognition. Specifically, we suggested that metacognitive compromise may contribute to the collapse of dialogue, which is experienced by some as a diminishment of sense of self and agency. We further argued that growth in metacognitive capacity would help pave the way for recapturing dialogue as persons are brought more fully into the relationships that constitute their lives: a life that is always ours, and never just mine. We have finally discussed how this work may point to underlying psychological processes that are necessary though not sufficient for what are called meta-positions in DST to emerge and persist over time.

Naturally, there are limitations to this approach. Schizophrenia involves heterogeneous experiences across individuals and it is possible, if not likely, that the kinds of alterations in self-experiences we focused on do not apply to all people diagnosed with schizophrenia spectrum disorders. The metacogni-tive research summarized above was also conducted among adults who were willing to consent to research and who were all enrolled in some form of treatment. It is not known if similar relationships would be observed among persons who would not consent to participate in research or treatment. Finally, these research methodologies are still developing and it may be that new, more effective ways of assessing metacognition and dialogue will lead to new insights.

References

Arnon-Ribenfeld, N., Hasson-Ohayon, I., Lavidor, M., Atzil-Slonim, D., & Lysaker, P. H. (in press). A meta-analysis and systematic review of the association between metacognitive abilities, symptoms and functioning among people with schizophrenia. *European Psychiatry*.

Andreasen, N. C. (1984). *The broken brain: The biological revolution in psychiatry.* New York: Harper & Row.

Andreasen, N. C., Paradiso, S., & O'Leary, D. S. (1998). "Cognitive dysmetria" as an integrative theory of schizophrenia: A dysfunction in cortical-subcortical-cerebellar circuitry? *Schizophrenia Bulletin*, 24(2), 203–218.

Andreasen, R., Oades, L., & Caputi, P. (2003). The experience of recovery from schizophrenia: Towards an empirically validated state model. *Australian New Zealand Journal of Psychiatry*, 37, 586–594.

Bakhtin, M. (1985/1929). *Problems of Dostoyevsky's poetics.* C. Emerson (Trans.). Minneapolis, MN: University of Minnesota Press.

Bargenquast, R. & Schweitzer, R. (2014). Enhancing sense of recovery and self-reflectivity in people with schizophrenia: A pilot study of metacognitive narrative psychotherapy. *Psychology and Psychotherapy: Theory, Research and Practice*, 87(3), 338–356.

Barham, P. (1993). *Schizophrenia and human value.* London: Free Association Books.

Buck, K. D., McLeod, H. J., Gumley, A., Dimaggio, G., Buck, B. E., Minor, K., ... Lysaker, P. H. (2014). Anhedonia in prolonged schizophrenia spectrum patients with relatively lower vs. higher levels of depression disorders: Associations with deficits in social cognition and metacognition. *Consciousness and Cognition*, 10(29), 68–75.

Cortina, M. & Liotti, G. (2010). The intersubjective and cooperative origins of consciousness: An evolutionary-developmental approach. *Journal of the American Academy of Psychoanalysis and Dynamic Psychiatry*, 38(2), 291–314.

Davis, L. W., Eicher, A. C., & Lysaker, P. H. (2011). Metacognition as a predictor of therapeutic alliance over 26 weeks of psychotherapy in schizophrenia. *Schizophrenia Research*, 129(1), 85–90.

de Jong, S., Donkersgoed, R. J. M., Aleman, A., van Der Gaag, M., Wunderink, L., Arends, J., ... Pijnenborg, G. H. M. (2016). The practical implications of Metacognitive psychotherapy in psychosis: Findings from a pilot study. *Journal of Nervous and Mental Disease*, 204(9), 713–716.

Dewey, J. (1988). Human nature and conduct. In *The middle works of John Dewey* (Vol. 14). Carbonodale, IL: Southern Illinois University Press. (Original work published 1922.)

Dimaggio, G., Salvatore, G., Azzara, C., & Catania, D. (2003). Rewriting self-narratives: The therapeutic process. *Journal of Constructivist Psychology*, 16, 155–181.

Firmin, R. L., Luther, L., Lysaker, P. H., Minor, K. S., & Salyers, M.P. (2016). Stigma resistance is positively associated with psychiatric and psychosocial outcomes: A meta-analysis. *Schizohrenia Research*, 175(1–3), 118–128.

Flavell, J. H. (1979). Metacognition and cognitive monitoring: A new area of cognitive-developmental inquiry. *American Psychologist*, 34, 906–911.

Gonçalves, M. M. & Ribeiro, A. P. (2012). Narrative processes of innovation and stability within the dialogical self. In H. J. M. Hermans & T. Gieser (Eds.), *Handbook of dialogical self theory* (pp. 301–318). Cambridge, UK: Cambridge University Press.

Hamm, J. A., Buck, B. E., & Lysaker, P. H. (2015). Reconciling the ipseity-disturbance model with the presence of painful affect in schizophrenia. *Philosophy, Psychiatry and Psychology*, 22(3), 197–208.

Hamm, J. A. & Firmin, R. L. (2016). Disorganization and individual psychotherapy for schizophrenia: A case report of metacognitive reflection and insight therapy. *Journal of Contemporary Psychotherapy*, 46(4), 227–234.

Hamm, J. A., Renard, S. B., Fogley, R. L., Leonhardt, B. L., Dimaggio, G., Buck, K. D., & Lysaker, P. H. (2012). Metacognition and social cognition in schizophrenia: Stability and relationship to concurrent and prospective symptom assessments. *Journal of Clinical Psychology*, 68(12), 1303–1312.

Hasson-Ohayon, I., Avidan, M., Mashiach-Eizenberg, M., Kravetz, S., Rozencwaig, S., Shalev, H., & Lysaker, P. H. (2015). Metacognitive and social cognition approaches to understanding the impact of schizophrenia on social quality of life. *Schizophrenia Research*, 161(2–3), 386–391.

Hermans, H. J. M. (1996). Voicing the self: From information processing to dialogical interchange. *Psychological Bulletin*, 119(1), 31–50.

Hermans, H. J. M. & Gieser, T. (Eds.). (2011). *Handbook of dialogical self theory*. Cambridge, UK: Cambridge University Press.

Hermans, H. J. M. & Hermans, K. (2010). *Dialogical self theory: Positioning and counter-positioning in a globalizing society*. Cambridge, UK: Cambridge University Press.

Kean, C. S. (2009). Silencing the self: Schizophrenia as a self-disturbance. *Schizophrenia Bulletin*, 35(6), 1034–1036.

Kierkegaard, S. (1949/1980). *The sickness unto death*. Princeton, NJ: Princeton University Press.

Kukla, M., Lysaker, P. H., & Salyers, M. (2013). Do persons with schizophrenia who have better metacognitive capacity also have a stronger subjective experience of recovery? *Psychiatry Research*, 209(3), 381–385.

Ladegaard, N., Lysaker, P. H., Larsen, E., & Videbech, P. (2014). A comparison of capacities for social cognition and metacognition in first episode and prolonged depression. *Psychiatry Research*, 220(3), 883–889.

Leonhardt, B. L., Benson, K., George, S., Buck, K. D., Shaieb, R., & Vohs, J. L. (2016). Targeting insight in first episode psychosis: A case study of metacognitive reflection insight therapy (MERIT). *Journal of Contemporary Psychotherapy*, 46(4), 207–216.

Leonhardt, B. L., Huling, K., Hamm, J. A., Roe, D., Hasson-Ohayon, I., McLeod, H., & Lysaker, P. H. (2017). Recovery and serious mental illness: A review of current clinical and research paradigms and future directions. *Expert Review of Neurotherapeutics*, 17 (11), 1117–1130.

Luther, L., Firmin, R. L., Minor, K. S., Vohs, J. L., Buck, B., Buck, K. D., & Lysaker, P. H. (2016b). Metacognition deficits as a risk factor for prospective motivation deficits in schizophrenia. *Psychiatry Research*, 245, 172–178.

Luther, L., Firmin, R. L., Vohs, J. L., Buck, K. D., Rand, K. L. & Lysaker, P. H. (2016a). Intrinsic motivation as mediator between metacognitive deficits and impaired functioning in schizophrenia. *British Journal of Clinical Psychology*, 55(3), 332–347.

Lysaker, J. T. (2006). I am not what I seem to be. *International Journal for Dialogical Science*, 1(1), 41–45.

Lysaker, J. T. (2017). *After Emerson*. Bloomington, IN: Indiana University Press.

Lysaker, J. T. & Lysaker, P. H. (2005). Being interrupted: The self and schizophrenia. *Journal of Speculative Philosophy*, 19, 1–22.

Lysaker, P. H., Carcione, A., Dimaggio, G., Johannesen, J. K., Nicolò, G., Procacci, M., & Semerari, A. (2005). Metacognition amidst narratives of self and illness in private schizophrenia: Associations with insight, neurocognition, symptom and function. *Acta Psychiatrica Scandinavica*, 112, 64–71.

Lysaker, P. H., Davis, L. W., & Lysaker, J. T. (2006). Enactment in schizophrenia: Capacity for dialogue and the experience of the inability to commit to action. *Psychiatry*, 69(1), 81–93.

Lysaker, P. H. & Dimaggio, G. (2014). Metacognitive capacities for reflection in schizo-phrenia: Implications for developing treatments. *Schizophrenia Bulletin*, 40(3), 487–491.

Lysaker, P. H., Dimaggio, G., Carcione, A., Procacci, M., Buck, K. D., Davis, L. W., & Nicolò, G. (2010). Metacognition and schizophrenia: The capacity for self-reflectivity as a predictor for prospective assessments of work performance over six months. *Schizophrenia Research*, 122(1–3), 124–130.

Lysaker, P. H., Dimaggio, G., Wicket-Curtis, A., Kukla, M., Luedtke, B. L., Vohs, J., . . . Davis, L. W. (2015). Deficits in metacognitive capacity are related to subjective distress and heightened levels of hyperarousal symptoms in adults with posttraumatic stress disorder. *Journal of Trauma and Dissociation*, 26, 1–15.

Lysaker, P. H., George, S., Chadoin-Patzel, K. A., Pec, O., Bob, P., Leonhardt, B. L., . . . Dimaggio, G. (2017). Contrasting metacognitive, social cognitive and alexithymia profiles in adults with borderline personality disorder, schizophrenia and substance use disorder. *Psychiatry Research*, 257, 393–399.

Lysaker, P. H., Gumley, A., Luedtke, B., Buck, K. D., Ringer, J. M., Olesek, K., . . . Dimaggio, G. (2013). Social cognition and metacognition in schizophrenia: Evidence of their inde-pendence and linkage with outcomes. *Acta Psychiatrica Scandinavica*, 127(3), 239–247.

Lysaker, P. H., Hamm, J., Hasson-Ohayon, I., Pattison, M. L., & Leonhardt, B. L. (2018). Promoting recovery from severe mental illness: Implications from research on metacogni-tion and metacognitive reflection insight therapy. *World Journal of Psychiatry*, 8(1), 1–11.

Lysaker, P. H., Johannesen, J. K., & Lysaker, J. T. (2005). Schizophrenia and the experience of intersubjectivity as threat. *Phenomenology and the Cognitive Science*, 4, 335–352.

Lysaker, P. H. & Klion, R. (2017). *Recovery, meaning-making, and severe mental illness: A comprehensive guide to metacognitive reflection and insight therapy*. New York: Routledge.

Lysaker, P. H., Kukla, M., Dubreucq, J., Gumley, A., McLeod, H., Buck, K. D., . . . Dimaggio, G. (2015). Metacognitive deficits predict future levels of negative symptoms in schizophrenia controlling for neurocognition, affect recognition, and self-expectation of goal attainment. *Schizophrenia Research*, 168(1–2), 267–272.

Lysaker, P. H., Leonhardt, B. L., Brüne, M., Buck, K. D., James, A., Vohs, J., . . . Dimaggio, G. (2014). Capacities for theory of mind, metacognition, and neurocognitive function as independently related to emotional recognition in schizophrenia. *Psychiatry Research*, 219(1), 79–85.

Lysaker, P. H. & Lysaker, J. T. (2001). Schizophrenia and the collapse of the dialogical self: Recovery, narrative and psychotherapy. *Psychotherapy: Theory, Research, Practice, Training*, 38(3), 252.

Lysaker, P. H. & Lysaker, J. T. (2002). Narrative structure in psychosis: Schizophrenia and disruptions in the dialogical self. *Theory and Psychology*, 12, 207–220.

Lysaker, P. H. & Lysaker, J. T. (2004). Schizophrenia as dialogue at the ends of its tether: The relationship of disruptions in identity with positive and negative symptoms. *Journal of Constructivist Psychology*, 17, 105–120.

Lysaker, P. H. & Lysaker, J. T. (2008). *Schizophrenia and the fate of the self*. Oxford: Oxford University Press.

Lysaker, P. H. & Lysaker, J. T. (2010). Schizophrenia and alterations in first person experience: A comparison of six perfectives. *Schizophrenia Bulletin*, 36(2), 331–340.

Lysaker, P. H. & Lysaker, J. T. (2011). Psychotherapy and recovery from schizophrenia: A model of treatment as informed by a dialogical model of the self-experience in psychosis. *Journal of Contemporary Psychotherapy*, 41(3), 125–133.

Lysaker, P. H., McCormick, B. P., Snethen, G., Buck, K. D., Hamm, J. A., Grant, M. L. A., ... Dimaggio, G. (2011). Metacognition and social function in schizophrenia: Associations of mastery with functional skills competence. *Schizophrenia Research*, 131(1–3), 214–218.

Lysaker, P. H., Vohs, J., Hamm, J. A., Kukla, M., Minor, K. S., De Jong, S., ... Dimaggio, G. (2014). Deficits in metacognitive capacity distinguish patients with schizophrenia from those with prolonged medical adversity. *Journal of Psychiatric Research*, 55, 126–132.

McCarthy-Jones, S., Marriott, M., Knowles, R., Rowse, G., & Thompson, A. R. (2013). What is psychosis? A meta-synthesis of inductive qualitative studies exploring the experience of psychosis. *Psychosis*, 5(1), 1–16.

McLeod, H. J., Gumley, A. I., MacBeth, A., Schwannauer, M., & Lysaker, P. H. (2014). Metacognitive functioning predicts positive and negative symptoms over 12 months in first episode psychosis. *Journal of Psychiatric Research*, 54, 109–115.

Nabors, L. M., Yanos, P. T., Roe, D., Hasson-Ohayon, I., Leonhardt, B. L., Buck, K. D., & Lysaker, P. H. (2014). Stereotype endorsement, metacognitive capacity, and self-esteem as predictors of stigma resistance in persons with schizophrenia. *Comprehensive Psychiatry*, 55(4), 792–798.

Nelson, B., Parnas, J., & Sass, L. A. (2014). Disturbance of minimal self (ipseity) in schizophrenia: Clarification and current status. *Schizophrenia Bulletin*, 40(3), 479–482.

Nietzsche, F. (1886/1966). *Beyond good and evil*. New York: Random House.

Parnas, J., Sass, L. A., & Zahavi, D. (2008). Recent developments in philosophy of psychopathology. *Current Opinions in Psychiatry*, 21(6), 578–584.

Popolo, R., Smith, E., Lysaker, P. H., Lestingi, K., Cavallo, F., Melchiorre, L., ... Dimaggio, G. (2017). Metacognitive profiles in schizophrenia and bipolar disorder: Comparisons with healthy controls and correlations with negative symptoms. *Psychiatry Research*, 257, 45–50.

Selten, J. P., van Der Ven, E., Rutten, B. P., & Cantor-Graae, E. (2013). The social defeat hypothesis of schizophrenia: An update. *Schizophrenia Bulletin*, 39(6), 1180–1186.

Semerari, A., Carcione, A., Dimaggio, G., Falcon, M., Nicolo, G., Procacci, M., & Alleva, G. (2003). How to evaluate metacognitive function in psychotherapy? The metacognition assessment scale and its applications. *Clinical Psychology and Psychotherapy*, 10, 238–261.

Snethen, G., McCormick, B. P., & Lysaker, P. H. (2014). Physical activity and psychiatric symptoms in adults with schizophrenia spectrum disorders. *Journal of Nervous and Mental Disease*, 202(12), 845–852.

Tomasello, M., Carpenter, M., Call, J., Behne, T., & Moll, H. (2005). Understanding and sharing intentions: The origin of cultural cognition. *The Behavioral and Brain Sciences*, 28, 691–735.

van Os, J. (2004). Does the urban environment cause psychosis? *British Journal of Psychiatry*, 184(4), 287–288.

Vohs, J. L., Lysaker, P. H., Francis, M., Hamm, J., Buck, K. D., Olesek, K., . . . Breier, A. (2014). Metacognition, social cognition, and symptoms in patients with first episode and prolonged psychosis. *Schizophrenia Research*, 153, 54–59.

WeiMing, W., Yi, D., Lysaker, P. H., & Kai, W. (2015). The relationship among the metacognitive ability, empathy and psychotic symptoms in schizophrenic patients in a post-acute phase of illness. *Chinese Journal of Behavioral Medicine and Brain Science*, 24(2), 128–131.

Part II
Methodological innovations

8 The dialogical self in grief therapy

Reconstructing identity in the wake of loss

Robert A. Neimeyer and Agnieszka Konopka

In the aftermath of life-changing bereavement, one's self, as the landscape of mind inhabited by a multiplicity of *I*-positions (Hermans, 2001), can become a desolate terrain where, together with the loved one, the features of a once familiar self and world may be eroded, shattered, or seemingly lost altogether. Viewing identity from the plural point of view of Dialogical Self Theory (DST; Hermans & Hermans-Konopka, 2010), we have observed how mourners can lose valued aspects of themselves that were anchored in the centrally important attachment relationship with the deceased.

However, our clinical and consulting practice, as well as a growing body of research on meaning reconstruction in bereavement (Neimeyer, 2016), also convince us that this same dialogical self can respond to the loss resourcefully from multiple positions, sometimes supported in this by a therapist who helps mobilize healing connections with the deceased as well as with parts of the client's self that are at risk of collateral extinction. Honoring all parts of one's self that suffer from the loss may create new room, a dialogical space (Hermans & Hermans-Konopka, 2010), in which a continuing symbolic bond to the deceased (Neimeyer, 2012a) can be nurtured and become a source of new and emerging meanings. DST offers conceptual, theoretical, and practical resources to understand and work with the complexity of such significant loss and transition. Our goal in the present chapter is to convey the utility of DST in grief therapy, illustrating some of its concrete implications through the use of actual vignettes of clinical practice. The following notions derived from this model can be especially useful in this respect: (1) the other in the self, (2) the multiplicity of self, (3) the contextual nature of *I*-positions, (4) relations with the self, (5) healing dialogues, and finally (6) the organization of the *I*-position repertoire. We will briefly describe each and offer an illustration of grief therapy that "puts them to work" with actual clients suffering impoverishment of self and close relationships in the wake of a wide range of losses arising from bereavement and other difficult life transitions.

The other in the self and the continuing symbolic bond

The landscape of mind in the dialogical self perspective is intertwined with the minds of other people (Hermans, 1996). A significant other is not only an "outside person," but also a part of the extended domain of the self; an *external position* in the self, the other in the self (Hermans & Hermans-Konopka, 2010). The other can be not only physically present, but also mentally present in the "room" of our selves. One can enter an internal dialogue with another who is physically distant, but within intimate reach in one's inner landscape.

When a significant person dies, he or she will never again be physically present to touch, smell, hear, or see, and the realization of this hard fact often evokes a formidable feeling of grief for this tangible loss, which an eternity will not return as a sensory reality. This confrontation with the irreversibility of death led proponents of twentieth-century approaches to mourning to emphasize the need of the mourner to say goodbye, let go of the relationship or bond with the one who died, and withdraw emotional energy from the deceased in order to invest it in other relations (Freud, 1917/1957). Recent developments in bereavement theory, however, display a growing recognition of the comforting role of continuing symbolic bonds with the deceased that survive their physical absence (Klass & Steffen, 2018). From a constructivist perspective, grieving the death of a loved one entails reaffirming or reconstructing a world of meaning that has been challenged by loss (Neimeyer, 2002). In this process finding a new way to reestablish and continue a cherished connection with the deceased is typically seen as more favorable than letting it go. To continue such symbolic relations it is helpful to acknowledge a significant other as an external position, the other in the self, whose internal presence is distinguishable from physical proximity. Remembering the deceased, recalling them in one's mind or in ongoing story-telling with others and entering into an inner dialogue with them maintains the deceased as members of the society of mind of the bereaved. Acknowledging the other as a part of the extended domain of the self can support reaffirmation or reconstruction rather than relinquishment of the relationship with a person who has passed on, in a way that mitigates grief and provides resources for adapting to a changed life.

Renewing the bond

When her father died two years earlier of a massive heart attack, Bobbie was disconsolate, stuck in an isolating grief that seemingly was frozen and unchanging since that fateful day. In a turbulent family rocked by her mother's alcoholism and infidelity, her father had been her "rock," the one secure base she had in a "scary" world. Now, even in her late thirties, having overcome her own 15-year struggle with drinking and having recently married the man to whom she was engaged in the final year of her dad's life, she vacillated between angry interactions with family and increasing self-isolation in the face of her father's absence.

Hearing the deep yearning in Bobbie's statement in her first session of therapy that she just wished she "could pick up the phone and talk to him," the therapist asked, if it were possible, whether Bobbie would be willing to reopen her conversation with her father now. As Bobbie expressed both intrigue and uncertainty about how she might do this, the therapist suggested gently that therapy could "bend the rules of the usual social world, and make things possible that otherwise might not be." He then suggested an imaginal conversation with her father, offering his own chair to the father opposite his daughter, and taking another chair just to the side from which he could help orchestrate the ensuing conversation. Prompting Bobbie to speak directly in "I-you" language to her dad, the therapist briefly paraphrased, accentuated, and asked Bobbie to repeat parts of what she said in order to encourage greater depth and honesty in her description of her life, her needs, and her feelings in the aftermath of his dying. What emerged was a detailed and tender evocation of all the commonplace conversations with him she missed, about the corn on sale at the store, about his reminders about the bus leaving soon to take her to work, and most especially about their shared struggles with her mother, for which he always seemed to have constructive advice.

As this touching opening statement reached a natural conclusion, the therapist gestured toward the empty chair holding her father, and suggested that she take the seat and "offer her father her own voice" to respond to his daughter's disclosure, which the therapist summarized in a few poignant phrases. Chuckling, Bobbie immediately asked, "What, are you nuts?!?" to which the therapist responded, "Go ahead, tell her more: Are you nuts?" Growing more serious, Bobbie's "father" then added, "You know I'm here with you," to which the therapist prompted, "Tell her more about how you are with her now." What followed was an evocative litany of ways that she could sense his presence, at the beach, in the boat, over morning coffee—the many contexts in which they had shared their lives together. The therapist then prompted "father" to tell Bobbie what he needed from her now. "I need you to go on," she replied, "to remember the things we learned together ... and to remember, she's still your mother."

As this loving paternal advice sunk in, the therapist gestured for Bobbie to return to her seat and process the interaction that had just occurred, as she wiped away tears, moved by the sweetness and solidity of a bond with her father than she once again was able to access tangibly, in the performance of the dialogue. She had known, Bobbie noted, that her father was still with her, but somehow speaking the words aloud from both perspectives "made it real," and "loosened" a kind of tightness and self-inhibition that she had carried in her chest for nearly two years. This initial chair work (Neimeyer, 2012a), then, had vividly restored a long-needed inner dialogue with the external *I*-position of her father, re-opening her to a source of support and understanding that she greatly needed in negotiating a world filled with his physical absence.

Multiplicity of the self

Multiple *I*-positions in the dialogical self create heterogeneous potential perspectives from which an experience of loss can be approached. A dominant or usual position from which one answers to bereavement can be limited and insufficient to reconstruct the world of meaning challenged by departure or transition. Rigid and limiting habitual positions can be seen as *I*-prisons (Hermans & Hermans-Konopka, 2010) that constrain ways of dealing with loss, as illustrated in the final vignette of this chapter. Accessing and inviting different positions to answer to the experience of loss can broaden one's perspective, create more dialogical space, and facilitate creation of new meanings.

Accessing and attending to those aspects of the self that act as *promoter positions* (Hermans & Hermans-Konopka, 2010) in the society of mind can be one of the process goals of grief therapy. Such positions help a person to integrate a broad range of other positions and contradictory feelings, establishing a new balance on the ground of the self that has been shaken by the earthquake of significant loss.

In a Japanese garden, the Daisen-In, a hermit's headstone (Semboseki) supports and guards with its wisdom the flow of life that is confronted with the experience of suffering.[1] Similarly, in the landscape of the mind, there may be dormant positions waiting that can assist the flow of one's life after an interruptive experience of bereavement. *I*-positions that are sources of supportive spiritual or secular belief can perform a promoter function by making sense of loss and life transitions. They can be intentionally accessed, allowed and voiced in therapeutic dialogue. These are not only well-known internal positions like "I as mother" or "I as wise," or familiar external positions (e.g. my partner or my cat). We can experiment with a broad range of possible positions by just inviting them into the therapy room, letting them speak, and be enacted by a client. They can be positions such as Buddha, Christ, soul, God, or even an unusual figure chosen by a client as a potential nourishing source of new meanings. Entering experientially such positions and speaking from within them can also help to access latent emotional resources that may not be available in habitual positions.

The flexibility of identity implicit in the notion of multiple *I*-positions reflects the potential variability and richness of the dialogical self. This richness can be introduced and enhanced in therapy to help clients rebalance and make sense of their anguish and torment.

When trying to access such positions in the self, we need to take into account that the deepest meanings are typically elusive and vague, accessing and expressing the unspeakable truths that lie at the heart of grief therapy (Neimeyer, 2010). In this process *I*-positions can gradually unfold from as yet unverbalized bodily sensed meanings. Such subtle processes of articulating an as yet unformed or undefined "felt sense" (Gendlin, 2012) may involve listening analogically (Neimeyer, 2012b) to the whisper of a new position, which may slowly evolve and become distinctive from others. This typically calls for symbolization of the position in figurative rather than literal forms. It requires recognition of the preverbal, embodied level of the self from which experiences can gradually take form and grow into new *I*-positions that later can be put in words and become sources of new meanings.

A dialogue with Suffering

In the six months since the death of her college-age son, Kyle, to an intractable cancer, Darla had managed to keep moving forward, but at great cost. In the first minute of her opening therapy session, she described the multiple dimensions of the pain she felt: the "encompassing pain" that forced her to lie down and rest herself, conveyed in wavy hand movements around her body, and the "void" that could not be filled in her abdomen, signaled by further hand gestures that placed it near her womb, where she once carried this child. When further reference was made to the pain of losing her son 15 minutes later, after Darla had shared proud stories of his character and accomplishments, the therapist asked her where she felt that pain now, in her body. Without hesitation she noted that it was deep in her torso, again gesturing toward it with her hands, and describing the dull ache that accompanied it. This then became the sensory portal through which the therapist guided Darla, as they sought a deeper contact with the felt sense of her grief and its implicit meanings.

Inviting Darla to close her eyes with him and scan her body for a sense of where and how she held her grief, the therapist asked her to stand close, but off to one side of it slightly, so as to be able to observe it closely, without being swallowed by it. Over the next ten minutes Darla, with eyes closed to minimize external distractions, described the form of what she encountered—"something with a lot of texture ... like a really fine sandpaper," which when contacted left her hand needing something to soothe it, like a cooling water or balm. Further prompting her to explore what Darla described as the "dimension" of the image, the therapist invited her to draw close and see whether there might be something beneath the sandpaper that needed to be seen or understood. Wrinkling her brow, Darla hesitated, reluctant to disturb the surface of the sandpapery grief. Sensing this resistance, the therapist inquired gently what she sensed might lie beneath it, though it was something not to be perturbed or moved. With a flood of tears, Darla replied, "all of my hopes and dreams ... the possibilities." "The possibilities," the therapist whispered, "all beneath that sandpaper." With this clearer image of the grief positioned within her, Darla then opened her eyes, and joined the therapist in exploring her understandable, but ultimately unsustainable attempt to keep it "compartmentalized" as an aching void, wrapped in sandpaper.

Some 20 minutes later, after relating poignant accounts of her caring for her son who bore his "suffering" with "dignity" during the time of his illness, Darla stated with conviction, "I'm not afraid to die anymore, but I'm afraid to suffer." But this posed a problem, as Darla explained, "Kyle didn't like to see me cry, so I would have to hide and cry," as she acknowledged this through her tears in the presence of the photograph of her son that she had brought to invite his presence in the session. The therapist recognized this as a potential problem in her grieving—that the very grief she keenly experienced needed to be hidden inside to keep faith with the dead son to whom she sought to remain bonded. The therapist formulated an incisive question, borrowing the key terms of her description of her son and herself: "Do you think it is possible to suffer with dignity?" "Good question, Bob," Darla replied, slowly repeating the question for herself. She then joined the therapist in exploring what such suffering might look like, suggesting that it would involve "not treating it as the enemy ... but as something that could be worked with." Alerted to this personification of suffering, in which it turned into an *I*-position, the therapist suggested an improvisational move: for Darla to have a conversation with Suffering, placed in an empty chair opposite her, to discover what she had to say to it, and it to her.

What ensued was a remarkable spontaneous dialogue between Darla and Suffering, with her enacting both parts, in which Suffering explained to her that it was not targeting her personally, but that she "was just the one who was there," whose "love for Kyle made my job so easy." From the sidelines, the therapist prompted, "Tell her more about what your job is in her life, now." After reassuring Darla that she would never have to go through anything else as difficult as the death of Kyle, Suffering paused, and with furrowed brow added slowly, "But . . . hmm . . . You needed to have me there . . . because letting me go, would be going into a place that would be without him," tears welling as she then looked to the therapist imploringly. Un-staging the chair work, the therapist gestured Darla back into her chair to consider the profound messages conveyed by Suffering that was less an enemy than a guide and ally, paradoxically revealing qualities of a promoter position. Most significantly, Darla began to take in the deep meaning and function of Suffering in providing a "bridge" of connection to Kyle, but also began to consider that it might not be the only such bridge, as she explored and embraced different ways of re-contacting the hopes, dreams, and memories contained in her son's life. The session concluded with the therapist acknowledging with subtle emotion how touched he was by what he had witnessed, as they jointly honored Darla's son and Darla's Suffering, and what each still had to tell her and teach her that she was now more ready to hear.

Contextual character of *I*-positions

In a relationship with a significant other, a person is a dynamic arrangement of *I*-positions, a version of himself or herself unique for this relation. With one person one can be courageous, open, and free while with another person one can feel anxious, trying to hide oneself in a cloistered inner world. Some people are surprised when in an encounter with another person they discover new areas of their inner landscape, gaining sudden access to some deeper, previously unknown dimension of themselves. With some people one can enter, discover, and cultivate deep and hidden areas of one's landscape of mind while in another interaction the same person stays on the surface, in a predictable flatland of the inner world. Some people seem to hold keys to important areas of one's inner landscape. When they die, or they are gone, the key seems to be lost and this area is hardly accessible. Stated differently, *I*-positions have a contextual character (Hermans, 2001) and they become prominent to a different degree in the context of varied interactions.

In this perspective the death of a significant other can also portend the death of this unique version of self that one was anchored in just this particular relationship. Who was the mourner in relation to this deceased loved one? It may be relevant for the process of grief therapy to see which parts of the self are themselves dying, fading away, or at risk of becoming inaccessible when a loved one is no longer there to engage them or call them forth. Moreover, some people also lose potential external positions, like children who were expected to be born from a relationship with a partner who has now died. In other processes of transition unrelated to literal death, for example the loss of a job, many social and personal positions may disappear from the personal repertoire. Metaphorically they can be seen as empty spaces in the landscape of mind that call for new positions to arise, even if a continuing bond with the deceased is cultivated. Taking into account a multiple view on the self, the loss also has a multifaceted character that includes, but goes beyond the focal loss.

Disentangling multiple loss

At 84, Dorothy had already lost many and much, but had coped resiliently with the normative deaths of parents, partner, and peers to age and infirmity over the last 30 years. Now, however, she found herself overwhelmed by a complex multifaceted grief in the aftermath of three untimely deaths in the past 15 months: of her youngest sister, Laura, who had succumbed to an illness exacerbated by a lifelong developmental disability; of her "golden" middle son, Bill, who died suddenly of a heart attack; and of her youngest grandson, Kenny, whose cause of death in his late teens was concealed by his mother, but that Dorothy suspected was drug related. In the midst of so much anguishing loss, she felt adrift in the pervasive sadness, unable to engage her characteristic resourcefulness and stay afloat in the sea of grief. Painfully, these deaths also brought on secondary losses, such as her relationship with her other grandson, Darren, Kenny's brother, in light of Dorothy being cut off from their mother.

After reviewing the general timeline of her bereavement experiences and how she was coping with them, the therapist returned to the three cardinal losses—of Laura, Bill, and Kenny—and began disentangling them (Neimeyer, 2016) by systematically focusing on each to discover (1) the special qualities of each of her loved ones, (2) their unique role relationship with her, (3) how Dorothy experienced herself in the relationship, (4) her dominant feeling in the wake of the loved one's death, and finally, (5) what would help with her grief for that specific loss now. Interviewing her about each loss in turn and its implications for each of these five themes, the therapist metaphorically combed down through the strands of the multiple losses, distinguishing what was unique to each, in terms of her relationship to Laura, Bill, and Kenny in turn, and what parts of her were engaged in each relation. For example, he began by asking about Laura's special qualities, summarizing Dorothy's answers in her own words on his notepad for later joint review ("She was smart, with strong opinions. But her disability could make life difficult, because she had no self-restraint"). To promote comparisons and contrasts to her other family members, the therapist then shifted to Bill, hearing stories of his sense of humor, soft heart, and caring nature. Finally, they turned to Kenny, as Dorothy smiled sadly but proudly, relating shared moments in which his musical talent, curiosity, and surprising maturity were evident from an early age. As the therapist nodded appreciatively, sometimes asking a brief follow-up question, they segued naturally to exploration of her own position relative to each of her family members, such as the loss of her "nurturing and guiding" self anchored in relation to Kenny in particular. Together, the two then finished with consideration of her grief-related feelings and her sense of what concrete step would help most in relation to each loss. The result was surprisingly enlightening, as Dorothy began to identify specific actions that could constructively address the needs implicit in each different loss, such as passing on her considerable collection of art books to Darren, who shared his brother's artistic inclination. As she began to implement these actions in the weeks that followed, Dorothy also discovered a cross-cutting theme that integrated her responses across the three strands of her relational web: her generative, giving role as the loving matriarch of a family that had known far too much traumatic loss. Enacting this role once more gave her back a part of herself that had seemingly died with her loved ones, as it also restored her relation to her remaining grandson.

Relation with one's self in the face of loss

A view of the self as multiple helps to differentiate not only varied *I*-positions emerging or diminished in the face of loss and transition, but also to bring to light relations between them. Multiplicity of the self allows people to develop relationships not only with other people but also with themselves (Hermans & Hermans-Konopka, 2010). They may entertain different relations with themselves ranging from self-hate, self-conflict, or self-neglect to self-appreciation, self-acceptance, and self-love. One has not only a relationship with a deceased one or something important, he or she also has a relationship with himself or herself that can be critically influenced by loss. Significant loss may, for example, evoke or deepen a split in one's self, in which a person may criticize, blame, or overburden the self. A person can become painfully stretched between two conflicting aspects of himself or herself, unable to take necessary steps in the journey of mourning.

Elzen (2017), applying the perspective of DST, explored two texts of grief memoirs that depicted the experience of young widowhood: *Unremarried Widow* by Artis Henderson (2015) and *When It Rains* by Maggie MacKellar (2010). She observed that the process of mourning was constrained by conflicting voices that arose from the lived experience of widowhood, and how widows positioned and juxtaposed their versions of selves that existed prior to their loss with their post-loss selves.

Differentiation of manifold parts of the self, exploring their relations and becoming aware of how one treats oneself in a situation of loss or transition are important steps towards a greater awareness and agency. Relations between conflicting parts of the self resulting in a negative self treatment can be further transformed in a dialogue, in which two differentiated aspects of the self are brought together in a dialogical interaction, engaged separately in relation to the deceased (e.g. in an imaginal dialogue with a deceased parent from the standpoint of the needy child the client once was and the adult he or she now is), or invited as a participant in a conversation with the deceased and then as a witness to it. Moving to this *meta-position* (Hermans & Hermans-Konopka, 2010) can help the client to become aware of the dynamic relations between different positions and further elaborate on *meaning bridges* created in a dialogue between them. The following vignette from the fourth session of therapy with a middle-aged male attorney illustrates this process.

Witnessing the relationship

Rob had entered therapy to sort out his life, an effort that had in the last two years moved him to adopt a deeply Buddhist perspective on the role of loving kindness in all relationships. This was a sharp departure from the fundamental Christian religiosity of his parents, with its strong emphasis on sin and the very real threat of eternal damnation. "Like a wild horse breaking free," Rob recalled jettisoning both his faith and family as he pursued his university and ultimately law school studies with a fierceness and "ego" that seemed the clearest alternative to the sanctimonious atmosphere of his home. Now, however, Rob realized that his cut-off from family left his little brother Jimmy without a "buffer" from a deeply unhealthy and alcoholic home environment. As Jimmy slipped into an adolescence saturated in substance abuse, Rob recalled that "I judged him ... and he felt it," expressing in these words a deep form of self-reproach for actions toward his brother that now seemed unresolvable. Ten years after Jimmy's ambiguous overdose, Rob now felt deep remorse but was stymied how to address it, "like an itch I can't scratch."

Having established a strong working alliance in the preceding three sessions, the therapist asked Rob if these were things he would feel ready to address with Jimmy now, were his brother able to join us in the session, fully ready to hear what he had to say. Bravely but uncertainly, Rob nodded his head. Gesturing to the empty chair positioned opposite him, the therapist asked him to close his eyes for a moment and envision Jimmy there, and then to open his eyes and speak to the broken heart of their relationship. Rob did so, his eyes growing moist:

> I'm sorry I didn't help you ... As ten years have gone by, my perspective has changed so much. I'm sorry for judging you ... I hope my love for you now helps carry you forward. You were always good to me, never judged me. I want to pay that forward with my own children.

"Try telling him," the therapist suggested, "I am loving my kids for you." Pausing and nodding seriously, Rob repeated this, and continued, "Yes ... Your memory, your essence, are still part of my family; you are forever in my life." "Try saying," the therapist offered, "You are still my brother." Tears welling, Rob repeated this, then fell silent with private emotion.

Gesturing to Jimmy's chair, the therapist then directed Rob to take his seat and respond to his older brother's honest and anguished comments. Responding as Jimmy, Rob answered lovingly, reassuringly:

> Rob, I've missed you greatly. I feel tremendous regret about my addiction . . . I just lost the battle. Grieve me . . . I'm happy you found beauty and purpose in your life. Love your children . . . thanks for keeping me in their minds and hearts . . . I accept your apology.

Moving Rob to a third chair at right angles to the two he had used in the dialogue, the therapist asked him from this "witness position" what he had observed about the conversation that had just taken place. Taking this meta-position, Rob responded that he was struck by the "earnest sincerity in the relationship, the genuine feeling. The relationship is tremendously significant. I think I carry it with me wherever I go." As we sat with this recognition, Rob was suddenly flooded with profound emotion, and sobbing deeply, stammered out, "Of all my family, my brother loved me the best. Now I see so much of my brother in me. Jimmy never had my mean streak, my severity." Recognizing the seeds of love that his brother had planted in him, which were only now growing and bearing fruit, Rob concluded, "So now I tell my children every time I see them that I love them just the way they are." Nine months later, as our therapy drew to a close, Rob reflected on that pivotal fourth session, which seemed to resolve a long-standing sense of guilt, install more securely a brother's love, and begin to prompt a more compassionate "witnessing" of those wounded souls— including his parents—who remained physically present for a deeper dialogue.

Healing dialogues

I-positions in the dialogical self, like in a society (Hermans, 2001), may entertain varied relationships, ranging from severe war-like conflicts, oppositions, alienation, and remoteness to helpful coalitions, cooperation, and relationships of care and love. In order to heal, transform, or develop some relations between different self-aspects, we as therapists facilitate not only a dialogue with a client but also different forms of dialogue between internal *I*-positions of a client. Dialogue in a DST perspective is seen as a highly innovative process (Hermans & Hermans-Konopka, 2010) that has the power to change interactions between internal, and between internal and external *I*-positions. In such dialogue, positions can learn from each other and become better integrated into the dialogical community of mind. Through changing relationships between distinct aspects of the self in a dialogue, positions themselves can be altered and developed. Such exchanges often evoke intense emotions, allowing the client to experience an *I*-position directly from within, and in this way experience it vividly, rather than merely talk about it abstractly. We see all significant moments of therapeutic change as experientially intense, and everything else that happens in therapy as merely commentary (Neimeyer, 2009). By itself, commentary may be necessary, but not sufficient for inducing a significant shift. As in classical Gestalt therapy (Perls, Hefferline, & Goodman, 1951), such dialogues may involve the deceased or two aspects of oneself that are in conflict or opposition.

As illustrated in the earlier case of Rob, a bereaved person can enter a dialogue with a deceased one as a way to nurture, develop, or transform the relationship. People burdened by "unfinished business" with the deceased (Klingspon, Holland, Neimeyer, & Lichtenthal, 2015) have an opportunity to express in the imagined presence of a significant other what has not been said in his or her physical presence. The still accessible voice of a loved one can be invited to enter this dialogue. Dialogue helps to reconstruct and continue attachment bonds (Klass & Steffen, 2018) with the departed. It may also open opportunities to realign those internal *I*-positions of a grieving person that were uniquely or especially prominent in a relationship with the deceased, for example the voice of a son after his parents died. While a significant loss can create a serious discontinuity in the self, dialogue may introduce a strong counter-force of continuity. When performing a dialogue, a person can pursue a symbolic bond with the other who is present in the extended domain of the self. Those *I*-positions that come to the fore, sometimes in a unique way in a relationship with the deceased, may still be given voice in this dialogue. A dialogue with a deceased person can take either the spoken form of imaginary conversations (Shear & Shair, 2005) or chair work (Neimeyer, 2012a), or the written form of correspondence with the deceased (Neimeyer, 2012c). The same can, of course, be true of dialogues between different *I*-positions in oneself, which can develop as a result of experiences of loss and further influence a variety of social relations.

The Controller and the Rebel

The many losses of Lauren's early life, including the death of her beloved grandmother and the contentious divorce of her parents, promoted two opposing forms of adaptation. On the one hand, Lauren learned to control her emotional displays, mediate intra-familial conflicts, and generally "keep the peace" by being genial, cooperative, and undemanding. On the other hand, she found herself secretly wanting to rebel, escape entanglements with family, have fun, and perhaps find love from someone who "really seemed to understand her." Now in her forties with three college-age children and a responsible, if not always exciting, husband, George, she sought therapy for the press of internal conflict, guilt, and self-doubt that attended her secret pursuit of an affair with a "wild and free" man named Nick, whose freedom was evident not only in the bedroom, but also in a succession of careers and relationships.

Exploring Lauren's relationships with both George and Nick, we quickly learned that each engaged one of her two dominant, but antagonistic *I*-positions: the Controller who efficiently ran her family, and the Rebel who passionately pursued the affair. Offering a chair to each, the therapist invited Lauren to first take the Controller position, and describe herself: in her forties, primly dressed, sitting upright—and fiercely angry at the Rebel in the chair opposite her. For her part, the

Rebel was 16, sloppily dressed, laid back in her chair—and angrily contemptuous of the Controller who seemed to want nothing more than to rein her into the same "boring" conformity that she required of herself. Orchestrating a dialogue between the two, the therapist deepened the Controller into a statement of not only her rage at Lauren's inner teen, but also into an acknowledgment of her fear for what the Rebel's behavior could cost them both: not only stability and respectability, but also the genuine love of her husband and children, who would be shocked and rejecting if the affair were discovered. Taking the Rebel's position, Lauren tearfully began tentatively to voice the "suffocation" she felt in the Controller's cold embrace, as well as the yearning she felt for liberation to live large, and be free of the oppressive responsibility and predictability associated with her home life. Going back and forth between these two dialogical positions, Lauren soon expressed the Controller's deeply loving and protective stance toward her teen self, a kind of "mothering" that she had experienced far too little in relation to her own mother. Likewise, in the Rebel position, she helped awaken the muted and in an ironic sense pseudo-mature stance of the Controller, who had carried over an emotionally inhibited, managerial, and people-pleasing style that had served her well as a teen, but that unnecessarily constrained her family life, contributing to simmering (but disowned) resentment. As this more self-compassionate rather than self-condemning stance consolidated over the next few sessions, she spontaneously and definitively ended the furtive affair, recommitted to her husband, and began to voice and live out more of her own desires in relation to her husband and children. The dialogue between two originally conflicting and distant positions resulted in a new, more encompassing, self-compassionate meta-position (Hermans & Hermans-Konopka, 2012).

Organization of the *I*-position repertoire

According to DST (Hermans, 2001), multiple *I*-positions create a dynamic whole, an organized *I-position repertoire*. This manifold assembly can be seriously influenced by an experience of loss. The complexity of loss of significant others or something very important in one's life can be more deeply investigated if we take into account not only the separate *I*-positions involved, but also their overall configuration and the pattern that they co-create. What is the influence of loss on the organization of the entire *I*-position repertoire? Does it become fragmented, disorganized, impoverished or dominated by splitting conflicts? Or does the shock or stress of an unwelcome position prompt a novel organization to emerge? The following case illustrates the disorganization of the *I*-position repertoire with the loss of a centrally organizing role, and suggests the relevance of grief therapy to a large range of "non-finite" losses that go beyond bereavement, per se (Harris, 2011).

Breaking out of prison

As he entered his fifties, Jakob was extremely involved in his highly successful business, but to a point that he experienced more and more dissatisfaction and fatigue and decided to give up his company. Before taking this radical step not only his agenda but also his total *I*-position repertoire was organized around the *I*-position "I as businessman," which was supported by a position of "I as perfectionist" and "I as anxious." Hence, the relinquishment of his business carried a ripple effect for a broad range of Jakob's *I*-positions. Multiple conflicts between *I*-positions emerged, and resulted in heavy guilt and anxiety feelings, which blocked him from giving space to new or dormant positions that were potential sources of novel meanings and fulfillment. Completing a *composition work* exercise (Konopka, Neimeyer, & Jacobs-Lenz, 2017), Jakob depicted the shifting alignment of his *I*-position repertoire by symbolizing each as a small rock, and placing them in alignment or opposition to one another on the table before him. By voicing the externalized positions, literally speaking aloud the words they would say, Jacob heard some of these voices for the first time. Speaking from his child position, Jakob painfully acknowledged, "I want to live, but I almost died," allowing him to feel the suffocation and grief created by years of unrelenting work and loss of his innocent playfulness. He was deeply touched by the sorrow of his child position and softly held the small stone representing it in his hands, embracing this part of himself also in his heart. Giving a voice to his position as an artist helped him hear his deep longing to live a life of beauty and purpose and acknowledge the intense sadness related to "not doing it for so many long years." Those voices were blocked by a critical *I*-position that dictated to him "how to be a man." In the eyes of this position the child and the artist were signs of disgusting softness while other positions like I as man, husband, and father lost their worth when he gave up his business. This critical position blocked his movement toward a new organization of his life by blaming him and scarring him. His businessman position had grown up on this demanding, critical voice and now was opposed by his artist position, which "felt like a prostitute in the world of commerce." The complex dynamic pattern of his composition showed a split, an *I*-prison in which he had become confined. The recognition of this tension in his *I*-position repertoire opened the prospect of creative realignment of his identity, which then became the goal of subsequent coaching sessions.

Conclusion

In the chapter we have argued that the integration of DST into grief therapy could deepen the latter by suggesting numerous nuances in the reconstruction of meaning and identity in the wake of loss, offering conceptual as well as practical tools for helping clients re-engage the external position of the deceased as an inner resource, discover adaptive promoter positions, inner witnesses or meta-positions to take perspective on a difficult transition, and to realign conflicting positions within the *I*-prison of the self to promote a more harmonious, flexible, and adaptive society of mind. Likewise, by offering actual vignettes of grief therapy and career consultation drawing upon these ideas, we have sought to broaden the scope of DST by applying it creatively to a universal human challenge: the unwelcome transition that comes with the loss of people, places, projects, and possessions that configure and validate our community of self. We hope that this tandem effort to suggest the mutual relevance of DST and a meaning reconstruction approach to grief therapy developed in previous writings (Neimeyer, 2012d; Neimeyer & Arvay, 2004) will encourage other helping professionals to respond creatively to clients facing unwelcome life transitions, in a way that recognizes both the challenge and prospects they imply for our evolving self-narratives.

Note

1 This statement is based on a Daisen-In temple publication that commemorates the 500th anniversary of Daisen-In.

References

Elzen, K. (2017). Exploring the nature of the dialogical self: The young widow memoir. *European Journal of Life Writing*, *6*, 40–61.

Freud, S. (1957). Mourning and melancholia. In J. Strachey (Ed.), *The complete psychological work of Sigmund Freud* (Vol. XIV, pp. 239–260). London: Hogarth Press. (Original work published 1917.)

Gendlin, E. T. (2012). *Focusing-oriented psychotherapy: A manual of the experiential method*. New York: Guilford Press.

Harris, D. (Ed.) (2011). *Counting our losses*. New York: Routledge.

Henderson, A. (2015). *Unremarried widow: A memoir*. New York: Simon & Schuster.

Hermans, H. J. M. (1996). Opposites in a dialogical self: Constructs as characters. *Journal of Constructivist Psychology*, *9*, 1–26.

Hermans, H. J. M. (2001). The construction of a personal position repertoire: Method and practice. *Culture & Psychology* (Special Issue: Culture and the Dialogical Self: Theory, Method and Practice), *7*(3), 323–365.

Hermans, H. J. M., & Hermans-Konopka, A. (2010). *Dialogical self theory: Positioning and counter-positioning in a globalizing society*. Cambridge, UK: Cambridge University Press.

Klass, D., & Steffen, E. M. (2018). *Continuing bonds in bereavement*. New York and London: Routledge.

Klingspon, K. L., Holland, J. M., Neimeyer, R. A., & Lichtenthal, W. G. (2015). Unfinished business in bereavement. *Death Studies*, *39*, 387–398.

Konopka, A., Neimeyer, R. A., & Jacobs-Lenz, J. (2017). Composing the self: Toward the dialogical reconstruction of self-identity. *Journal of Constructivist Psychology*. doi: 10.1080/10720537.2017.1350609

MacKellar, M. (2010). *When it rains: A memoir*. North Sydney: Random House Australia.

Neimeyer, R. A. (2002). Traumatic loss and the reconstruction of meaning. *Journal of Palliative Medicine*, *5*, 935–942.

Neimeyer, R. A. (2009). *Constructivist psychotherapy*. London: Routledge.

Neimeyer, R. A. (2010). Reconstructing the continuing bond: A constructivist approach to grief therapy. In J. D. Raskin, S. K. Bridges, & R. A. Neimeyer (Eds.), *Studies in meaning 4: Constructivist perspectives on theory, practice and social justice* New York: Pace University Press.

Neimeyer, R. A. (2012a). Chair work. In R. A. Neimeyer (Ed.), *Techniques of grief therapy* (pp. 266–273). New York: Routledge.

Neimeyer, R. A. (2012b). Analogical listening. In R. A. Neimeyer (Ed.), *Techniques of grief therapy* (pp. 55–57). New York: Routledge.

Neimeyer, R. A. (2012c). Correspondence with the deceased. In R. A. Neimeyer (Ed.), *Techniques of grief therapy* (pp. 259–261). New York: Routledge.

Neimeyer, R. A. (2012d). Reconstructing the self in the wake of loss: A dialogical contribution. In H. Hermans & T. Gieser (Eds.), *Handbook on the dialogical self*. Cambridge, UK: Cambridge University Press.

Neimeyer, R. A. (2016). Meaning reconstruction in the wake of loss: Evolution of a research program. *Behaviour Change, 33*(2), 65–79. doi: 10.1017/bec.2016.4

Neimeyer, R. A., & Arvay, M. J. (2004). Performing the self: Therapeutic enactment and the narrative integration of traumatic loss. In H. Hermans & G. Dimaggio (Eds.), *The dialogical self in psychotherapy* (pp. 173–189). New York: Brunner Routledge.

Perls, F., Hefferline, G., & Goodman, P. (1951). *Gestalt therapy*. New York: Julian Press.

Shear, K., & Shair, H. (2005). Attachment, loss, and complicated grief. *Developmental Psychobiology, 47*(3), 253–267.

9 Innovation and ambivalence

A narrative-dialogical perspective on therapeutic change

Miguel M. Gonçalves, António P. Ribeiro,
Catarina Rosa, Joana R. Silva, Cátia Braga,
Carina Magalhães, and João Tiago Oliveira

Innovative moments and therapeutic change

Over a decade ago (Matos & Gonçalves, 2004), departing from the narrative therapy concept of *unique outcomes* (White & Epston, 1990), we operationalized the concept of innovative moments (IMs) as instants during the therapeutic conversation in which exceptions to the maladaptive framework of meaning emerge. The concept of the dialogical self as a "dynamic multiplicity of relatively autonomous *I*-positions" (Hermans, 2001, p. 248) offered a privileged background for the initial innovative moments' conceptualization and for the theoretical model of change that we have been developing from that moment on. The narrative and other communicative outputs (e.g., signs of tension in the session) observed in psychotherapeutic conversation are the result of different *I*-positions voicing their own perspectives (for a model with similar features, see also Stiles, 2002, 2011; Stiles et al., 1990). A client's statement in therapy such as "I am not sure whether I will be able to do things differently" may be voicing an internal *I*-position ("I as an unable and incompetent person"), and external *I*-positions of others (e.g., "my mother always told me that I was worthless"). The interactions between these *I*-positions constitute the dialogical processes underpinning what can be observed in psychotherapy (e.g., complete or incomplete narratives, brief emotional reactions). Moreover, the arrangement between specific internal and external *I*-positions provides the content and structure for the client's self-narrative or, as we have most recently designated it, the client's framework of meaning. Recapturing Wittgenstein's (1922) famous dictum, "The limits of my Language mean the limit of my world" (5.6), this framework of meaning establishes the limits of the client's world, i.e., what is possible, what is conceivable, what is plausible, how interpretations emerge, the favorite outcomes, etc. Thus, it is easily conceivable that whenever some *I*-positions are systematically silenced and overshadowed by the dominant ones, this framework may become too narrow or inflexible, leaning towards the monological polo of the continuum between dialogical and monological relationships (Gonçalves & Guilfoyle, 2006; Hermans & Hermans-Konopka, 2010). Thus, in the case of a monologized self-system, an innovative moment could be conceived as an expression of an alternative *I*-position that challenges the dominant and problematic framework of meaning, potentially expanding the limits of the client's inner world. These alternative *I*-positions may be previous silenced ones or new *I*-positions emerging from new experiences (see the concept of corrective experience in psychotherapy, Castonguay & Hill, 2012). For example, let us take the fictional example of John, a client whose maladaptive framework of meaning is centered on the need to be superior to others in order to avoid being in a fragile interpersonal position, and target of imagined humiliation. This position may become problematic as it leads John to constantly monitor his power relationship with others, searching for signs of anxiety and vulnerability in the self. This pattern is typical of clients suffering from social anxiety. An alternative experience would occur if John was able to express what he sees as a vulnerable self (often highly exaggerating what this vulnerability is), without feeling attacked or humiliated by significant others. The consistent expression of alternative *I*-positions throughout treatment (e.g., "I as a person who accepts my flaws," "my friends as trustworthy") might create a new dialogical tension between *I*-positions, promoting a more democratic self, with an increased flexibility (see Hermans, Konopka, Ooster-wegel, & Zomer, 2017 on the democratic organization of the self). Thus, as illustrated through John's example, as innovative moments are expanded and elaborated, they stimulate the centrifugal movement of *I*-positions towards flexibility and change, setting the stage for the construction of a more adaptive framework of meaning and a more open, resourceful and flexible self.

Tracking the narrative innovation

The innovative moments coding system (Gonçalves, Ribeiro, Mendes, Matos, & Santos, 2011) is a methodological tool that allows the identification of innovative moments in the clients' discourse throughout psychotherapy. Although the development of this coding system was inspired from the narrative therapy tradition (White & Epston, 1990), its application has not been restricted to this therapeutic model. Besides narrative therapy (e.g., Gonçalves, Ribeiro, Silva, Mendes, & Sousa, 2016), this methodology has been reliably applied to client-centered therapy (Gonçalves et al., 2012), emotion-focused therapy (Mendes et al., 2010), constructivist therapy (Alves et al., 2014), Cognitive behavioral therapy (Gonçalves, Silva et al., 2016), and more recently to psychodynamic brief therapy (Nasim et al., 2017). Beyond psychotherapy, this method has been applied to the study of spontaneous change in daily life (Meira, Salgado, Sousa, Ribeiro, & Gonçalves, in press), vocational counseling (Cardoso, Gonçalves, Duarte, Silva, & Alves, 2016), group counseling of underachieving university students (Esposito, Ribeiro, Alves, Gonçalves, & Freda, 2016), and more recently to the deradicalization process in terrorism (da Silva, Fernández-Navarro, Gonçalves, Rosa, & Silva, 2018).

Through the empirical studies on psychotherapy, conducted mainly with depression samples, but also complicated grief or victims of intimate violence samples, the coding system has been reformulated and updated to encompass the idiographic nature of psychotherapeutic processes. We categorized seven different types of innovative moments (e.g., actions, cognitive products; for a further description of the coding system's specificities see Gonçalves et al., 2017) but recently, and more relevant to this chapter, we have proposed a categorization of this diversity of types into three groups, according to their main developmental function towards change: level 1 innovative moments, in which exceptions are characterized by the creation of distance from the maladaptive framework of meaning; level 2 innovative moments centered on the elaboration and expansion of the change process; and level 3 innovative moments corresponding to meta-positions. While level 1 innovative moments involve actions, cognitive or emotional occurrences in which the maladaptive framework is challenged, level 2 innovative moments involve behavioral, cognitive, or emotional changes, in which change is elaborated and expanded, most of the time assuming two main forms: description of a contrast between a previous problematic position and a more adjusted one, termed contrasting self (CS) (e.g., before I did X, now I do Z); and/or the description, from an agentic position, of the process that allowed this change to unfold, which we termed transformation process (TP) (e.g., I'm more clear about my needs and this allows me to do X), (Fernández-Navarro et al., in press). Level 3 innovative moments correspond to meta-positions in which the two components described above (contrast and transformation process) emerge in articulation. This articulation usually takes the following form: "Before I felt/saw/behaved (or some other form) X, now I feel/see/behave (or some other form) Y, and this was possible because I start realizing/doing/thinking (or some other form) Z." Where X was the problematic *I*-position, Y is the newer adaptive *I*-position (i.e., contrast), and Z is the proactive process that allowed the contrast to occur (i.e., transformation process) (see also Gonçalves & Ribeiro, 2012, in which level 3 innovative moments were termed reconceptualization).

Dialogically, level 1 innovative moments could be perceived as a centrifugal movement towards flexibility and change, while level 2 and 3 innovative moments could represent a centripetal movement of change construction (see Hermans & Hermans-Konopka, 2010 on centripetal and centrifugal movements, or centering and decentering).

As we have stated, this three-level categorization was constructed from a bottom-up approach, grounded on the empirical data collected over more than one decade of innovative moments research. Interestingly, though, the developmental function towards change implied by each level is in close consonance with the theoretical conceptualization of adult development proposed almost 30 years ago by Freeman and Robinson (1990). These authors assumed that development in adults takes place not by a pre-fixation of ends (as it occurs in traditional developmental theories), but through the revision and construction of new ends. From a dialogical perspective, this means a disruption in the previous equilibrium of *I*-positions (the previous end), and the emergence of a new temporary equilibrium (the new end). Moreover, Freeman and Robinson (1990) proposed that this creation of a new end occurs along four stages of change, which are strikingly congruent with what we have found at an empirical level. These four stages are as follows:

1. *Recognition*, that is, "some semblance of a disjunction or contradiction between what exists and what is posited as representing a more ideal state" (Freeman & Robinson, 1990, p. 64). This is a necessary condition for development, and also for psychotherapeutic change. When the client is aware of the need to change, this notion is present from the onset of therapy. In fact, in the absence of this recognition, it is very difficult to actively involve the client, a condition that overlaps with what Prochaska and DiClemente (1982) have termed pre-contemplation stage, that is, a stage in which the client does not even consider the possibility of change.

2. *Distanciation*, that is, "some 'removal' from one's current existential situation" (Freeman & Robinson, 1990, pp. 64–65). In our model, this is akin to level 1 innovative moments, that is, events in which new understandings of the problem emerge, prompting the client to express new feelings and intentions, or to develop new actions. A tension is created here between a former problematic arrangement of *I*-positions, and an alternative and more adaptive one. But this tension has no form yet, and an alternative framework of meaning is still far from having a distinct structure.

3. *Articulation* is

   a movement wherein the aforementioned tension [present in the former stage] is given some measure of form ... one comes to identify the difference between the new and the old. One's narrative and, by extension, one's self is being reconstructed here.

   (Freeman & Robinson, 1990, p. 65)

   At this stage, which is clearly related to level 2 innovative moments, the dialogical relationships are being reappraised, and new or formerly silent *I*-positions now have more power, creating the possibility of a new framework of meaning to emerge.

4. *Appropriation* is "the process of 'taking in' newly constructed ends by incorporating them into the fabric of subjectivity" (Freeman & Robinson, 1990, p. 66). This is an extension of the previous stage, in which the unfamiliar becomes integrated and in a sense, automatic. While articulation may be prompted by the emergence of level 3 innovative moments, for appropriation to take place, it will probably be necessary for level 2 innovative moments to keep repeating themselves along therapy, facilitating the transformation of the unfamiliar into the familiar until this centripetal movement culminates into a new and consolidated version of the self-system. In order to consolidate this appropriation, meta-positions are needed, connecting what has changed (contrast) with how this change has been developing (transformation process) (see Gonçalves & Ribeiro, 2012 on the functions of meta-positions and reconceptualization, or level 3 innovative moments).

From a dialectical perspective, if the maladaptive framework of meaning is A, level 1 innovative moments are *non*-A (the step that allows access to the vast field of possibilities beyond A), level 2 and 3 innovative moments are B (the definition of a new framework of meaning). If we retrieve the example of John, an example of a level 1 innovative moment could be his expression throughout therapy of something like: "Yesterday I finally got the courage to tell my sister what I thought." This specific action shows a behavioral movement towards change. John could also state that, "Now I realize that I observe myself all the time, and that I avoid to express myself freely. I'm getting tired of that." This also would be a level 1 innovative moment (in the form of a cognitive product) and clearly expresses what we termed a protest against the problematic framework of meaning. Level 2 would represent expanding the centrifugal movement of level 1 and the setting in motion of a new centripetal movement. Level 2 innovative moments could emerge as a contrast or as transformation process. For instance, John could state: "Lately I've been feeling different, not so worried about what others think of me." As clients perform and author their change process, they will be able to reestablish both the sense of coherence (centripetal movement) and the self-system's permeability to innovation (centrifugal movement), two crucial building blocks of a new and more resourceful framework of meaning, which leads to level 3 innovative moments. An example of this in John's case could be the following example: "Now I feel capable of fighting my own battles and stand up for what I believe, nota mere reflection of what I fantasized others thought of me anymore" (in which we have both components, contrast, and process). This is a representation of the already ongoing flow of change, but it is not a mere by-product of that; it is also a performance of change, *giving shape to a new end*, to use Freeman and Robinson's (1990) term referred above. Despite this differentiation, it should be underlined that the three levels represent a clear disruption regarding the maladaptive framework of meaning that brought the client to therapy, becoming opportunities for new (or previously silenced) *I*-positions to emerge.

The body of empirical data gathered so far allowed us to reach two main conclusions concerning innovative moments and therapeutic change. The first one derives from correlational studies (e.g., Gonçalves et al., 2012; Matos, Santos, Gonçalves, & Martins, 2009; Mendes et al., 2010) and refers to the assumption that clinical recovery is associated with a higher presence of innovative moments, namely levels 2 and 3. The second one results from longitudinal studies (e.g., Gonçalves, Ribeiro et al., 2016; Gonçalves, Silva et al., 2016) pointing to the hypothesis that innovative moments precede change in symptoms. In these studies, levels 2 and 3 (and not level 1) emerged as predictors of symptomatic improvement, thus reinforcing the crucial importance of this type of innovation in the process of change.

Nevertheless, the process of change is hardly a smooth one. Innovations imply a kind of "peek experience," which represents a challenge to the usual (even if problematic) framework of meaning. Next we will address a possible and rather typical counter reaction to the challenge imposed by innovative moments, the process of ambivalence.

Ambivalence and therapeutic stability

As suggested in the previous section, the clinical relevance of innovative moments resides in their potential to lead off a process of increased innovation in the self, reaching a point in which an alternative framework of meaning is constructed (level 2) and consolidated (level 3). However, change is a challenging process and clients often get trapped in a loop between striving for innovation and dialogue within the self-system and pulling back towards monologue and conservatism (Hermans, 2003). We termed these instances as ambivalence markers and empirically operationalized them as moments in which clients elaborate an innovative moment (e.g., I was finally able to do X) and, immediately after it, they attenuate, devalue, or refuse its meaning (e.g., but it probably will not make any difference) (Gonçalves, Ribeiro, Stiles et al., 2011). An example of an ambivalence marker in John's case would be:

> Yesterday I finally got the courage to tell my sister what I thought [level 1 innovative moment]. However, I have not been able to do that with anyone else, I guess I am still the good old passive person that I have always been [ambivalence marker].

Dialogically, this process is characterized by a cyclical movement between two opposing *I*-positions: one representing a centrifugal movement, led by a non-dominant and innovative *I*-position, and another one representing a centripetal movement, led by a dominant *I*-position that organizes the client's problematic framework of meaning. This process reflects the client's need for change, his or her ability to create distance from the maladaptive framework of meaning (centrifugal movement), but also his or her urge to maintain self coherence that was, until that point, organized around the maladaptive but familiar framework of meaning (centripetal movement), thus preventing him/her to expand this distance by giving shape to a new framework of meaning. In Freeman and Robinson's (1990) terms, distanciation is occurring, but articulation is paralyzed. Consistently, according to Hermans and Hermans-Konopka (2010) the overshadowing prevalence of one of these movements puts the client at risk of rigidity and stagnation. Thus, the significant presence of ambivalence markers is a clear indicator of a client's current difficulty to promote change; and their persistent emergence throughout the therapeutic process might be perceived as a red flag regarding the course of therapy, potentially compromising the therapeutic outcome if left unattended and unresolved (Gonçalves, Ribeiro, Stiles et al., 2011; Ribeiro et al., 2014).

Ambivalence can be the result of a diversity of processes. Three common possibilities will be suggested here, but it is essential for the therapist to make sense of ambivalence in each specific case to effectively deal with it (see Miller & Rollnick, 2002). The first possibility refers to the presence of a dilemma in which we have *I*-positions claiming that the maladaptive pattern is negative, but also *I*-positions seeing this pattern as an advantage. Several therapists have addressed this phenomenon of a dilemmatic internal organization (Ecker &

Hulley, 1996; Feixas, Montesano, Erazo-Caicedo, Compañ, & Pucurull, 2014). For instance, a person who is in a grieving process can face the "It's not ok to be ok" dilemma. One *I*-position holds that the person should be able to be well again, to enjoy life, even in the absence of the lost person; while another *I*-position affirms that it would be preferable to suffer and stay connected with a lost loved one through the suffering (Alves et al., 2016; Neimeyer, Baldwin, & Gillies, 2006).

The second possible scenario involves the cluster of problematic *I*-positions being so fused with the client's identity that he or she may feel that it is better to stay the same, keeping his or her sense of stability, than promoting a change that is perceived as potentially chaotic and unpredictable. This is probably the case when problematic *I*-positions have been dominant for a long period and have emerged as a response to very disruptive environments (e.g., personality disorders and chronic depression, see Dimaggio, 2006; Dimaggio, Ottavi, Popolo, & Salvatore, Chapter 10, this volume).

Finally, the problematic internal *I*-positions could be highly valued by some relevant external *I*-positions (my wife, my mother), making it difficult for the client to find social validation (Frank & Frank, 1991) in the change process. The dilemma here is not entirely internal since change could be perceived as a betrayal of significant others. Early parental abuse could be a good example. The person, as an adult, may wish to be assertive toward an abusive parent (that does not recognize or even trivializes the past abuse) but simultaneously be afraid of further damaging the fragile ties that sustain this relationship. Here we have a triad of positions that keep the system in a problematic stability: two internal (one favoring change, another favoring stability), and a very powerful external position supporting stability (in this case the abusive parent).

Ambivalence markers have been tracked in several clinical samples with the ambivalence coding system (Gonçalves, Ribeiro, Stiles et al., 2011). The body of empirical data resulting from the application of this coding system (Gonçalves, Ribeiro, Stiles et al., 2011) led us to two main conclusions: (1) the presence of ambivalence markers is lower in successful psychotherapy, suggesting that these clients' motivation to change is high; or (2) presents a consistent decreasing tendency, suggesting that the ambivalence was high at the onset but resolved throughout treatment (Alves et al., 2016; Gonçalves, Ribeiro, Stiles et al., 2011; Ribeiro, Gonçalves, Silva, Brás, & Sousa, 2015; Ribeiro et al., 2014).

One final remark on the possible meaning of absence of ambivalence at the onset of therapy: We speculate that ambivalence may be low as the dialogical self-system is already flexible enough for the client to mostly consider the advantages of change (the first stage proposed by Freeman & Robinson, 1990, previously described); but low levels of ambivalence may also mean that the system is so rigid that the client is not even able to consider change and all centrifugal movements are boycotted. In this last case, ambivalence is absent because there is not enough tension between opposed *I*-positions, and the system is leaning towards the monological end. How ambivalence can come to be resolved in psychotherapy is the topic of the next section.

Innovative moments as opportunities for ambivalence resolution

The study of the processes of ambivalence resolution assumes theoretical and clinical importance as ambivalence constitutes a frequent process in psychotherapy, and one that must be addressed and resolved for sustained change to take place (Miller & Rollnick, 2002). The ambivalence resolution coding system (Braga, Oliveira, Ribeiro, & Gonçalves, 2016) was developed in order to allow the empirical exploration of the dialogical processes involved in ambivalence resolution. Studies with this coding system (Braga et al., 2016; Braga et al., 2018) have proposed that ambivalence can be overcome through, at least, two distinct processes: (1) the dominance of the innovative *I*-position and consequent inhibition of the problematic *I*-position, and (2) the negotiation and engagement in joint action between both *I*-positions (for a similar distinction see Nir, 2012), resulting in a new position (on the concept of third position see Hermans & Hermans-Konopka, 2010; Konopka, Hermans, & Gonçalves, Chapter 2 in this volume).

In the dominance process, the innovative *I*-position struggles to control the problematic *I*-position by mimicking the strategy of its rival, that is, by affirming the innovative position's power in an authoritarian way. Coming back to John's case, a dominance type of ambivalence resolution could be: "I do not care what people think about me anymore, what I do with my life is totally up to me!" In an effort to overcome the problematic *I*-position's power, the innovative *I*-position severely imposes its control, upholding its authority.

In the negotiation process, the conflicting *I*-positions seem to be respectfully communicating with one another, promoting a dynamic flow between opposites, rather than the dominance of one of them (Braga et al., 2016). An example of the negotiation process in John's case could be: "Of course, what other people think of me is important, mainly the people that have a significant role in my life; but I don't need to be approved by every person in the world." The negotiation process implies that both *I*-positions contribute to the meaning making process, establishing a dialogical relationship that is substantially different from the previous confrontational one; they now seem to be collaborating to resolve the conflict (e.g., "What they think is important to me, but that does not mean I must live by what they say").

The assimilation model (Stiles, 2002; Stiles et al., 1990) suggests that in successful psychotherapy the non-congruent position is progressively integrated in the community of voices through the eight levels of the Assimilation of Problematic Experiences Scale (APES). Successful cases often reach a level in which a *meaning bridge* emerges (Detert, Llewelyn, Hardy, Barkham, & Stiles, 2006), that is, a common language between the problematic *I*-positions and the innovative *I*-positions, allowing the negotiation processes to take place. Congruently with the assimilation model, in the innovative moments' model, level 3 innovative moments have been more closely associated with successful cases. Thus, level 3 innovative moments are a form of insight in which a meaning bridge is established between the problematic *I*-position and the innovative *I*-position.

We assume that ambivalence is resolved through the cumulative process of repetitive *momentary resolutions*, that is, moments when there is an agentic and determined resolution of ambivalence, even if it is a momentary one (Braga et al., 2016). Empirical studies (Braga et al., 2016; Braga et al., 2018) revealed that both dominance and negotiation processes of ambivalence resolution can be found in different psychotherapeutic approaches and no significant differences have been found between the different models in terms of these processes' evolution (Braga et al., 2018). However, distinct paths have been observed for successful and unsuccessful psychotherapy cases. In recovered cases the dominance process tends to be less frequent and negotiation gradually increases as treatment evolves. In unsuccessful psychotherapy, this apparent gradual shift between dominance and negotiation does not seem to happen; dominance is frequently used from the beginning to the end of treatment, and negotiation is scarce at any stage of therapy. These results are theoretically coherent with theories that have been proposing an increasing integration of opposing elements of the self along the therapeutic process (e.g., the assimilation model, emotion-focused therapy).

Practical implications: how can IMs inform clinical practice?

The studies described above have demonstrated important differences between recovered and unsuccessful cases in terms of the production of narrative innovation, levels of ambivalence experienced by clients throughout treatment, as well as the strategies used by these clients to resolve ambivalence. The main question that emerges at this moment is: in what way can this knowledge serve to inform therapists in their clinical practice?

We believe that the line of empirical research we have been developing allowed for some important insights into the dialogical-narrative processes involved in psychotherapeutic change, regardless of the therapeutic modality. In order to clarify the possible contribution that this line of research can offer, we use the example of Mary (a pseudonym), a young 32-year-old married woman who comes to therapy referring to herself as "dumber than all other people" and "cognitively limited." Her maladaptive framework of meaning was informed mostly by these dominant *I*-positions that led Mary to avoid several tasks in her work, avoid asking for help, and constantly agreeing with others' opinion. Also, she frequently compared her performance with that of others, criticizing herself for being slower and for making many mistakes.

Throughout therapy, she presented some centrifugal movements towards flexibility, as other supressed *I*-positions emerged. Two examples of this movement were the following: "Yesterday I called a colleague for help with the computer programme and he had the same doubt" or "This week I was able to feel differently when I had to present my work, I felt some competency" (two level 1 innovative moments). However, these movements were constantly inhibited by the dominant *I*-position, consolidating further the problematic framework of meaning: "He didn't know how to solve the problem because his work functions are different from mine. He is not supposed to know that but I am, I should have known"; "although everyone can have some doubts, these doubts aren't even similar to the ones I have, so ridiculous and so frequent!" The previous examples are instances of ambivalence markers, neutralizing previous IMs. The inner tension between these forces was very clear when the client was talking about her final project for her Master's degree:

> I was able to present my project in the meeting but no one made questions. It was easy. However, if they had asked any questions I think I would not have been able to answer, I would have blocked. I am not so clever as they think.

Mary's case represents a typical example of an unsuccessful case, where level 1 innovative moments dominate as the only form of innovation, being frequently aborted by ambivalence markers, while level 2 and 3 are almost absent. In this kind of psychotherapeutic processes if therapists are able to be attentive and acknowledge these processes they may attune themselves to the client needs, which in this case implies the promotion of level 2 innovative moments. Of course, deciding when a therapist may try to promote level 2 innovative moments is a matter of timing. The therapist may think that elaborating and understanding further the maladaptive framework of meaning is necessary before prompting more and more complex innovation. Promoting level 2 innovative moments is possible if the therapist tries to elicit contrasts and transformation processes components. Contrasts may be elicited around the theme "what is better/different than before?" or "what were the main changes in therapy?" while transformation processes are related to the question(s) of "how did you achieve those changes?" or "what helped you getting to where you are now?" So, returning to the case of Mary, her therapist's first effort could be centered on promoting these components. For instance, when the client said:

> I was able to present my project in the meeting but no one made questions. It was easy. However, if they had asked any questions I think I would not have been able to answer, I would have blocked. I am not so clever as they think.

The therapist could have asked Mary to recall the episode in detail, in order to avoid generalized memories that would disrupt the recalling (see the role of generalized auto-biographic memories in depression, Boritz, Angus, Monette, Hollis-Walker, & Warwar (2011). During the recalling, the therapist could be attentive to any difference in her feelings, actions, or thoughts compared to other times, searching for the possibility of prompting innovative moments. Another possibility would be to elicit connections between the way she felt in this situation with other level 1 innovative moments described before: "Remember when you felt competent presenting your work last week? Was there any similarity between the two episodes?" If similarities emerged the therapist may further ask "How do you think you managed to do this?" trying to elicit the process component, thus prompting a level 2 innovative moment.

After the emergence of level 2 innovative moments, therapists may try to connect contrasts with transformation processes, promoting level 3 innovative moments. Along these lines, therapists might be more effective if they asked questions that invite the client to relate a particular contrast ("now I feel that I can do X") with a specific transformation process ("I was able to do X, because now I Y").

The second point to keep in mind is the promotion of ambivalence resolution. The process mostly used by Mary to resolve her inner tension was dominance: "From now on I'm going to stop worrying about others' opinions about my work," As referred previously, in order to resolve ambivalence, *I*-positions need to communicate with one another promoting the integration of the non-congruent position. This integration is akin to what Hermans and Hermans-Konopka (2010) described as a promoter position. Considering this knowledge, the therapist should be able to early identify the presence of ambivalence, promoting the understanding of each one of the *I*-positions that are in conflict and constantly validate both of them in order to clarify their existence to the client and decrease the emergence of resistance to change (Lewis & Osborn, 2004; Oliveira, Gonçalves, Braga, & Ribeiro, 2016). Integrating elements from different approaches to ambivalence resolution (e.g., Engle & Arkowitz, 2006; Sato, Hidaka, & Fukuda, 2009), including well-established techniques such as two-chair work (Greenberg, Rice, & Elliott, 1993; Perls, Hefferline, & Goodman, 1951), Oliveira and colleagues (2016) have suggested ten steps (see Table 9.1) that may guide therapists in conceptualizing their clients' ambivalence.

Until the present time, our research program has allowed the clarification of several processes associated with clinical change and stagnation throughout psychotherapy. Currently, we recognize it is crucial to deal with the challenge of transposing this empirical data to the daily clinical practice. Lambert, Whipple, Smart, Vermeersch, and Nielsen (2001) have argued that pre-post evaluations of therapy are a kind of post-mortem evaluation, as they are not useful for the current client. Although our research is not about outcomes but about psychotherapy

Table 9.1 Guidelines to conceptualize clients' ambivalence in psychotherapy

1. Define and gather information about the client's problematic self-narrative
2. Define an alternative, more adaptive, self-narrative
3. Identify movements towards change
4. Identify movements away from change
5. Conceptualize these oscillatory movements as a dialogue between voices
6. Present both identified voices to the client (towards and away from change)
7. Isolate each voice and explore them separately
8. Express validation regarding each voice
9. When present, identify the processes used by the client to overcome ambivalence
10. Promote the dialogue between the identified voices

Note: Adapted from Oliveira et al. (2016, p. 134).

processes, we still need to avoid only offering "post-mortem" explanations for what is going on in therapy. Thus, we expect that the previous lines of application could soon inform the therapeutic practice, feeding back to new research, and so forth.

The therapeutic process can be seen as an opportunity to reconstruct a dialogical space that allows all relevant *I*-positions to be audible, to reestablish a productive communication between them and to reorganize their dynamics in an adaptive way. The dialogical interaction between the *I*-positions is the best way to protect the multiplicity of meanings and to allow the person to remain the co-author of their own process of change. However, innovative methods and therapeutic strategies are needed to access, understand, and change the complex processual dynamics that occur in the self-system. In this sense, we have suggested some therapeutic guidelines resulting from our current effort of transposing our research program empirical data to clinical practice. Although the effectiveness of these intervention guidelines is still to be tested, we assume that task as an important and prioritized line of future research.

References

Alves, D., Fernández-Navarro, P., Batista, J., Ribeiro, E., Sousa, I., & Gonçalves, M. M. (2014). Innovative moments in grief therapy: The meaning reconstruction approach and the processes of self-narrative transformation. *Psychotherapy Research*, *24*(1), 25–41. 10.1080/10503307.2013.814927

Alves, D., Fernández-Navarro, P., Ribeiro, A. P., Ribeiro, E., Sousa, I., & Gonçalves, M. M. (2016). Ambivalence in grief therapy: The interplay between change and self-stability. *Death Studies*, *40*(2), 129–138. doi: 10.1080/07481187.2015.1102177

Boritz, T. Z., Angus, L., Monette, G., Hollis-Walker, L., & Warwar, S. (2011). Narrative and emotion integration in psychotherapy: Investigating the relationship between autobiographical memory specificity and expressed emotional arousal in brief emotion-focused and client-centred treatments of depression. *Psychotherapy Research*, *21*(1), 16–26. doi: 10.1080/10503307.2010.504240

Braga, C., Oliveira, J. T., Ribeiro, A. P., & Gonçalves, M. M. (2016). Ambivalence resolution in emotion-focused therapy: The successful case of Sarah. *Psychotherapy Research*, Advance online publication. doi: 10.1080/10503307.2016.1169331

Braga, C., Ribeiro, A. P., Gonçalves, M. M., Oliveira, J. T., Botelho, A., Ferreira, H., & Sousa, I. (2018). Ambivalence resolution in brief psychotherapy for depression. *Clinical Psychology & Psychotherapy*, *25*(3), 369–377. doi: 10.1002/cpp.2169

Cardoso, P., Gonçalves, M. M., Duarte, M. E., Silva, J. R., & Alves, D. (2016). Life design counseling outcome and process: A case study with an adolescent. *Journal of Vocational Behavior*, *93*, 58–66. doi: 10.1016/j.jvb.2016.01.002

Castonguay, L. G., & Hill, C. E. (2012). *Transformation in psychotherapy: Corrective experiences across cognitive behavioral, humanistic, and psychodynamic approaches.* Washington, DC: American Psychological Association.

Da Silva, R., Fernández-Navarro, P., Gonçalves, M. M., Rosa, C., & Silva, J. (2018). Disengagement from political violence and deradicalisation: A narrative-dialogical perspective. *Studies in Conflict and Terrorism*. doi: 10.1080/1057610X.2018.1452709

Detert, N. B., Llewelyn, S., Hardy, G. E., Barkham, M., & Stiles, W. B. (2006). Assimilation in good-and poor-outcome cases of very brief psychotherapy for mild depression: An initial comparison. *Psychotherapy Research, 16*(4), 393–407. doi: 10.1080/10503300500294728

Dimaggio, G. (2006). Disorganized narratives in clinical practice. *Journal of Constructivist Psychology, 19*(2), 103–108. doi: 10.1080/10720530500508696

Ecker, B., & Hulley, L. (1996). *Depth-oriented brief therapy: How to be brief when you were trained to be deep—And vice versa.* San Francisco, CA: Jossey-Bass.

Engle, D., & Arkowitz, H. (2006). *Ambivalence in psychotherapy: Facilitating readiness to change.* New York: Guilford Press.

Esposito, G., Ribeiro, A. P., Alves, D., Gonçalves, M. M., & Freda, M. F. (2016). Meaning coconstruction in group counseling: Development of innovative moments. *Journal of Constructivist Psychology, 30*(4), 404–426. doi: 10.1080/10720537.2016.1238789

Feixas, G., Montesano, A., Erazo-Caicedo, M. I., Compañ, V., & Pucurull, O. (2014). Implicative dilemmas and symptom severity in depression: A preliminary and content analysis study. *Journal of Constructivist Psychology, 27*(1), 31–40.

Fernández-Navarro, P., Rosa, C., Sousa, I., Ventura, H., Ribeiro, A. P., & Gonçalves, M. M. (in press). Reconceptualizing the self during treatment for depression: Latest findings and future directions. *Clinical Psychology and Psychotherapy.*

Frank, J. D., & Frank, J. B. (1991). *Persuasion and healing: A comparative study of psychotherapy* (3rd ed.). Baltimore, MD: Johns Hopkins University Press.

Freeman, M., & Robinson, R. E. (1990). The development within: An alternative approach to the study of lives. *New Ideas in Psychology, 8*(1), 53–72.

Gonçalves, M. M., & Guilfoyle, M. (2006). Therapy as a monological activity: Beliefs from therapists and their clients. *Journal of Constructivist Psychology, 19,* 251–271. doi: 10.1080/10720530600691723

Gonçalves, M. M., Mendes, I., Cruz, G., Ribeiro, A. P., Sousa, I., Angus, L., & Greenberg, L. S. (2012). Innovative moments and change in client-centered therapy. *Psychotherapy Research, 22*(4), 389–401. doi: 10.1080/10503307.2012.662605

Gonçalves, M. M., & Ribeiro, A. P. (2012). Therapeutic change, innovative moments and the reconceptualization of the self: A dialogical account. *International Journal of Dialogical Science, 1,* 81–98.

Gonçalves, M. M., Ribeiro, A. P., Mendes, I., Alves, D., Silva, J., Rosa, C., ... Oliveira, J. T. (2017). Three narrative-based coding systems: Innovative moments, ambivalence and ambivalence resolution. *Psychotherapy Research, 27*(3), 270–282.

Gonçalves, M. M., Ribeiro, A. P., Mendes, I., Matos, M., & Santos, A. (2011). Tracking novelties in psychotherapy process research: The innovative moments coding system. *Psychotherapy Research, 21*(5), 497–509. doi: 10.1080/10503307.2011.560207

Gonçalves, M. M., Ribeiro, A. P., Silva, J. R., Mendes, I., & Sousa, I. (2016). Narrative innovations predict symptom improvement: Studying innovative moments in narrative therapy of depression. *Psychotherapy Research, 26*(4), 425–435. doi: 10.1080/10503307.2015.1035355

Gonçalves, M. M., Ribeiro, A. P., Stiles, W. B., Conde, T., Matos, M., Martins, C., & Santos, A. (2011). The role of mutual in-feeding in maintaining problematic self-narratives: Exploring one path to therapeutic failure. *Psychotherapy Research, 21*(1), 27–40.

Gonçalves, M. M., Silva, J. R., Mendes, I., Rosa, C., Ribeiro, A. P., Batista J., Sousa, I., & Silva, C. F. (2016). Narrative changes predict a decrease in symptoms in CBT for depression: An exploratory study. *Clinical Psychology & Psychotherapy.* doi: 10.1080/10503307.2010.507789

Greenberg, L., Rice, L., & Elliott, R. (1993). *The moment-by-moment process: Facilitating emotional change.* New York: Guilford Press.

Hermans, H. J. M. (2001). The dialogical self: Toward a theory of personal and cultural positioning. *Culture & Psychology, 7*(3), 243–281.

Hermans, H. J. M. (2003). The construction and reconstruction of a dialogical self. *Journal of Constructivist Psychology, 16,* 89–130.

Hermans, H. J. M., & Hermans-Konopka, A. (2010). *Dialogical self theory: Positioning and counter-positioning in a globalizing society.* Cambridge, UK: Cambridge University Press.

Hermans, H. J. M., Konopka, A., Oosterwegel, A., & Zomer, P. (2017). Fields of tension in a boundary-crossing world: Towards a democratic organization of the self. *Integrative Psychological and Behavioral Science, 51*(4), 505–535.

Lambert, M. J., Whipple, J. L., Smart, D. W., Vermeersch, D. A., & Nielsen, S. L. (2001). The effects of providing therapists with feedback on patient progress during psychotherapy: Are outcomes enhanced? *Psychotherapy Research, 11*(1), 49–68. doi: 10.1080/713663852

Lewis, T. F., & Osborn, C. J. (2004). Solution-focused counseling and motivational interviewing: A consideration of confluence. *Journal of Counseling & Development, 82* (1), 38–48. doi: 10.1002/j.1556-6678.2004.tb00284.x

Matos, M., & Gonçalves, M. M. (2004). Narratives on marital violence: The construction of change through re-authoring. In R. Abrunhosa (Ed.), *Assessment, intervention and legal issues with offenders and victims* (pp. 161–170). Brussels: Politea.

Matos, M., Santos, A., Gonçalves, M., & Martins, C. (2009). Innovative moments and change in narrative therapy. *Psychotherapy Research, 19*(1), 68–80. doi: 10.1080/10503300802430657

Meira, L., Salgado, J., Sousa, I., Ribeiro, A., & Gonçalves, M. (in press). Psychological change in everyday life: An exploratory study. *Journal of Constructivist Psychology.*

Mendes, I., Ribeiro, A., Angus, L., Greenberg, L., Sousa, I., & Gonçalves, M. M. (2010). Narrative change in emotion-focused therapy: How is change constructed through the lens of the Innovative Moments Coding System? *Psychotherapy Research, 20*(6), 692–701. doi: 10.1080/10503307.2010.514960

Miller, W., & Rollnick, S. (2002). *Motivational interviewing: Preparing people for change* (2nd ed.). New York: Guilford Press.

Nasim, R., Shimshi, S., Ziv-Beiman, S., Peri, T., Fernández-Navarro, P., & Gonçalves, M. M. (2017). *How is change constructed in time limited psychodynamic psychotherapy? An innovative moments' perspective.* Manuscript in preparation.

Neimeyer, R. A., Baldwin, S. A., & Gillies, J. (2006). Continuing bonds and reconstructing meaning: Mitigating complications in bereavement. *Death Studies, 30*(8), 715–738.

Nir, D. (2012). Voicing inner conflict: From a dialogical to a negotiational self. In H. J. Hermans & T. Gieser (Eds.), *Handbook of dialogical self theory* (pp. 284–300). Cambridge, UK: Cambridge University Press.

Oliveira, J. T., Gonçalves, M. M., Braga, C., & Ribeiro, A. P. (2016). How to deal with ambivalence in psychotherapy: A conceptual model for case formulation. *Revista de Psicoterapia, 27*(104), 119–137.

Perls, F., Hefferline, G., & Goodman, P. (1951). *Gestalt therapy.* New York: Julian Press.

Prochaska, J. O., & DiClemente, C. (1982). Transtheoretical therapy: Toward a more integrative model of change. *Psychotherapy: Theory, Research and Practice, 19,* 276–288. doi: 10.1037/h0088437.

Ribeiro, A. P., Gonçalves, M. M., Silva, J., Sousa, I., & Brás, A. (2015). Ambivalence in narrative therapy: A comparison between recovered and unchanged cases. *Clinical Psychology and Psychotherapy, 23,* 166–175.

Ribeiro, A. P., Mendes, I., Stiles, W. B., Angus, L., Sousa, I., & Gonçalves, M. M. (2014). Ambivalence in emotion-focused therapy for depression: The maintenance of problematically dominant self-narratives. *Psychotherapy Research*, *24*(6), 702–710. doi: 10.1080/10503307.2013.879620.

Sato, T., Hidaka, T., & Fukuda, M. (2009). Depicting the dynamics of living the life: The trajectory equifinality model. In J. Valsiner, P. Molenaar, M. Lyra, & N. Chaudhary (Eds.), *Dynamic process methodology in the social and developmental sciences* (pp. 217–240). New York: Springer.

Stiles, W. B. (2002). Assimilation of problematic experiences. In J. C. Norcross (Ed.), *Psychotherapy relationships that work* (pp. 462–465). New York: Oxford University Press.

Stiles, W. B. (2011). Coming to terms. *Psychotherapy Research*, *21*(4), 367–384. doi: 10.1080/10503307.2011.582186

Stiles, W. B., Elliott, R., Llewelyn, S. P., Firth-Cozens, J. A., Margison, F. R., Shapiro, D. A., & Hardy, G. (1990). Assimilation of problematic experiences by clients in psychotherapy. *Psychotherapy: Theory, Research, Practice, Training*, *27*(3), 411–420. doi: 10.1037/0033-3204.27.3.411

White, M., & Epston, D. (1990). *Narrative means to therapeutic ends*. W. W. Norton & Company.

Wittgenstein, L. (1922). *Tractatus logico-philosophicus*. London: Routledge & Kegan Paul.

10 Metacognitive interpersonal therapy as a dialogical practice

Experiential work in session with personality disorders

Giancarlo Dimaggio, Paolo Ottavi, Raffaele Popolo, and Giampaolo Salvatore

Introduction: metacognitive interpersonal therapy as a dialogical psychotherapy

Psychological health and adaptation depend on the capacity to be open and flexible, and see the world from multiple perspectives. Humans need a series of self-narratives to deal with social challenges and scripts that guide them in adaptive decisions in the relational world. These scripts need to include how to deal with a conflict, how to court a potential romantic partner, how to respond to a colleague who is pressing with requests we would prefer to avoid, and so forth. According to proponents of Dialogical Self Theory (DST; Hermans & Dimaggio, 2004; Hermans & Hermans-Konopka, 2010; Hermans & Gieser, 2011; Hermans et al., 1992; Lysaker & Lysaker, 2002), the self is made up of a series of *I*-positions, as a society of mind (Mead, 1934), which interact and continuously negotiate the course of action to be undertaken and the meaning to ascribe to events.

Every *I*-position has its own goals, motives, and preferences and can take control of action. The person is guided at one moment by the devoted father position, then shifts to the committed worker and then, when playing tennis, to the pleasure seeker. In order to grant unity and coherence humans need higher-order stances, termed meta-positions (Hermans & Hermans-Konopka, 2010). A person might have a meta-position whose macro-narrative sounds like:

> I want to raise my kids in a well-knit family and in order to do so I have to be successful at work. Enjoying my leisure time helps me soothe my distress and remember I can still live without the responsibilities the father role involves and remain playful.

Positions can be recognized as self, "I as a victim," "I as weak" "I as independent," or be external: "My controlling mother," "My angry boss," "My cheerful son." Both in the mental landscape – see Konopka, Hermans, and Gonçalves (Chapter 2 this volume) for its description – and in real-world positions interact with each other. One's inner dialogue can sound like:

I want to spend a night by the sea with my colleagues but my jealous wife would overreact. I have to give up because I could not stand her anger. I have her voice and face in my mind: jumpy, smoking, asking me endless questions and just going on and on. I say to myself to not surrender as it makes me feel depressed and frustrated, but I'm unable to stand up for myself.

The outcome of this same dialogue can have a wider impact and be included in a life script: "I'm unable to do things my own way. I'm weak and doomed to slavery."

Personality disorders (PD) patients tend to ascribe meaning according to stereotyped dialogical relationship patterns (Dimaggio et al., 2003), which we will frame according to metacognitive interpersonal therapy (MIT) (Dimaggio, Montano et al., 2015a).

Interpersonal motives

In order to assess the dominant theme, a clinician has to try to understand what the patient's wish or motive is. MIT assumes that the most important motives are shaped evolutionarily and suffering comes from forecasts that these motives remain unmet (Fassone et al., 2016; Gilbert, 1989; Lichtenberg, 1989; Liotti & Gilbert, 2011; Panksepp, 1998). Motives include the following:

a) *Attachment* (Bowlby, 1969): the need for love, protection, safety, and attention.
b) *Caregiving*: the tendency to lend help when we perceive someone as scared, vulnerable, or suffering. It can be activated by children, relatives, or persons in distress.
c) *Autonomy/independence and exploration*: activated in order to explore the environment and find resources, associated with curiosity and playfulness (Panksepp, 1998).
d) *Social rank*: triggered when resources are limited, warranting access to them after a hierarchy has been established. Driven by social rank, persons can experience anger when they perceive someone is defying them or threatening their status, pride, or contempt when they feel superior, shame when humiliated, or sadness when they lose.
e) *Group inclusion/affiliation*: refers to the basic need to belong (Baumeister & Leary, 1995; Lichtenberg, 1989). Humans cannot live without a sense of being part of a larger community, of which they share the values, interests, and rites.
f) *Sexuality*: more than its more basic counterpart, that is to say mating behavior. Sexuality regulates behaviors relating to attracting a partner with the goal of forming long-term bonds where primary sexual drives can be met and yield erotic pleasure.
g) *Cooperation*: fundamental for the formation of stable bonds and the maintenance of cohesive groups (Tomasello et al., 2005). It aims at forming alliances and combining resources to meet shared goals.

Persons enter into dialogues with others, in their mental landscape and in the society, driven by these motives. If they predict or perceived that others are not responding so their motive is fulfilled, they are prone to maladaptation and suffering. Once PD sufferers imagine the others will react negatively to a wish, for example to be appreciated (social rank) or to be supported in exploration, they have difficulties forming open-ended dialogues as they have limited access to alternative and healthier *I*-positions, which will imagine the wish can possibly be met.

Schemas

MIT understands schemas consistently with the core conflictual relationship theme (CCRT; Luborsky & Crits-Christoph, 1998; see also Batista et al., 2017). Once a clinician has detected the dominant(s) motive(s) in patients' autobiographical memories, the elements of the schemas are: (a) the core *I*-position underlying the wish, for example "I as not deserving love," "I as unworthy," "I as alone"; (b) the "if … then …" procedure (Baldwin, 1992) to fulfill the basic wish; for example: "I want to be appreciated so if I show what I did then the other …"; (c) the expected or appraised *response of the other*, which corresponds to other-positions in the landscape of the mind. The other's response triggers (d) the *self's response*, including cognitions, affects, bodily sensations, which trigger maladaptive coping procedures. Underlying the basic wish, there are usually at least two nonintegrated *I*-positions. When one is driven by attachment, she can see things from a dominant *I*-position: "I as not deserving love." At the same time, a suppressed and less easy to contact *I*-position can be "I as lovable." The first *I*-position triggers fear of rejection, the second ignites hope. When in her imaginal dialogue the person anticipates or appraises a real response by the other as impending rejection, the negative *I*-position is reinforced and takes control. Thus, if the other is positioned as neglecting, the self experiences sadness, demoralization, and impotence. Different *I*-positions shift between taking control; for example, after a moment of sadness, the *lovable I*-position can take center stage and experience anger in face of the other perceived as unjust and mean.

PD patients' inner dialogue and their exchanges with real others tend to be repetitive and they have a paucity of *innovative moments* (Gonçalves et al., 2017). Their dialogues lack a capacity for flexibility and schemas tend to dictate how the dialogues unfold. Such schema-driven attributions narrow tendencies to openness and innovation, which are typical features of a dialogical self (Hermans et al., 1992). A clinician's task is to enliven this capacity.

PD patients' dialogues also lack meta-positions that would allow them to see themselves with a bird's-eye view and realize that things can appear different when seen from a different angle. For example, a patient with avoidant PD endorses an "I as unworthy" position, and positions the other as harsh, critical, or tyrannical. He lacks the capacity to recognize the presence of different *I*- and other-positions in other moments of the relationships. Said otherwise, they lack a meta-position speaking as: "Sometimes I feel unworthy and imagine the others will despise me, but there are situations in which I have a sense of worth and capacity, I am proud of myself and think I deserve praise from others."

We take the case of a young woman driven by the autonomy motive: she wants to move to another town to begin university. She imagines her parents will undermine her independence. Her father will think she is arrogant and disrespectful because she is betraying family traditions, her mother will feel abandoned. We consider both parents' reactions as other-positions, which correspond to the *other's response* in the CCRT. In the face of these reactions, the *I*-position underlying the wish for independence becomes "I as paralyzed," "I as hurting," and "I as disappointing the other." Autonomy is now switched off and caregiving is turned on, at the cost of renouncing to pursue one's deep-seated goal. The self's response includes guilt, shame, and sadness (for not having been supported), with a likely reduction in feelings of agency, enthusiasm, and fulfillment.

Impaired metacognition

Metacognition is the capacity to identify, reflect upon, and regulate mental states, both of the self and of the others (Dimaggio & Lysaker, 2015; Semerari et al., 2003, 2014). It includes *metacognitive mastery*, the ability to use information on mental states to find solutions to everyday life social challenges and soothe suffering (Carcione et al., 2011). Humans engage in *metacognitive activity* by identifying and understanding how they feel and what drives them to act, and by forming an integrated view of themselves in face of *I*-positions continuously alternating in their mental landscape. They identify contents based on different cues. They realize they are experiencing a specific emotion because they link a bodily sensation to a particular situation and a thought that is passing through their mind: a stomach ache and the idea of failing mean they are worried about the outcome of an exam.

Humans use metacognitive capacities when trying to understand how others feel and what intentions drive their behavior. One guesses others' emotions by observing facial expressions, posture, and prosody. Lastly, metacognition includes the ability to use an understanding of mental states to regulate them. Mastery is at stake when we try to calm down, concentrate, relax, or enjoy ourselves. A knowledge of mental states is beneficial for the maintenance of relationships, because it helps us foresee what will probably occur through a rich and deep understanding of our own and the other's mind, while trying to solve any relational conflicts, and achieve mutual goals. At its highest level, metacognition includes the capacity to adopting meta-positions from which to observe the different *I*- and other-positions and integrate them in a coherent self. Evidence is that PD patients have poor metacognitive capacity, which is more impaired when the PD is more severe (Semerari et al., 2014). There is preliminary evidence that metacognition increases in good outcome therapies (Popolo et al., 2018) and predicts therapy outcome (Maillard et al., 2017).

MIT aims at increasing awareness of mental states when recalling specific autobiographical memories or in the heat of important social exchanges. Persons can be helped to name the affects they are experiencing, instead of speaking of "tension" or "uneasiness," so that they realize they experience shame, guilt, sorrow, or anger. MIT focuses on understanding the complex interplay between cognition, affects, and behaviors in specific narrative episodes. A woman might describe herself as a caring mother, but when invited to report episodes, her therapist can help her realize that, when she has to take care of children, she feels frustrated and belittled. She then experiences a mixture of shame, constriction, and anger, which points to the existence of another *I*-position, "I as an independent worker," which was previously unacknowledged and not validated because it met a *judgmental* other-position.

Maladaptive coping

PD sufferers tend to deal with suffering and problems caused by others' expected or actual responses by adopting maladaptive coping procedures. When PD sufferers position the others as malevolent, rejecting, abusing, humiliating, neglecting, needy, and so forth, they first experience feelings such as sadness, guilt, and shame. Then they try to regulate these feelings but they fail and enact maladaptive behaviors, including avoidance, aggression, and submission. These behavioral reactions to emotions elicited in interpersonal contexts further deteriorate relations and consolidate maladaptive schemas. Another form of coping is cognitive and includes worry, rumination, and various forms of repetitive thinking (Wells, 2009). Repetitive thinking is a set of mental strategies, used purposefully or automatically without awareness, aimed at regulating emotions (Borkovec et al., 2004). We describe here the case of interpersonal rumination: when a person thinks she has disappointed the other, she experiences shame. She focuses on the episode where she acted inadequately and thinks: "Why did she behave like that?" "What did she expect from me?" "Was the fault mine or hers?" A frequent variant is counterfactual rumination, where patients try to modify certain aspects of a distressing memory in order to achieve a different outcome: "If only I'd done ..." or "If I'd told him ..." (Ottavi et al., 2016). The contents of rumination change according to the type of PD. For the sake of clarity we focus on what happens in obsessive-compulsive PD (OCPD) consistently with the case we discuss later in the chapter. An OCPD sufferer may ruminate about having made mistakes at work that will threaten his position of "I as honest, trustworthy, and reliable." At the same time he ruminates about others having failed to do their job because they were unreliable or selfish. Interpersonal rumination takes the form of a stereotyped and repetitive dialogue where the different positions repeat the same sentences without any solution to pointless conversations. As a result, negative affectivity increases.

Metacognitive interpersonal therapy (MIT) structure and procedures

MIT is mostly about making persons aware of typical positions they ascribe to both the self and others and how this positioning drives social behavior, thus improving metacognition. Dialogically speaking, this means first understanding what oneself and the others think and feel, and why. MIT then helps clients to build meta-positions allowing for a cohesive self that makes them see themselves and society from a broader perspective. Thanks to these meta-positions patients become capable of openness and innovation. MIT also tries to form new *I*-positions and other-positions, with the goal of re-opening a dialogue, both among internal positions and with real others. With such new dialogical relationships patterns, the influence of old maladaptive ones is reduced, and clients are more able to experience agency and hope to fulfill their innermost wishes.

MIT (Dimaggio, Montano et al., 2015a; Dimaggio et al., 2012) is made up of *shared formulating of functioning* and *change promoting*. Shared formulating includes (a) eliciting specific autobiographical episodes with clear space and time boundaries where positions are well described and interact; (b) searching for affects and their links with thoughts and actions; (c) collecting other autobiographical memories that patients feel to be associated with the first, so that they realize that recurrent meaning-making patterns exist and this helps them see they are driven by stereotyped and crystallized dialogical relationship patterns, instead of thinking that suffering comes from reality; and the final step is (d) to devise together with patients a formulation of the schema and use awareness of this to plan change. During formulation, clinicians try to foster early access to healthy self-aspects, and point them out to patients. The purpose is to make patients aware as early as possible that their narratives include innovative moments (Gonçalves et al., 2017), in which they hope they will meet their goal. In order to elicit healthy *I*-positions and let innovative moments emerge, clinicians very early set up behavioral experiments, which are not aimed at behavioral change, but just at attempting to counteract behavioral routines and then increase awareness of mental states when reflecting on these experiments (Dimaggio, Salvatore et al., 2015b; Dimaggio & Shahar, 2017; Gordon-King et al., 2017).

Change promoting includes (e) fostering differentiation between fantasy and reality. Clinicians try to make clients realize their ideas are subjective and do not necessarily reflect reality; (f) increasing access to healthy *I*-positions. These *I*-positions can be of different kinds, ranging from the positive side of the same construct, for example "I as lovable" vs. "I as unlovable," or "I as powerful" vs. "I as powerless"; they include the capacity to be driven by personal preferences and desires instead of letting oneself be guided by the need to please others; (g) encouraging new behaviors in line with patients' innermost wishes; (h) understanding that others' inner worlds are complex and nuanced; and (i) forming meta-positions that lead to coherence and dialogical connections among various *I*-positions and other-positions. Change promoting happens eliciting what in DST has been named the *promoter position*, which is able to trigger curiosity and exploration and, thanks to repeated enactment of new behaviors, to generate new *I*-positions and foster innovative outcomes in personal narratives.

MIT is undergoing an experiential turn, which is the main novelty introduced in this chapter. Clinicians invite patients to remember significant narrative episodes from their lives and enact them during exercises such as guided imagery and rescripting (Hackmann et al., 2011), two-chair work (Greenberg, 2002), and role-play. This means re-opening the dialogue with the way patients imagine the others will react or with parts of the self that were previously suppressed or ignored, and guiding them to construct a new dialogical relationship.

MIT focuses on the regulation of the therapy relationship (Dimaggio, Montano et al., 2015a; Safran & Muran, 2000). Therapy is about promoting new forms of internal dialogue and interacting in different ways with real others. Patients and therapists often start their journey positioning the other in ways that are consistent with their own patterns, but therapists need to see patients as unique human beings, rather than reflections of their own tendencies to position the other. Therapists try and detect any problem in the relationship, disengage from repetitive patterns, and promote the capacity to recognize the otherness in the other (Buber, 1970).

Rewriting the dialogical self in the imaginal world: the experiential work

The self undergoes continuous rewriting and this mostly happens through inner dialogues. MIT therapists invite clients to recall specific problematic autobiographical memories in which interaction with others was difficult. These memories include a reactivation of the conversation with the internalized others, that is with other-positions. The problem is, as we noted earlier, that these conversations tend to have predetermined outcomes, with a paucity of innovative moments (Gonçalves et al., 2017). To promote change, MIT therapists invite clients to re-experience episodes during guided imagery, role-play or two-chair exercises. The purpose is to open an imaginal space, detached from everyday life experience, where clients can see the plot that unfolds as belonging to their mental landscape, rather than a mere reflection of past events. During imaginal re-enactment, clients likely experience intense emotions and clinicians have more room to work suffering through.

Guided imagery is used with different purposes. A typical example is therapy for post-traumatic stress disorder, where clients relive their memories and then either discover they can tolerate exposure to painful emotions they previously avoided or dissociated (Foa et al., 2007) or, thanks to imagery rescripting (Arntz et al., 2007; Hackmann et al., 2011), inhabit different *I*-positions and therefore cope differently with distressful interpersonal situations. Many negative memories of interpersonal events can be processed, for example when trying to rewrite the relationships with one's parents or close relatives. In this case, the imagery work is not just aimed at overcoming trauma, but at changing dialogical relationship patterns.

Imagery work may focus on future scenarios. Therapists can suggest to clients to relate to others in previously unexplored situations: meeting a group of friends and imagining how the conversation might be, or dating a person they like. Clients can safely experience new forms of relating that are likely to elicit positive emotions. For example, one client with fear of social exposure can discover the pleasure of joking with another or experience a position of "I as nice" vis-à-vis another positioned as "accepting and welcoming."

MIT follows a series of steps when using guided imagery and rescripting, in order to foster a secure atmosphere. The sequence begins with the therapist proposing re-experiencing a specific episode: "This episode appears significant to me, do you agree? I'd like to imagine being in it; do you feel like trying?" The therapist should seek client's feedback and give any information requested if using this technique for the first time. The client should be aware that he or she can interrupt the experience at any moment, or decline the invitation. Once the client accepts, the experience begins with some relaxation or mindfulness technique. The goal is to create a hiatus between external world and the flow of the therapy conversation on the one hand, and immersion in the imaginal landscape on the other. When the client is ready, the therapist asks if she can reenter the memory, not just by recalling, but by being there as if it was happening now. The client needs to speak in the present tense and not reason about what unfolds. She is instead invited to describe what she sees and feels and what every character does. Typical questions are: "Can you describe what you see to me?" "In which room of your family house are you now?" "Can you hear your mother's voice? How her tone sounds? What do you see in her face?" Other questions are focused on internal reactions: "Your friend is saying she won't be there for you, how are you feeling?" Associations with other memories or reflections about the story are noted, but the client is gently discouraged to explore them further, as therapists avoid as this stage promoting any kind of cognitive reflection. They do not ask, "Are you sure that your mother wants to blame you?" but rather, "So you notice she is blaming you. Where do you see this judgment in her face or hear it in her voice? What do you think and feel in front of her attitude?"

The goal of imagery work in this phase is to increase awareness of inner states, and potentially make emotional arousal mounts, although remaining tolerable. Once therapists have gathered enough information, they stop the exercise and start reflecting with the client about the experience. They can invite the client to notice aspects of her inner world that were previously unnoticed, for example emotions that were not there before the experience, or reactions she did not expect. The last stage is rescripting, which can either lead on immediately from the original imagery experience or occur after the break we have just described. The therapist proposes the client to go back into the scene with the goal of doing something different. When there is no break, the therapist says to the client something like: "Ok, we know what happened and how you felt. Now breathe deeply and then try to say that …"

Imagery rescripting moment is the core of the dialogical exercise. Clients are invited to repeat the dialogue with the others in the narrative, while responding differently and exploring and regulating their emotions and cognitions. Therapists keep a stable focus on what clients experience when they attempt to engage them in a new form of dialogue with significant others: "How do you feel when speaking with this tone of voice?" "How does saying to your mother 'I want to be listened to' sound to you?" "Where is fear placed in your body while you reply to bullies?" "You say you feel more powerful now, after telling your father to not beat you again. Can you tell me more? Do you feel it in your muscles, guts, face?"

At the end of guided imagery and rescripting, client and therapist jointly reflect about the episode and try to integrate the new dialogical experience into the client's self. This helps in understanding that new *I*-positions – e.g. "I as strong," "I as worthy," "I as free" – and other-positions – e.g. "the supporter," "the protector," "the caring girlfriend" – exist in the imaginal landscape. Therapists should invite clients to remember these new positions in-between sessions and to realize they belong to their inner world. Clients learn that embodying these new positions allows for more flexible responses and grants safety, relief, and relaxation and constitutes solid ground for exploratory behaviors. We now illustrate the basic steps in MIT with one clinical vignette, highlighting the dialogical component of the imagery experience.

Dario's case

Dario, a 24-year-old university student, met DSM V (APA, 2013) criteria for obsessive compulsive disorder (OCD) and OCPD. He underwent two years of weekly MIT, attending more than 90% of the scheduled weekly appointments. He sought psychotherapy because of severe OCD: when he walked through the streets, he was worried that his looking at men meant he was gay and became very anxious at the idea. In the second session he told the therapist that the day before he had gone to the university to get some documents. In a corridor he met some students and thought: "You are looking at them all; you're a dirty fag." He became anxious and imagined that all the others were convinced "Dario is a fag." He then considered that his anxiety was a sign that he really was homosexual, thus creating a vicious cycle. He usually thought that he needed to inhibit the thought he was homosexual because if he was unable to control his thoughts he would become mad. This controlling strategy also increased his anxiety.

With regard to metacognition, Dario had problems in many domains. He was aware he was anxious, but could not perceive that his anxiety was connected to the emergence of a specific *I*-position, that is "I as inadequate." He was poor at understanding what the others were thinking and feeling and at the same time differentiating, that is adopting a meta-position from which to reflect on his own assumptions and question them or consider them just interpretations and not facts. For example, he was sure that his university colleagues criticised or scorned him because they thought he was gay. For this reason he adopted avoidance as a form of behavioral coping and did not attend his courses. He spent much time home alone, studying and doing a lot of physical workouts. Dario had poor metacognitive mastery and was unable to use mental strategies to soothe suffering, calm down, concentrate, relax, or enjoy himself. The only strategy he used to regulate anxiety, at the beginning of his therapy, was calling the therapist when in despair.

He entered therapy with little hope that his obsessions could be cured. The therapist dealt with this by telling him that the therapy could offer tools to diminish the problem, once there was an understanding of the mechanisms underlying his suffering so that solutions could be found. The therapist readily explained that the primary goal of the therapy was symptom-centered, that is by reducing his intrusive thoughts and anxiety, and that they would then try to understand the interpersonal mechanisms underlying his suffering in order to change them. This second goal was more about overall personality change in order to prevent a symptom relapse and live a more fulfilling life. Dario accepted the therapy contract and was relieved by this formulation.

With regard to his symptoms, the therapist gave him both antidepressive and low-dosage antipsychotic medication (Sertraline, 100 mg/day and Olanzapine, 5 mg/day). Dario had some fears about becoming dependent on medication and was worried about the stigma "It means I'm crazy," but was readily reassured by the therapist and took the drugs regularly, with some benefit. A next step was to find strategies to cope with his symptoms by explaining the mechanisms underlying the three perseverative thinking strategies accountable for their maintenance, that is, worry, threat monitoring and suppression, and how to stop them. Importantly, repetitive thinking includes endorsing problematic *I*-positions that adopt positive and negative cognitions about own cognitive processes. These cognitions about own cognitions are named metacognitive beliefs. One example of this was "worrying saves me from being taken off guard." The therapist provided psychoeducation about the existence of these metacognitive beliefs and how they tend to maintain suffering instead of solving problems. Then he helped the patient realize how the more he worried, the more the idea of being gay got stronger and the associated shame more intense. The therapist then produced written diagrams where the process of worrying was portrayed. The first step was having intrusive thoughts, such as "If I pay attention to men's muscles this means I'm gay," triggering self-critical statements, such as "If I'm gay I'm immoral and deserve rejection." This thought generated anxiety and was accompanied by a constant monitoring of his thoughts – "Am I thinking about men now?" – and by attempts to suppress his thoughts about men. The only result of this monitoring and suppression was again a symptom rebound and feeling fragile. Feeling vulnerable increased his anxiety, which Dario tried to solve by further attempting to control his thoughts. The end result was a feeling of anxiety, impotence, and being overwhelmed by thoughts. Dario could recognize himself in such a formulation and started to realize that the real problem was not so much being gay or not, but the very process of worrying.

With this formulation the therapist offered Dario a series of strategies to interrupt worry, threat monitoring, and suppression, and gain control over his mind: (1) read reminders written during sessions in order to remember that having an intrusive thought is not a sign of homosexuality, but moments in which Dario needs to stop worrying; (2) phone the therapist, or write a message or an email, should he not be able to calm down his anxiety and need to hear the therapist's voice repeating the formulation; (3) divert attention from the worry coming from the vicious cycle: "If I'm anxious about being gay this means I'm gay, which makes me anxious." In order to break this cycle, the therapist used techniques imported from detached mindfulness (Wells, 2009) and attention training (Moritz et al., 2011). First, the therapist engaged Dario in some simple mindfulness exercises, for example increased awareness of bodily signals and of external sounds during short meditations. Then he asked Dario to purposefully think about being gay, and then learn how not pay attention to this, by increasing his attention to other stimuli, such as bodily signals and external sounds. This was repeated until his anxiety disappeared during the experiment, so that Dario could think of terms like "gay," "homosexual," and "faggot" as just words without the associated meaning and his painful reactions. Once his anxiety was well regulated, the therapist passed to cognitive restructuring. Dario thus came to understand that thoughts are just thoughts that can simply pass through one's mind without meaning anything special about oneself. He also learnt that anxiety is just a reaction to a feared outcome but not a sign that an event is real. Dario also took a critical distance from the idea that we should be able to control our thoughts or suppress them, because otherwise we risk going crazy, and accepted that thoughts just pass through our mind. The therapist reinforced these ideas with self-disclosures, such as: "At this moment I am thinking about many things, for example that I'd love a pizza. Do you think this means I'm crazy or not a good therapist because I cannot keep my thoughts under full control?" Dario soon realized he considered the therapist's functioning normal, and therefore accepted his mind could function that way too.

During the first three months, the symptom improved significantly, which permitted passing to the next step of identifying and revising maladaptive dialogical relationship patterns. Initially, Dario had difficulties reporting episodes with clear space and time boundaries in which he interacted with others, and all the dialogue unfolded in his imaginal landscape and involved worry. Given his difficulties in reporting narrative episodes, the therapist first worked through the therapy relationship. During one session, the therapist asked Dario how his workouts were going. Dario described his weightlifting, and the therapist in an interested, non-judgemental way asked him what weight he was lifting. All of a sudden, Dario blushed as if he was embarrassed. The therapist noticed the change and asked what was passing through his mind and if the change depended on his question. Dario said that he had passed from a sense of feeling appreciated by the therapist to the idea that: "Now he'll think I'm a weakling and a wimp." This is a typical alliance rupture, unwillingly provoked by the therapist's question, which elicited the maladaptive dialogical pattern in the patient. In line with procedures to solve ruptures (Safran & Muran, 2000), the therapist first took responsibility for the rupture: "I realize my question may have induce a sense of being judged/criticised." Then he provided cues about how he actually thought of the patient:

> Dario, I really didn't think you are weak, not even for a moment. It's just that I do a lot of training too and was curious about it. I realize that

something may have happened inside you: it's like you hoped to be appreciated by me (*wish*). You first had an idea that I did appreciate you (*response of the other 1: other-position as benevolent judge*). Then you imagined, after my question, that I broke this illusion and you turned to the usual thing you think about the others, that is that they despise you (*response of the other 2: other-position as harsh and spiteful*). This made you feel inadequate, unworthy, and ashamed (*core maladaptive position: "I as worthless"*). Then, you shied away and withdrew in order to protect yourself from further negative judgment (*maladaptive coping: withdrawal*). What do you think about my reconstruction?

Dario nodded sadly and recognized himself in this pattern. At this point, the therapist could use this narrative episode, that is the therapy relationship exchange, as the cue for eliciting associated memories. This time Dario was able to retrieve autobiographical episodes he felt had the same problematic dialogical relationship structure. Dario reported a memory of a few months before. He was at the university bar and he met a girl he liked, a colleague, who he had never dared to approach before. She was with some friends and she smiled at him when their eyes crossed. Encouraged by her smile, Dario said "hi," but almost whispering. She did not reply and turned her face towards her friends, who giggled. Dario was convinced they were laughing at him: "They were convinced I'm not a real man and cannot approach a woman the way a man would."

In keeping with MIT procedures, the therapist did not consider this an irrational belief. Instead, he first validated Dario for the shame he felt, and then started a joint reconstruction of the episode, noting it had the same structure as the therapeutic incident. Again, Dario could see himself clearly in the reconstruction of the pattern and started to realize that he had this tendency to either discard perception of the other as benevolent – lack of a stable, internalized, benevolent other-position – or ascribe criticism to others.

Connecting the therapy incident with this recent one, there was enough material for the final step of the *shared formulation of functioning* part. The full formulation sounded like:

It looks like you are continuously striving to be appreciated, which is completely human. But then you focus more easily on, or expect to receive, reactions in which others say: "You're no real man, you're a fag." Then you experience worthlessness and shame, because of your core idea of being wrong. At the same time, there are some rare moments in which you experience being appreciated by others and feel ok, but this does not last and your mind is quickly flooded with the negative aspect of the pattern. Once you are in this state, you think you cannot enter a dialogue with despising others, and prefer to withdraw, isolate yourself, or try to become perfect by continued training in order to increase your muscle mass. You think: "If I'm perfectly fit, people will not despise me." But this does not work and when you focus on other men's bodies, your obsessions appear and you think you deserve criticism again.

One of the steps in MIT is to note and highlight healthy *I*-positions early and this is a crucial driver of therapy success. In this case, the therapist asked Dario to perform a short, guided imagery exercise. He asked him to return to the scene and to focus on the moment in which he noticed the girl smiling at him. When Dario retrieved the memory, the therapist asked him to scan the girl's face. Dario did it and noticed she seemed to like him. The therapist asked how he felt and he said: "Fine, I'm ok." At the end of the exercise, the therapist helped Dario notice that he endorsed a different pattern, where he still longed for approval (wish), which is supported by an "I-as-valid" position facing an accepting other. Both act as promoter positions, one is internal, the second external. Dario could then experience a sense of self-confidence and happiness at the idea that the other considered him worthy.

Dario now understood even better the roots of his obsessions, and they decreased further. Subsequent steps at this point were to increase differentiation, which in DST terms can be described as leaving aside negative and crystallized constructions of self and others, and let a richer repertoire of *I*- and other-positions come to the fore. The desired outcome is to use this broader repertoire to achieve flexible dialogicality, including the capacity to see the world from multiple perspectives instead of continuing to endorse one's own negative view of self and others and firmly believing these attributions to be true and accurately describe reality. With this new functioning, patients can see themselves in more benevolent, compassionate ways, access feelings of strength and competence and be driven by *I*-positions where fulfilling higher-order wishes – such as social rank and attachment – and specific goals, such as dating or doing a job that one likes, are perceived within their reach.

Together with differentiation, the first goal of *change promoting* is the consolidation of the emerging healthy self, which means allowing for new *I*-positions filled with positive feelings and capable of cooperative interactions to emerge. This happens in the context of the promotion of exploratory behavior, involving becoming curious and finding avenues for self-actualization and for fulfilling one's innermost desires.

One important moment in this respect happened when Dario retrieved a remote memory, which made him further understand how the pattern got formed and where. Dario remembered when he was 6 and playing football, with his father in the audience. He was afraid of his father's criticism, so he played badly and made a lot of mistakes, though he also remembered playing sometimes very well. The match was a draw, and he was satisfied, but his father came into the dressing room and said that a real defender has to be much ruder and meaner and that Dario had behaved like a "faggot." Dario felt humiliated when remembering this episode, which quickly turned into self-protective anger.

The therapist asked Dario to re-experience the episode in a guided-imagery and rescripting exercise. The therapist said:

This episode appears significant to me, do you agree? I'd like to enter that scene in your imaginal landscape, do you feel like trying? If it is too distressing, just tell me and we either don't do it or we stop whenever you want.

Dario accepted with curiosity and some anxiety. After some minute of diaphragmatic breathing, eyes shut, the therapist invited Dario to describe what was unfolding.

D: I'm in the locker room with my teammates. We joke and laugh. My father steps in. He is laughing with the other relatives. I'm not hearing what he says.

T: What do you see in his face?

D: The face of one who mocks everyone. He turns to me and says: You behaved like a faggot! A real defender is like a rock and needs the guts you'll never have!

T: (*notes anger and further explores feelings*): You look upset. Is there anything else you are feeling?

D: Sadness. I feel humiliated.
The re-experiencing part was now complete and the therapist tried to engage Dario in rescripting work:

T: Now breathe again deeply, until you feel in control ... well ... now try and reply to your father. Tell him whatever you want.

D (*HESITATES, VOICE TREMBLES*): It's difficult

T: No worry, keep trying

D: (*looks angrier though voice is still low*): Dad, I did my best and I want you to acknowledge it. You are humiliating me in front of my friends instead. That's unfair.

T: Breathe again, lift your shoulders and raise your chin. Ok?

D: Ok

T: Try again, put more energy into your voice.

D (*LOUDER, ALMOST YELLING*): You shouldn't treat me this way. You humiliated me!

T: How do you feel now?

D: Stronger.

T: Where do you feel the strength?

D: In my legs and my arms, kind of when I lift weights. I'm stronger and my father seems smaller.

Thanks to this experience, the quality of the inner dialogue changed, letting a stronger *I*-position to emerge, not subjugated by a spiteful and domineering other.

MIT does not consider in-session dialogical change to be the only driver of improvement. Behaviors sustain change, in line with a model cycle involving planning change, performing new behaviors, and reflecting about them in the next sessions (Hermans & Hermans-Jansen, 1995; Kolb, 1984). New behaviors are about enacting in everyday life new forms of dialogical relationship, in order to fulfill innermost wishes.

Dario realized that physical training was not enough for him as he longed for more contact with peers. As an exploratory exercise they planned on participating in a *powerlifting* class and going there once a week. The task was just to try to go and report either his inner experience or actual conversations. This time the therapist used guided imagery to promote adaptive anticipatory dialogues. Dario imagined asking someone for advice about how to best execute one exercise. Dario positioned this imaginal other as welcoming, accepting, and driven by the same enthusiasm. Real exposure went well and Dario started participating in social events with the class, experiencing a sense of belonging and sharing. After one and a half years the therapy terminated with good outcome. Dario was not anxious any more, and whenever his anxiety increased, he was able to regulate it without much effort. He did not have either OCPD or OCD.

Conclusions

Promoting change in patients with PD involves opening their minds to new forms of dialogical relationship. Therapy aims at making patients realize that they observed the world from the eyes of problematic *I*-positions but those were only ideas and other forms of positioning exist. MIT for PD attempts to let new and more adaptive *I*-positions emerge and meet different Other-positions, perceived as welcoming, accepting, nurturing, and supporting, act as promoter positions. Rewriting dialogues requires preliminary steps, which are increasing awareness of self-states and of the way others are constructed. Patients need to realize how crystallized and repetitive forms of dialogue have been guiding their lives. In order to achieve such a change, experiential work makes change possible or faster. In the clinical case we have described, the client re-experienced past episodes during guided imagery and rescripting, where he first re-experienced pain coming from previously noxious dialogical interactions. He then discovered how he was able to respond differently, adopting new *I*-positions and positioning the others in ways that made him feel he could fulfill his wishes. There are promising signs that this approach is effective when treating persons suffering with PD but research is needed in the field. To date there are preliminary outcomes showing that MIT is helpful in treating these disorders (Dimaggio et al., 2017; Gordon-King et al., 2017; Popolo et al., 2018). This strengthens the idea that a dialogical understanding of mind can be a useful guide for therapy with difficult-to treat individuals.

References

American Psychiatric Association (APA). (2013). *Diagnostic and statistical manual of mental disorders* (5th ed.). Washington, DC: APA.

Arntz, A., Tiesema, M., & Kindt, M. (2007). Treatment of PTSD: A comparison of imaginal exposure with and without imagery rescripting. *Journal of Behavior Therapy and Experimental Psychiatry*, *38*, 345–370. doi: 10.1016/j.jbtep.2007.10.006

Baldwin, M. W. (1992). Relational schemas and the processing of social information. *Psychological Bulletin, 112*, 461–484.

Batista, J., Silva, J., Freitas, S., Alves, D., Machado, A., Sousa, I., . . . Gonçalves, M. M. (2017). Relational schemas as mediators of innovative moments in symptom improvement in major depression. *Psychotherapy Research, 5*, 1–12. doi: 10.1080/10503307.2017.1359427

Baumeister, R., & Leary, M. (1995). The need to belong: Desire for interpersonal attachment as a fundamental human motivation. *Psychological Bulletin, 117*(3), 497–529.

Borkovec, T. D., Alcaine, O., & Behar, E. (2004). Avoidance theory of worry and generalized anxiety disorder. In R. G. Heimberg, C. L. Turk, & D. S. Mennin (Eds.), *Generalized anxiety disorder: Advances in research and practice* (pp. 77–108). New York: Guilford Press.

Bowlby, J. (1969). *Attachment and loss. Volume I: Attachment*. London: Penguin Books.

Buber, M. (1970). *I and Thou: A new translation with a prologue "I and You" and 10 notes by Walter Kaufmann*. Edinburgh: T & T Clark.

Carcione, A., Semerari, A., Nicolò, G., Pedone, R., Popolo, R., Conti, L., . . . Dimaggio, G. (2011). Metacognitive mastery dysfunctions in personality disorder psychotherapy. *Psychiatry Research, 190*, 60–71.

Dimaggio, G., & Lysaker, P. H. (2015). Metacognition and mentalizing in the psychotherapy of patients with psychosis and personality disorders. *Journal of Clinical Psychology: In-Session, 71*, 117–124. doi: 10.1002/jclp.22147

Dimaggio, G., Montano, A., Popolo, R., & Salvatore, G. (2015a). *Metacognitive interpersonal therapy for personality disorders: A treatment manual*. London: Routledge.

Dimaggio, G., Salvatore, G., Azzara, C., Catania, D., Semerari, A., & Hermans, H. J. M. (2003). Dialogical relationships in impoverished narratives. From theory to clinical practice. *Psychology and Psychotherapy: Theory, Research and Practice, 76*, 385–410.

Dimaggio, G., Salvatore, G., Fiore, D., Carcione, A., Nicolò, G., & Semerari, A. (2012). General principles for treating the overconstricted personality disorder. Toward operationalizing technique. *Journal of Personality Disorders, 26*, 63–83.

Dimaggio, G., Salvatore, G., Lysaker, P. H., Ottavi, P., & Popolo, R. (2015b). Behavioral activation revised as a common mechanism of change for personality disorders psychotherapy. *Journal of Psychotherapy Integration, 25*, 30–38. doi: 10.1037/a0038769

Dimaggio, G., Salvatore, G., MacBeth, A., Ottavi, P., Buonocore, L., & Popolo, R. (2017). Metacognitive interpersonal therapy for personality disorders: A case study series. *Journal of Contemporary Psychotherapy, 47*, 11–21. doi: 10.1007/s10879-016-9342-7

Dimaggio, G., & Shahar, G. (2017). Behavioural activation as a key principle of change in the psychotherapy of adult mental disorders. *Psychotherapy, 54*(3), 221–224. doi: 10.1037/pst0000117

Fassone, G., Lo Reto, F., Foggetti, P., Santomassimo, C., D'Onofrio, M. R., Ivaldi, A., . . . Picardi, A. (2016). A content validity study of AIMIT (assessing interpersonal motivation in transcripts). *Clinical Psychology & Psychotherapy, 23*, 319–328. doi: 10.1002/cpp.1960

Foa, E. B., Hembree, E. A., & Rothbaum, B.O. (2007). *Prolonged exposure therapy for PTSD*. New York: Oxford University Press.

Gilbert, P. (1989). *Human nature and suffering*. London: Psychology Press.

Gonçalves, M. M., Ribeiro, A. P., Mendes, I., Alves, D., Silva, J., Rosa, C., . . . Braga, C. (2017). Three narrative-based coding systems: Innovative moments, ambivalence and ambivalence resolution. *Psychotherapy Research, 3*, 270–282. doi: 10.1080/10503307.2016.1247216

Gordon-King, K., Schweitzer, R. D., & Dimaggio, G. (2017). Behavioural activation in the treatment of metacognitive dysfunctions in inhibited-type personality disorders: A case study. *Psychotherapy, 54*, 252–259. doi: 10.1037/pst0000120

Greenberg, L. S. (2002). *Emotion-focused therapy: Coaching clients to work through their feelings.* Washington, DC: American Psychological Association.

Hackmann, A., Bennett-Levy, J., & Holmes, E.A. (2011). *Oxford guide to imagery in cognitive therapy.* Oxford: Oxford University Press.

Hermans, H. J. M., & Dimaggio, G. (Eds.). (2004). *The dialogical self in psychotherapy.* London: Brunner-Routledge.

Hermans, H. J. M., & Gieser, T. (Eds.). (2011). *Handbook of dialogical self theory.* Cambridge, UK: Cambridge University Press.

Hermans, H. J. M., & Hermans-Jansen, E. (1995). *Self-narratives.* New York: Guilford.

Hermans, H. J. M., & Hermans-Konopka, A. (2010). *Dialogical self theory: Positioning and counter-positioning in a globalizing society.* Cambridge, UK: Cambridge University Press.

Hermans, H. J. M., Kempen, H. J. G., & Van Loon, R. J. P. (1992). The dialogical self: Beyond individualism and rationalism. *American Psychologist, 47,* 23–33.

Kolb, D. A. (1984). *Experiential learning: Experience as the source of learning and development.* Englewood Cliffs, NJ: Prentice Hall.

Lichtenberg, J. D. (1989). *Psychoanalysis and motivation.* Hillsdale, NJ: Analytic Press.

Liotti, G., & Gilbert, P. (2011). Mentalizing, motivation, and social mentalities: Theoretical considerations and implications for psychotherapy. *Psychology and Psychotherapy: Theory, Research and Practice, 84,* 9–25.

Luborsky, L., & Crits-Christoph, P. (1998). *Understanding transference: The core conflictual relationship theme method.* New York: Basic Books.

Lysaker, P. H., & Lysaker, J. (2002). Narrative structure in psychosis: Schizophrenia and disruptions in the dialogical self. *Theory and Psychology, 12,* 207–220.

Maillard, P., Dimaggio, G., de Roten, Y., Despland, J.-N., & Kramer, U. (2017). Metacognitive processes and symptom change in a short-term treatment for borderline personality disorder: A pilot study. *Journal of Psychotherapy Integration.* doi: 10.1037/int0000090

Mead, G. H. (1934). *Mind, self, and society.* Chicago, IL: University of Chicago Press.

Moritz, S., Wess, N., Treszl, A., & Jelinek, L. (2011). The attention training technique as an attempt to decrease intrusive thoughts in obsessive-compulsive disorder (OCD): From cognitive theory to practice and back. *Journal of Contemporary Psychotherapy, 41*(3), 135–143.

Ottavi, P., Passarella, T., Pasinetti, M., Salvatore, G., & Dimaggio, G. (2016). Mindfulness for anxious and angry worry about interpersonal events in personality disorders. In W. J. Livesley, G. Dimaggio, & J. F. Clarkin (Eds.), *Integrated treatment for personality disorders: A modular approach.* New York: Guilford Press.

Panksepp, J. (1998). *Affective neuroscience: The foundations of human and animal emotions.* Oxford: Oxford University Press.

Popolo, R., MacBeth, A., Canfora, F., Rebecchi, D., Toselli, C., Salvatore, G., & Dimaggio, G. (2018). Metacognitive interpersonal therapy in group (MIT-G) for young adults personality disorders. A feasibility, acceptability and clinical significance randomized controlled trial. *Psychology and Psychotherapy: Theory, Research & Practice.* doi: 10.1111/papt.12182

Safran, J. D., & Muran, J.C. (2000). *Negotiating the therapeutic alliance: A relational treatment guide.* New York: Guilford.

Semerari, A., Carcione, A., Dimaggio, G., Falcone, M., Nicolò, G., Procacci, M., & Alleva, G. (2003). How to evaluate metacognitive functioning in psychotherapy? The metacognition assessment scale and its applications. *Clinical Psychology and Psychotherapy, 10,* 238–261.

Semerari, A., Colle, L., Pellecchia, G., Buccione, I., Carcione, A., Dimaggio, G., ... Pedone, R. (2014). Metacognition: Severity and styles in personality disorders. *Journal of Personality Disorders*, *28*, 751–766. doi: 10.1521/pedi_2014_28_137

Tomasello, M., Carpenter, M., Call, J., Behne, T., & Moll, H. (2005). Understanding and sharing intentions: The origin of cultural cognition. *Behavioral & Brain Sciences*, *28*, 675–691.

Wells, A. (2009). *Metacognitive therapy for anxiety and depression*. New York: Guilford Press.

11 Developing a dialogical approach to analysing psychotherapy

Eugenie Georgaca and Evrinomy Avdi

The view of the self as dialogical and of psychotherapy as a dialogical practice has gained increased prominence in the last few decades in psychotherapy theory and practice (Hermans & Dimaggio, 2004). Research on psychotherapy based on dialogical principles, however, is not yet as developed. In this chapter, we present an approach to analysing psychotherapy sessions using dialogical principles and analytical tools. In what follows we briefly discuss the central tenets of dialogical approaches to the study of psychotherapy, outline and demonstrate through an example our approach, and discuss its usefulness for making sense of dialogical processes in psychotherapy.

Trends in dialogical psychotherapy research

To date a number of distinctive trends in dialogical psychotherapy research have been articulated, from the earlier personal positioning repertoire (Hermans, 2006), dialogical sequence analysis (Leiman, 2004) and the voices reformulation of the assimilation model (Leiman & Stiles, 2001) to the more recent investigation of innovative moments (Gonçalves et al., 2016), positioning microanalysis (Salgado, Cunha, & Bento, 2013), dialogical investigations of happenings of change (Seikkula, Laitila, & Rober, 2011), and dialogic discourse analysis (Martínez, Tomicic, & Medina, 2014). All these approaches treat psychotherapy as a semiotic process, focusing on the way meaning is created, negotiated, and transformed in the course of therapy. They all start from the premise that the self is complex and polyphonic, and attempt to empirically trace the emergence and negotiation of the positions or voices articulated in psychotherapy sessions. Some modes of analysis adopt a macro-level approach (e.g. Hermans, 2006; Salgado et al., 2013) and produce descriptions of the self-positions that appear in relatively long stretches of talk in therapy; these approaches usually examine the content of talk, i.e. how positions are being talked about. This type of analysis can provide a comprehensive description of the main dialogical features of the client's self and trace their development through therapy, thus providing a description of the outcome of therapy in dialogical terms. On the other hand, a few approaches start from the premise that the self is not a preformed entity expressed through the person's speech but a dynamic ongoing process, which is enacted in every encounter (Avdi & Georgaca, 2009). In other words, it is assumed that the client does not describe their self but rather *performs* it in the here and now of the therapeutic interaction. This requires the analysis to move to the examination of the form and function of speech, which can only be done through qualitative micro-analysis, an approach adopted by some, but not many, of the existing dialogical research trends (e.g. Leiman, 2012; Martínez et al., 2014; Seikkula et al., 2011).

Despite the acknowledgement in dialogical theory that meaning is interactionally constructed, this is not always followed through in the actual analysis of psychotherapy sessions, which in most trends focuses exclusively on the client's talk. We would argue that in psychotherapy research several interrelated aspects of the therapist's position could be analysed, including the therapist as an interactional addressee of the client's talk, as a counter-position to the client's self positions, and as an institutional voice that functions to facilitate the transformation of the client's dialogical self and foster the work of therapy (Georgaca, 2012). Finally, the formative and normative aspects of psychotherapy as an institution shaping contemporary subjectivity should be acknowledged and the ways in which these are actively played out and pursued in the minutiae of the therapeutic exchange could be examined. This, again, seems not to be at the forefront of most current dialogical research trends.

Overall, we would argue that dialogical research in psychotherapy has been heavily influenced by constructivism and post-positivism in focusing on internal dialogues as individual constructions, while neglecting the role of discursive and sociocultural processes in the construction of the self. In our view, dialogical research would be significantly enriched by taking into account the interactional and wider sociocultural constitution both of the client's subjectivity and of psychotherapy as a process and institution (Georgaca, 2012). It is worth noting that the newer approaches to the dialogical investigation of psychotherapy seem to develop much more complex, dynamic, and micro-analytic modes of analysis, which weave together the internal constitution of the self with the interactional context of its ongoing development, thus paving the way for future developments in this direction.

Concepts and principles of dialogical research

Central to dialogical analysis is the concept of *dialogical position*, a term used to denote the variety of *I*-positions present in the therapeutic exchange, including internal and external positions, personal and social positions, observing positions, and meta-positions (Hermans & Hermans-Konopka, 2010; Raggatt, 2011). In the context of psychotherapy research, it is important to identify observing positions, that is dialogical positions that have as an object other dialogical positions. Moreover, we use the term 'meta-positions' for those observing positions that have an overseeing and integrating function in the dialogical self. Fostering observing positions and developing meta-positions are often considered an aim of therapy, since they are associated with self-reflection and the reorganisation of the self. Dialogical positions entail an agent, a recipient, and a referential object, all of which are reciprocally positioned and interrelated (Leiman, 2012). In contrast to more static, noun-based formulations used by other dialogical approaches, we find that the use of active verb phrase constructions to denote dialogical positions does justice to their dynamic and relational character.

Dialogical positions tend to coalesce together forming *dialogical patterns*. Mapping the dialogical patterns, as they appear in long stretches of talk, effectively amounts to charting the landscape of the client's dialogical self. Although we recognise the usefulness of the concept of 'voices' as material enactments of positions, which many dialogical research approaches rely on (e.g. Leiman, 2012; Leiman & Stiles, 2001; Seikkula et al., 2011), we tend to privilege the notion of 'position', which is theoretically commensurate with discursive approaches (Avdi & Georgaca, 2007) and entails a spatial dimension, in line with the metaphor of the internal landscape of the mind (Hermans, 2001). A distinction we underscore is between the level of actual interaction (act of narrating, enunciation), which includes a speaker (narrator, subject of enunciation) and correspondingly a listener (interlocutor), and the level of the text (narrative, utterance), in which the subject of the utterance and correspondingly the recipient and the referential object can be found. When focusing on the level of the text, we seek to identify the protagonists of the action described, the content of what is said, the referential object, the timing of the action, who speaks and whose words are being used, what voice is expressed, and the kind of agent articulated. This kind of analysis is useful for identifying dialogical positions and patterns, and for charting the gradual development of patterns through sequences of utterances. This more macro-analytic process results in mapping the landscape of the client's dialogical self and tracing its development in the course of therapy.

Another central analytic concept is that of *subject position*, which refers to the position that the speaker speaks from, the position constructed for the speaker, which the speaker occupies (Guilfoyle, 2016). Every subject position constructs a counter-position, which the listener is invited to inhabit. This we refer to as the *addressee*. The subject position and the addressee are usually not apparent in the text; they are deduced through micro-analysis, by observing aspects of talk, such as the speaker's authorial stance, the content and form of talk, features of the interaction, and the discourses employed.

A defining aspect of positioning is the speaker's *authorial stance*, which refers to the relation of the speaker to what is being said, how the speaker is positioned with regard to their own speech. Here we draw from positioning theory (Harré & Van Langenhove, 1991) and the concept of footing (Goffman, 1981), discourse analytic notions mainly around the construction of agency and the rhetorical functions of talk (Georgaca & Avdi, 2012), and critical discourse analysis (Fairclough, 1989). Central to determining the speaker's authorial stance is the degree of authorship and responsibility the speaker assumes with regard to what they say. The speaker can achieve differing degrees of distance from the statements made and positions performed through layers of reflexive positions, evaluative comments, attributions of statements to other authors, and rhetorical disclaimers. Conversely, a speaker can assume certain dialogical positions in the text and can even enact them in the here and now of the session.

The term addressee refers to how the interlocutor is positioned in the actual interaction. The interlocutor, the therapist in our case, can be positioned in different ways, usually in multiple ways simultaneously. For example, the therapist can be positioned as the other of the dialogical pattern (e.g. in the position 'I am afraid I will be punished' as a punishing other) or in line with the therapist's institutional role, as an expert on human suffering, who is expected to listen, reflect, and support (Guilfoyle, 2006).

In order to identify the subject position and addressee, apart from taking into account the authorial stance, it is useful to examine the *action orientation of speech*, that is the function of what is being said, which is deduced primarily through examining the rhetorical organisation of talk. Discourse analysis (Harper, 2006) and conversation analysis (Rapley, 2012) enable the examination of the rhetorical devices that the interlocutors use and the discursive moves they make, in order to present their versions of events as true and themselves as credible and morally accountable. The properties of the actual interaction between client and therapist can be analysed drawing upon conversation analysis (Peräkylä, Antaki, Vehviläinen, & Leudar, 2008), dialogical investigation of happenings of change (Seikkula et al., 2011) and dialogic discourse analysis (Martínez et al., 2014). Finally, it is important to consider the context that shapes the therapeutic interaction, in this case both the institution of psychotherapy and broader socio-cultural discourses about the self, values, a good life, etc. Here, discourse analysis can be utilised to examine the ways in which discourses are drawn upon and used by client and therapist as well as the effects of these discourses for the client's subjectivity and the direction of therapy (Avdi & Georgaca, 2007).

This mode of analysis is useful for highlighting the mutual relation between intrapersonal aspects of the self (internal dialogues between different *I*-positions of the self) and interpersonal aspects of the self (real dialogues with interactional others), and exploring the processes through which the self is enacted, rather than just described, in the here and now of the session. It allows us to explore in further detail and complexity the processes of active construction and co-construction of the self in the process of therapy.

Analysing a case of psychoanalytic psychotherapy

Our focus in this chapter is methodological, aiming to showcase the analysis and demonstrate its usefulness for psychotherapy process research, at the expense of a more substantive account of findings and their clinical relevance. The therapy presented was conducted a few decades ago at the Menninger Clinic, as part of a set of three therapies that were used by researchers at the Menninger Clinic for a project on psychoanalytic psychotherapy of borderline patients (Horwitz et al., 1996). Eugenie Georgaca had obtained the therapies with permission to use for her research, and had only used one of the three for a previous research project (Georgaca, 2001, 2003). For the current project, we chose to work on one of two non-analysed psychotherapies, a long-term psychoanalytic psychotherapy with a female client in her late twenties, diagnosed as borderline. Out of the 207 sessions conducted in this therapy, 17 sessions from all phases of the therapy were randomly selected, transcribed, and anonymised by the Menninger team.

In the analysis of these 17 sessions, we focus both on the client's talk and on the unfolding interaction. When focusing on the client's talk, the aim is to examine the client's dialogical positions as they are formed in the sessions.

The analysis comprises of three inter-related levels; each of these levels can address different questions and highlight different clinical phenomena, and we see these as complementary. The first level consists of *mapping the client's dialogical position patterns*, that is the constellations of *I*-positions and observing positions and the relationship between them, and tracing their development in the course of therapy. The second level comprises a *sequential analysis of dialogical positions and patterns*, where we examine the sequential organisation of the exchange between client and therapist, focusing on the processes of positioning, re-positioning, and counter-positioning, as they unfold in the therapeutic dialogue. The third level of analysis consists of *microanalysis* of selected extracts, with an emphasis on the processes through which dialogical positions are mutually constructed between client and therapist. Starting from a broader macro-level of analysis helps us limit and organise the material, by identifying the key dialogical positions implicated in the therapy, and thus select the material for more detailed micro-analysis. Below we present each level of analysis.

Level 1: mapping dialogical positions and dialogical patterns

The aim of this level of analysis is to reach a broad but comprehensive description of the client's main dialogical positions and dialogical patterns that emerge in the sessions. The analysis starts with the meaning units identified in the preliminary preparation of the data; initially, a summary, including the main topics and the main relational incidents, is written for each meaning unit. Then, following grounded theory principles (Henwood, 2006), the relational episodes are thematically categorised and these themes form the basis for deducing the client's main dialogical positions. This categorisation is bottom-up, i.e. categories are gradually built, 'grounded' in the data, descriptive, and close to the original material, i.e. we often use the participants' own wording (Joffe, 2012). Drawing upon the spatial metaphor of the self as a landscape of mind (Hermans, 2001), we produce pictorial depictions of the main dialogical positions that emerge and the relationships between them. We find a diagrammatic representation preferable to a narrative description, as the shifts between dialogical positions and dialogical patterns are more readily discernible. Dialogical positions are placed in boxes, including all the expressions through which a certain position is manifested in the text, with the main gist of the position denoted in **bold** (see Figure 11.1). In the boxes in the middle of the figure we place the dialogical positions that have as agent the client's self, in the boxes on the left-hand side the observing positions, which have as their object/referent another dialogical position, and in the boxes on the right-hand side the representation of others in the client's talk.

In the case example, the analysis of all relational episodes across 17 sessions yielded 23 maps in total; a relatively small number of these dialogical positions were found to recur; shifts were observed both in the ways in which these positions combined to form dialogical patterns and in the dominance of different patterns over time. In this chapter, we will use one dialogical pattern from this therapy to illustrate our method of analysis. This was a dominant dialogical pattern, which entailed two dialogical positions, namely 'being hurt → hurting others'. This pattern appeared frequently and consistently throughout the sessions, as it emerged in 10 of the 23 maps. In Figure 11.1, a map of the first instance of the 'being hurt → hurting others' pattern is illustrated; this occurs in an exchange that takes place at the start of the fourth session, which is the first recorded session.

This process of mapping positions allows us to examine the manifestation and transformation of the client's dialogical self through the process of therapy. It provides a systematic way of studying the main dialogical positions and dialogical patterns that emerge in the sessions, leading to a description of the client's *dialogical position repertoire*. Essentially, this is a dialogically informed formulation of the client's inner world and inner dynamics. Based on this, one can examine which dialogical positions are dominant, appear most often, or are discussed more extensively at different stages in therapy. Moreover, one can study how the client's dialogical self is transformed through the process of therapy (e.g. how different positions gradually become linked to form more complex formulations, how one dialogical pattern becomes transformed into another, and track the development of dialogical patterns through time), thus providing a dialogically informed description of therapy outcome.

In sum, mapping the dialogical positions and patterns provides an overall picture of the client's dialogical position repertoire and how it may change in the course of therapy. This can be used as a method of analysis in its own right, if a macro-level description of the client's dialogical self is the aim of the study. This mapping can also be used as a first step for further analysis. Using the maps as a guide, we can select extracts for further analysis, which can elucidate how the dialogical pattern is constructed in the clinical interaction, as well as explore its functions and effects. Next, we present the analysis of one relational episode, depicted in the map shown in Figure 11.1, and contained in the extract shown in Box 11.1. The main dialogical positions are marked in **bold** and the extract is part of the exchange that formed the basis of the map, extensively shortened here in the interests of brevity.

Level 2: sequential analysis

This level of analysis is concerned with examining in detail *how* selected dialogical patterns are built up within specific interactions; in other words, it

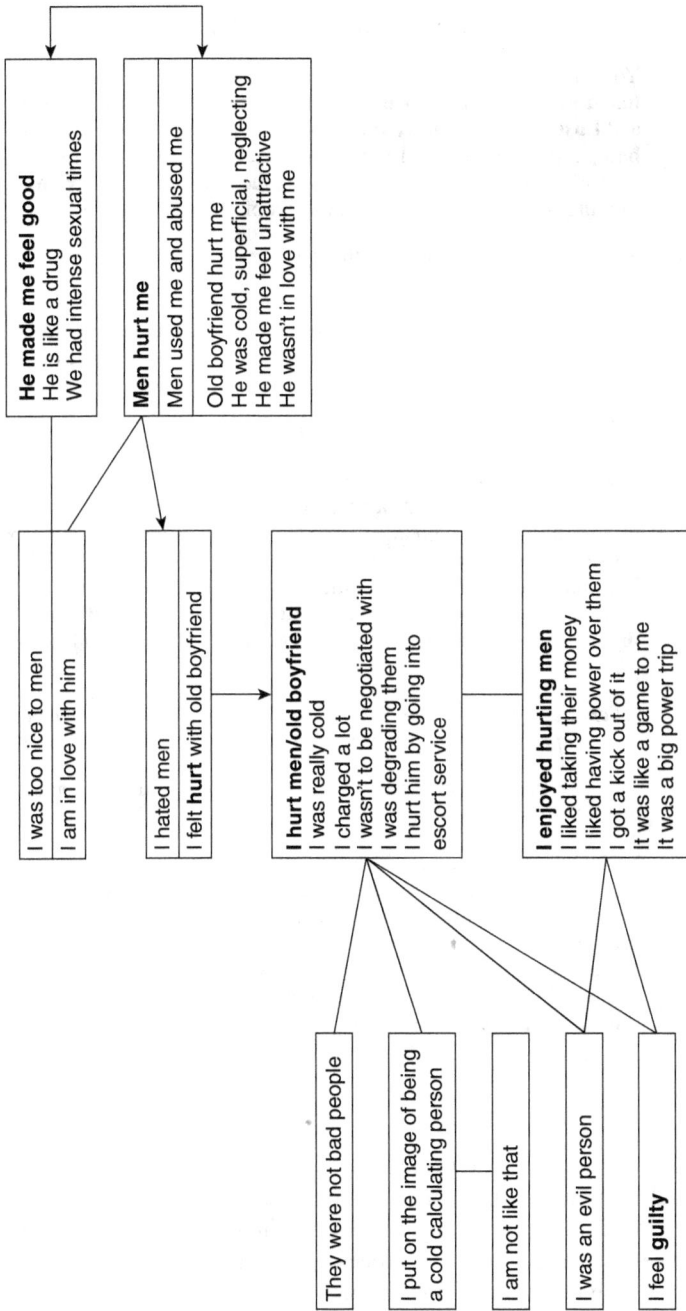

He made me feel good
He is like a drug
We had intense sexual times

Men hurt me
Men used me and abused me
Old boyfriend hurt me
He was cold, superficial, neglecting
He made me feel unattractive
He wasn't in love with me

I was too nice to men
I am in love with him

I hated men
I felt **hurt** with old boyfriend

I hurt men/old boyfriend
I was really cold
I charged a lot
I wasn't to be negotiated with
I was degrading them
I hurt him by going into
escort service

I enjoyed hurting men
I liked taking their money
I liked having power over them
I got a kick out of it
It was like a game to me
It was a big power trip

They were not bad people

I put on the image of being
a cold calculating person

I am not like that

I was an evil person

I feel **guilty**

Figure 11.1 Map of the dialogical pattern 'being hurt/hurting others'.

Box 11.1 Extract of dialogical position: being hurt/hurting others.

1   C   You know, when I worked for the escort service . . . I did it cause **I really hated men . . . and I . . . I used to like, you know, to take their money** and **I used to like to have that power over them** . . . and **they weren't bad people,** but I mean, **I really got a kick out of it** . . . you know and I . . . **I was kind of an evil person** . . . in the sense that **I really enjoyed hurting them** . . . and I think that's part of the reason **why I feel guilty**

2   Th   So all of your relationships with men were . . . with that sort where you're involved with hurting?

3   C   Right [. . .] **I really put on the image of being a very cold, calculating person** . . . **I'm not really** but that's the kind of image that I put forth

4   Th   Why do you think you came across that way?

5   C   **It was like a game to me** . . . you know . . . it was really like a game, because I mean . . . I made a lot of money . . . and ah . . . I . . . **I enjoyed taking the cash** . . . you know . . . I really enjoyed that [. . .] and **it was just a big power trip** . . . I just liked having . . . you know, I think I felt like **men had abused me** . . . I did feel that **men had used me** . . . **and abused me** and that **I had been too nice** . . . and that **I had to pay back the whole** . . . **you know, the whole gender** by just being calculating and . . .

        [client describes how she stopped working in the escort service because she was pregnant by her boyfriend at the time]

6   Th   But your working in the escort service, then, occurred in the context of that relationship with him?

7   C   Yeah . . . I . . . I . . . although he never has found out about it . . . **I really did it to hurt him** . . . I did it because **he made me feel so unattractive,** because **he wasn't in love with me** . . . that I just had to get the intention [*sic*] elsewhere [. . .] **I have been in love with him** since I've been about 16 years old [. . .] **he's very cold** . . . **he's very superficial** . . . he **neglected me** a lot [. . .] Deep down inside **I wanted to be able to hurt someone like I had been hurt**

focuses on the *processes* of positioning, repositioning, and counter-positioning, through which the patterns are constructed. This is mainly achieved through examining the sequence in which dialogical positions appear, the links between positions and the process of co-construction, i.e. who introduces each dialogical position and makes links between positions and how the other responds. In Box 11.2 we present an outline of sequential analysis of the above extract.

Box 11.2 Examining the sequence of positions in the client's talk.

Turn 1: The client's narration centres on the position 'I enjoyed hurting men' and this is interspersed with observing positions and distancing markers (hesitations, repetitions, repeated use of a past construction 'I used to …')

Turn 3: Following the therapist's question, the client elaborates on the position 'I hurt men' and then distances herself from it explicitly ('I'm not really'). The distancing devices employed in turns 1 and 3 may be seen to indicate that the positions 'I hurt men' and 'I enjoyed hurting men' are uncomfortable for the client to sustain.

Turn 5: In response to the therapist's question, the client initially elaborates on the position 'I enjoyed hurting men' and then shifts to articulating a dialogical pattern around 'I hurt men':

I was too nice to men → men hurt me → I hurt men

Turn 7: The client responds to the therapist's invitation to link her working in the escort service with her relationship with her ex-boyfriend through formulating a dialogical pattern regarding her relationship that parallels the pattern described in her previous turn in relation to men in the escort service:

I'm in love with old boyfriend → he hurt me → I hurt him

She then very clearly articulates it as an abstract and generalised dialogical pattern.

Based on an examination of the above sequence, a shift can be observed in the client's dialogical self. At the start of the extract (turns 1–3), the client's self-description centres around the positions 'I hurt men' and 'I enjoyed hurting men'; here, the client occupies an agentic position but her actions are evaluated from an observing position as shameful and guilt-inducing. In the second part of the extract (turns 4–7), the position 'I hurt men' is constructed as a response to the position 'men hurt me'; in this formulation, relational meaning is attributed to her shameful actions, which are now represented as a justifiable response to having been hurt. It is worth noting that in the last two client turns no distancing devices are evident, which is in contrast to the start of the extract; this could be seen to indicate that this dialogical pattern, which functions to provide an explanation for the client's shameful self-positions, is less threatening than the previous positions. In a sense, by articulating a dialogical pattern, and thus providing meaning to her actions, the quality of the position 'I hurt men' seems to change; this could be described as a change in the client's dialogical organisation.

Next, we turn to the therapist's talk and explore the interactional dynamics that have contributed to shifts in the client's dialogical self (see Box 11.3).

Box 11.3 Examining interactional processes.

Turn 2: The therapist selectively focuses on the position 'hurting men' and uses a question format that constructs 'hurting men' as a generalised and recurring pattern. This reflects a key psychoanalytic intervention, whereby early relational patterns are seen as important for understanding both the client's inner world and the client's problematic relational patterns in adulthood. The therapist subtly shapes the direction of the conversation, by selectively responding to one of the positions in the client's talk, while sidestepping others. We could speculate that his selective focus on the position 'hurting men' (rather than e.g. on 'enjoying hurting men') reflects a strategy for managing potentially threatening topics and fostering the therapeutic alliance.

Turn 4: The therapist enquires about the reasons for the client adopting a specific position, thus implying that there is an inner motivation reflected in unarticulated positions that precede the 'hurting men' position. In addition to fostering reflection, this utterance is an example of technique based on the psychoanalytic notion of unconscious motivation and the conceptualisation of therapy as a process of making the unconscious conscious. In dialogical terms, the therapist invites the client to articulate dialogical positions that precede the 'hurting men' position, which the client responds to by formulating a whole dialogical pattern in her next turn.

Turn 6: The therapist provides a tentative link between patterns, through a question format; this tentative interpretation invites further elaboration and reflection on the client's part. It is arguably a successful interpretation, in the sense that it leads to the articulation by the client of a clear dialogical pattern in the next turn.

Through analysing the therapist's turns, it becomes clear that the therapist's contributions here centre in selectively attending to specific dialogical positions, eliciting narrative elaboration of selected dialogical positions, and forging dialogical patterns through connecting disparate dialogical positions, in line with therapeutic aims and technique.

In sum, sequential analysis leads to a narrative description of the dynamic process through which dialogical positions are formed and negotiated within specific interactions. It adds detail and nuance to the information contained in the maps, explicating *how* the map – which is a static representation of the client's dominant dialogical patterns – has developed, as well as illustrating the interactional features that have led to its development. Moreover, this level of analysis allows us to examine the therapist's contribution to the unfolding dialogue. In this way, we can trace the interactional processes through which change takes place in the client's dialogical position repertoire, as well as examine psychotherapeutic technique and its effects on the interaction.

Level 3: micro-analysis

Micro-analysis relies on the use of the analytic tools drawn from discourse and conversation analysis (Georgaca & Avdi, 2012; Peräkylä et al., 2008); as such it is difficult to describe in terms of specific steps to be followed. Broadly speaking, we examine each utterance in terms of its grammatical, syntactical, and stylistic features as well as in terms of the context in which it occurs, and we ask two broad questions: The first is, 'Why is this said in this way at this point?' thus orienting the analysis towards the functional aspect of language and its action orientation. The second set of questions concerns the subject positions of the speaker and the addressee. Here we ask questions like: 'What is the authorial stance of the speaker with regard to what she says?' 'What position does the speaker speak from?' and correspondingly: 'Who is the talk addressed to?' or 'What kind of addressee does the talk entail?' This level of analysis allows us to examine in detail the interactional dynamics of the clinical encounter and adds depth and complexity to the study of therapy process. In Box 11.4, we illustrate some of the ways in which this level of analysis can be conducted and the types of questions it can address, by discussing a very small part of the extract. Due to space constraints, we regrettably are not able to discuss broader conclusions drawn from the rest of the extract or this therapy as a whole. In the example of analysis shown in Box 11.4 we focus on several inter-related questions, namely how the client's inner dynamics get played out in the interaction, from what position the therapist responds to the client's 'position calls', and a discussion of different types of observing positions.

Looking at the above turn in terms of *subject positioning*, the client constructs an agentic position for herself, which is evaluated in a negative way and represented as 'evil'. Through the turn the position is gradually built up and intensified (I liked taking their money → I liked having power over them → I really got a kick out of it) and culminates in the position 'I really enjoyed hurting men'. At the same time, the self-reproaching subject position also becomes gradually intensified and more clearly articulated, culminating in the position 'I was kind of an evil person'. These two positions alternate and both escalate through the turn, leading to 'I was kind of an evil person' because 'I really enjoyed hurting men'.

Drawing from the above, there is evidence in this turn of two subject positions. The first is a self-reproaching subject position, from which the utterance 'I was an evil person' is spoken; its addressee, i.e. the therapist, is accordingly positioned as a criticising and possibly tormenting other. In psychoanalytic terms this would be seen as the enactment of a punitive transferential pattern. The second subject position could be described as a more neutral observing position, one that observes links and provides explanations, without

Box 11.4 Micro-analysis of client talk.

You know, when I worked for the escort service …

In the opening of her turn the client topicalises her narration around a specific theme, her working in the escort service, thus marking the start of a new narrative. By clearly locating the topic in the past, she distances herself from what she is about to describe. This topic was introduced at the start of the session as something shameful and difficult to talk about. In this opening phrase, the client announces her decision to talk about something difficult, marking the narrative that follows as a disclosure of a delicate topic. Implicitly, the therapist is positioned as a potentially accepting other.

I did it cause I really hated men … and I …

The client continues with a clause describing an *I*-position imbued with acting ('I did it') and feeling ('I really hated men'); her actions are, thus, attributed to strong feelings, in a formulation that is in line with psychotherapeutic discourse. This clause implies the presence of an observing position that provides a psychological explanation for her reprehensible actions.

I used to like, you know, to take their money and I used to like to have that power over them …

This narration is again clearly located in the past; the speaker thus distances herself now form herself in the past.

The repetitive structure of the sentence underscores the point the client makes. She refers to two things she enjoyed doing, one a more observable/ concrete action and the other more abstract/relational. Structured this way, the sentence implies that what she actually enjoyed was the power she had over men, rather than the money.

Here we see the first instance of the repeated relational pattern, where the client is positioned as an active agent, who harmed and enjoyed harming men, and men are positioned as victims/recipients of these actions, which in recent relational psychoanalytic theories about borderline states has been described as a 'doer-done to' dynamic (Howell, 2002).

and they weren't bad people

The client continues with an utterance, spoken from an observing position, which can be seen as an indication of the construction of a self-blaming sequence. We could say that this evaluative statement is spoken from a self-reproaching subject position, which from a psychoanalytic perspective could be seen as a reflection of a harsh and punitive super-ego.

but I mean, I really got a kick out of it … you know

Starting with 'but' this utterance juxtaposes the client's morally reprehensible actions with men not being 'bad people'.

and I … I was kind of an evil person …

This is a strong, negative self-evaluation, moderated by being located in the past and through the use of the expression 'kind of'.

in the sense that I really enjoyed hurting them …

Here the client defines the actions previously described ('I liked taking their money' and 'I liked having that power over them') as 'hurting', a term that will be used repeatedly in the therapy.

Moreover, a clear link is articulated between being 'an evil person' and 'enjoying hurting men'; this is articulated from an observing position that again evaluates and judges the self.

and I think that's part of the reason why I feel guilty

This is a reflective utterance on multiple levels: (a) 'I feel guilty' is an observing position, in the sense that its referential object is another position (i.e. 'enjoying hurting men') and it is worded in the present tense, being close to the 'I' of the speaker; (b) the phrase 'that's part of the reason why I feel guilty' expresses an observing position that explains 'feeling guilty'; (c) in the phrase 'I think that's part of the reason why I feel guilty' the 'I' of 'I think' is a direct expression of the speaker in the here and now and is in line with the primary position of a psychotherapy client, a thinking/reflecting client.

necessarily evaluating or criticising. It is most clearly articulated through the utterance 'and I think that's part of the reason why I feel guilty'. The therapist is accordingly positioned as a benign co-observer.

A contribution of microanalysis to this extract is the discernment of two distinct observing subject positions in the client's talk. The dominant subject position in this turn is a self-reproaching subject position; this is actually part of a problematic dialogical pattern that recurs in the early sessions of this therapy, expressed in a highly critical, punitive, and tormenting voice. This is in line with arguments that there are different layers of observing positions, some of which are part of the problematic pattern, while others are more aligned with the aims of therapy (Leiman, 2012).

The self-reproaching subject position is associated with a reproaching other/ addressee. This dynamic was introduced by the client in the beginning of the session, where she described having been criticised and tormented by others when she'd spoken about her reprehensible past. In this framework, the therapist would be expected to be reproaching too. Moreover, from a discursive perspective, we would argue that the client's turn is structured in such a way as to pre-empt potential blame, by the client blaming herself. From examining the therapist's response there is evidence that this rhetorical manoeuvre is indeed successful (see Box 11.5).

This is an example, out of many in this therapy, where the therapist adopts an observing position, whereby he summarises and reflects what the client has said, and correspondingly positions the client in an observing position. Encouraging the articulation of observing positions is considered an important therapeutic process, as it is a crucial step in developing meta-positions in the client's dialogical self. From a psychoanalytic perspective, this could be seen as a process of fostering the client's observing ego capacities and promoting mentalising (Bateman & Fonagy, 2006). At the same time the therapist sidesteps the judgemental/reproachful aspect of the client's utterance, thus avoiding a reproaching position himself. This could be seen as an example of the therapist managing the transference without interpreting it and rather fostering collaboration, which was an explicit mode of working in this therapy (Horwitz et al., 1996).

Box 11.5 Micro-analysis of therapist talk.

So all of your relationships with men were … with that sort where you're involved with hurting?

This brief response by the therapist is very skilfully constructed. First, as already mentioned, the therapist selectively attends to the topic of 'hurting men' rather than that of 'enjoying hurting men'. Moreover, the therapist responds from a curious observing subject position, and invites the client to an associated observing subject position. From a discursive perspective, the therapist responds to the client's self-blaming turn as theoretically expected. From a clinical perspective, we would speculate that the therapist selects a less delicate topic to discuss, in the service of the therapeutic alliance. Moreover, the therapist manages to avoid being drawn into a reproaching position and encouraging in any sense the problematic position of self-reproach.

With the phrase 'all of your relationships with men were' the therapist generalises the pattern to one that concerns all her relationships with men in the past. At the point where the therapist is about to characterise the client's relationship with men, he hesitates and carefully manages this delicate issue; he pauses briefly, and then uses a series of non-descript words that delay and moderate the characterisation. In this way, the client's strongly worded statement 'I enjoyed hurting men' is transformed into 'that sort of relationship where you're involved with hurting', where it is unclear who does what to whom.

In sum, micro-analysis enables a fuller examination of the interactional co-construction of dialogical positions and patterns, as well as the functions of these constructions. It produces a complex and nuanced account of how the client's inner dynamics are 'played out' in the psychotherapeutic dialogue and how the therapist actively manages the implications of the client's position calls. In this way, it highlights the emergent, dynamic, and co-constructed nature of the self as a society of mind (Hermans & Hermans-Konopka, 2010) and the role of the therapist's interventions in shaping it.

Discussion

In this contribution, we have argued that dialogically inspired psychotherapy process research would benefit from broadening its scope from a description of the landscape of the client's mind and its development through therapy, to the examination of the dynamic processes of therapeutic dialogue, through which the client's subjectivity is constituted and reformulated. We have attempted to present and illustrate what we have found to be a comprehensive dialogical analysis of psychotherapy, which includes both a macro-analytic mapping of the client's dialogical self and a micro-analytic examination of the dialogical processes through which this is shaped in the course of therapy. We contend that a dialogically inspired analysis of psychotherapy, while guided by the concepts of dialogical self theory, can fruitfully utilise concepts and analytical tools from other, albeit compatible, methodological traditions. Along with other dialogical research approaches, we have found thematic and grounded theory-based modes of analysis useful for organising the research material (Henwood, 2006), but we also draw heavily upon the social constructionist methodologies of discourse (Harper, 2006) and conversation analysis (Rapley, 2012) to delineate the processes of negotiation of the client's subjectivity in and through the clinical dialogue.

We see the different levels of analysis presented above as complementary, each building upon the previous one in order to compose a complex picture of the dynamic formation of the client's self as a society of mind through the process of psychotherapy. Each level, though, could be utilised separately, or in different combinations, depending on the research material and the research question. We do not claim to have devised a method, and this is why we have not given our endeavour a name; we have rather collected together a research toolkit and proposed some analytic notions that we think might be useful for investigating psychotherapy from a dialogical perspective. Its usefulness, of course, as well as its relevance to the dialogical self approach to psychotherapy, remain to be proven by future research.

Acknowledgements

Eugenie Georgaca would like to express her gratitude to Dr L. Horwitz for kindly allowing her access to transcripts from psychotherapy sessions conducted at the Menninger Clinic. The views presented in this chapter and the analysis of the transcripts reflect the authors' perspective on subjectivity and psychotherapy and should not be attributed to the therapist or the researchers who initially analysed these sessions (Horwitz et al., 1996).

References

Avdi, E., & Georgaca, E. (2007). Discourse analysis and psychotherapy: A critical review. *European Journal of Psychotherapy and Counselling, 9*(2), 157–176. doi: 10.1080/14780880802146896

Avdi, E., & Georgaca, E. (2009). Narrative and discursive approaches to the analysis of subjectivity in psychotherapy. *Social and Personality Psychology Compass, 3*(5), 654–670. doi: 10.1111/j.1751-9004.2009.00196.x

Bateman, A., & Fonagy, P. (2006). *Mentalization-based treatment for borderline personality disorder: A practical guide*. Oxford: Oxford University Press.

Fairclough, N. (1989). *Language and power*. London: Longman.

Georgaca, E. (2001). Voices of the self in psychotherapy: A qualitative analysis. *British Journal of Medical Psychology, 74*, 223–236. doi: 10.1348/000711201160939

Georgaca, E. (2003). Exploring signs and voices in the therapeutic space. *Theory and Psychology, 13*(4), 541–560. doi: 10.1177/09593543030134005

Georgaca, E. (2012). The essential elements of dialogically based research on psychotherapy: A proposal. *International Journal of Dialogical Science, 6*(1), 161–171.

Georgaca, E., & Avdi, E. (2012). Discourse analysis. In A. Thompson & D. J. Harper (Eds.), *Qualitative research methods in mental health and psychotherapy: A guide for students and practitioners* (pp. 147–162). Chichester, UK: Wiley.

Goffman, E. (1981). *Forms of talk*. Philadelphia, PA: University of Pennsylvania Press.

Gonçalves, M. M., Ribeiro, A. P., Mendes, I., Alves, D., Silva, J., Silva, C., & Oliveira, J. T. (2016). Three narrative-based coding systems: Innovative moments, ambivalence and ambivalence resolution. *Psychotherapy Research, 18*, 1–13. doi: 10.1080/10503307.2016.1247216

Guilfoyle, M. (2006). Using power to question the dialogical self and its therapeutic application. *Counselling Psychology Quarterly, 19*(1), 89–104. doi: 10.1080/09515070600655189

Guilfoyle, M. (2016). Subject positioning: Gaps and stability in the therapeutic encounter. *Journal of Constructivist Psychology, 29*(2), 123–140. doi: 10.1080/10720537.2015. 1034815

Harper, D. (2006). Discourse analysis. In M. Slade & S. Priebe (Eds.), *Choosing methods in mental health research* (pp. 47–67). London: Routledge.

Harré, R., & Van Langenhove, L. (1991). Varieties of positioning. *Journal for the Theory of Social Behaviour, 21*(4), 393–407.

Henwood, K. (2006). Grounded theory. In M. Slade & S. Priebe (Eds.), *Choosing methods in mental health research* (pp. 68–84). London: Routledge.

Hermans, H. J. M. (2001). The dialogical self: Towards theory of personal and cultural positioning. *Culture & Psychology, 7*(3), 243–281.

Hermans, H. J. M. (2006). The self as a theatre of voices: Disorganization and reorganizations of a position repertoire. *Journal of Constructivist Psychology, 19*, 147–169. doi: 10.1080/10720530500508779

Hermans, H. J. M., & Dimaggio, G. (Eds.) (2004). *The dialogical self in psychotherapy*. New York: Brunner/Routledge.

Hermans, H. J. M., & Hermans-Konopka, A. (2010). *Dialogical self theory: Positioning and counter-positioning in a globalizing society*. Cambridge, UK: Cambridge University Press.

Horwitz, L., Gabbard, G. O., Allen, J. G., Frieswyk, S. H., Colson, D. B., Newsom, G. E., & Coyne, L. (1996). *Borderline personality disorder: Tailoring the psychotherapy to the client*. Washington, DC: American Psychiatric Press.

Howell, E. F. (2002). Back to the 'states': Victim and abuser states in borderline personality disorder. *Psychoanalytic Dialogues, 12*(6), 921–957. doi: 10.1080/10481881209348713

Joffe, H. (2012). Thematic analysis. In A. Thompson & D. J. Harper (Eds.), *Qualitative research methods in mental health and psychotherapy: A guide for students and practitioners* (pp. 209–223). Chichester, UK: Wiley.

Leiman, M. (2004). Dialogical sequence analysis. In H. J. M. Hermans & G. Dimaggio (Eds.), *The dialogical self in psychotherapy* (pp. 255–270). London: Brunner/Routledge.

Leiman, M. (2012). Dialogical sequence analysis in studying psychotherapeutic discourse. *International Journal of Dialogical Science, 6*(1), 123–147.

Leiman, M., & Stiles, W. B. (2001). Dialogical sequence analysis and the zone of proximal development as conceptual enhancements to the assimilation model: The case of Jan revisited. *Psychotherapy Research, 11*(3), 311–330.

Martínez, C., Tomicic, A., & Medina, L. (2014). Psychotherapy as a discursive genre: A dialogic approach. *Culture & Psychology, 20*(4), 501–524. doi: 10.1177/1354067X14551292

Peräkylä, A., Antaki, C., Vehviläinen, S., & Leudar, I. (Eds.) (2008). *Conversation analysis and psychotherapy*. Cambridge, UK: Cambridge University Press.

Raggatt, P. T. F. (2011). Positioning in the dialogical self: Recent advances in theory construction. In H. J. M. Hermans & T. Gieser (Eds.), *Handbook of dialogical self theory* (pp. 29–45). Cambridge, UK: Cambridge University Press.

Rapley, M. (2012). Ethnomethdology/conversation analysis. In A. Thompson & D. J. Harper (Eds.), *Qualitative research methods in mental health and psychotherapy: A guide for students and practitioners* (pp. 177–192). Chichester, UK: Wiley.

Salgado, S., Cunha, C., & Bento, T. (2013). Positioning microanalysis: Studying the self through the exploration of dialogical processes. *Integrative Psychological and Behavioral Science, 47*(3), 325–353. doi: 10.1007/s12124-013-9238-y

Seikkula, J., Laitila, A., & Rober, P. (2011). Making sense of multi-actor dialogues in family therapy and network meetings. *Journal of Marital and Family Therapy, 37*, 1–21. doi: 10.1111/j.1752-0606.2011.00238.x

12 From dissociation to dialogical reorganization of subjectivity in psychotherapy

Claudio Martínez and Alemka Tomicic

Contemporary psychoanalysis, and its emphasis on the relational and intersubjective field, shares with the dialogical approach the notions of a decentered self and a view of the mind as a set of discrete states of consciousness. From the perspective of relational and intersubjective psychoanalysis, the human mind is regarded as a non-unitary configuration; that is, as the conjunction of discontinuous states of consciousness that follow a nonlinear course. These states reach a level of coherence that surpasses this discontinuity and leads to the experiencing of a cohesive feeling of personal identity and oneness: the healthy illusion of being "oneself" (Bromberg, 1998, 2011). From another perspective – the dialogical approach – and taking into account Bakhtin's theory and his polyphonic metaphor, Hermans (1996, 2003, 2004) conceptualized the self as "a dynamic multiplicity of relatively autonomous *I*-positions in an imaginal landscape" (Hermans, 1996, p. 33). This multiplicity of positions constitutes the identity of a person, which not only emerges from the dialogue with another person but also from the dialogue with other positions of his or her own inner world. For its part, this multiplicity of the self is not only embodied in a social and cultural structure: it also has a neurobiological representation. For instance, LeDoux (2002) proposes a connection between the multiplicity of the self and brain processes, observing that each component of the self correlates with the activation of specific brain systems, which are not always synchronized. This represents a major difference between the idea of the self as an emergent unit or state and the view of the self as a non-unitary process. With respect to the latter point, we know that not all aspects of the self manifest themselves simultaneously, and that these multiple aspects may even be contradictory.

In turn, these self-states, namely subjective positions or *I*-positions (Hermans, 2014), may be thought of as expressions of relational patterns developed during early attachment and subsequently modeled by new significant relationships within a given social and cultural context. As a result of the quality of past interactive experiences, these self-states will remain disconnected – dissociated – or will become dialogically connected.

Pathological dissociation, trauma, and psychotherapy

Pathological dissociation is defensive in nature and undermines a person's reflective ability by decoupling the mind from the self. Donnel Stern (1997,

2010) describes what he calls "passive dissociation" as a rigidity that, due to various unconscious reasons – defensive, traumatic, or a combination of both – causes certain narratives to occupy a person's description of his/her own identity and other narratives to become unimaginable to him/her. This is a non-conscious rejection of certain meanings that remain unsaid, linked to unformulated experiences in interactions with significant others in early childhood (Stern, 1997). Unlike repression, this defense does not affect the conscious being or the narration of a certain feeling, fantasy, thought, or memory; instead, it is a response to a state of identity, a way of being, a self-state. This is what Bromberg (2006) refers to as a *not-me* state: one that is unable to participate in relational discourse and that usually represents the effects of traumatic life situations or events. In other words, these correspond with aspects rejected by the self, which appear not to participate consciously in the behavior of the individual, although they influence it from the shadows – in DST terms, a "shadow position" (Hermans & Hermans-Konopka, 2010).

Trauma is not just a special situation, but a continuous process that demands our attention only when it interrupts or threatens the continuity of the self experience. All of us are vulnerable to the experience of having to deal with something that exceeds what we can psychologically handle, and it is common to observe differences in this coping ability among patients receiving psychotherapy. For some people, experiences with others can be too stressful for their psychological functioning – too stressful to deal with during a state of internal conflict – and so the mind attempts to relieve this stress through the defensive use of a normal brain process: dissociation (Bromberg, 2011). Dissociation allows certain experiences to be adaptively kept in separate self-states with no connection with one another, at least for some time. This period may be brief for some, but permanent for others. For the latter, dissociation is not only a mental process aimed at dealing with everyday stress, but a structure that organizes their life, reducing the range of experiences that can be lived. Therefore, this mechanism – capable of structuring a person's experience – ensures the preservation of the continuity of the self but at the same time limits reflective capacity. In the therapeutic relationship, these patients need to recognize their most dissociated aspects rather than only understand them. In turn, therapists must accept this act of recognition, both in the patients' development and in the psychotherapy (Bromberg, 2004). In fact, Bromberg (2011) calls *structural change* the process that, via psychotherapeutic intervention, allows a patient to gradually move from dissociation to conflict, which may be clinically represented by his/her increasing ability to adopt a reflective position in which one aspect of the self observes and reflects – often with some degree of displeasure – on other aspects that were dissociated in the past.

Psychotherapy contributes to the modulation of and to the dialogue between the multiple *I*-positions of the patient, activating the relationship between them, allowing those less conscious or dissociated positions of the patient to become more conscious and integrated. The aforementioned constitute an intra- and intersubjective *regulatory process* that occurs in the patient–therapist exchange (Martínez, 2011b; Martínez, Tomicic, & Medina, 2012; Martínez, Tomicic, Medina, & Krause, 2014).

From this perspective, psychotherapy is regarded as a process of articulation of what is left unformulated, by means of the dialogical experience of generating, together with the patient, a space for him/her to learn about him/herself through the other's *ears* and eyes. The therapist acts as an emotionally responsive witness who recognizes the patient's dissociated and unformulated self-states (Stern, 2010). The recognition and witnessing operation that patient and therapist direct to these dissociated states allows the patient's self to expand by naming, formulating, and mentalizing them (Martínez, 2011a; Tronick, 1998). In other words, this operation makes it possible for multiple positions and voices of the self to communicate and engage in a dialogue, which enables them to struggle and negotiate with one another in the safe exploration space provided by psychotherapy (Duarte, Fishersworring, Martínez, & Tomicic, 2017; Fonagy & Allison, 2014; Martínez et al., 2012).

Recognizing voices: model of analysis of discursive positioning in psychotherapy (MAPP)

Upon the basis of the aforementioned theoretical backgrounds, we have created a method that makes it possible to depict the way in which the multiple subjectivities of patients and their therapists are organized in their speech and participate in an active dynamic of mutual recognition.

In the field of psychotherapy research, several methods have been advanced to make multivocality visible and reveal the relationship between voices and their unfolding throughout the psychotherapeutic process (Hermans, 2008). All of them have in common the notion of self-multiplicity and approach subjective positioning by means of the participants' narratives. Even though some of them consider both patient and therapist self-states (see Seikkula, Laitila, & Rober, 2012), most of them focus only on the patient's dialogical dynamics.

We have developed a model of analysis of discursive positioning in psychotherapy (MAPP) based on the notion that a discursive position is equivalent to a subjective position or an *I*-position, because it is a point of view or a way of being in the world that is expressed through utterances that shape the discourse of an individual (Larraín & Medina, 2007; Martínez et al., 2012).

The MAPP is a three-level system (see Figure 12.1). The first level is composed of the *voices* of an individual, patient, or therapist, which constitute the most idiosyncratic – and therefore embodied – expression of subjectivity in discourse. The second level is formed by the *personal positions* of a patient or therapist, which group together repertoires of voices that voice them. Lastly, the third analytic level of the MAPP is an abstract *taxonomy* that represents the typical organization of the personal positioning of patients and therapists accounting for a level of social organization of these positions or social positions (Martínez & Tomicic, 2017).

Regarding the first level of the MAPP, we consider that patients and therapists can express different points of view in an utterance by means of voices. Thus, a voice not only expresses spoken contents, but also the perspective from which those contents are addressed. Patients or therapists talk by means of a set or repertoire of voices that constitutes the essential elements used by each of them to construct versions or interpretations of reality; these, when weaved into discourse, preserve the coherence of such interpretations (see Wetherell & Potter, 1988). The repertoire of voices usually is diverse and unique in the case of patients: it represents the very specific way everyone's subjectivity is organized (see Table 12.1). In the case of therapists, because their voices express their point of view within their professional role, they show much less diversity, with the *inquirer, meta-analytic, confrontational,* and *assertive* voices being frequent (see Morán et al., 2016).

In the second level of the MAPP, the patient's and the therapist's voices are regarded as jointly voicing a recurrent perspective, labeled "personal position," namely a self-state. In other words, a specific repertoire of voices involves a shared subjectivity as part of the multiple self-states of the patient or the

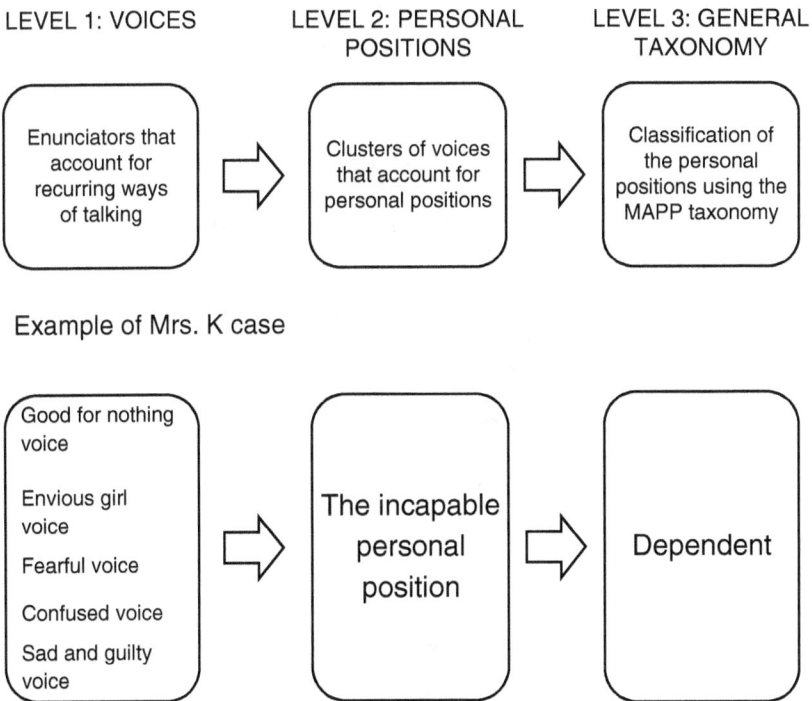

LEVEL 1: VOICES   LEVEL 2: PERSONAL POSITIONS   LEVEL 3: GENERAL TAXONOMY

Example of Mrs. K case

Figure 12.1 Three analytical layers of the MAPP.

Note: The Mrs. K case will be used to illustrate the dialogical analysis using MAPP therapist. Again, at this level there is a difference when comparing the specificity and idiosyncratic features of the positions of patient and therapist. Pushed by the uniqueness of their voices, the patients' positions reveal the very idiosyncratic perspectives and ways of being of each one of them. On the other hand, the positions of the therapists are linked to their specific role (Martínez, Tomicic, & Medina, 2014), and in that regard, reveal the perspectives that can be adopted within their "social positions," for example "I as therapist, helper, counselor, psychologist" (Hermans, 2001, 2004).

As mentioned above, the third level of the MAPP proposes a general and very abstract taxonomy representing the configurations of positions that are typically adopted by the participants of the therapeutic encounter. This taxonomy emerged from the categorization of the personal positions of both patients and therapists resulting from the analysis of several psychotherapies (see Table 12.1; Martínez & Tomicic, 2017). In the case of patients, three general positions represent the typical configuration: reflective, dependent, and independent. As for therapists, two general positions do so: proposer and professor.

Table 12.1 Mrs. K.'s and her therapist's voices, personal positions, and MAPP taxonomy

Therapies	*Patient's personal positions and voices*	*Therapist's personal positions and voices*	*MAPP taxonomy*
Mrs. K.'s therapy	**1 The integrative**	**1 The proposer**	**Patient**
	1.1 Continuity voice	1.1 Inquirer voice	1 The reflective
	1.2 Self-dialog voice	1.2 Confrontational voice	2 The dependent
	1.3 Down-to-earth/ grounded voice	1.3 Metaanalytical voice	3 The independent
		1.4 Self-revealing voice	**Therapist**
	2 The incapable	**2 The expert**	1 The proposer
	2.1 Good for nothing voice	2.1 Asserting voice	2 The professor
		2.2 Specialist's voice	
	2.2 Envious girl voice		
	2.3 Fearful voice		
	2.4 Confused voice		
	2.8 Sad and guilty voice		
	3 The detached		
	3.1 The voice of duty		
	3.2 Disaffectionate voice		
	3.3 Angry voice		
	3.4 Carefree voice		

Therefore, for patients, a triadic organization of positions has been described. First, the *dependent* general category is characterized by the patient's self-positioning as needy, weak, damaged, and/or vulnerable. In contrast, the second general position – called *independent* – is characterized by the patient's positioning as someone strong and self-sufficient and/or as someone who does not need help from others. These two general positions speak upon the basis of a single truth in a more monological manner (see Martínez, Tomicic, Medina, & Krause, 2014).

Finally, the *reflective* general positioning category accounts for a subjective stance in which the patient is able to have a distant – but not disconnected – perspective of emotional situations, listening and critically looking at other positions while encouraging dialogue between them in the manner of a meta-position (e.g. Bertau & Gonçalves, 2007; Georgaca, 2001). This meta-position has been regarded in Dialogical Self Theory (DST) with some qualities similar to the reflective positioning described here. For example, it allows a distancing from other positions, which in turn allows a panoramic vision and simultaneously of the different positions of self, thus providing a dialogical space for conversation between voices and opposing positions. (Hermans, 2003).

In turn, the first general position of therapists is called *the proposer*, in which the practitioner positions him/herself as someone who shows the patient what he or she observes and offers him/her a new perspective, thus generating a dialogical space between the patient's positions. In addition, the general positioning category labeled *the professor* is more dominant and monological, establishing the therapist as someone in possession of a truth or knowledge that can be presented, taught, or sometimes imposed on the patient as the only alternative.

In sum, the three levels of the MAPP reflect a view of the self as a dialogical entity that encompasses the multiple expressions (i.e. voices) of the patient's and the therapist's subjective positioning (i.e. personal positions), which in turn reflect a socially and culturally determined organization of subjectivity (i.e. MAPP taxonomy). In the MAPP taxonomy, multiplicity is believed to reflect certain aspects of the personality and development of individuals that constitute a supra-organization, a notion already proposed in other theoretical models as a way of organizing subjectivity (see polarities of experience, advanced by Blatt, Shahar, & Zuroff, 2001; or attachment categories such as *avoidant* and *preoccupied*, advanced by Main, 2000).

Trauma and dissociation in the case of Mrs. K.

To illustrate the MAPP, we will present two fragments of a long-term psychotherapy with Mrs. K., a patient diagnosed with a personality disorder and whose issues allow us to examine in greater depth the dialogical dynamics at work in a context of trauma and pathological dissociation. The therapy took place in an outpatient psychological clinic in a public psychiatric institute in Santiago, Chile. The psychotherapy lasted approximately 18 months, with weekly sessions. The psychotherapist has a psychodynamic orientation and over 25 years of experience.

Mrs. K. was 31 years old at the time of the first session. She was a married housewife with two school-age children. She was seeking psychological help due to her severely aggressive behavior towards her 6-year-old daughter. The last time she beat her daughter, she became aware of the excessive force used and the damage that she had caused her. In the first session, she reports that she no longer beats her daughter, but that she sometimes grabs her and yells violently at her; she says that sometimes she does not recognize herself while performing these acts. This also happens to her when she drinks alcohol at weekends, as she becomes someone else: a more disinhibited, daring, and sensuous person. The rest of the time, she describes herself as a shy, bashful, and rather foolish woman. She finished secondary school, but has been unable to practice any of the trades that she learned afterwards.

Mrs. K. was born in a very poor family and is the youngest of four daughters. She was raised in an environment that bestowed upon her the importance of cleanliness, order, and good habits (e.g. personal hygiene, table etiquette), but that at the same time harmed her through physical and psychological abuse, parental alcoholism, a lack of safety, and an uncaring attitude from her care-givers. She was sexually abused twice when she was aged between 8 and 9 years of age, by friends of the family who came to drink with her parents at the weekend. Mrs. K.'s mother had committed suicide five years before the patient sought help, while her father has a severe case of cirrhosis.

In the first interviews, she comes across as an intelligent patient with a very high motivation for psychotherapy. She conveys a very marked feeling of identity diffusion, which causes her much anguish and has even led her to consider suicide.

Mrs. K.'s discursive voices and discursive positions

We identified three personal positions in Mrs. K.: the incapable, the detached, and the integrative (see Table 12.1).

In the *incapable* personal position, Mrs. K. becomes a person who establishes herself, before herself and others, as a worthless person who lacks skills for tackling the challenges of everyday life and who is trapped beneath feelings of fear, confusion, sadness, and guilt, which, as a whole, reflect her vulnerability. Speaking from this position, she comes across as someone who is unable to take responsibility for herself and others who require that she behave like an adult; also, she expresses the need to be aided and understood. While in the *incapable* position, Mrs. K. appears to express her motivations for requesting psychological help and suggests foci for the psychological intervention. This position is expressed through a variety of voices: a *good-for-nothing voice*, an *envious girl voice*, a *fearful voice*, a *confused voice*, and a *sad and guilty voice*. According to the MAPP taxonomy, the *incapable* personal position of Mrs. K corresponds to the *dependent* general positioning category (see Figure 12.1 and Table 12.1).

Within the variety of voices expressing the *incapable* position, the *confused* and *fearful* voices appear to be the main bearers of trauma – her history of maltreatment and abuse. The *confused* voice appears to express or embody the patient's personality disorder. Mrs. K. is locked in a dissociation state, not knowing what she is doing or why, "not feeling her identity," all of which results in a loss of agency. Using this voice, she reports actions and desires that she finds alien, expresses her feeling of bewilderment at what she does or says, and notes the key importance of other people's gaze for her to "become aware [of things]." For its part, the *fearful* voice allows Mrs. K. to express anxious aspects that interfere with her everyday life. She permanently conveys anxiety, nervousness, and a feeling of being in a rush. With this voice, Mrs. K. positions herself as a woman who is unable to take responsibility for herself. This is a voice that transmits weakness, a need to get help, and at times even panic. In addition, it expresses fear and nervousness in her interactions with the outside world (fear of needles, of elevators, of being on the street): "I'm afraid of everything," "And I start getting nervous and my hands start sweating," "and then with someone else it's like I get nervous . . . or I walk down the street and I'm scared . . . so it's like . . . it's like everything's weird," "Like, I'm sort of in a hurry all day . . . I'm never calm when I'm doing things . . . I'm like a very nervous person."

In the *detached* position – which could be regarded as contrary to the *incapable* position – Mrs. K. comes across as someone who does without affective bonds and who finds it easier to live without others. In addition, with this position she is able to reveal her ability to function in the world according to the norms of what must be done, while also managing to push aside the painful aspects of her life that could make her weak and vulnerable. Thus, from this position, the patient displays agency and autonomy, although by sacrificing her innermost desires, feelings, and needs. This position is expressed through four discursive voices: the *voice of duty*, the *disaffectionate voice*, the *angry voice*, and the *carefree voice*. According to the MAPP taxonomy, this idiosyncratic position constitutes the *independent* positioning category.

In the case of this position, the *disaffectionate* and *carefree voices* appear to manifest the dissociation of the painful and debilitating aspects resulting from Mrs. K.'s traumatic childhood experiences. In other words, these voices appear to contribute to the preservation of a strong self with a high level of agency; however, this task has a major impact on her feeling of well-being. Specifically, she uses the *disaffectionate voice* to refer to her relationships with significant others, mainly her daughter and husband. With this voice, she expresses how unnatural her maternal role feels to her and how uninterested she is in adopting it: she simply does not feel like giving or expressing affection; she is never moved. This is especially visible when she refers to her daughter, as she conveys not only her lack of concern and interest but also her strong feelings of rejection regarding her requests for affection. This voice allows Mrs. K. to express egotistical, self-centered, non-empathetic, and detached aspects of herself. She avoids emotional and physical contact and considers such actions to be embarrassing signs of weakness:

> I feel I don't love her [her daughter]. Sometimes she cries, and I feel like laughing. I see her crying and I think "oh, she's so dramatic." That's the sort of

thing I say. I'm also rather cold towards him [her husband]. He is always worried about me and everything, and I buy things for myself but I never think of him. I buy things, but just for myself, I don't get anything for my children, nothing. It's like I only care for myself. It's like I never think of others.

For its part, the *carefree voice* allows Mrs. K. to minimize the issues affecting her, which she has not managed to or does not know how to solve. With this voice, she adopts an indifferent or apathetic attitude towards issues that are clearly important to her; she uses expressions such as "that's the way things are" or "why should I bother?" Thus, she stops trying to solve or examine in detail what is hurting or affecting her, avoiding these painful or pending aspects. She comes across as a strong person in contrast to the possibility of allowing herself to be affected, of "overthinking things," an approach to which she gives a negative connotation: "being weak." With this voice, she moves from worry and anxiety to a detached and carefree attitude:

> Oh, no, not that, no. Right! I remember now that my mom had a shorter fuse, she was quick-tempered . . . she was . . . um . . . and no, the fact that my mom died doesn't affect me now. I feel . . . it's like . . . it's like . . . it's a distant thing . . . as you say . . . it's like . . . that's it, why should I bother?

In the *integrative* position, Mrs. K. articulates several aspects of herself and her circumstances. Here – speaking from this meta-position – she comes across as someone capable of describing and reflecting on her dissociated aspects and generating an understanding of the origin and dynamics of her problems, in which she incorporates other voices of her self. While in this position, Mrs. K. manifests her commitment and responsibility regarding herself and others, which causes her to live enthusiastically. For its part, this position is expressed through three discursive voices: the *continuity voice*, the *self-dialogue voice*, and the *down-to-earth/grounded voice*. In the MAPP taxonomy, this idiosyncratic position constitutes the *reflective* discursive position.

Throughout the psychotherapy, the *self-dialogue* and *down-to-earth/grounded* voices were particularly interesting. The former is characterized by its integrative nature: this is the voice with which Mrs. K. refers to and reflects on her dissociated aspects – which are present in other discursive voices. With this voice, she distances herself and adopts a perspective grounded on a coherent and regulated emotional state. With this discursive voice, she devises theories and notions regarding the origin of what is happening to her and what she does, while also challenging herself in her self-dialogue:

> Maybe that happens to me because I feel bad inside and that's why I do things. It's like I take it out on others. Maybe it's that? I take it out on others. With my son, he's small, and why do I wash him so aggressively? It's like I want to clean myself.

For its part, the *down-to-earth/grounded voice* allows Mrs. K. to express commitment and responsibility towards herself and others, especially her children. Also, she uses this voice to express a feeling of well-being and her identification of a core in which "she is herself"; she expresses her pride in being able to function in a grounded manner, while also experiencing a feeling of "normality." The *down-to-earth/grounded voice* reveals that Mrs. K. knows what is happening to her and why; with it, she validates and accepts her feelings, is able to be flexible and adapt to situations, gives affection without feeling weak, and takes an interest in living:

> "No, I'm fine ..." I said, but after some time I said, "No, I'm not okay. I'm not okay with myself. I'm not at peace with myself." So I came here [to get therapy] and I kept coming, I always come here, I think I have never abandoned this, it's like I'm really interested in this, because, I mean, I need to heal.

A confused self: "I can't say who I am"

The following extract was taken from the very beginning of the first therapy session. In this fragment, Mrs. K. presents the central issue that led her to seek psychological help: her difficulties for recognizing herself in her own behaviors.

44.   Mrs. K: But I still haven't noticed that; it's like I don't think I have – I don't notice it. It's that I don't know who I am – it's like I act differently later I'm someone else in another place.
45.   Therapist: What do you mean? Let's have a look at that.
46.   Mrs. K: Like, for example when I'm talking and all ... but then umm ... I don't feel that nervous and then with someone else it's like I get nervous or I walk down the street and I feel sort of scared it's like; it's all quite weird. I don't know ... it's like I feel I'm this way and I'm cranky or I'm nice or I'm umm short-tempered ... I don't know I can't tell.
47.   Therapist: Uh-huh.
48.   Mrs. K: ... who I am because sometimes I say I'm not cranky ... I'm happy ... I'm nice ... I have everything – it's like I say, I have everything mixed together so I think it shouldn't be so ...
49.   Therapist: Uh-huh.
50.   Mrs. K: It's as if everything – since I don't – I don't feel my identity – it's like I can't say who I am.
51.   Therapist: Uh-huh.
52.   Mrs. K: It's like I'm acting; like for example I get together with some friends who ... who drink, who like to party and all and I like start drinking and I become a party animal and all ... then I get together with other friends who are ... who don't drink or smoke or anything and I stay with them there and I don't I don't drink and it's like I lie to them like I tell them that I don't drink, that I'm a quiet person – I tell them those things.
    (...)

59. Therapist: So maybe you get to think it's not a lie when you're telling your friends "No, I don't like to drink. I don't party, in fact."
60. Mrs. K: It's a lie, right?
61. Therapist: Yes, why?
62. Mrs. K: Because it's true. I drink.
63. Therapist: Okay but I'm thinking that the one who says that maybe umm, in fact doesn't: doesn't drink.
64. Mrs. K: It's that I don't know – but I say why do I? Lie, I mean. Why do I say that?
65. Therapist: You see it as a lie.
66. Mrs. K: Yes, I do.
67. Therapist: Okay.
68. Mrs. K: And then I ask myself why; I ask myself because I even ask questions and I answer myself (ha).
69. Therapist: Uh-huh.
70. Mrs. K: It's like I ask why I am; why do I tell them I don't drink? Why do I lie? Why don't I show myself as I am?
71. Therapist: Uh-huh ... but you say you don't know?
72. Mrs. K: It's that I don't either and when I drink I also say that I say I'm not like that. I mean, I don't drink. I'm not a heavy drinker but I drink anyway.

Two moments can be identified in this extract of the dialogue between Mrs. K. and her therapist. First, between speaking turns 44 and 58, the conversation is mainly led by the patient's *confused voice* (see Table 12.1), which converses with the therapist, who adopts the *proposer* position, expressed through the *inquirer voice* (speaking turn 45).

The fragment starts with the patient speaking with the *confused voice*, through which she presents her central problem – her lack of recognition of herself in this self-state: "I don't know who I am." The therapist, adopting his role and using his *inquirer* voice, participates only minimally and invites the patient to explain and *show* him what she is talking about: "Let's have a look at that." In speaking turn 46, Mrs. K. responds from a single position – the *incapable* – but expresses it through two different discursive voices. One of them, the *confused voice*, shows how the patient behaves differently in various situations and how this reinforces another voice – the *fearful* one – that expresses the affects and emotions that are activated due to this confusion, that is, feeling scared and nervous. In other words, the appearance of these two discursive voices of the patient at this point of the conversation reinforces and adds nuances to this self-state – that of inability and vulnerability. In the following three speaking turns (48, 50, and 52), Mrs. K. uses the *confused voice* to narrate more events of her life that stress her confusion; in them, the recurrent expressions "I don't" and "I can't tell" seem to indicate the first recognition of the *me and not-me* of dissociation.

In the second moment of this first extract, the dialogue transforms between speaking turns 59 and 74, displaying a greater diversity of voices and positions, mainly of the patient.

This fragment starts in speaking turn 59, where the therapist proposes an interpretation identifying a link between the patient's actions and her mental functioning, highlighting with his *metaanalytic voice* that this may not be exactly a "lie." This leads to a shift in the patient's position in speaking turns 60, 62, and 66. Here, using her *voice of duty* – part of the repertoire of the *detached* discursive position – the patient reinforces the notion that her behavior is deceitful and that she is therefore committing an offense. For his part, the therapist switches positions, using his *asserting voice* to identify and reaffirm the right of another position to exist in Mrs. K. ("the one who says that"), a position that also tells the truth ("in fact doesn't: doesn't drink"). This intervention by the therapist lays the groundwork for a process in which the participants acknowledge the patient's multiple voices; this process, one year later, would manifest itself through one of the most relevant therapeutic changes for Mrs. K., as shown in the following fragment of session 30. Nevertheless, at this initial stage of the therapy, this intervention by the therapist only seems to cause tension and conflict between some of the patient's voices and positions. On the one hand, her first reaction in speaking turns 64 and 66 is again expressed through the *voice of duty*, as if she were trying to reassert, monologically, the truth of her lies. On the other hand, in her two subsequent speaking turns (68 and 70), the *self-dialogue voice* rears its head: "but I say why do I? ... I ask myself why." This voice, though weakly, manages to pose the question about the patient's *me* ("why don't I show myself as I am?"), but then quickly yields to the power of the *confused voice* (speaking turn 72).

These difficulties telling who she really is mark a key point in Mrs. K.'s psychotherapy; however, the situation starts changing towards the end of her psychotherapeutic process. The fragment analyzed below illustrates this change.

An integrated self: "but now I feel like it's mine like it's ..."

In this second extract, taken from session 30, a year later, Mrs. K. returns to talk about her internal voices. However, this time she refers to her voices from a different position: an *integrative* one, mainly expressed through the *down-to-earth/grounded* and *self-dialogue* voices.

328. Mrs. K: and I know that I can't go on living like this and that I cannot be sad and because I no longer feel that sadness that misfortune ... I can no longer have that grief. I said that sadness it's because it's not so much anymore (...)

336. Mrs. K: Not anymore because now I feel grief – we all feel grief – but I mean not that grief; that normal grief, I think, and it's like I no longer have that ... What was that thing that I said to myself? Something about

my head that I wanted to do something and it's like someone else. I don't know, a feeling, like another person said to me.

337. Therapist: I remember that at the beginning you told me you had lots of dialogues inside you.

338. Mrs. K: Yes.

339. Therapist: Like with yourself but it was a confusion that left you feeling that you didn't know who you were. Do you remember? (. . .)

344. Mrs. K: Like, I was telling myself that I wanted to do something: "Don't. Don't do that because that's not like that," or "Just do it. Because, what's wrong with it? If you are you are nice, you are" I hear sort of many voices which talk to me like that. (. . .)

348. Mrs. K: I was secretive. I mean – like, I used to drink and I didn't make a big deal of it but my voice wanted to do something and said, "Do it. Nothing, nothing will happen. Yes, yes, you're pretty. Right, you are"; I felt like the greatest person in the world when I drank. I felt sort of the best, the prettiest, the most gorgeous. And later now the week, the week before last, I drank and drank and that thing of feeling like, like someone else was talking to me, didn't happen to me.

349. Therapist: okay

350. Mrs. K: Like, I felt – I felt sort of, sort of normal like it was me who was drinking.

351. Therapist: Uh-huh.

352. Mrs. K: Something like that.

353. Therapist: Okay.

354. Mrs. K: And sometimes I'm fine. I'm normal and I want to do something but I think about it first anyway.

355. Therapist: Uh-huh.

356. Mrs. K: Like, what do I say? oh "do I do it or not"? Umm but now I feel like it's mine like it's . . .

Mrs. K. starts the fragment (turn 328) using the *down-to-earth/grounded voice* to talk about her sorrow, which does not seem to overwhelm her as it used to and that she currently accepts as a part of her life. Later, in speaking turn 336, along with normalizing her current grief, she refers to another of her internal voices – the *confused* one – alluding to it as "that thing that was said to me" or "another person said to me." In speaking turn 337 the therapist intervenes from a *proposing position*, recalling the patient's internal voices and alluding to them as "dialogues" within the patient. Then, specifically in speaking turn 339, he reminds her that those dialogues made her feel confused. In speaking turns 344 and 348 Mrs. K. responds from an *integrative position* that is expressed with the *continuity voice*, providing material that supports what the therapist says, such as memories that allude to "talking with herself" and the "many voices which talked to me like that." However, she no longer speaks from a position of confusion, but from a more integrated place that appears to acknowledge and accept these dialogues within herself. In the following turns, she reinforces the idea that she no longer feels that she is another person pulling her in a different direction; instead, she accepts that she can have contrary ideas within her, but she realizes that they are hers, that they belong to her. The fragment ends on speaking turns 354 and 356. Here, with this *down-to-earth/grounded voice*, she highlights the fact that now, when she wonders whether she should do something, she thinks and decides, certain that this dialogue is hers – that she is talking with herself: "like what do I say oh do I do it or not? Umm but now I feel like it's mine. Like it's …."

Conclusions

As human beings, we move within cultural spheres, which envelop and constitute the individual (Joerchel, 2011; Slunecko & Hengl, 2007). This implies that the dialogical self resonates in a specific social and cultural context that, for its part, provides a structure that organizes the space in which the voices and positions of the self move and influences the dialogical interactions among them (Joerchel, 2011; Slunecko & Hengl, 2007). Individuals flourish due to their participation in social and cultural spheres, which necessarily occurs with others. One of these emerges very early on and has been entitled intersubjective intimacy of early life (Trevarthen & Aitken, 2001), that is, the mother–infant space that is itself already within a certain cultural atmosphere (Joerchel, 2011).

Mrs. K., severely traumatized during her childhood, is part of a discursive chain (Bakhtin, 1986) in which her subjectivity has been organized in a dissociated manner, and that originated in the cultural spheres that constituted her, first as a daughter and later as a mother. These spheres, dominated by a mother who provides a dissociated discourse – cleanliness versus chaos – constitutes in the patient a self dominated by a position of inability that, through pathological dissociation, keeps her in a state of confusion that shifts alternately from *me* to *not-me*, thus restricting her cultural and social existence. Psychotherapy, as another cultural sphere, provides her with a space of recognition and acknowledgment of other relegated voices of herself. Thus, the patient manages to move from dissociation to a dialogical reorganization of her subjectivity – a reorganization in which she integrates her internal dialogues, gains agency, and broadens her experience of her own self and of herself as a person in her social and cultural world.

By means of this case, we illustrated the MAPP as a tool that gathers and nourishes itself from the DST in the conception of self as a concert of *I*-positions or states of self that can or cannot dialogue with each other. Likewise, from the background of relational psychoanalysis, the application of the MAPP allows us to analyze the way in which these aspects are dissociated from the self (e.g. shadow positions) and are integrated in the inner dialogues between the voices and positions of a patient, building bridges between this psychotherapeutic theory and the DST. Thus, through the Mrs. K case, we exemplified the idea that a new organization of the inner dialogue between the patients' voices and positions – a form of self-regulatory behavior – could constitute an important element of the psychotherapeutic process of change.

References

Bakhtin, M. (1986). *Speech genres and other late essays*. Austin, TX: University of Texas Press.

Bertau, M.-C., & Gonçalves, M. M. (2007). Looking at meaning as movement in development: Introductory reflections on the developmental origins of the dialogical self. *International Journal for Dialogical Science, 2*(1), 1–13.

Blatt, S., Shahar, G., & Zuroff, D. (2001). Anaclitic (sociotropic) and introjective (autonomous) dimensions. *Psychotherapy: Theory, Research, Practice, Training, 38*(4), 449–454. doi: 10.1037/0033-3204.38.4.449

Bromberg, P. M. (1998). *Standing in the spaces: Essays on clinical process, trauma and dissociation*. Hillsdale, NJ: Analytic Press.

Bromberg, P. M. (2004). Standing in the spaces: The multiplicity of self and the psychoanalytic relationship. In H. J. Hermans, & G. Dimaggio (Eds.), *The dialogical self in psychotherapy* (pp. 13–28). Hove, UK: Brunner-Routledge.

Bromberg, P. M. (2006). *Awakening the dreamer: Clinical journeys*. Mahwah, NJ: Analytic Press.

Bromberg, P. M. (2011). *The shadow of the tsunami: And the growth of the relational mind*. New York: Routledge.

Duarte, J., Fishersworring, M., Martínez, C., & Tomicic, A. (2017). "I couldn't change the past; the answer wasn't there": A case study on the subjective construction of psychotherapeutic change of a patient with a borderline personality disorder diagnosis and her therapist. *Psychotherapy Research, 3*, 1–18. doi: 10.1080/10503307.2017.1359426

Fonagy, P., & Allison, E. (2014). The role of mentalizing and epistemic trust in the therapeutic relationship. *Psychotherapy, 51*(3), 372–380. doi: 10.1037/a0036505

Georgaca, E. (2001). Voices of the self in psychotherapy: A qualitative analysis. *British Journal of Medical Psychology, 74*, 223–226.

Hermans, H. J. M. (1996). Voicing the self: From information processing to dialogical interchange. *Psychological Bulletin, 119*(1), 31–50.

Hermans, H. J. M. (2001). The dialogical self: Toward a theory of personal and cultural positioning. *Culture and Psychology, 7*, 243–281.

Hermans, H. J. M. (2003). The construction and reconstruction of a dialogical self. *Journal of Constructivist Psychology, 16*, 89–130.

Hermans, H. J. M. (2004). The dialogical self: Between exchange and power. In H. J. M. Hermans & G. Dimaggio (Eds.), *The dialogical self in psychotherapy* (pp. 13–28). Hove, UK: Brunner-Routledge.

Hermans, H. J. M. (2008). How to perform research on the basis of the dialogical self. Special issue on the dialogical self. *Journal of Constructivist Psychology, 21*(3), 185–199.

Hermans, H. J. M. (2014). Self as a society of *I*-positions: A dialogical approach to counseling. *Journal of Humanistic Counseling, 53*, 134–159. doi: 10.1002/j.2161-1939.2014.00054.x

Hermans, H. J. M., & Hermans-Konopka, A. (2010). *Dialogical self theory: Positioning and counter-positioning in a globalizing society*. Cambridge, UK: Cambridge University Press.

Joerchel, A. C. (2011). Locating the dialogic self within a cultural sphere. In M. Martsin, B. Wagoner, E.-L Aveling, I. Kadianaki, & L. Whittaker (Eds.), *Dialogicality in focus: Challenges to theory, method and application*. New York: Nova Science.

Larraín, A. Y., & Medina, L. (2007). Utterance analysis: Operative distinctions for a dialogical discourse analysis. *Estudios de Psicología/Studies in Psychology, 28*, 283–301. doi: 10.1174/021093907782506443

LeDoux, J. (2002). *The synaptic self.* New York: Viking.

Main, M. (2000). The organized categories of infant, child, and adult attachment: Flexible vs. inflexible attention under attachment-related stress. *Journal of the American Psychoanalytic Association, 48*(4), 1055–1127.

Martínez, C. (2011a). Mentalización en psicoterapia: Discusión sobre lo explícito e implícito en la relación terapéutica [Mentalizing in psychotherapy: Discussion on explicit and implicit of the therapeutic relationship]. *Terapia Psicológica, 29*(1), 97–105.

Martínez, C. (2011b). *Regulación mutua y dialogicidad en psicoterapia: Un análisis empírico de la subjetividad e intersubjetividad en el discurso terapéutico [Mutual regulation and dialogue in psychotherapy: An empirical analysis of subjectivity and intersubjectivity in thetherapeutic discourse].* Saarbrucken: EAE Publishing.

Martínez, C., & Tomicic, A. (2017). *Model of analysis of discursive positioning (MAPP): A method for researching discourse in psychotherapeutic interactions.* Publication under review.

Martínez, C., Tomicic, A., & Medina, L. (2012). Dialogic discourse analysis (DDA) of psychotherapeutic dialog: Microanalysis of relevant psychotherapy episodes. *International Journal for Dialogical Science, 6*(1), 99–121.

Martínez, C., Tomicic, A., & Medina, L. (2014). Psychotherapy as a discursive genre: A dialogic approach. *Culture & Psychology, 20*, 501–524. doi: 10.1177/1354067X14551292

Martínez, C., Tomicic, A., Medina, L., & Krause, M. (2014). A microanalytical look at mutual regulation in psychotherapeutic dialogue: Dialogic discourse analysis (DDA) in episodes of rupture of the alliance. *Journal Research in Psychotherapy: Psychopathology, Process and Outcome (RIPPPO), 17*(2), 73–92.

Morán, J., Martínez, M., Tomicic, A., Pérez, J. C., Krause, M., Guzmán, M., . . . de la Cerda, C. (2016). Verbal and nonverbal expressions of mutual regulation in relevant episodes of psychotherapy. *Estudios de Psicología/Studies in Psychology, 37*(2–3), 548–579. doi: 10.1080/02109395.2016.1204784

Seikkula, J., Laitila, A., & Rober, P. (2012). Making sense of multi-actor dialogues in family therapy and network meetings. *Journal of Marital Family Therapy, 38*(4), 667–687. doi: 10.1111/j.1752-0606.2011.00238.x

Slunecko, T., & Hengl, S. (2007). Language, cognition, subjectivity: A dynamic constitution. In A. Rosa & J. Valsiner (Eds.), *Handbook of sociocultural psychology* (pp. 40–61). Cambridge, UK: Cambridge University Press.

Stern, D. B. (1997). *Unformulated experience: From dissociation to imagination in psychoanalysis.* Hillsdale, NJ: Analytic Press.

Stern, D. B. (2010). *Partners in thought: Working with unformulated experience, dissociation, and enactment.* New York: Routledge.

Trevarthen, C., & Aitken, K. J. (2001). Infant intersubjectivity: Research, theory and clinical applications. *Journal of Child Psychology and Psychiatry, 42*, 3–8.

Tronick, E. (1998). Dyadically expanded states of consciousness and the process of therapeutic change. *Infant Mental Health Journal, 19*, 290–299.

Wetherell, M., & Potter, J. (1988). Discourse analysis and the identification of interpretative repertoires. In C. Antaki (Ed.), *Analyzing everyday explanation: A casebook of methods.* London: Sage.

Part III
Bridging cultures

13 Compositionwork

Working with dialogical self in psychotherapy

Agnieszka A. Konopka and Wim van Beers

Compositionwork (Hermans, 2014; Konopka & van Beers, 2014) is a contemplative-artistic method of work with identity and emotions, used in therapy, counseling, coaching, and training. It is based on Dialogical Self Theory (DST) (Hermans, 2003; Hermans & Hermans-Konopka, 2010), as a creative way of working with the landscape of mind populated by the multiplicity of *I*-positions. The method is also inspired by contemplative traditions, especially the tradition of Japanese Zen gardens (Berthier & Parkes, 2000). The contemplative aspect encourages an attitude of openness and receptivity to the multiplicity of self as it emerges in one's experience. The artistic aspect is a process of expressing and shaping this plurality in a creative form, within which different elements are *composed*. Emphasized in contemplative traditions, and later on in Gestalt therapy (Perls, Hefferline, & Goodman, 1951), the present moment oriented, receptive attitude comes together here with acknowledging an agentic role in creating one's experience, as in constructivist perspective (Neimeyer, 2009). Taking into account the important role of emotions in self organization and change (Greenberg, 2011), the method also incorporates some recent developments in the psychology of emotions as presented in emotion-focused therapy and the dialogical view on emotions, as part of DST.

In Compositionwork the multiplicity of *I*-positions (Hermans, 2014) is often accessed via direct embodied experience, or via choosing *I*-positions from a narrative or a standard list. Then it is symbolized and externalized by non-verbal natural elements, typically stones, which are positioned, re-positioned and 'composed' in a space, usually a box with sand, sometimes on paper. The emerging composition reflects the quality of the separate elements, their interrelations and the overall pattern. The nonverbal language of stones and sand and their spatial arrangement allows for the expression and exploration of the complexity of the dialogical self in a figurative, nonlinear, simultaneous, and dynamic way. This symbolizing way of working aims to also involve those *I*-positions that are not yet verbalized or voiced, in order to address the unspeakable in the self, which can be a source of deep and transformative meanings (Neimeyer, 2010).

The process of externalization, central in Compositionwork (Konopka & van Beers, 2014), facilitates a working distance, which helps to regulate emotions and creates optimal conditions for taking a meta-position (Hermans, 2003).

Moreover, looking at a composition from a meta-position a client can see every element in the context of its broader pattern (Hermans & Hermans-Konopka, 2010). Such a pattern has features of abstract art and may facilitate an aesthetic, metaphorical way of approaching one's experience. Seeing a composition may evoke a new bodily felt appeal, which often encloses a message, a question that facilitates an unfolding dialogue between nonverbally and verbally depicted *I*-positions, which co-create the polyphony of the dialogical self.

First we will describe how DST is introduced in Compositionwork. Next we will discuss the affective and contemplative aspects of work with the dialogical self in Compositionwork. Finally we will present a case example that illustrates the micro-processes of positioning and repositioning in process of Compositionwork.

Basic theoretical concepts guiding Compositionwork

The landscape of mind as a composition

DST depicts the self as a *landscape of mind* populated by a multiplicity of *I*-positions (Hermans, 2001). Compositionwork introduces the landscape of mind not only as a concept or metaphor, but also as a concrete creation, in which multiple *I*-positions are symbolized, externalized, composed, and re-composed. Clients are invited to express their inner world by creating a symbolic land-scape using a variety of stones that represent *I*-positions and that are placed in a box of sand or on a sheet of paper. In this way the landscape of mind is *externalized* with the effect that it can 'speak back' to the person who created it. It speaks back in colours and forms, structures, and overall pattern, which may gradually 'come to words', expressing their personal meanings. When the landscape of mind is externalized in the form of a composition, this also creates optimal conditions to take a meta-position (Hermans, 2003), what permits an overview of juxtaposed positions and their patterns. The meta-position results from making one's inner world physically placed in front of oneself, by looking at it from some distance and seeing different positions simultaneously. From this perspective the client can explore their interrelations and its total pattern.

'Landscape of mind' introduced in metaphorical and concrete form in Compo-sitionwork offers a rich spectrum of related natural metaphors. The richness of geographical images, words like 'volcano' or 'storm', fosters the use of a poetic pictorial language that transcends the descriptive language and invites one 'to speak poetically, rather than prosaically for maximum impact' (Neimeyer, 2012, p. 8). Compositionwork is an invitation to an artistic dialogue that takes place on a nonverbal and verbal level and in which one's inner word can be differentiated, enriched, and transformed.

Creating a landscape of mind via Compositionwork can take two basic forms: (a) as an identity focused landscape, in which *I*-positions are derived from a narrative, or from a list of *I*-positions; and (b) as a 'now-scape', a direct-experience focused landscape, in which *I*-positions derive from present moment experience. In this chapter we will focus on the latter.

The micro-process of positioning

In DST the self is seen as a dynamic process of *positioning, counter-positioning,* and *repositioning* (Hermans & Hermans-Konopka, 2010). In this process *I*-positions come to the fore and go. We see developmental and therapeutic change as a shift from a fixed, rigid, usually conceptually based sense of self, to a sense of self derived from dynamic direct experience of positioning. In order to enhance this shift we pay attention to this dynamism on the micro-level by addressing the process of positioning and repositioning, based on moment-to-moment experience. Working on this micro level allows for *I*-positions to be addressed in a relatively direct way, as experientially accessible in a moment and bodily felt.

Implicit, bodily felt I-positions

In present moment oriented Compositionwork, *I*-positions are accessed via direct embodied experience and not from a narrative or a list of *I*-positions as it is practised in a more identity oriented way of working. Focusing on the embodied experience stimulates access to *implicit I*-positions and emotions. These parts of the self may not yet be fully available through one's narrative, and not yet verbalized. They may be at the edge of one's awareness, but can already be bodily sensed. These partly known *I*-positions can be especially rich sources of new meanings, growth, and innovation. In Compositionwork implicit positions are explored by contacting embodied affective experience, especially on the level of the felt sense (Gendlin, 2012) in a way that is similar to 'analogical listening' (Neimeyer, 2012), which will be further elaborated on later in the chapter.

Emotional aspects of dialogical self in compositionwork

Bi-directional relation with one's emotions

The way a person relates to his or her emotions is of utmost relevance in therapy. As described in DST (Hermans & Hermans-Konopka, 2010) this relation has a bi-directional character. Emotions influence, organize, and reorganize the self. At the same time a person relates to his or her emotions, by reacting/answering to them. Pathology can be based on problems in emotion regulation, like for example avoiding or supressing affective states. On the other hand, acceptance of all emotions can have a healing effect, which has been emphasized in therapeutic approaches like acceptance and commitment therapy (Hayes, Strosahl, & Wilson, 2012), mindfulness-based interventions (Kabat-Zinn, 2003), or emotion-focused therapy (Greenberg, 2004).

In Compositionwork the awareness of one's relation with emotions is facilitated by externalization, which helps to notice impulses towards symbolized and externalized emotions. Simply observing how people react to, or what they tend to do with stones that symbolize their emotion may be quite revealing. Some clients may express aggressive impulses and actions towards particular emotions, like a client who smashed a stone representing his anxiety with another heavy stone, crushing it to pieces. Another client covered his *sadness stone* deep down under a layer of sand. Such symbolic actions often reflect the ways in which people relate to their emotions. Moreover, the feeling one has towards an externalized emotion can help to make one become aware of a secondary emotion, that is an emotion felt towards another emotion, like for example anxiety about one's sadness (Greenberg, 2004). It is important to notice that there can be a difference between what people may *do* with an emotion and the *need* connected with an emotion. When for example one rejects a part of oneself that needs soothing, it only increases psychological suffering. Compassionate presence and listening to the voice of a need that is enclosed in an emotion can often be a way to transform one's relation with it into a more dialogical one. In this way we also facilitate our 'inner democracy' (Hermans, 2018), in which all parts of our selves can receive a voice and be heard in the society of mind.

Emotion regulation

According to Greenberg (2011) emotion regulation is an important aspect of emotion change and Compositionwork supports emotion regulation in several ways. Externa-lization and taking a meta-position helps to create a working distance and thus supports emotion regulation. Symbolizing emotions by stones and giving them a place in the larger context of other emotions not only allows them to be acknowledged but also helps to contain them. When a person can see an externalized emotion in the context of his larger *I*-position repertoire, this may also influence how it is experi-enced. A client expressed the experience of giving a place to her fear as follows[1]:

> Now my fear has a place . . . [*When you are seeing it, what are you feeling?*] It is a relief . . . I see that I have more: here is a tender feeling, here an angry one. Here is my creative side. I am not alone with my fear. [*How is it to be not alone with your fear?*] I am stronger, not so afraid anymore.

When people are less afraid of their emotions, they become stronger, as they see that they have enough resources to regulate and deal with these emotions. Labelling on the verbal level also has a function of emotion regulation (Green-berg, 2011). Giving an emotion-position a form and a place in a composition has a similar supportive function on the nonverbal level.

I-position and emotion scheme

The dynamic and flexible notion of the *I*-position is closely related to emotion. First, every *I*-position has an affective connotation. At the same time, emotions, organizing the self in specific ways, can be seen as temporary ways of positioning (Hermans & Hermans-Konopka, 2010). It may be useful to look at *I*-positions from the perspective of emotion-focused therapy (Elliot, Watson, Goldman, & Greenberg, 2015). Any *I*-position can be seen and explored in terms of an *emotion scheme*, which consists of the following aspects: motivational, bodily expressive, perceptual-situational, and conceptual, organized around the particular emotion. The advantage of such exploration is that all elements related to an emotion can be more differentiated. We select here the motivational aspect to illustrate it. In Compositionwork the motivational aspects of an emotion scheme can be explored by experimenting with moving the stone symbolizing an emotion. This movement happens in the context of other positions, so that any movement simultaneously has contextual meaning. An example: '[*Where does that energy want to be or move?*] It wants to move up. Closer to this white restful stone in my chest. It wants to connect with my peace'. In Compositionwork every other aspect of an emotion scheme is seen in the context of its surrounding dynamic multiplicity.

External positions and emotions

A composition can be organized not only by emotions of the client but also an emotion of a significant other. From the perspective of DST external *I*-positions are seen as parts of the extended domain of the self (Hermans, 2003). Likewise, emotions of significant others can also be relevant parts of this extended domain. Including an influential emotion of a significant other in a composition helps to explore and map its impact on the organization of the self. Some clients can be dominated by such internalized emotions in a way that their own adaptive emotions are silenced. An emotion of a significant other can have a lot of power and influence on the organization of the *I*-position repertoire and significantly influence the pattern of a composition.

Dialogue and emotional change

Differences and oppositions between *I*-positions are a common characteristic of the multiplicity of the self and are not seen as a problem. However, for example, hostile relations between *I*-positions often lead to severe psychological suffering. Like in regular society, in the society of mind (Hermans, 2002) good dialogue and understanding between involved parties is crucial for well-being, creativity, and growth. Compositionwork acknowledges the innovative potential of dialogue as it has been extensively described in DST. In emotion-focused therapy (Greenberg, 2011) the dialogue between emotions has also been defined as a fundamental factor of change, but no dialogue is possible if two emotions or *I*-positions are not separated and clearly distinguished from each other.

Compositionwork helps prepare the ground for such a dialogue by concrete spatial differentiation of the two parts: giving them distinguishable places and symbols. An externalized emotion can receive a voice, just by letting its symbol (a stone) speak for itself. Things that people do not dare to say while talking themselves can sometimes more easily be said when they are voiced by a stone. Giving voice to a stone can also be a preparatory step for other forms of dialogue, like for example two-chair dialogue.

Emotions as an artistic composition

Inviting an artistic attitude in Compositionwork can support further differentiation of emotions and also promote a more constructive attitude towards one's emotional experiences. The artistic vision on the self is a way to look at the self as an artistic project (Hermans & Hermans-Konopka, 2010). Acknowledging the uniqueness of one's self- composition may lead to a greater integration and self-acceptance.

By approaching emotions as a form of 'inner art' we try to discover their unique richness and complexity that can be caught by artistic forms and metaphorical language. In their turn, emotions differentiated in an artistic form can become richer experiences. Artistic attitude and expression potentially help to celebrate experience in its uniqueness and discover its health-promoting aspects, which may also be latent in negative emotions. Stimulating an artistic attitude can reduce defensiveness towards emotions and invite a greater openness and acceptance.

The role of figurative, nonverbal elements in Compositionwork

Nonverbal elements introduced in Compositionwork (Konopka, Neimeyer & Jacobs-Lentz, 2017) can support differentiation of emotions, helping one to become aware and express not yet verbalized, implicit emotions and those aspects of emotional experience that are not easily caught by words. By introducing nonverbal materials the process of naming an emotion can slow down and become more nuanced. This can be especially important in case of vague feelings and for people who are used to intellectual processing of experience, quick labelling, and in this way run a risk of losing contact with the bodily felt level of experience. When an emotion is symbolized by a stone, it 'speaks back' with it's nonverbal qualities, like e.g. size, colour, texture, or position in the space.

As Neimeyer (2010) points out 'the deepest meanings with which our clients struggle, as well as fresh possibilities for constructing and doing life differently, are typically elusive and call for articulation in figurative rather than literal forms' (p. 73). Stones and their compositions act as a non-verbal, figurative vocabulary that may be very helpful in accessing deep, illusive, sensed but not yet verbalized meanings and differentiate vague and complex feelings. Stones are useful materials because of their sensoric nonverbal qualities (Konopka & van Beers, 2014). According to Jaffé and Jung (1964), stones can be used as universal symbols of the psyche. They had symbolic meaning for ancient and primitive societies, and they still speak to the psyche of modern humans.

According to Jung (Hannah, 1997) stones can act like bridges between unconscious and conscious levels and in our view they help to access implicit not yet verbalized *I*-positions and emotions. In this sense Compositionwork can be a complementary method to more verbally oriented approaches, which tend to address more explicit and verbalized levels of experience.

Contemplative aspects of Compositionwork

The now-scape of mind

In contemplative traditions waking up from 'the dream of thoughts' to the present moment is often seen as part of the awakening or enlightenment process. From a therapeutic perspective, contacting the present moment experience is also an important factor for well-being and psychological health. Present moment focused attention is cultivated in mindfulness training (Shapiro, Carlson, Astin, & Freedman, 2006), both for spiritual and psychological purposes. Gestalt Therapy (Perls et al., 1951) emphasizes that people often build a wall of thoughts and concepts that isolates them from the environment and themselves. Contacting present moment, direct experience can be liberating from narrowed concepts and a mentally constructed world. According to Stern (2004), therapeutic work focused on the here and now has the greatest transforming potential. Direct contact and relation with feelings and life in fact only happens in the present moment. At the same time 'it is remarkable how little we know about experience that is happening right now' (p. 3). Contacting present moment experience can increase the quality and richness of life and self. Moreover, as Stern emphasizes, the micro pattern of the present moment often reveals a broader pattern in which a person functions and in this way it can be a source of important insights.

Present moment oriented Compositionwork focuses on a special type of landscape of mind, the 'Now-scape': the affective landscape that emerges from moment to moment, out of direct embodied experience. In making a composition in this way, present moment experiences are symbolized and externalized and create a symbolic landscape of mind that reflect aspects of the self that come to the fore from direct experience.

Affective now-scape and felt sense

Attention in present moment oriented Compositionwork is often directed towards the inner areas of the body, the places where people usually feel their feelings. This aspect of the practice is partly based on focusing as developed by Gendlin (2012). According to Gendlin (2012), therapeutic change can happen if a client can make contact with his or her inner experience on the level of their 'felt sense'. Felt sense is often experienced as an atmosphere, like a vague feeling, accessible in the inner spaces of the body. When contacted and attended to it may become a source of implicit emotions and *I*-positions. Approaching the felt sense allows one to work with the dialogical self on the implicit level. In this process implicit positions can unfold, gradually 'ripening' towards becoming a verbal expression. According to Leijssen (1998), attention directed at the felt sense has a contemplative character, similar to Zen or Taoist traditions. It enhances a presence and receptive openness to not yet verbalized or formed aspects of experience emerging in the present moment.

There is a difference between the focusing attitude as introduced by Gendlin (2012) and approaching the felt sense in Compositionwork. While focusing practice often starts from addressing a variety of problematic experiences and then focuses on one specific personal problem, Compositionwork puts more emphasis on a Zen like 'not-knowing', open, curious attitude in the present moment without conceptualizing any experience as problematic or otherwise but rather trying to temporarily put aside any assumptions about it. Anderson and Goolishian (1992) proposed a not-knowing approach to therapy, in which the development of new meanings is based on the therapists' attitude of not knowing. The therapist practices asking questions from a position of not knowing, communicating curiosity. In an analogical way we facilitate a not-knowing attitude of the client towards his own experience. The not-knowing attitude of the therapist and his curiosity can stimulate a similar curiosity and not-knowing attitude of the client, which create a space for newness to emerge.

Mindful awareness and self as process

According to Mamberg and Bassarear (2015) nonjudgemental attention focused on unfolding moment-to-moment experience (mindfulness) enhances an experience of self as process. Mindful attention introduced systematically in mindfulness-based stress reduction training (Kabat-Zinn, 2003) helps to shift the sense of self from a fixed, reified self to a sense of self as a changing process. Likewise Gestalt therapy highlights the value of present awareness understood as spontaneous sensing of what arises in one's self, in contrast to an evaluating, correcting, or in any way manipulating form of dealing with experience (Perls et al., 1951). This kind of awareness is invited in Compositionwork. One of the purposes of it is to enhance a sense of self based on the dynamic process of experience, which is in contrast with a sense of self based on fixed concepts. We see the shift from a reified self to a self as a dynamic experiential process – or from the identification with a rigid narrative about one's self to one that is open to new experiences (Gonçalves, Matos, & Santos, 2009) – as the core of therapeutic change and a source of psychological health.

Externalization and the 'depositioned self'

In mystical, contemplative traditions increasing inner freedom is not related to solving one's problems or changing negative emotions, but rather to enhancing the differentiation between the content of mind and awareness itself. This is reflected by many authors in relation to psychotherapy. Deikman (1982) distinguishes between an 'observing self' (awareness as such) and an 'observed self' that in his view is the content of mind. From this position a new, freer, and more spacious relation with experiences, including painful ones, can be established.

From the perspective of Japanese culture, such relation with experience can be characterized by expanding '*ma*' (space between), which, according to Morioka (2012), is an important factor of therapeutic change. Likewise in the practice of focusing ('clearing space practice') enhancing such space is

> an attempt at establishing a better relationship, whereby the client gets more space to look at problems instead of coinciding with them and whereby the energy and healing power of the observing self becomes free to face the problems and get a hold of the situation.
>
> (Leijssen, 1998, p. 132)

In Compositionwork the act of externalization emphasizes the distinction between the content of the mind and the awareness of it (as in acceptance and commitment therapy; Hayes et al., 2012). Just by the act of placing experience in a concrete, symbolic form 'out there', a person may move from coinciding with the experience towards relating to it in a freer and more spacious way, that allows to answer to it rather than automatically react on it.

The 'not-knowing mind'

Compositionwork invites the contemplative attitude of '*not knowing mind*' towards one's experience. In Zen tradition this is sometimes called 'beginners mind' (Suzuki, 2010). 'Not knowing mind' is a way to relate to one's experience characterized by openness and receptivity. New experience and new emerging *I*-positions can only be received if there is mental space for them. Suzuki (2010) argues that a full cup cannot receive more tea and relates this metaphor to the mind. If we are full of concepts about ourselves we cannot receive the fresh liquid of new direct experience. Beginner's mind ideally has no assumptions, apart from the following: 'I know that I do not know what will emerge in my experience in the next moment'. It is an experimental, 'child-like', 'curious way of being', similar to White's 'exocitization of the domestic' (White, 1993), when usual experiences are specially attended to and examined, and reveal something unusual, special, uniquely distinctive. It is also the readiness of the mind to encounter experience directly and the ability to be with the uncertainty of the not yet known or not yet formed. The beginner's mind can also be seen as a gap in one's narrative, a window that allows the novelty of experience to come in. According to Morioka (2015) such a gap can be important for therapeutic change: 'We may say that the turning point in a personal narrative does not have a linear form. Paradoxically, it is the gap [. . .] in the language of linearity' (p. 88). The gap that is opened by not knowing increases contact with direct experience by reducing the tendency to impose knowledge on experience. As a result the self can be experienced as a process that is changing from moment to moment. Not knowing mind can also be seen as the door to the knowing body, which is the source of implicit positions and emotions. When explicit knowledge about one's self can be put aside, this helps to contact the implicit. New, innovative positions that are sources of new personal meanings can be accessed via the gap of 'not knowing mind'.

Procedure

Working in a present moment focused way we access *I*-positions by giving attention to the bodily affective experience. A person is invited to turn his attention internally, in a curious, 'not-knowing' way, trying to put aside what he already knows, as if entering a new continent, taking a receptive position by staying inside, and openly waiting for any feeling or sensation to arise. Emerging experiences can be differentiated by questions until they take a form that can be symbolized by a stone. *I*-positions can also be accessed via choosing stones that spontaneously attract attention. The variety of stones symbolizing positions are externalized and composed in the box of sand (or on paper). By placing every position in the box, a client gives it a place in the context of other *I*-positions. All *I*-positions can be further differentiated and explored in terms of the their qualities, focusing on (a) single *I*-positions, (b) their interrelations, (c) the pattern they form. The qualities of every emotional *I*-position can be further differentiated in terms of its emotion scheme (Greenberg, 2011). When a person is looking at his or her composition and experimenting with movement of positions this may evoke further experiences. New elements often appear and are added to the existing composition and a person can take a meta-position that encompasses a broader bandwidth of *I*-positions.

Case example

Miriam (pseudonym) suffers from lack of energy and motivation in her work. She has lost her enthusiasm and interest. During 11 sessions we practice Compositionwork in combination with two-chair work (Elliott et al., 2015). The trajectory also includes homework exercises (recorded by the therapist, Agnieszka Konopka), meant to increase Miriam's 'emotion awareness' and mindfulness. In order to present some relevant micro-processes specific for Compositionwork, here we focus on two sessions and then reflect on the process.

Compositionwork session 3

The client makes a composition starting from her direct bodily experience. I ask her to slow down and turn her attention inside to focus on the feelings that emerge in the inner areas of her body.

In the first phase of the session the following parts are emerging: (1) '*frozen rock*', a heavy feeling in the belly, represented by a big dark stone; (2) '*peaceful warmth*' in her chest, represented by a pink stone; (3) a small vivid warm feeling in the belly represented by a small red stone, defined later as '*my life power*'; (4) a '*cool, fresh feeling*' represented by blue and yellow stones (see Figure 13.1). After all those parts have emerged, her attention goes to the *frozen rock*. It appears to be 'almost frozen, no emotion inside'. Under the *frozen rock* is blocked a small red stone (*life energy*). When she sees it she feels a tension inside and an impulse to remove the frozen rock. There is a lively energy in the red stone that wants to expand. I ask her what it needs to expand. She indicates that something needs to happen with the *frozen rock*. I invite her to give it attention. She describes it as 'dense and complex'. It contains many 'not naturally glued together parts'. The parts need to be disconnected: 'There needs to be more space between them, so this little red can come up'. In order to differentiate the parts of the stone we explore which part of the stone needs attention first. It appears to be the lowest part of the *frozen rock*, the '*bedrock*'. It is the 'oldest part' and it needs warmth. It is possible to give this warmth from: the *peaceful warmth* stone. We focus on warming the *bedrock* stone with the help of the *peaceful warmth* stone. In this process the *bedrock* is changing: disconnecting from the *frozen rock* and moves to the left. Here we can see that a compassionate interaction between two *I*-positions can change an *I*-position and stimulate a new movement in the composition. While looking at this composition a new feeling is evoked. The *bedrock* is now felt as warmer and more

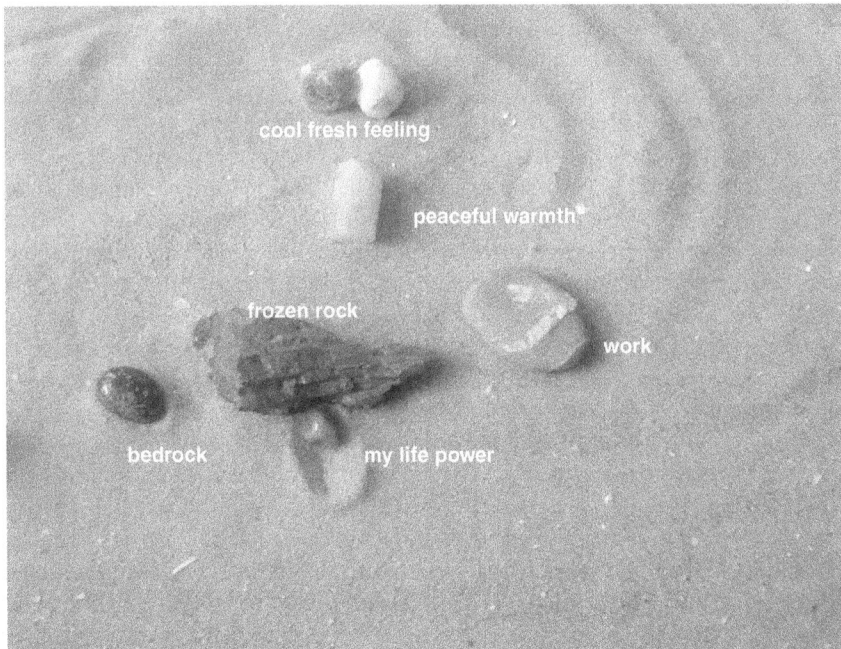

Figure 13.1 Compositionwork session 3

restful. The *frozen rock* needs to be warmed slowly, piece by piece. In order to work with such metaphors we need to be sure that a person has access to a position. Giving attention to bodily sensations helps to check and facilitate access to a position from direct experience. A person also needs to be able to stay involved in the metaphor as if it were real, which was possible in this case.

Further, I ask her what the *bedrock* is about. An image that relates to the sickness of her father appears, when she had to take care for him, not receiving any support. The need of support is still there, in her present situation. She is moved realizing this. I validate the pain that is related to this unmet need and we explore it further, which leads to the insight that she also needs self-support and care and to become milder towards herself. This mildness is accessible in the *peaceful warmth* position.

Slowly the *frozen rock* becomes differentiated, developing into a small composition in itself. The upper part of the frozen rock still needs attention. It is as if it is glued on the main body of the *frozen rock*. It is rather new and is not very hard. I check if it still resonates in her body and she indicates an uncomfortable feeling in her belly related to it. There is some plasticity in it, but it feels 'not mine'. Miriam's work feels like this stone. She feels tiredness related to this stone (*work* stone), which tells her that she is going against her needs doing things for others and not for herself. (The demanding voice is addressed later and included in a two-chair dialogue in the fifth session. In Compositionwork an inner conflict can be made explicit and differentiated. A person deepens the embodied awareness of the split and learns to take a working distance to it. A two-chair dialogue can be a necessary continuation of this process to transform the relation between two conflicted *I*-positions).

She feels self-alienation looking at her *work* stone, expressed as 'it is not me'. 'My work is not really mine', she says. It is opposite to the *peaceful warmth* stone that relates to a feeling of 'being me and just me'. There is a genuine feeling, warmth, and aliveness in this stone. She needs to nurture and follow this feeling. We explore how to do this: 'By feeling it, by feeling what I need here ... giving it attention'. It seems to be an adaptive feeling that includes the very important need of self-care and creativity. The voice given to the stone says: 'I would like to make music, to be creative again'. There is a strong, creative impulse in this pink stone. Since it seems to be a promoter position (a position that has the capacity to organize other positions of the repertoire and is even able to generate new ones; Hermans & Hermans-Konopka, 2010). I try to acknowledge and support this position in her. Miriam comes for the eleventh session after having made the decision to stop with her current job. The composition includes the following positions: *my life/power, gradual action, creative, my new place, I as compassionate, I as weak* and *I as dynamic* (see Figure 13.2). Her decision relates to a feeling of a relief, regaining her life and energy. This position, called *my life/power*, is represented by a big red stone. She feels strong in her upper body, her arms also feel strong and she has a feeling that she can use them to shape her life. The red energy of *my life/power* radiates to her arms. It is the same energy that she felt before (see Figure 13.1, *my life power*) but then it was

Figure 13.2 Compositionwork, session 11

smaller and blocked by the *frozen rock*. Now it is stronger and makes her feel stronger. This energy wants to move to the world, gradually ... (*gradual action* stone). She needs to feel the movement of this energy, but not press it. She does not want to be in the old position when she was pressing herself. She sees two colours in the *gradual action* stone: a yellow/orange tone, which is related to nurturing herself, being soft and a red one related to a need for action. She wants to get a new job, but do it in a way that is soft to herself. 'Now I need time to find *my new place* (...) It is not yet clear what this place is, but what I feel is that I can act from what *I want*, not automatically'. This evokes a feeling of peace. She realizes that she was used to doing things as expected by others. Now she wants to 'give myself space to feel what I want for myself'. The *life/power* position is related to her growing agency, in contrast with her earlier reactive way of approaching life. The symbol of an egg of *life/power* relates to a perspective of new life. She places the stone deeper in the sand. This move-ment evokes a feeling of peace, symbolized by the sand. *Life/power* needs to be grounded, it needs to feel more support of her body. We explore which parts of her body need attention. The feeling in her belly is like a soft material. It is weak, has no resistance and can easily be pushed (*I as weak*). She places a white stone to represent *I as weak* and feels tenderness. *I as weak* needs care.

She is able to relate to it from her *compassionate* position represented by a yellow stone. *I as weak* has something to do with food: 'I was not eating good enough. I need a good diet, sports'. She is contrasting two positions towards herself: 'Some time ago I did not care, but now I am much more *compassionate* with myself: it is like the sun'.

The *life/power* position also needs something that is symbolized by a lazur stone. It turns to be her *creative/social* side. 'It also has been neglected in my life, so it was not able to grow', she comments. When she is looking at it she feels a soft energy in her chest. It is about the possibility of learning something new that expresses her creativity, 'living my creativity and connecting with others'. She would like to make a new study to nurture this side.

Reflections on the process

Various *I*-positions emerge from direct experience in different areas of the client's body. Using stones as symbols for these emerging positions helps to carry the process further. Looking at the composition easily evokes new feelings, which, if attended to, often facilitate the process. Externalized *I*-positions become further differentiated by giving them attention, exploring their qualities and feelings and the needs related to them. Such differentiation creates a more sophisticated internal map of inner multiplicity. Differentiation of an initial *I*-position can lead to the reorganization of a composition, e.g. when the *frozen rock* became differentiated, the *life energy* stone was able to change position for a more suitable place. In Compositionwork work one *I*-position is easily related to the broader context of the other positions, since they are com-posed in one space.

Differentiation between an impulse *towards* a position and an impulse/need *enclosed* in this position helps to change the relation with this position (e.g. from rejection to compassion towards the *frozen rock*). As a consequence the organization of the self becomes more democratic (Hermans, 2018). Focusing on differences among stones in the composition the client becomes aware of contrasts between her own *I*-positions. By attending to the feelings and needs enclosed in the various, spatially distinguished positions the client develops a new, more compassionate relation with herself, which may act as a promoter position (Hermans & Hermans-Konopka, 2010).

The *life/power* position has a promoter function, being a source of many adaptive needs, which were attended to in the therapy. *My life/power* is like a gravity point in her self where she could become anchored and feel her needs, neglected in the earlier period of her life. Some adaptive needs are more easily accessed by symbolization via a stone, before they are ready to be named. In this way a stone became a bridge between not yet verbalized experience and its verbal meaning.

Change in the organization of the self is also facilitated by attending to relations and space between different internal *I*-positions and experimenting with movement of stones (e.g. *my life energy* wants to meet the *peaceful warmth* so that they could merge together as one strong river).

The composition vividly reflects the qualities of different positions and their dynamic relations, e.g. the coalition between *I as dynamic* and *I as compassionate* in session 11. It facilitates the possibility to work directly on the relations between *I*-positions (e.g. one position can symbolically care for the other).

A change in the pattern of the composition can be observed that reflects the change in the organization of the self. The last composition is more centred, which suggests that a centripetal movement in the self has become stronger (Hermans & Hermans-Konopka, 2010). While the composition from session 3 showed more conflicts (e.g. between *life/strength* and *work*), the last composition shows coalitions between many positions (e.g. *life/power* and *new place*).

Conclusion

People develop themselves in a dynamic movement between openness to experience and its co-creation. Receptivity and creativity are sources of change and growth that often need to be restored and enhanced in the process of therapy. Compositionwork typically invites receptivity to the inner process, needed for the discovery of experience; on the other hand it stimulates creativity inviting the client to be 'a composer', who has an agentic role in giving form to his own self. Enhancing receptive openness to embodied experience facilitates the emergence and accessibility of a broad bandwidth of *I*-positions. Some positions, which are not yet verbalized or restricted by a dominant narrative, can be accessed via embodied experience and be expressed in nonverbal forms. Compositionwork is a dialogical process of unfolding and composing one's inner landscape. It helps to access, experience, and relate to the complexity of the inner world by spatial and symbolic differentiation of *I*-positions, bringing them in relation and placing them in an artistic encompassing gestalt. Compositionwork helps to get an overview of the complex relational field of the society of mind and differentiate it.

Creation of new meaning takes place in a process of com-posing. It results from relating to the multiplicity of internal and external *I*-positions and bringing them into a dialogue. The relational and complex field of the dialogical self, the landscape of mind – which is not easily depicted in linear speech – can become more accessible in a pictorial form where *I*-positions are juxtaposed, simultaneously seen and placed in the context of its broader *I*-position repertoire (Hermans, 2003).

Compositionwork can be a complementary method to more verbal and linear methods of work with the dialogical self. It can easily be combined with, or be a preparation for other methods and interventions focused on work with the multiplicity of self, like e.g. one- or two-chair work (Elliott et al., 2015) or the more verbally oriented personal position repertoire (Hermans, 2003).

Note

1 Italic text within square brackets in this and later dialogues in this chapter are spoken by the therapist.

References

Anderson, H., & Goolishian, H. (1992). The client is the expert: A not-knowing approach to therapy. In S. McNamee & K. J. Gergen (Eds.), *Therapy as social construction* (pp. 25–39). London: Sage.

Berthier, F., & Parkes, G. (2000). *Reading Zen in the rocks: The Japanese dry landscape garden*. Chicago, IL: University of Chicago Press.

Deikman, A. J. (1982). *The observing self: Mysticism and psychotherapy*. Boston, MA: Beacon Press.

Elliott, R., Watson, J. C., Goldman, R. N., & Greenberg, L. S. (2015). *Learning emotion-focused therapy: The process-experiential approach to change*. Washington, DC: American Psychological Association.

Gendlin, E. T. (2012). *Focusing-oriented psychotherapy: A manual of the experiential method*. New York: Guilford Press.

Gonçalves, M. M., Matos, M., & Santos, A. (2009). Narrative therapies and the nature of 'unique outcomes' in the construction of change. *Journal of Constructivist Psychology, 22*, 1–23.

Greenberg, L. S. (2004). *Emotion-focused therapy: Coaching clients to work through their feelings*. Washington, DC: American Psychological Association.

Greenberg, L. S. (2011). *Emotion-focused therapy*. Washington, DC: American Psychological Association.

Hannah, B. (1997). *Jung: His life and work*. Wilmette, IL: Chiron.

Hayes, S. C., Strosahl, K. D., & Wilson, K. G. (2012). *Acceptance and commitment therapy: The process and practice of mindful change* (2nd ed.). New York: Guilford Press.

Hermans, H. J. M. (2001). The construction of a personal position repertoire: Method and practice. *Culture & Psychology* [Special Issue: Culture and the Dialogical Self: Theory, Method and Practice], *7*(3), 323–365.

Hermans, H. J. M. (2002). The dialogical self as a society of mind introduction. *Theory & Psychology, 12*(2), 147–160.

Hermans, H. J. M. (2003). The construction and reconstruction of a dialogical self. *Journal of constructivist psychology, 16*(2), 89–130.

Hermans, H. J. M. (2014). Self as a society of *I*-positions: A dialogical approach to counseling. *Journal of Humanistic Counseling, 53*(2), 134–159.

Hermans, H. J. M. (2018). *Society in the self: A theory of identity in democracy*. New York: Oxford University Press.

Hermans, H. J. M., & Hermans-Konopka, A. (2010). *Dialogical self theory: Positioning and counter-positioning in a globalizing society*. Cambridge, UK: Cambridge University Press.

Jaffé, A., & Jung, C. G. (1964). *Man and his symbols*. New York: Dell.

Kabat-Zinn, J. (2003). Mindfulness-based interventions in context: Past, present, and future. *Clinical Psychology: Science and Practice, 10*(2), 144–156.

Konopka, A., Neimeyer, R. A., & Jacobs-Lentz, J. (2017). Composing the self: Toward the dialogical reconstruction of self-identity. *Journal of Constructivist Psychology*, 1–13.

Konopka, A., & Van Beers, W. (2014). Compositionwork: A method for self-investigation. *Journal of Constructivist Psychology, 27*(3), 194–210.

Leijssen, M. (1998). Focusing microprocesses. In L. S. Greenberg, J. C. Watson, & G. Lietaer (Eds.), *Handbook of experiential psychotherapy* (pp. 121–154). New York: Guilford Press.

Mamberg, M. H., & Bassarear, T. (2015). From reified self to being mindful: A dialogical analysis of the MBSR voice. *International Journal for Dialogical Science, 9*(1), 11–37.

Morioka, M. (2012). Creating dialogical space in psychotherapy: Meaning-generating chronotope of ma. In H. J. M. Hermans & T. Gieser (Eds.), *Handbook of dialogical self theory* (pp. 390–404). Cambridge, UK: Cambridge University Press.

Morioka, M. (2015). How to create ma – The living pause – In the landscape of the mind: The wisdom of Noh theatre. *International Journal for Dialogical Science, 9*, 81–95.

Neimeyer, R. A. (2009). *Constructivist psychotherapy: Distinctive features.* New York: Routledge.

Neimeyer, R. A. (2010). Reconstructing the continuing bond: A constructivist approach to grief therapy. In J. D. Raskin, S. K. Bridges, & R. A. Neimeyer (Eds.), *Studies in meaning 4: Constructivist perspectives on theory, practice and social justice.* New York: Pace University Press.

Neimeyer, R. A. (2012). *Techniques of grief therapy: Creative practices for counseling the bereaved.* New York: Routledge.

Perls, F., Hefferline, G., & Goodman, P. (1951). *Gestalt therapy.* New York: Souvenir Press.

Shapiro, S. L., Carlson, L. E., Astin, J. A., & Freedman, B. (2006). Mechanisms of mindfulness. *Journal of clinical psychology, 62*(3), 373–386.

Stern, D. N. (2004). *The present moment in psychotherapy and everyday life* (Norton series on interpersonal neurobiology). New York: W.W. Norton & Company.

Suzuki, S. (2010). *Zen mind, beginner's mind.* Boston, MA: Shambhala Publications.

White, M. (1993). Deconstruction and therapy. In S. Gilligan & R. Price (Eds.), *Therapeutic conversations* (pp. 22–61). New York: W.W. Norton & Company.

14 On the constitution of self-experience in the psychotherapeutic dialogue

Masayoshi Morioka

This chapter examines the dynamic movements intrinsic to self-experience in a therapeutic conversation from the perspective of Dialogical Self Theory (DST). To illustrate this theme, the author presents a clinical vignette of a severely traumatized female client. This client had encountered a very serious life event but remained able to talk about it, creating meaning, and integrating it into a narrative.

The constitution of self-experience in the client's narrative may be described in terms of *I*-positions in DST. This process of appropriation creates unity and continuity in a self that is spatially and temporally distributed in which the "I" participates in the process of positioning and repositioning (Hermans & Hermans-Konopka, 2010, p. 139). The therapeutic meaning is also generated through the dynamism between positioning and repositioning in the spatial nature of the self (landscape of mind).

Self-experience is temporal, as expressed in narrative accounts (Bruner, 1990). Individuals try to connect one event to another in the act of creating meaning and may reconstruct their meanings, collaborating with their therapist. Self-experience in the therapeutic context is also marked by the characteristic of its space. The psychotherapist pays attention to create a free and safe dialogical space, which is called "*ma*" (Morioka, 2015). The unique Japanese word *ma* has multiple meanings. It can indicate a space between two things or a space between one moment and another. *Ma* is a concept that includes both time and space. The word *ma* is also used to describe the quality of interpersonal relationships. The process of talking and listening creates unique *ma* between persons.

I have introduced the Japanese cultural concept of *ma* to explain the characteristics of therapeutically shared space (Morioka, 2012). Concerning the context of psychotherapy, I argue that the in-between *ma* not only refers to a person's relationship with an individual but is also concerned with the distance from voice to voice in an internal dialogue. When one remains in an internal dialogue, a distance is created between the narrating and the narrated self in one's internal world. This distance can also be called *ma*. Therefore, *ma* is generated in both internal and external relationships, in taking a pause, maintaining silence, and experiencing a deepened chronotope (time-space). As Hermans and Hermans Konopka (2010, p. 294) put it, "Silence, too, giving space for inner recapitulation, rehearsal, and imagination, is a facilitating factor in dialogical relationships." The silence that gives this space can be called *ma*. *Ma* is to be understood as the shared reality of an intersubjective sphere.

A therapeutic meaning may be generated through semiotic activity in this space. Chronotope literally means "time-space." Bakhtin (1981, pp. 84–85) defines it as the intrinsic connectedness of spatial and temporal relationships that are artistically expressed in literature. The temporal and spatial determinants are inseparable and always colored by emotions and values. The chronotope expresses this inseparability of space and time. A narrative is closely integrated into a unique "spatial-temporal" frame (the chronotope) that plays a key role in the production of meaning and sense. The chronotope organizes and binds the ongoing dialogues that make a movement of meaning.

Basic concepts from DST for the dialogical constitution of the self

DST is suitable for researching multiplicity of the self and their dynamic relationship as it appears in the process of psychotherapy (Dimaggio, 2012; Gonçalves & Ribeiro, 2012; Rowan, 2012). It is particularly prominent in visibly drawing the deepening process of the therapeutic reflection by the dynamic multiplicity of *I*-positions.

From the DST perspective, the dialogical conception of the self is based on the existence of differences, multiplicity, and discontinuity (Hermans & Hermans-Konopka, 2010). These characteristics are expressed in the following four concepts (p. 191).

(i) *I-position*: The unity and continuity brought into the self are dependent on the capacity of the self to assign positions. As positioned in time and space, the self is multiple and changing. The unity and continuity within the self are created amid multiplicity.

(ii) *Meta-position*: The "I" can leave specific positions and move to a meta-perspective from which the specific positions can be observed from the outside as an act of self-reflection.

(iii) *Coalition of positions*: Positions do not work in isolation. As in a society, they can cooperate and support each other, thereby creating strong forces of the self that may dominate the others.

(iv) *Third position*: A conflict between two positions can be reconciled by creating a third position that has the potential of unifying the two original ones without denying or removing their differences.

From this perspective, a psychological problem may be considered the result of fragmentation between the *I*-positions and/or structural dominance of one *I*-position over others. "The 'natural' process of positioning and repositioning assumes a movement from one position to another as a dynamic feature of life" (Hermans & Hermans-Konopka, 2010, p. 197). Yet, most of all, the clients are supposed to have some experiences of "stress, which is particularly felt when the person is actually located in one position but feels that he should be in another one" (p. 197). In an extreme case, it is supposed that any specific position is experienced as limiting or blocking for a client. Hermans and Hermans-Konopka (2010) call such a situation "*I*-prison."

The landscape of mind is a metaphor that pictures the self as a spatially organized multiplicity of *I*-positions involved in mutual interchange. The spatial metaphor invites one to think about processes that are happening in the self simultaneously rather than sequentially. *I*-positions are not only *horizontally* (e.g., opposed to each other) but also *vertically* organized; the positions on the surface can be influenced by deeper, not immediately accessible positions that may be, for example, sources of resistance and need to be addressed in the process of psychotherapy (see Gonçalves, Konopka, & Hermans, Chapter 1 this volume).

Raggatt (2010) indicates that "reality is constructed between the participants in a conversation, in a space that is empty that, in a way, waits to be filled with new words" (p. 1). One's experience is structured like a conversation. How, then, is the self-experience structured as a conversation? One of the distinctive features of the conversation is the temporal-space matrix, the chronotope where the dynamism of decentering and centrifugal force is generated through the turn-taking movement of speech. For Hermans (2004, p. 13), the "notion of the 'dialogical self' considers the self as a multiplicity of parts (voices, characters, positions) that have the potential of entertaining dialogical relationships with each other." The same multiplicity is often referred to as a chronotopically organized "position repertoire" (Hermans, 2001, p. 350).

From the viewpoint of DST, clients' narratives concern the dialogues between the characters in the narrative. In the dialogue of the *I*-positions, each narrative organizes a vector of experience along a temporal horizon that spans the past, present, and possible realms whereby the corresponding *I*-position gains its positioning relative to the other positions. This narrative organizing process can be said to be a dialogical constitution of self-experience.

Movable *I*-positions

The transformation of self-experience along with the client's narrative may be described in terms of *I*-positions. A short review on the theory of *I*-positions is first necessary. Each *I*-position creates a voice that relates to other voices (of other *I*-positions) in a dynamic relation to dialogue. Each position is given a voice. From a Bakhtinian perspective, we can say that a word has many voices in a dialogical situation (Bakhtin, 1981). We can hear different voices in a word. One's speech occurs when being in contact with the other. Conceptualizing the self as a dynamic interplay among voiced positions opens a range of possibilities for recognizing individual and situational differences (Hermans, 1996). The voices of the particular *I*-positions "function like interacting actors in a story" and each voice "has a story to tell about experiences from its own stance" (Hermans, 2004, p. 19). Each voice must be taken care of in the therapeutic dialogue (Morioka, 2012). Various other voices may be latent in the client's silence. It is fundamental to therapeutic progress to voice suppressed aspects of the self.

Unity and integration can also be realized by the construction of a *third position*. Hermans and Hermans-Konopka (2010) indicate that, when there is a conflict between two positions in the self, this can be reconciled by the creation of a *third position*. The third position has the potential to articulate the two originals without denying or removing their differences. This dynamic movement between positions creates a dialogical space where a *third position* can be activated.

Positions have contextual character (Hermans, 2001), which means that, at different times, varied contexts and distinct positions come to the fore and to different degrees. In one relationship, a person can easily position him or herself as playful, while in another relationship, he or she is more controlled or anxious. People are different versions of themselves in different relationships. The quality of their relationships determines the functioning and organization of the *I*-positions and vice-versa. The contextual nature and bandwidth of *I*-positions are supposed to be basic dynamic concepts for explaining how the therapeutic change can be generated. Considering the points mentioned above, we will examine them in a case vignette.

Case vignette

Ms. A is a woman in her early forties and a former company employee, currently unemployed. The referring therapist told me that she was recovering from two severe traumas.

Around one year before our first appointment, she had a car accident. Ms. A was driving when a large truck struck her. The truck driver had fallen asleep. Ms. A's car had been demolished. Miraculously, she had survived. She lost the ability to grip with her right hand due to paralysis. A lawsuit related to the accident was pending. After the accident, Ms. A developed agoraphobia, became wary of people, and was unable to concentrate at work. She tended to stay shut up in her home.

Ms. A had divorced 11 years previously. Her husband had been abusive. Physical violence had begun soon after they got married, 25 years ago. From this marriage, she had a daughter now in her early twenties and a son who had drowned six years ago at the age of 18. The death had been treated as a suicide, although Ms. A questioned that conclusion. Ms. A suggested that her son's girlfriend was involved in the incident.

Both of Ms. A's parents were still living. Ms. A had a negative image of her mother. She reported about her mother: "She's someone with no interest in her children."

Period 1

During her initial sessions, Ms. A spoke about not feeling alive, feeling not understood, helplessness, and forgetfulness. In a detached way, she lamented,

> Even if I try to convey to others the state I am in, they don't seem to be able to understand my feelings. I seem to appear very courageous and strong to

people. On the other hand, I feel I get stuck listening to how other people are doing. When I am with others, I just passively go along with whatever they say. (...) When I get home, I become a different person. I do a 180-degree turn and return to my useless, unable-to-do-anything self. I am horribly forgetful.

In this way, she noticed and described different positions in herself.

Ms. A expressed intense dominant feelings of guilt, clearly reported self-blame, and anxiety related to the death of her son. She was able to talk about her feelings of guilt; however, the way of expressing her emotions was restricted. She said,

> After my son died, I visited his grave every day. I thought I might try to continue to do that for a thousand days. I blame myself, thinking that this is my fault for having gotten married. What could I do so he would forgive me? I did visit the grave for a thousand days, but no forgiveness came. I lie on my futon at night not letting myself fall asleep. I flop over and lie on the tatami floor. I've fallen into the habit of moving around in order to stay awake. The day my son died, I happened to have had a sound sleep. I learned that unlucky things happen when you feel good and let your guard down.

On the seventh anniversary of her son's death, she did nothing. She said about the death of her son,

> It made my brain cells harden. Even though my son is dead, I think that I shouldn't enjoy things or be cheerful. It's different from if he had died from a disease. I still don't try to look squarely at the reality. I keep reality at bay by trying to keep myself busy.

She was clearly dominated by feelings of anxiety and had developed an unsecure sense of self. She thought that, if she started to feel secure, something terrible was bound to happen. She was on the watch all the time. "Security doesn't last; something always happens!" Her son's accident happened just after he succeeded in getting a new job, which supported her belief that she should not relax even in a positive situation: "As soon as you relax, you can be sure that the next misfortune or something wrong is going to happen." She reported that many things belonging to her son were left as they were before the accident and that the past and the future had become disconnected. She herself felt not alive anymore. "I haven't been alive since that time. I only live for today and now. The past and the future don't connect. Even just hearing my son's name makes me freeze up."

Period 2

Over the course of about ten sessions, Ms. A had gradually begun to talk about her family of origin. In parallel, we began to focus on the constraints she imposed on herself and her position in the family.

Ms. A felt that life had been unfair to her compared to her younger sister: "I feel totally inferior to my sister." Even though she was wild and irresponsible in high school, she married someone who works for the government and has a comfortable life. "I've kept myself under control and stayed out of trouble. I always obey my mother. In spite of that, nothing good has come of it!" She talked about two different opposite positions in herself. Ms. A thought about herself as having, on the one hand, a "resilient me" and, on the other, a "pathetic me." She said,

> I tried to show myself a better image than the actual self. There are two people in my mind: one is amicable and overly adaptive in company; the other is weak and does not wish to live. I have two versions of me: one who walks around actively and one who stops because of anxiety about anything.

Ms. A began to explain.

> The "weak me" can never be shown to anyone. There is a me who can't say "it hurts!" That's been with me for a long time and is at the root of my relationship with my mother. My mother left me with my grandmother around the time I was six months old and came alone to city X. She visited my father more than she visited her children. She is a person without "motherliness." My father is also unreliable.

During another session, Ms. A said, "But I guess my fluctuation is affected by my mother's constraint. I feel a strong constraint from my mother." She gradually came to express natural affect such as anger. I asked how she usually expressed herself when she became angry. She said that nobody knew she was so angry. I asked, "Now then, . . . from whom does your feeling of anger stem?" Ms. A talked about an episode in which her mother had tried to prevent her divorce because she was afraid about decency, despite Ms. A's suffering.

Ms. A spoke graphically about her marriage and abuse by her husband:

> He went so far as to strangle me. I couldn't even tell my mother about that abuse. On the contrary, she stopped me from divorcing. In front of others, my ex-husband was a serious-minded person. He puts on a good face. His family, too, blames me rather than him, saying I "have a way with words." Anyway, I am made out to be the bad one. I separated from my husband, and the three of us lived more or less peacefully for the next six years until my son graduated from high school.

She came back to the issue of her son's accident and reported disorientation, telling me that she didn't know how to "become a mother like any other who has lost a son." She repeatedly spoke about the girlfriend who was with her son until just before his sudden accident. She spoke about her with anger and feelings of unfairness.

> I wonder why my son got stuck on a girl like that. I feel it had to do with our marriage problems. The police viewed the reason for his drowning as suicide, but the girl got her friends to tell a story that was more favorable to her.

Her anxiety and insecurity related to the death of her son showed up again and was also expressed by the irrational belief, "Do not drop your guard. Never be satisfied when you are well."

Period 3

Afterward, as Ms. A talked during the sessions, her image of her family gradually changed. In particular, when she thought about the place of her birth and where she was raised, her attachment to her grandfather came back to life. Ms. A began to talk about her grandfather as if he were next to her.

> City Y is not my hometown, but it is the city where my grandfather was. He was kind to me. He had been adopted through marriage into my grandmother's family, and, at the time, her family was living in the house. Our days passed trouble free. He was the kind of person who spent money on neighborhood rituals like washing away evil spirits. Grandpa grew a lot of figs and gave me some every year!

One impression that remained from those stories was that her grandfather had taught her the proper way to visit a grave.

After approximately 20 sessions, she spoke again about her feelings toward her mother: "My mother wouldn't do anything for me. She gave good meat to my sister, and I was told to do without. I couldn't ask for anything!" When I asked her what happened if she asked for something, she was silent and then tearfully replied,

> The child inside me is stifling the voice that wants to scream. To compensate, I've created a parent/guardian inside me on my own. So that's why, in reverse, other people want me to take care of them like a parent! Speaking like this, various things have become clear to me. In my childhood, I think I was more good-natured. In classes and in sports, I was above average. I was probably an easy child. Compared to not wanting to lose to anyone, I don't want to lose to myself.

As a result of our work, Ms. A now can say that she can recognize herself. After the sessions ended, she would make contact occasionally, and, being busy with her daughter's wedding and other things, it seemed she had been able to get her life back. She enrolled in a distance-learning course to become qualified in social welfare.

Analysis of the case

Recovery of the reflexive space for dominant–subdominant voices

First, we attempt to review the process of the treatment. In the initial sessions, the event that precipitated Ms. A's seeking treatment was her inability to recover from a traffic accident. Chronologically, her son's death had happened much earlier, but that event was not yet "in the past" for her. It appeared that the event had not yet been positioned in Ms. A's life narrative. Here, rather than understanding Ms. A's symptoms from the point of view of trauma, I took care to accompany her in the way she was constructing her world and trying hard to manage difficult circumstances.

In the first period of therapy, Ms. A spoke about not feeling alive, what seems to be related to a loss of the sense of temporality. "I haven't been alive since that time. I only live for today and now. The past and the future don't connect." She said that, even six years later, she hadn't recovered.

The focus of the psychotherapy was to accept the experience of injury and suffering and to recover her sense of agency. Looking from the dialogical self perspective, it may be a question of how she can contact and position the suffering self. To realize it, it is necessary to organize and connect the different positions in the self. The self is structured based on hierarchically organized voices (dominant–subdominant relation) together with the need for dialogical interactions between those voices. The self needs to create a multi-voiced structure by interacting with an organized or disorganized living world. The subject undertakes this project through re-experiencing the narratives about the self as a central topic of the conversation. In the therapeutic situation, the therapist remains receptive when the different positions of the self begin to talk and enter into a dialogue with one another. The therapist makes an effort to receive the expression of the client's authentic sense of self at any given moment.

It seems that, during period 1, Ms. A was developing and imposing constraining rules on herself. She could not distance from her dominant positions that were the sources of her negative relation with herself (e.g. self-blame). A reflexive space was generated in the therapeutic situation. She could reflect on the dominance–subdominance dynamism of such restricting voices as: "Security doesn't last; something always happens" or "I do not have a future," which included dominance of positions. Here, it may be helpful to deepen the characteristics of the reflexive space by taking a detour and investigating the Japanese concept *ma* (Morioka, 2012). *Ma* can be recovered by the coherent exchange between the participants in a natural conversation. Intrinsically, the conversation is the temporal-space matrix, the chronotope where the dynamism of decentering and centrifugal force is generated through the turn-taking movement of speech. The potential chronotope facilitates internal self-to-self dialogue (Morioka, 2008). In the psychotherapeutic process, participants open a space in which they may create something new. There is a movement in which the self's will is de-occupied and shifts into intermediation in the intervening space. This area guides our conversation. That is *ma* within the dialogical conversation.

One aspect of emergence of *ma* in the therapeutic conversation is concerned with the dialogical space between positions created and enhanced. In period 3, Ms. A's image of her family gradually changed, especially when she talked about her grandfather. She behaved as if she was really talking with her grandfather, entering a dialogical space with him in the counseling room. The character of significant other appeared in the "here and now" of the session.

The second aspect of *ma* is a moment between one action and the next. For example, in period 3, at the moment she spoke again about her feelings toward her mother, I asked her, "What happened if you asked for something (to you mother)?" She was silent and then tearfully replied—this is *ma*, a pause or a moment between one action and the next.

Remembering in I-positioning

Remembering means both recalling and remembering or bringing people or things back together (Hedtke & Winslade, 2004; White, 2007). In the act of remembering, not only cognitively but also emotionally, in a shared space, Ms. A took quite an active role in bringing together the members of her world, whether living or dead, imaginary or real. From the point of view of *I*-positioning, it is suitable for the practice of remembering. We can take the process of remembering as an ongoing constant repositioning of *I*-positions.

The utterance of Ms. A in the session addressed many persons she remembered. She seemed to go through silent dialogues with them. It is indicated that figures close to her in her narrative became part of her own cohesive story—and this included her dead son. In an individual's narratives of his or her experiences, the grim disconnectedness between the living and the dead is temporarily set aside, because the living carry on. The living must adjust to how both the living and the dead are positioned within their stories.

A person matches his/her *I*-positions with external positions. Each person is spatially positioning him/herself in a characteristic way in the space of Ms. A's self. Depending on this multiplicity of addressees, the positional configuration in any utterance can be dynamic and movable. Once the living and the dead take form in Ms. A's internal world, each equally deals with *I*-positions. Each position is given a voice. These en-voiced positions take concrete figures and are enacted in the field of practice. The therapist accompanies the patient into the enactment of *I*-positions. Ms. A's experience was gradually structured by connecting the fragmented life events. The *I*-positions animate inner and outer dialogues that trigger the need for local self-narrative plots (Gonçalves & Ribeiro, 2012). The therapeutic process was gradual, enabling Ms. A to obtain enough distance from her life events, yet also connect with her feelings and experiences.

Her family image was steadily transformed. In Ms. A's case, several people appeared who she clearly recalled, including her abusive husband. Although her narrative was accompanied by complicated and negative emotions, it enabled her to improve her sense of self. Her dead son and family members appeared in her thoughts and feelings. She placed these figures in her stories in reference to herself. Her internal dialogue with them might have gradually transformed into an actual conversation with the therapist. She learned to feel real feelings in the process of dissolving her tension. Gradually, Ms. A grew warmer toward herself. In the internal conversation, a new narrative was generated.

In the second period of the session, she coherently talked about her comparison to her young sister and, later on, her marriage in which she was abused by her husband. These conversations were serious, working through her past events. The external positioning of family figures can be grasped in DST. Ms. A kept her dialogue with these external positions. In the last section of the second period, she tried to confront her concerns regarding her son's death. The confused and fragmented events in Ms. A's life were connected in the new narrative.

It can be seen that the *meta-positioning* was recovered in this period, which enabled her to distance herself from the stream of experiences. In parallel, we began to focus on the constraints she imposed on herself. Through our work, Ms. A was able to discover her own themes. In this way, the therapist takes the position of reworking the words of the other.

In the case of Ms. A, her mother's image had gradually changed in the therapeutic conversation from period 2 to 3. The therapist and Ms. A mutually elaborated the words of the response and mutually explored words that could regulate her negative affect derived from her interpersonal relationships. In period 2, Ms. A said, "But I guess my fluctuation is affected by my mother's uneasiness. I feel a strong constraint from my mother." I asked how she usually expressed herself when she became angry. She said that nobody knew she was so angry. When asked where her anger stemmed from, Ms. A remembered the story of her marriage.

In period 3, she spoke again about her feelings toward her mother. "My mother wouldn't do anything for me. She gave good meat to my sister, and I was told to do without it. I couldn't ask for anything!" When I asked her what would have happened if she asked for something, she was silent and then tearfully replied, "The child inside me is stifling the voice that wants to scream." In this instance, she could be aware of her self-structure. "I have created a parent/guardian inside me on my own. Therefore, in reverse, other people want me to take care of them like a parent!"

The awareness of one's sense of self emerges in a specific mode of relationship and in a particular context of conversation. The client can recover her subjective appropriation through co-experience in which her sense of agency is supported. This is a typical possibility of taking a *meta-position* that permits an overview of diverse other positions. Hermans and Hermans-Konopka (2010) explain that a meta-position has several specific qualities:

a) It provides an overarching view of several positions.
b) It enables participants to link the positions as part of their personal history.
c) It helps people find a direction of change.

The diverse *I*-positions play roles in the story, appearing in characters. Each *I*-position formed and articulated within the dialogical self is ruled by a *coalition of positions*. The possibility of engaging in the therapeutic dialogue may be a significant movement. With the help of this *coalition of positions*, Ms. A. recovered her lost voice and addressed her mother. Ms. A said, "The child inside me is stifling the voice that wants to scream." The last part of the third period of the session seems to be the core moment of the therapeutic dialogue. It might open an insight into herself. At this moment, Ms. A's repressed voice of her internal *I*-position got a new link to the external *I*-position of her mother and that of her young sister. She had awareness because, to compensate, she had created a parent/guardian inside her on her own because she expressed that "that is why other people want me to take care of them like a parent."

This can be reconciled by the creation of *a third position*. At period 2 in the internal conversation as a self-talk between I and me, Ms. A could create another person in her mind that served as a double for her. Ms. A said, "But I guess my fluctuation is affected by my mother's constraint. I feel strong constraint from my mother." She gradually came to express natural affect such as anger. This dynamic movement between positions creates a dialogical space where a third position can be activated. In the third position, she could really feel her anger as her own. This experience lays the groundwork for warm and full acceptance of oneself.

Recreate self-experiencing

It was characteristic of the experience of self in Ms. A to be disturbed by others. Internal *I*-positions of Ms. A were easy to reverse into the opposite position. Ms. A had opposite *I*-positions—on the one hand, a "resilient me" and, on the other, a "pathetic me." She said the weak me could never be shown to anyone and that there was a "me" who could not say "it hurts."

For the first period of the session, she said, "I seem to appear very courageous and strong to people" and "When I am with others, I just passively go along with whatever they say." There is supposed to be no dialogical exchange between opposite *I*-positions in the self of Ms. A. The remembered facts and events were fragmented and without plot, lacking temporality. Ms. A said, "I haven't been alive since that time. I only live for today and now. The past and the future don't connect." She could not experience the natural passage of time since her son's accident.

Ms. A had severed her emotional connection to the past. First, she lost any commitment to interlinked contexts and situations of previous events. She was disentangled and alienated from her personal having-been. This alienation from one's own past is typical with severely traumatized clients. Usually, they lose the ability to self-narrate. Facts and events told of her past were fragmented. They were meaningless in her life. It was necessary to recover temporalized narrative through which she could recreate her sense of coherence of life. But how?

The course of psychotherapy involves moving from a limited inner space (I-*prison*: Hermans & Hermans-Konopka, 2010) towards a living, open, and varied landscape of mind. The therapist gradually throughout the sessions focused on the emotional experiences associated with her relevant life events. There were gaps and disconnects in the memories and continuity of Ms. A's life history. As if to fill in those gaps, she continued to blame herself for her son's sudden death. After her son had died, she imposed on herself a thousand daily visits to his grave. This stemmed from a feeling of guilt and the necessity to compensate for her son's death. Despite her efforts, no forgiveness came. She was exactly constricted in the I-*prison*.

In period 3, when the therapist asked Ms. A what happened if she asked her mother for something, she was silent and then tearfully replied, "The child inside me is stifling the voice that wants to scream." In this instance, the internal position of her child obtained an emotional voice. The therapist tried to focus on the counter-emotion. After deep silence, Ms. A spoke: "To compensate, I've created a parent/guardian inside me on my own. So that's why, in reverse, other people want me to take care of them like a parent."

An emotional counter-position—in combination with a meta-position (closely related to taking a reasonable position)—will be an especially powerful tool changing dominant emotions. When the dominating emotion has a particular perspective, the counter-emotion has a different perspective. A dialogical relationship between emotions implies that different emotions have something to tell and can send out different messages to the self and to each other. In the space of the dialogical self, where the individual generates awareness of his/her own life history in the context of emotions, the individual can recreate the self-experience.

When one creates self-narratives for one's own experiences, a significant distance will appear between the different voices of the self. Telling a story in the therapy session is a way of yielding to maintain distance from the inner disturbance (Rennie, 1992). For example, in the first period of the session, there were two voices that indicated a negative relation to herself. Ms. A. held in her mind such two voices repetitively. One was "Even though my son is dead, I think that I shouldn't enjoy things or be cheerful." The other was "As soon as you relax, you can be sure that the next misfortune or something wrong is going to happen." The second voice seems to be a position that frightens her. Keeping a distance from these positions and creating *ma* was important to allow a warm self to be created.

The change in psychotherapy includes a process of distancing (*ma*) from oneself. The quality of this distancing must be varied. When a voice contacts the actual other's voice, a dialogical process is facilitated. One's voice can get the overtones mingled with another's voice. It is the spontaneous living moment of the therapeutic conversation.

Concluding remarks

Psychotherapy represents a specific mode of joint action that is deeply dialogical. Most clients come to therapy because they do not understand their complaints, cannot control them, and are disturbed by them. The client's partly disowned experiences lie buried in these complaints, which can be regarded as meaning-laden signs. Even if not available for self-reflection, the client's problematic experiences are an inseparable aspect of his or her personality, echoing the events that formed them (Stiles, 1999).

To articulate the process of therapeutic meaning generation, the author paid attention to the positional meaning-making activity in utterances of a client in a psychotherapeutic session. It is useful to examine the frame of *I*-positions in DST, its characteristic in the therapeutic action. It is thus one of the main goals of psychotherapy to initiate a dialogue between positions. In psychotherapy, such work is ongoing, jointly looking for an adequate word for the meaning of the experiences narrated in the dialogue.

In this study, the dynamic movement of self-experience in a therapeutic conversation was investigated through a clinical vignette of a severely trauma-tized client. As a result, several remarks are articulated as follows.

1 For the treatment of the traumatized client, the course of the psychotherapy moves from a limited inner space (I-*prison*) towards a living, open, and varied landscape of mind. For the first period, the remembered facts and events were fragmented and without a plot.

2 The constitution of the self in psychotherapy is to create new meanings within the fragmented events that could be related to the emerging of new positions of the self and bring them together in a *meta-position*.

3 The psychotherapeutic relationship can facilitate the living area generated between two persons where a potential chronotope—*ma*—is generated. The therapist works to facilitate the reorganization of the client's *I*-positions in the area.

4 In the narrative of the client's experiences, a space can be created to talk to both the living and the dead positioned within their stories. The coherence of self-experience rests on the continuing interpretation of everyday events. It proceeds even if one experiences negative life events.

5 Once the living and the dead take a form in the client's internal world, each equally deals with *I*-positions. Each position is given a voice in which strong emotions are fixed. *I*-positions have contextual character. In the new context of a therapeutic situation, the dialogical movement and a broader bandwidth of *I*-positions can be generated. This is the core moment for explaining how the therapeutic change occurs.

References

Bakhtin, M. M. (1981). *The Dialogic Imagination: Four Essays* (ed. Holquist, M., trans. Emerson, C. & Holquist, M.). Austin, TX: University of Texas Press.

Bruner, J. S. (1990). *Acts of Meaning*. Cambridge, MA: Harvard University Press.

Dimaggio, G. (2012). Dialogically oriented therapies and the role of poor metacognition in personality disorders. In Hermans, H. J. M. & Gieser, T. (eds.), *Handbook of Dialogical Self Theory* (pp. 356–373). Cambridge, UK: Cambridge University Press.

Gonçalves, M. M. & Ribeiro, A. (2012). Narrative processes of innovation and stability within the dialogical self. In Hermans, H. J. M. & Gieser, T. (eds.), *Handbook of Dialogical Self Theory* (pp. 301–318). Cambridge, UK: Cambridge University Press.

Hedtke, L. & Winslade, J. (2004). *Remembering Lives: Conversations with the Dying and the Bereaved*. London: Routledge.

Hermans, H. J. M. (1996). Voicing the self: From information processing to dialogical interchange. *Psychological Bulletin*, 119, 31–50.

Hermans, H. J. M. (2001). The construction of a personal position repertoire: Method and practice. *Culture and Psychology*, 7, 323–365.

Hermans, H. J. M. (2004). The dialogical self; between exchange and power. In Hermans, H. J. M. & Dimaggio, G. (eds.), *The Dialogical Self in Psychotherapy* (pp. 13–28). New York: Bruner-Routledge.

Hermans, H. J. M. & Gieser, T. (eds.) (2012). *Handbook of Dialogical Self Theory*. Cambridge, UK: Cambridge University Press.

Hermans, H. J. M. & Hermans-Konopka, A. (2010). *Dialogical Self Theory: Positioning and Counter-Positioning in a Globalizing Society*. New York: Cambridge University Press.

Morioka, M. (2008). Voices of the self in the therapeutic chronotope: Utushi and ma. *International Journal of Dialogical Science*, 3, 93–108.

Morioka, M. (2012). Creating dialogical space in psychotherapy: Meaning-generating chronotope of ma. In Hermans, H. J. M. & Gieser, T. (eds.), *Handbook of Dialogical Self Theory* (pp. 390–404). Cambridge, UK: Cambridge University Press.

Morioka, M. (2015). How to create ma—the living pause—In the landscape of the mind: The wisdom of Noh theatre. *International Journal for Dialogical Science*, 9, 81–95.

Raggatt, P. (2010). Space and time in the dialogical self: Personal chronotopes in life history data. Paper for the Sixth International Conference on the Dialogical Self, Athens, Greece.

Rennie, D. L. (1992). Qualitative analysis of client's experiences of psychotherapy: The unfolding of reflexivity. In Toukmanian, S. G. & Rennie, D. L. (eds.), *Psychotherapy Process Research: Paradigmatic and Narrative Approaches* (pp. 211–233). Thousand Oaks, CA: Sage.

Rowan, J. (2012). The use of *I*-position in psychotherapy. In Hermans, H. J. M. & Gieser, T. (eds.), *Handbook of Dialogical Self Theory* (pp. 341–355). Cambridge, UK: Cambridge University Press.

Stiles, W. B. (1999). Signs and voices in psychotherapy. *Psychotherapy Research*, 9, 1–21.

White, M. (2007). *Maps of Narrative Practice*. New York: Norton.

15 North American indigenous concepts of the dialogical self

Lewis Mehl-Madrona and Barbara Mainguy

The world's indigenous psychologies are rich and varied and rarely considered by academic psychology. In this chapter, we present a North American vision of self and mind that is similar to the dialogical self of Hubert Hermans and colleagues. We highlight the similarities and the differences with Dialogical Self Theory (DST) and therapy.

DST (Hermans & Gieser, 2012) locates the self and identity in space and time. Relationships exist between a person and other people in their world, but also with additional characters, who are not visible, and are intrapsychic forces. The dialogical self has been defined as a "complex narratively structured self with many '*I*- positions' that can be occupied by the same person, a multi-voiced self that includes internal dialogues and expands the possibilities for experience with others" (Maria & Largoza, 2008, p. 57). Hermans' dialogical self deconstructs the idea of a core self, the central "I" to a perspective of multiple positions of self in relationship. The self is a "society of mind" (Hermans & Hermans-Konopka, 2010). The indigenous North American concept of the self is equivalently dialogical, predating Bakhtin, Bruner, and others.

Foundational concepts

Understanding the North American indigenous concepts of self and mind requires some underlying philosophy. Lakota philosopher Viola Cordova (2007) described the universe as an interconnected field of energy in motion. Occasional "pooling" occurs to create "'events': being, peopling, mountaining, and so on" (p. 117). Self is not static, but part of a flow, iterating in space and time, depending on the forces that construct it at a given moment. These forces have ontological validity and exist as beings. The self resides "in a highly personalized universe that includes the world of plants, animals, insects, fish, stones, the earth, fire, air, water, wind, and spirit entities" (Voss et al., 1999, p. 239). Existence is nested in the cosmological structure of the four directions, which have their own identities and energetic shape (Burkhart, 2016) and that serve as meta-positions in the terms of DST. We come to know and understand self and others through dialectic engagement in iterative and occasional contacts sometimes involving community counsel (Fixico, 2003). Health arises in the balanced co-creation of self by these elements. Self can emerge in a balance with the energies that create it, or out of balance, requiring adjustment or healing.

The *nagi* as a community of *I*-positions

This sense of a constructed mind that is interactive and "in play" in a torrent of forces, resembles the community of *I*-positions found in Hermans' dialogical self. The Lakota call this community *nagi*. It contains aspects of all the forces that shape us as human beings. These forces are often presented in storied form, causing some to describe the *nagi* as the swarm of stories surrounding a body that inform the being who occupies that body how to be in the world. Stories are purposive and relational, for they require an audience to be told. Some stories in the *nagi* are invisible, lying outside our conscious awareness. They are discovered in dialogue, particularly with others who are different from us. These stories exist in a community of storytellers, which are equivalents of the *I*-positions of Hermans. The community of stories and storytellers is anchored to the body, but is distinctly non-local. It can extend far afield from the body.

The *nagi* parallels Bakhtin's vision of mind as a polyphonous, cacophonous concatenation of disparate voices, each struggling to achieve dominance – collaborating, defecting, and cooperating with each other to gain control (Bakhtin, 1929/1984, p. 63). Bakhtin's idea of mind consists of a collection of voices that are attempting to achieve dominance over the mind. Within the concept of the *nagi*, we would refer to these voices as storytellers or avatars or characters. Hermans calls them *I*-positions.

The forces that create mind act through the stories they tell. The *I*-position is the storyteller, who exists in the vicinity of the body in constant interaction and creates new instantiations as the stories shift. As in Hermans' conception, members of this community negotiate. They criticize each other or themselves, they consult each other, they love or hate each other (Hermans, 2013). People form relationships with other human beings who can be seen and touched but also with invisible beings, who cannot be seen and touched. The stories exist in layers, from the small stories that parts of our body can tell, to the stories told by extended family, to the cultural stories that form the tribal psyche, to the political and global stories that are part of everyone's consciousness and the environmental stories that are spoken by the rocks, trees, and rivers. Being is a verb, and the self is thrown into this tumult of stories by virtue of existence in space and time. Consistent with the Lakota language in which verbs are more important than nouns (and more plentiful), what matters is the relationship with the storyteller and the story. The body itself is conceived as an occasional instantiation, one of Cordova's incidences of "pooling" (Cordova, 2007), a physical object that allows us to be located in space and time. Some characters (voices, parts, avatars, etc.) are closer to the body than others. Some are our internal avatars, some are spirits, and the spirits can be ancestors, elements of nature, mythological beings, or helpful strangers. Any character can argue with any other character. Identity is maintained through a continued dialogue among the beings within us who are grounded in the physical world and the beings who speak to us from the spirit world. This philosophy lacks an ego that organizes meaning and identity. Cordova (2007) tells us that consciousness in the form of awareness exists as a matrix supporting the dialogue among the elements of the *nagi*.

Native American philosophy and scholarship are conceptualized by writers as "holistic, contextualized, relational, personal, concrete, and We-centered" (Waters, 2004, p. xv). Implicit in the North American aboriginal perspective is the embeddedness of the person in the group. The integration of the individual and the collective, the particular and the general is part of the very nature of the universe and goes to the very heart of being human (Burkhart, 2016). The being or spirit of a human is both an individual essence and a universality. In Lakota philosophy, human beings have two existential positions: the small and the specific and the large and the universal (Deloria, 1999, p. 229). We dialogue back and forth between the individual and the collective, seeking balance (*wicozani*) for health, harmony, and well-being.

Hermans described each person as a polyphonic society (Hermans, 2002). This is consistent with the *nagi*. Each of these storytellers (or avatars) is a relatively independent being, attempting to negotiate its relationships with other beings in the swarm. Salgado and Hermans (2005) emphasize the dialogical nature of the self over its many voices. North American thought emphasizes both – that there are many storytellers and many conversations among those storytellers. Others (Lewis & Todd, 2004; Salgado and Hermans, 2005) have wondered if the many metaphors (parts, schema, internal objects) that exist for the components of the self, have any value of one over any other. We think of these metaphors in the same manner that our elder, Uncle Albert, spoke of story. He said that over 500 creation stories exist, and all are true. They are true for the people who tell them in the place where they are told. The North American version grants full ontological validity to each of these storytellers, avoiding the question as to what is internal and what is external, what is real or what is imagined. In this perspective all is real.

The work to be done is to engage in meaningful dialogue with the positions, voices, or characters. Konopka and Van Beers (2014) call this work "Compositionwork" (p. 194), and it is elsewhere evoked as a discussion of "parts" therapy (Hunter, 2015), ego work (Frederick & McNeal, 2013), internal family systems therapy (IFST) (Schwartz, 1995), and voice dialogue (Stone & Stone, 1998). Differences inhere in the way the positions are constituted and in the structure and philosophy of the dialogical engagement. Compositionwork, for example, engages clients with linguistic and sensory representations through the use of stones as externalizing elements. Both indigenous North Americans and Europeans share with these therapies the recognition of the multiplicity of the components of self, but, as Rowan (2012) recognized, any entity or construct with which one can dialogue can become an *I*-position, even spirits and ghosts, which he considers an essential advantage above other therapies. *I*-positions are dynamic, flexible, and contextual. They help us avoid reification and permit a fluid self that is ever changing. *I*-positions can be personified and explored through dialogue. Rowan says that something or someone becomes an *I*-position in a dynamic way, in a particular moment and situation, so that an *I*-position changes or even disappears, depending on the situation, opening new possibilities of enriching, innovating, and broadening one's self, as new voices together with affective qualities can be included in the self and contribute to its content and organization. The dialogical self is not a fixed and isolated entity; it opens itself to the world, creating possibilities of traveling through unknown experiential spaces. For example, we often work with the "voices" that people hear as ontologically valid "*I*-positions," which begs the question of whether or not they are real. Everything is real in the dialogue.

The North American approach facilitates a dialogue among the "*I*-positions" or storytellers similar to the negotiational self method of Nir (2012), who describes the creation of a dialogical space in which conflicting *I*-positions can negotiate. Similar to Nir's approach, traditional healers identify the beings or storytellers who have a stake in a decision about which there is conflict. They encourage all these beings to tell their origin story as well as any other story to justify their position. They dialogue with these beings to learn their needs, beliefs, desires, and intentions. Healers pose questions such as, "How did you come to learn that?" Gradually the details emerge and shared interests are identified, which leads to a negotiated coalition of beings or storytellers who can move forward in the face of conflict. Sometimes a coalition forms to achieve dominance over a strident, minority voice or to render some voices/beings ineffective or unable to participate in the actions involved in deciding and carrying out a decision. The elders recognize that campaigning by *I*-positions or storytellers is continuous. Each being is interviewed in dialogue with external others and the others within the *nagi*. Some members of the swarm are always trying to convert other members to their points of view. When a sufficiently strong consensus coalition arises, a decision can occur and be enacted. Hermans and Hermans-Konopka (2010) argue that "strong coalitions produce strong motivation" (p. 337) and traditional elders would agree. Each time we hear a story, the story enters into our *nagi* along with a spark of the storyteller. As they say, "we live in an era in which the self is 'visited' by an increasing number and heterogeneity of positions or voices, leading to an increase of possible contradictions and conflicts within the self." This is similar to what Hermans (2001b) calls multivoicedness. The *nagi* is the space in which the negotiations occur.

The four directions dialectic

The Four Winds present the perspectives of mythological beings, sacred beings, who have a meta-perspective rendering them capable to act as narrators. Maintaining a dialogue with these beings supports balance and harmony. The east is associated with spirituality and guidance and direction from the spirit world. The south is associated with emotions and relationships (especially love and family) and the virtues of kindness, compassion, and generosity. The west is associated with courage and the physical body. The north is associated with wisdom, the community, strength, and endurance. These Four Directions always imply three more – upwards, which is associated with the sky spirits and protection; downwards, which is associated with the earth, who gives us healing, sustenance, and nurturing; and the center, which is the place from which we connect to everything around us. The balanced human relates equally to these directions in a dialogical manner, speaking to the beings that inhabit these directions (the Four Sons of the Wind). The personalization of these beings allows them to incorporate into one's *nagi*. While some general guidelines exist, the relationship of anyone to these directions is dynamic and interactive, not static.

According to Hermans (2001a), the term meta-position, "creates a certain distance toward the other positions; it provides an overarching view; it enables the participants to interrelate the positions as part of their personal history; it provides an opportunity for evaluating the several positions and their organization" (p. 354). The culture encourages ongoing dialogues with these beings through conversations and also, for cosmological and spiritual consultancies, through ceremony and songs. People are encouraged to incorporate the meta-perspectives of these beings to see themselves from different perspectives.

The incorporations of these meta-positions into the ongoing dialogical negotiations provide a source of wisdom that can be quite psychotherapeutic. While relationships with these beings are generally immediate and don't require an intermediary, some messages can be baffling on an individual level and are brought to elders for a community validation process. This moderates individualism and prevents extremism, ensuring that thought serves the whole.

The relational nature of the self

Cordova (2007) argues that human beings are fundamentally in relation, bound in the energetic fabric of the cosmological energy field. Humans, she insists, are *in* the system, and no part of the system stands outside, including no spiritual being. The complex notion of simultaneous independence and interdependence is intrinsic to the Native American perspective in which individuals are always in dialogue within a community. Consider the "talking circle" procedure, which was used to create consensus in communities, to create tribal consciousness, and in healing work (Mehl-Madrona & Mainguy, 2014). In this procedure, people sit in a circle. The person convening the circle introduces the question while holding a decorated staff, called a "talking stick" when translated into English. Once the convener has phrased the question or concern, he or she passes the stick to the left and that person talks as long as he or she wishes without interruption. Importantly, the speaker does not speak to anyone in the group, but to the center of the circle. No one in the circle responds to the speaker with noises, words, or micro-expressions. Responses are only appropriate when the stick comes to a person. The process continues until the group comes to a consensus and no one has anything further to say. Never does anyone speak directly to another person or respond immediately to what another person says. The process itself is necessarily dialogical, an exchange of ideas that is shaped by the members of the circle as the stick is passed. The circle is both decentering in that the stick moves to the individual apeakers and centering in that speakers address the center of the circle, moving toward consensus. The de-centered voices on the periphery instantiate the central "collective" energetic pool of voices and speakers. The whole moves forward in time. Circle processes are an integral part of North American indigenous healing practices, and are used with the multiple *I*-positions within the self, as well. Circle processes also presage the democratization of organizations in involving all stakeholders in a process in the dialogue.

From a North American indigenous perspective, the self is ever changing as more stories and tellers of stories are added to the *nagi*. In DST terms, the self is a dynamic multiplicity of *I*-positions. In North American indigenous philosophy, the self can change by expanding what DST calls the *I*-position repertoire. We routinely do this therapeutically when we tell stories that introduce new characters for the person to incorporate. Elders frequently teach lessons through telling such stories and the characters can be internalized as new *I*-positions. Change occurs through expanding the *I*-position repertoire of the person.

Traditional stories expand this *I*-position repertoire. In one, an evil spirit has taken over the dominant mountain to the west and hoards all the rain. The village is dying. The people have fallen into despair and lost their will. Only one young man and one young woman are left who have the capacity to go on a quest to vanquish the evil spirit. As they climb the path to the mountain, they encounter a demon guardian who forbids their passage and seems determined to eat them. The young man prepares to battle the demon. The young woman immediately realizes that he cannot win and prays to the thunderspirits (*wakinyan*) for intervention. They come, and their lightening arrows destroy the evil creature. They alight in their classic, visible form of the Swallow, and proceed to chide the young man for not following the guidance of the woman and for not asking for help, for having the arrogance to think that he doesn't need help. The first lesson, they say, is that help is not provided unless it is requested. The result is the incorporation of the *wakinyan* into the repertoire of the self as an external *I*-position.

Norton-Smith (2010) writes that human beings are not essentially persons, but spirits instantiated in a human body who can become persons "by virtue of their participation in social and moral relationships with other persons" (p. 86). Norton-Smith (2010, pp. 82–83) uses a Lakota story to illustrate this morality. In the story, Coyote gives *Inyan* (the Rock) his thick, wool blanket, only to steal it back when he feels cold. Outraged, *Inyan* chases Coyote and rolls over him, flattening him in true Wiley Coyote style, and then delivering the moral principle: once something is given, it cannot be taken back. This personalizes mythological beings and integrates them into the repertoire of the self. The incorporation provides a moral position. The incorporation of such positions in the form of mythological beings (the *wakinyan*, for example) is a strong centering movement that counters the decentering influences of contemporary post-modern culture, or, in the indigenous concept, the European invasion and imposition of epistemologies and value systems alien to North America.

Native American relational healing

Native American healing is fundamentally relational since we are formed through the dialogue of the constituent beings who occupy our *nagi*. The concepts of the individual and of privacy are relatively foreign to these practices for the community exists around us and within us. Psychotherapy does not exist apart from body therapies, spiritual therapies, and community therapies, for the mind does not exist apart from body, spirit, and community. The word "treatment" has no counterpart in the North American Native world, because one person does not fix another. Healing results from interaction and is an emergent property arising from that interaction among people and non-people. It occurs when mind, body, spirit, and community are balanced. It can occur in ordinary-appearing interactions among people or in highly scripted ceremonies.

Traditional healers operating within indigenous communities would not necessarily have had the English language skills to describe their healing activities (Mehl-Madrona, 2004; Mehl-Madrona & Kennedy, 2009). Indigenous healers working within their communities are progressively becoming more educated and cognizant of other techniques (Mehl-Madrona, 2010; Mehl-Madrona & Kennedy, 2015). They are incorporating an eclectic range of practices into their work (Linklater, 2014).

Community focus

Much of traditional healing takes place in community. Rarely do healers work alone. Centering and decentering occurs in the context of the dialogues among the personal, interpersonal, and the universal, which takes place in ceremony. Healers tell traditional stories, engaging in metaphors that are relevant in the life of the client. Relationships are formed with sacred beings through these practices and these sacred beings become storytellers (avatars, *I*-positions) within the *nagi* (in DST, the multiplicity of the dialogical self). Sophisticated communication occurs under the rubric of prayer, when people pray, one after the other, in a circle format. Again, the interaction between the personal and the universal creates communication, this time with the "divine." The *nagili* is translated as "that which arises from communication with the divine." In this way, the ineffable is bound to the *nagi*, with its acknowledgment of respect and acceptance of the forces of the "great mysteries," the spirits who engage with humans.

Traditional elders tell stories that emphasize fulfilling one's duties to the community, accepting a degree of pain and suffering for the benefit of others, and honoring one's relationships. Counseling often takes the form of storytelling and sometimes direct instructions for how to behave.

Circles are considered sacred among indigenous North American cultures. The tribal consciousness that arises through a talking circle process instantiates the collective consciousness. We could say that the community is a larger relational self, for it is formed from all of our relations. The circle provides a healing crucible to contain the collective creation of a new relational order. Common practice is to routinely ask people to bring all those they know to the talking circle process, in this way inviting external *I*-positions (Hermans & Hermans-Konopka, 2010) into a dialogue. This includes all the stakeholders in a problem. This circle represents an externalization of the dialogue that is already occurring within the person and allows for an enrichment of the other. The person's internal *I*-position or representation (or avatar) for the other becomes more accurate through engaging in the talking circle process. The dialogical process invites relationships to form in this created community setting. The circle "center" becomes a location for the creation of a new relationship, a healing *nagi*, a physical and psychic space into which are invited the participating beings, including the embodied spirits (humans) involved and the invited entities (*I*-positions) entailed in the question, as well as other spirits and ancestors who may wish to comment or contribute. The contributions from the circle literally create a new reality.

Listening

Burkhart (2016) writes that, "Native American philosophy ... opens up a space ... to find meaning and understanding but does not make or declare truth or meaning" (p. 231). The elders would agree with the French psychoanalyst, Jacques Lacan (1988), who taught that the greatest gift we can give another is to listen deeply without judgment or interpretation. Some of our most profound experiences have occurred while being heard by an elder. They have heard everything. They accept everything. Nothing produces micro-expressions, eye-rolling, or dismissive gestures. Respect and dignity pervades their interactions. When a question is presented to an elder for consideration, rarely does the elder respond immediately, which is different from the mainstream world. Typically, the elder holds the question for four days or more. Responding to a question involves prayer, discussions with other elders, and contemplation. Answers come when they come and in dialogue with the entire universe potentially (or at least those portions of it that condescend to interact with we instantiated humans). Indigenous Native American healing begins with this creation of a deeply respectful, radically accepting relationship, whether with an elder or a more contemporary practitioner.

Two-eyed seeing

Contemporary psychology is firmly ensconced in positivism, which refuses to acknowledge the existence of perspectives that contradict its fundamental assumptions (Martin, 2012). Positivism assumes that there is only one reality, which can be discovered through scientific procedure. Anything that falls outside of scientific reasoning is disregarded as inconclusive and ideological (Marker, 2003). Thus, studies that cannot be replicated, which use tools or methods that have not been standardized or verified, or that reach conclusions that veer away from the questions asked are dismissed as unscientific and lacking in credibility. Within health research specifically, certain "types" and styles of research are viewed as having more credibility than others (e.g. the randomized controlled trial continues to be the gold standard of Western health research, whereas storytelling may be interpreted as anecdotal and lacking in evidence) (Marker, 2003).

Indigenous approaches to knowledge are more dialogical, slower, and admit multiple perspectives, leading to what Nova Scotia M'iqmaq elder, Albert Marshall, has called "two eyed seeing," expressed by the word *etuaptmumk* in his language. These approaches to knowledge parallel approaches to healing. Two-eyed seeing welcomes multiple perspectives and knowledges and promotes explanatory pluralism. Multiple levels of explanation are accepted and each need not be logical to the other.

Two-eyed seeing allows both explanations to be true without one being privileged over the other. This is the spirit in which the elders approach people who are suffering. A multiplicity of stories exist to explain the suffering and all have validity. All have characters who tell the stories, who have stories themselves. The task of healing is to reveal these many storytellers and their own stories so that more healthy coalitions can be formed for less friction for living in the world. Through dialogue, the person gains a better understanding of the many voices/characters commenting on his or her problem and can be more selective about which ones to accept. The elder or therapist provides a meta-position for the person to incorporate that helps him or her to see the situations and the stories from a greater distance and perspective.

Moving and meditation

Meditative techniques similar to mindfulness exist in the making of prayer ties (*chanli pata*), which are strings of colored fabric containing small pinches of tobacco into which prayers are placed; sitting in nature for varied lengths of time (the *hanblechiya*), singing, and walking meditations. One Lakota elder, Carol Iron Rope-Herrera, told us that tracking an animal is meditation. Dancing is meditation. Praying is meditation. She resented outsiders coming onto the reservation and telling her that she had to learn mindfulness meditation, since that was evidence-based, unlike the local practices. Carol told us that most aspects of Lakota life are moving meditations. Hunting, for instance, requires learning all the stories about the animal one plans to hunt, so that the animal and the many storytellers who speak about the animal become incorporated as *I*-positions for the hunter. Hunters are supposed to follow an animal for a year to develop a story for how it lives through the four seasons before actually killing the animal. The Lakota sundance involves four days of dancing without food or water, which is highly trance inducing. The goal is to come as close to the spirit world as is humanly possible so as to give thanks for someone's life being saved or to pray for someone to be saved. The mythological characters in the sundance also become *I*-positions that are incorporated into the community's *nagi*, as well as that of the individual dancer. These moving meditations all involve symbolic enactment of historical *I*-positions in relation to others enacting other *I*-positions that creates a dramatic tableau for the negotiation of perspectives and for healing to occur, which happens regularly at a sundance.

Story is central

At an *inipikaga* ceremony,[1] hot stones are brought into a covered shelter, to create a portal for communication with spirits and for praying. In such a ceremony held in a Canadian prison, Lewis overheard an inmate saying he would be released soon, and that the doctors had told him he would return to prison quickly. He was diagnosed as having attention deficit disorder, conduct disorder, bipolar disorder, and antisocial personality disorder. The elder shrugged off this pronouncement. "You don't have any of those things," he said.

> You just grew up with bad stories. You come spend time with us (referring to the extended community of his helpers and relatives), and we'll give you good stories to replace those bad stories. We'll keep you out of here.

A number of his helpers present at the ceremony had been in that prison and proceeded to attest to the success of this elder's approach, for it had kept them from returning. The elder illustrated the broad principle of surrounding the person with community, hearing the "bad" stories that were living through the person, and replacing those bad stories with "good" stories, meaning stories more compatible with a healthy, friction-free, self-world interface. I have heard elders talking with people to learn the stories in which they grew up and telling them healthier stories for living to compete with those less healthy stories.

The elders would say that we manage the relationships among our avatars (*I*-positions) through the stories they tell to influence each other. To understand the dynamics of our internal world, we must hear the stories that the characters are telling and sometimes incorporate new stories (new *I*-positions into our repertoire). DST would describe this as the person repositioning him or herself through absorbing these new stories leading to the incorporation of new *I*-positions that allows the person to take new and different positions in relation to a personal problem.

We focus on the stories that live through the person. We identify the stories that shaped the person's childhood and early family life. We look at the pervasive stories abounding in the culture. We look at the contemporary stories that are being performed in the world by the person. We make maps (drawings, collages, etc.) of the beings who told or are telling those stories. We identify the coalitions of avatars or storytellers who are working for or against greater ease of function and less suffering in the world. We create interactive dialogues with these storytellers/avatars and began to reshape the map of the person's world. We describe this in more detail in *Remapping Your Mind* (Mehl-Madrona & Mainguy, 2015).

Manual medicine or bodywork plays an important role in eliciting the stories held in the body. This accompanies some degree of what is being called energy psychology. The bodywork that Lewis learned came from Cherokee people who taught him in the traditional manner. Later, we learned that this method of hands-on healing was common to all the tribes of Missouri and Kansas in the time period from 1850–1880 and became the inspiration and the foundation for American Osteopathy as developed by Andrew Taylor Still, who is considered the founder of osteopathic medicine, and lived with these tribes during that period, learning their methods of healing, as he developed osteopathy (Mainguy et al., 2017)

Our primary focus is to create dialogue among the characters or avatars who populate the person's *nagi*, to become aware of the stories they are telling, to selectively evaluate what stories are working and what stories are not, and to create new coalitions within the *nagi* to improve function and reduce suffering.

I observed an elder speaking to a young woman who had been diagnosed with anorexia nervosa. He asked her to speak about the part of her who thought she was fat. She named it Toni. He asked if a part of her thought she was thin. She called that part Tommie. He said he wanted to get to know both of them. He burned sage and blessed her with the smoke. He sang and asked her to pray for Toni and Tommie. He invited sacred beings to join the efforts for healing thereby reminding Toni of previously neglected *I*-positions who could be strengthened. Later that week, he asked Toni what made her think she was fat. She talked about her father sexually abusing her for six years while her mother ignored it all. The elder just listened. He invited her to name that wounded young woman who lived within her and felt betrayed. Then he spoke to that young woman, and encouraged the others to join in the discussion. Eventually, he brought together everyone involved in her suffering for a talking circle and then an *inipikaga* ceremony in which the ancestors were consulted, and everyone prayed for her healing. Over time, she gained weight and began to live comfortably in her community.

Narrative therapy

Narrative therapy is considered indigenous-friendly and is more accepted by indigenous people than conventional, mainstream psychotherapies. Narrative therapy focuses upon the stories we tell ourselves and others about who we are and how the world functions. An abundance of negative stories leads people to overly identify with problematic life narratives (White & Epston, 1990). When we change these stories, we change and our relationship to the world changes. Narrative therapy may or may not include a dialogical self. Elders naturally do narrative therapy without being taught.

In narrative therapy, storytellers construct new meaning through creating opposi-tional stories, focusing upon stories of positive outcomes instead of problem-saturated stories like those told by conventional medicine that render people equal to their diagnosis (White & Epston, 1990; Morgan, 2000). Contemporary indigen-ous people identify with the resistive, liberational element of narrative therapy, which can be utilized to empower people to separate from the dominant culture saturated story of indigenous people (rarely positive) and find counter-stories that lead toward health and wellness despite ongoing oppression and injustice (Freeman et al., 1997). People are encouraged to live their stories of strength and success as opposed to their stories of weakness and disability (Drewery & Winslade, 1997). One can appreciate the overlap of indigenous theories of mind with narrative approaches. Both are storied, and both use stories as teaching tools and as therapeutic devices. Both listen and tell stories. However, classic narrative therapy does not ask who tells the negative and disabling stories lived by the person but focuses instead on finding new stories rather than locating new storytellers. Classic narrative therapy can miss the greater depth of possibility available from within the indigenous model of mind (similar to DST and therapy).

Conclusions

North American indigenous thinking about self and others is remarkably similar to DST. The results of working in this format are exciting (Mehl-Madrona et al., 2014) and point toward many future studies on efficacy and outcome. The North American indigenous perspective makes psychotherapy accessible to those people in the world who find conventional Western methods of psychotherapy unappealing. The approach minimizes stigmatizing diagnoses in favor of creating a topology of characters (called *I*-positions by Hermans) who dwell within the *nagi* (mind), interacting, coalescing, collaborating, and defecting just as described by Bakhtin, and can be reorganized to function more effectively on behalf of the body to whom these beings are attached. The approach is fundamentally embedded in community, which for the *nagi* is a reflection of the exterior world, and new stories must be enacted in community and accepted and approved by one's community in order to become stable. The approach is fundamentally relational, emphasizing the manner in which dialogue creates the human world. The consideration of spirit allows the voice of unknown and unknowable to be present, accounting for the mystery of those things we cannot comprehend, except in a sense of the impact of their energy in the shaping of the self. As we have presented in this chapter, DST walks alongside these indigenous ideas.

Note

1 The *inipikaga* is a circle process that takes place in darkness and heat created by hot stones upon which water is poured. It is a considered a portal between the human and the spirit worlds.

References

Bakhtin, M. M. (1984). *Problems of Dostoevsky's poetics*. C. Emerson (Trans.). Minneapolis, MN: University of Minnesota Press. (Original work published 1929)

Burkhart, B. Y. (2016). Red wisdom: Highlighting recent writing in Native American philosophy. *Confluence: Journal of World Philosophies, 1*, 227–239.

Cordova, V. (2007). Time and the universe. In K. Moore, K. Peters, T. Jojola, & A. Lacy (Eds.), *How it is: The Native American philosophy of V. F. Cordova*. Tucson, AZ: University of Arizona Press.

Deloria, V., Jr. (1999). *Religion and revolution among American Indians for this land: Writings on religion in America*. New York: Routledge.

Drewery, W., & Winslade, J. (1997). The theoretical story of narrative theory. In G. Monk, J. Winslade, K. Crocket, J. Winslade, G. Monk, & D. Epston (Eds.), *Narrative therapy in practice: The archaeology of hope* (pp. 3–31). San Francisco, CA: Jossey-Bass.

Fixico, D. L. (2003). *The American Indian mind in a linear world: American Indian studies and traditional knowledge.* New York: Routledge.

Frederick, C., & McNeal, S. A. (2013). *Inner strengths: Contemporary psychotherapy and hypnosis for ego-strengthening.* London: Routledge.

Freeman, J., Epston, D., & Lobovits, D. (1997). *Playful approaches to serious problems: Narrative therapy with children and their families.* London: Norton.

Hermans, H. J. M. (2001a). The construction of a personal position repertoire: Method and practice. *Culture & Psychology, 7*(3), 323–366.

Hermans, H. J. M. (2001b). The dialogical self: Toward a theory of personal and cultural positioning. *Culture & Psychology, 7*(3), 243–253. doi:10.1177/1354067X0173001

Hermans, H. J. M. (2002). The dialogical self as society of mind: Introduction. *Theory & Psychology, 12*(2), 147–160.

Hermans, H. J. M. (2013). A multi-voiced and dialogical self and the challenge of social power in a globalizing world. In R. Tafarodi (Ed.), *Subjectivity in the twenty-first century: Cultural, philosophical, and political perspectives* (pp. 41–65). Cambridge, UK: Cambridge University Press.

Hermans, H. J. M., & Gieser, T. (2012). *Handbook of dialogical self theory.* New York: Cambridge University Press.

Hermans, H. J. M., & Hermans-Konopka, A. (2010). *Dialogical self theory: Positioning and counter-positioning in a globalizing society.* New York: Cambridge University Press.

Hunter, R. (2015). *What is parts therapy? Roy Hunter's hypnosis and hyponotherapy.* www.royhunter.com.

Konopka, A., & Van Beers, W. (2014). Compositionwork: A method for self-investigation. *Journal of Constructivist Psychology, 27*(3), 194–210.

Lacan, J. (1988). *The seminar of Jacques Lacan: Book II The ego in Freud's theory and in the technique of psychoanalysis 1954–55.* S. Tomaselli (Trans.), J.-A. Miller(Ed.). New York: Norton.

Lewis, M., & Todd, R. (2004). Toward a neuropsychological model of internal dialogue: Implications for theory and clinical practice. In H. J. M. Hermans, &G. DiMaggio (Eds.), *The dialogical self in psychotherapy* (pp. 43–59). Hove, UK: Brunner-Routledge.

Linklater, R. (2014). *Decolonising trauma work: Indigenous practitioners share stories and strategies.* Winnipeg, MB: Fernwood.

Mainguy, B., Conte, J., & Mehl-Madrona, L. (2017). *The indigenous roots of osteopathy.* Paper presented at the North American Primary Care Research Group, Montreal, Quebec, Canada. Retrieved from https://drive.google.com/file/d/0B6SaV2FuGlVJcXRhc3ZzYjVhY0k/view

Maria, M. A. S., & Largoza, G. L. (2008). On the non-distinction of self and other in the notion of personhood. *International Journal for Dialogical Science, 3,* 55–68.

Marker, M. (2003). Indigenous voice, community, and epistemic violence: The ethnographer's "interests" and what "interests" the ethnographer. *Qualitative Studies in Education, 16*(3), 361–375.

Martin, D. H. (2012). Two-eyed seeing: A framework for understanding Indigenous and non-Indigenous approaches to Indigenous health research. *Canadian Journal of Nursing Research, 44*(2), 20–42.

Mehl-Madrona, L. (2004). *Coyote healing: Miracles from Native America.* Rochester, VT: Bear & Company.

Mehl-Madrona, L. (2010). *Healing the mind through the power of story: The promise of narrative psychiatry.* New York: Simon & Schuster.

Mehl-Madrona, L., Jul, E., & Mainguy, B. (2014). Results of a transpersonal, narrative, and phenomenological psychotherapy for psychosis. *International Journal of Transpersonal Studies, 33*(1).

Mehl-Madrona, L., & Kennedy, C. (2009). What Aboriginal elders believe mental health workers should know to work with Aboriginal people. *EXPLORE: The Journal of Science and Healing, 5*(1), 20–29.

Mehl-Madrona, L., & Mainguy, B. (2014). Introducing healing circles and talking circles into primary care. *The Permanente Journal, 18*(2), 4.

Mehl-Madrona, L., & Mainguy, B. (2015). *Remapping your mind: The neuroscience of self-transformation through story.* Rochester, VT: Bear & Company.

Morgan, A. (2000). *What is narrative therapy? An easy-to-read introduction.* Adelaide, South Australia: Dulwich Centre Publications.

Nir, D. (2012). Voicing inner conflict: From a dialogical to a negotiational self. In H. J. M. Hermans & T. Gieser (Eds.), *Handbook of dialogical self theory* (pp. 284–300). New York: Cambridge University Press.

Norton-Smith, T. (2010). *The dance of person and place: One interpretation of American Indian philosophy.* Albany, NY: State University of New York Press.

Rowan, J. (2012). The use of *I*-positions in psychotherapy. In H. J. M. Hermans & T. Gieser (Eds.), *Handbook of dialogical self theory* (pp. 341–355). New York: Cambridge University Press.

Salgado, J., & Hermans, H. J. M. (2005). The return of subjectivity: From a multiplicity of selves to a dialogical self. *E-Journal of Applied Psychology, 1*(1), 3–13.

Schwartz, R. C. (1995). *Internal family systems therapy.* New York: Guilford Press.

Stone, H., & Stone, S. (1998). *Embracing ourselves: The voice dialogue manual.* Novato, CA: New World Library.

Voss, R., Douville, V., Little Soldier, A., & Twyss, G. (1999). Tribal and shamanic-based social work: A Lakota perspective. *Social Work, 44*(3), 228–231. doi:10.1093/sw/44.3.228

Waters, A. (2004). *American Indian thought: Philosophical essays.* Malden, MA: Blackwell.

White, M., & Epston, D. (1990). *Narrative means to therapeutic ends.* New York: Norton & Company.

16 Mindfulness-based interventions de-reify self

DST clarifies a new therapeutic voice

Michelle H. Mamberg and Donald McCown

Group mindfulness-based interventions (MBIs) are educational courses in which participants learn formal meditation practices to develop new ways of being. Mindfulness-based stress reduction (MBSR), the earliest, most researched and most widely taught of these programs, was designed to help participants develop present moment, non-judgmental awareness via training in contemplative practices (Kabat-Zinn, 1990, 2009/2017; Santorelli, 1999). This highly experiential course uses an eight-week, semi-structured curriculum that weaves together dialogue about stress reactivity, a systematic body scan, mindful movement, sitting, walking, and loving-kindness meditations. Each of these practices employs some degree of focused concentration (e.g., upon breathing) and open monitoring of perceptions as they arise (Lutz, Slagter, Dunne, & Davidson, 2008). This MBI was widely adopted because its founder, Jon Kabat-Zinn (1990, 2003), advocated for objective assessment of the program's effectiveness.

The psychological literature is now replete with outcome studies validating MBSR as an adjunct to treatment in numerous clinical populations as well as for improved quality of life in non-clinical populations (Salmon et al., 2004; Salmon, Santorelli, Sephton, & Kabat-Zinn, 2009). This empirically supported program, used in conjunction with traditional medical and psychological interventions, has clear psychotherapeutic qualities and effects, yet, it is not a psychotherapy. Because MBIs were not designed exclusively for diagnosed patients, instructors are not expected to have clinical training. While MBIs are not seen as psychotherapies among clinicians (or insurers),[1] researchers have been keen to identify their therapeutic properties. For years, outcome research has looked for the intrapsychic "mechanism" (Kabat-Zinn, 2003; Shapiro, Carlson, Astin, & Freedman, 2006) of mindfulness (a single, hoped-for, seemingly secret, ingredient). Whether MBIs are viewed as psychotherapies or not, as clinical theorists we seek to identify the underpinnings of their psychotherapeutic benefits. Such understanding requires a new approach that clarifies the relational aspects of MBI pedagogy, moving away from narrowly mechanistic views of individuals, toward a theoretically sound framework.

Self in psychotherapy and mindfulness-based interventions

The MBI research and pedagogical literatures lack systematic articulation of key aspects of the major (Western) psychological approaches they incorporate. Since MBSR's creator (Kabat-Zinn, 1990) was a molecular biologist trained in meditation, rather than a clinician, he was not constrained by any particular psychological theory. Yet, as a product of the American zeitgeist of the late twentieth century, MBSR was steeped in the US cultural milieu. Psychotherapies of the day were generally related to one or more of five theoretical frameworks: psychodynamic, behaviorist, cognitive, humanistic, or existentialist. Within MBSR teacher training, too, this intentionally integrative program can be seen to reflect its cultural context: each of these psychological perspectives can be identified within the MBSR curriculum. It may be seen as a flowering of the best of all approaches: skillfully weaving together many threads, without allegiance to any one particular theory. Such integration made MBSR a novelty in the mental health field (psychiatry, psychology, and social work), as it was quickly dubbed the "next wave" in some quarters. Resonance with a variety of psychotherapy approaches may explain why so many clinicians embraced MBSR – its non-aligned approach not only broke down academic silos, but also fitted with significant aspects of most professionals' prior training, while offering something quite new.

It is from within this cultural context that we take up a dialogical perspective to tease out those novel aspects of the MBIs[2] that we believe make them therapeutic. Given their specific cultural context, how do MBIs reframe participants' self-experiences from those of the reductionistic, isolated self toward a contextualized, interactive self-as-process? Our purpose here is to argue that a key psychological component of the MBIs is to highlight the fluid processes of direct experience, thereby shifting participants away from self-reification. Dialogical Self Theory (DST; Hermans & Dimaggio, 2004; Hermans & Gieser, 2012; Hermans, Kempen, & van Loon, 1992) serves as a contextualizing theory (Freeman, 2014) through which we can review these therapeutic aspects of MBIs and the Buddhist psychological insights upon which they rest. Having articulated those theoretical connections, we use DST to facilitate an understanding of methods suited to analyzing the MBIs' therapeutic aspects.

A comprehensive overview of how the self has been constituted within psychotherapeutic theories was articulated by Cushman (1990) nearly three decades ago. As he described the "empty self" constituted by psychotherapy in the United States during the late twentieth century, the implicit indictment of the field was clear. American psychotherapy aimed to alleviate suffering, yet inadvertently perpetuated suffering by reifying an individualistic self. Steeped as it has been in consumerism, materialism, and superficial change, American psychology has yet to shift out of this paradigm to critique its own contribution to this decontextualized and increasingly alienated self. Hermans et al. (1992) noted then how a dialogical approach could address this problematic individualism by reconceptualizing self "as a dialogical narrator ... spatially organized and *embodied* ... [as well as] *social* ... resulting in a multiplicity of dialogically interacting selves" (p. 23, italics in original).

Contemporaneously, clinical researchers were noting that key psychotherapeutic mechanisms are the therapist's capacity to set a warm and non-judgmental environment, to listen with open attention, to validate the client's suffering, and to convey unconditional positive regard (Rogers, 1947). Without these common factors, assumed to undergird nearly all techniques (Frank & Frank, 1991), therapeutic progress is stunted. Also during this time, clinicians of all persuasions began integrating Eastern contemplative approaches (Epstein, 1995; Fromm, Suzuki, & DeMartino, 1960/1974; Linehan, 1987; Watts, 1961). On their own, merely exploring unconscious material, modifying behavior, or challenging the content of thoughts, were implicitly acknowledged as insufficient to reduce suffering. Despite psychotherapists having recognized the limits of individualism, academic psychology, via theories and research methodologies, increasingly reified the self. Psychotherapy became reduced to a clinician applying specific techniques to change the contents of a client's mind or alter behavior; this was accompanied by a drive toward manualizing treatments and focusing exclusively on symptom reduction in health care (Cushman & Guilford, 2000). In this context, MBIs arose, utilizing a humanistic and existential approach combined with an inherently relational discourse, offering participants new ways to meet their physical and psychological distress. Thus, MBIs return a potential for self-growth and a sense of agency to even the most demoralized clients (Frank & Frank, 1991). To understand how MBIs implicitly challenge Western psychological assumptions, we briefly review some conceptual underpinnings.

Non-self in Buddhist psychology

There has been widespread confusion about mindfulness in Western health care and the larger culture. Contrary to popular representations, meditation is not oriented toward "blanking out" thoughts or achieving perpetual bliss. Rather, the insight meditation taught within MBIs entails staying present with all experience, including disturbing thoughts, difficult emotions, and physical discomforts. Concentration on one domain of sensation is emphasized, usually focusing on an anchor (e.g., bodily sensations). Thoughts are neither suppressed nor avoided, but *related to* in new ways that de-emphasize their content, while prioritizing an exploration of the non-conceptual process of knowing (Gunaratana, 1996; Kabat-Zinn, 1990). Mindfulness practices encourage inquiry into, and acceptance of, all perceptual phenomena, whether pleasant, unpleasant, or neutral. Practitioners are encouraged to experience incoming sensory information, thoughts, and emotions *directly*, i.e., without assuming some stable self exists to mediate those states. By thus focusing attention, the meditation practitioner does not reject or cling to any sensation, rather each is observed to arise and dissipate. An attitude is adopted that is not merely non-judgmental, but is accepting, even embracing, of change. Meditation becomes practice for letting each self-story arise and pass away. In this way, formal mindfulness practice reduces attachment to self. Gunaratana (1996) captures the process well, depicting how discomfort engenders self-reification, whereas mindfulness dissolves the reified self:

You find yourself thinking of it as "the pain". That is a concept ... a label, something added to the sensation itself. You find yourself building a mental image, a picture of the pain ... Most likely, you will probably find yourself thinking: "I have a pain in my leg." "I" is a concept. It is something extra added to the pure experience.

When you introduce "I" into the process, you are building a conceptual gap between the reality and the awareness viewing that reality ... When you bring "me" into the picture, you are identifying with the pain ... If you leave "I" out of the operation, pain is not painful. It is just a pure surging energy flow ... If you find "I" insinuating itself in your experience of pain or indeed any other sensation, then just observe that mindfully.

(p. 132)

The Buddhist concept of *anatta*, non-self, describes a key aspect of the MBIs' therapeutic effect: perceiving the self not as an entity, but as a process. During meditation, practitioners observe transient moments of "selfing" (i.e., the fabrication of a fixed self; Olendzki, 2010), linking the reality of constant change to the inevitable realization that self is not permanent. Addressing the concept of impermanence, Gunaratana (1996) goes on to give mindfulness practitioners a way to think about the observational process:

Mindfulness is awareness of change ... observing the passing flow of experience. It is watching things as they are changing. It is seeing the birth, growth, and maturity of all phenomena. It is watching phenomena decay and die. Mindfulness is watching things moment by moment, continuously ... observing all phenomena – physical, mental or emotional – whatever is presently taking place in the mind. One just sits back and watches the show. Mindfulness is ... seeing how that thing makes us feel and how we react to it ... observing how it affects others. In Mindfulness, one is an unbiased observer whose sole job is to keep track of the constantly passing show of the universe within ... Mindfulness is participatory observation. The meditator is both participant and observer at one and the same time ... Mindfulness is not an intellectual awareness. It is just awareness ... Mindfulness is objective, but it is not cold or unfeeling. It is the wakeful experience of life, an alert participation in the ongoing process of living.

(p. 141)

Here the pronoun "one" depicts the observational process that we typically refer to as self. The sense of some unified entity managing experiences is deconstructed; the observer is not involved in mental content, nor is any perspective prioritized over others. Returning to the psychotherapeutic aspects of the MBIs, we contend that reified self-stories of clients as dysfunctional are challenged in the process of change. The open, accepting atmosphere found in all effective psychotherapies provides a context in which clients adopt a parallel discourse that is open to the fluid nature of self, accepting of one's challenges or weaknesses, and does not cling to ideas about how one "should" be. Through its assumptions of *anatta* and the impermanence of self, MBSR can be seen as having served as a practical intervention that helped precipitate a cultural shift out of modernist psychological theory towards acceptance of post-modern perspectives. Scholars now need alternative methods to explore such a dramatically different view of self. We propose a dialogical framework and discursive methods to shift Western psychology out of self-reification so as to better align with the assumptions inhering in mindfulness approaches (Stanley, 2008).

DST de-reifies self

DST (Gonçlaves, Konopka, & Hermans, Chapter 1 this volume) facilitates a clearer understanding of constitutions of self in context. Using this theory, we show how the MBIs bridged the gap between traditional psychotherapies and a post-modern constitution of selfhood. In addition to clarifying what makes MBIs therapeutic, integration of dialogicality within psychotherapeutic frames helps move the field away from its individualistic focus (e.g., Dimaggio, Ottavi, Popolo, & Salvatore, Chapter 10 this volume; Georgaca & Avdi, Chapter 11 this volume). MBIs de-reify self through dialogue, yet MBI research that is based in realist assumptions and positivist methods still reifies self. By providing the theoretical constructs to discuss de-reification, DST provides a framework for more fruitful research into MBI processes. Hermans (2004, 2011) describes a meta-positioning of "I as observer," which we see as capturing mindfulness practitioners' observing of direct experience. Recognizing this fluid taking up of varying *I*-positions maps on well to Gunaratana's (1996) mindful awareness. During meditation, practitioners watch the ongoing shifting of positions, from a neutral distance, without rigid identification with any one. The observing process itself may be variously termed *attention, awareness*, or *consciousness*. Western psychology has often collapsed observing processes into nouns, whereas DST prevents us from seeing such meta-positions (continual observation) as static. Mindful awareness, then, may best be seen as perpetual "de-positioning": the process of taking up and letting go of various (meta-)positions can be noted directly, in the moment. Hermans-Konopka (2012), in her exploration of emotions from a DST perspective, coined the term "*I*-prison," which can logically be expanded to the reified self as a whole, in persons who are unable to de-position, to deliberately leave positions, or are otherwise locked into a constrained and inflexible story of a unitary, unchanging self. DST terminology thus provides a language for describing the process of mindful awareness, without risk of reification. DST and MBIs both employ discourses aimed at moving beyond limited and limiting, conceptual self-stories in order to point to the process of directly experiencing the phenomenological flux.

Similarly, DST is inherently social, relational, and discursive. When Hermans and Gieser (2012), building on Hermans' earlier works, framed DST as a bridging theory, they were in essence creating a space for psychological theorizing in which the interiorized self of Western psychology could be seen as inherently interactive while, in parallel, society would be seen as an ongoing dialogue of mind(s). The implications they saw were that "changes and developments in the self automatically imply changes and developments in society at large and reversed ... self and society are not mutually exclusive but inclusive" (p. 2). Their landscape metaphor, a spatialization of mind as interiorization of discourse into a multiplicity of positions, resonates with MBI classroom dialogues known as *inquiry*. These teacher-directed discussions treat all present as "thou," in Buber's (1958/1970) sense; participants learn to treat each *I*-position as a thou within, even those an observing-I might disown. Much as in psychotherapy, then, MBI practitioners interiorize what Cooper (2004) has called an "I–I ... mode of self-relating" (p. 62). Classroom discourse that de-reifies self is taken up as participants accept and dispassionately explore the phenomenological flux through a friendly lens. Morioka (2015, Chapter 14 this volume) has used the Japanese word, *ma*, to describe the open space and time characterizing therapeutic dialogues in which clients and therapists move toward meaning reconstruction. He focuses on the observing meta-position as integral to understanding forward movement in therapy; MBI classrooms provide similar space for practitioners to integrate a process approach to their varied momentary experiences. Relatedly, Neimeyer and Buchanan-Arvay (2004) and Neimeyer and Konopka (Chapter 8 this volume) integrate DST with a meaning reconstruction model where psychotherapy supports dialogue with lost others. Grief work yields re-integration of the relationship disrupted by the loved one's death. Such a therapeutic approach resonates with how the social and discursive space created within the MBI classroom is adopted by practitioners, reducing reification by highlighting how distress-inducing self-positions can be met in kinder, more flexible ways.

Additionally, Bertau's work (2007, 2014) offers the concept of *voice*, conveying an interiorized aspect of the embodied nature of positioning. Her dialogical framework provides a language to examine the inherently social nature of speech, allowing us to treat the talk of practitioners and of meditation instructors as together instantiating a larger social discourse, embedded in a particular context. The pedagogy outlined by McCown, Reibel, and Micozzi (2010) instantiates a voice that challenges participants' conditioned notions of self-as-entity in the open, yet highly focused, community of an MBI group (McCown, 2013). By continually noting momentary sensations and the ephemeral nature of thoughts and emotions, teachers voice acceptance of all that occurs. They highlight non-self, which practitioners then cultivate through contemplation of ever-changing experience. Attitudes of open acceptance and curiosity displayed in meditation guidance and classroom inquiry develop practitioners' de-positioning capacity. In this way, we consider the teacher's de-reification of self to serve as a *promoter position* (Hermans & Hermans-Konopka, 2010). Interacting with a teacher who relates to her own and others' experiences without recourse to a fixed self, practitioners interiorize her way of being: a promoter of self-as-process. Throughout the program, numerous brief interactions enable them to become familiar with prioritizing the fluid process of de-positioning rather than identifying with any particular *I*-position.

Discursive-dialogical methods examine the MBI voice

DST's formulations of mind as a society or a landscape challenge traditional conceptualizations of the self as a decontextualized entity with fixed qualities (e. g., ongoing coherence or unity through time). Since the framework reveals how MBIs bridged twentieth-century psychology's individualistic notions of self to the Buddhist concept of non-self, we propose using dialogical and discursive methodologies to examine first-person empirical data about how mindfulness is learned. Discursive analyses grounded in DST provide an alternative, non-reductive, research methodology to better examine the relational nature of self-hood imbued in the MBIs. We suggest three approaches to studying MBIs dialogically: (1) discursive analyses of practitioners' talk, (2) explication of the languaging found in guided meditation instructions, and (3) examining classroom inquiry dialogue. Such qualitative methods depict the MBIs' therapeutic aspects, which shift practitioners' typical reification of self toward formulating self-as-process. A voice unique to the MBIs de-reifies the self embedded in traditional psychology by creating a dialogical space of friendliness toward human suffering.

Discursive analyses of mindfulness practitioners' talk

As the MBIs were increasingly researched during the 2000s, and small outcome studies were replaced by larger randomized controlled trials, an imbalance in the scholarly literature became apparent. Grossman (2011) cogently critiqued the quantitative assessment inventories then in vogue (and still in use today); his concerns about their unclear definitions of mindfulness and assumptions within their methods, paved the way for more qualitative approaches. Unfortunately, many of these retained the reductive approach to self seen in quantitative, third-person research. In response, we combined content analysis (Charmaz, 1995) and discursive approaches (Edwards & Potter, 1992; Harré & Gillett, 1994) to examine interviews with MBSR practitioners. By studying micro-narratives, participants' retrospective accounts of how they learned mindfulness meditation were explored with particular attention paid to self-portrayals, resulting in explication of an "MBSR voice" (Mamberg & Bassarear, 2015, 2016). Participants reported deriving benefits from dialoguing with their own intentions to cultivate mindfulness, intentions observed to shift over time (Field, Mamberg, & Bassarear, 2014). The teacher's engaged presence and encouragement of discussion was deemed pivotal to helping participants develop mindful awareness (Mamberg, Bassarear, & Schubert, 2013). These close examinations of practitioners' accounts then clarified a concept unique to mindfulness studies: *reperceiving* (Shapiro et al., 2006). This term depicts practitioners' development of a novel, slightly distanced, relationship toward their own reactivity, wherein experiences are recognized as momentary, rather than treated as qualities of oneself (Mamberg, Madonna, & Bassarear, 2017). Reperceiving captures how practitioners come to notice the constant moving beyond positions, gaining broader perspective of their own experiences; DST theorists would consider this de-positioning.

By examining this MBSR voice taken up by practitioners, these studies differentiated that voice from typical American discourse about cognitions and behavior and interviewees' languaging varied from monological and reified to more dialogical and fluid portrayals of self (Mamberg & Bassarear, 2015). A developmental sequence was laid out that ran from rigidly fixed self-portrayals (e.g., absolute language, first-person pronouns) to a de-reified self seen in more developmentally advanced statements (e.g., awareness conveyed without recourse to a personal pronoun). This research program captured how teachers' languaging promotes a formulation of self-as-observer that is taken up quickly and persists after the course has ended. If there is a 'mechanism' of mindfulness, it appears to be the capacity to move fluidly in and out of varying *I*-positions without reifying any given position.

The languaging of guided meditation instructions

Verbal mindfulness meditation instructions repeat and rehearse (i.e., practice) the flexible shifting of attention from one's automatic selfing to the process of noting sensory experience. Language is employed that encourages participants to take up more compassionate and accepting ways of relating to their thoughts, emotions, and sensations. Formal mindfulness practice highlights the universal human predilection to resist change, thus emphasizing that meditators are connected to each other and a larger community of practitioners. This community shares a dedication to maintaining awareness that the conditioned self is not an entity and a present moment recognition of self-stories being no more than mere thoughts. How does this occur?

MBI pedagogy entails specific languaging of meditation instructions; MBI teachers' verbal and nonverbal guidance conveys an open and accepting approach to experience. To understand how practitioners might interiorize such discourse, a particular guided meditation was examined as a text. The body scan is a 45-minute, sequential exploration of different body regions in which participants are encouraged to carefully observe all physical sensations, and to note the affective valence attached to each, as well as judgmental cognitions arising in response to those sensations (Dreeben, Mamberg, & Salmon, 2013). Discursive analysis of the instructor's languaging highlighted aspects not previously articulated in the scholarly literature. Beginning with the assumption that teaching is dialogical – that teachers implicitly frame the selves of learners and encourage the taking up of specific self-portrayals – the research question, "How is the practitioner's self portrayed in the body scan instructor's discourse?" was applied to a transcript of Kabat-Zinn's recorded body scan (Mamberg, Dreeben, & Salmon, 2014). As with all MBI guidance, instructors lead the body scan while attending to their own experience of bodily sensations in the moment, rather than by relying on a script. Unique features of MBI discourse were identified in Kabat-Zinn's recorded guidance, which systematically direct practitioners toward awareness of self-as-process and thus subvert reification. Three discursive patterns were identified: *inclusivity*, where plural pronouns ("we," "us," "our") de-emphasized separation between instructor and practitioner; *process focus*, where definite articles ("*the* breathing" or "*an* awareness of") replaced "your," emphasizing the observing agent; and *actions without agents* where present participles replaced both possessive pronouns ("breathing" in place of "your breath") and imperatives ("noticing," rather than "now notice how"), de-emphasizing the self by minimizing the sense of an observer who prefers some sensations or rejects others.

Describing these discursive patterns clarifies the relational nature of de-reification. Guided meditation instructions might appear to be a monologue simply spoken by a teacher, but they are inherently dialogical. As the participants listen to and interiorize the spoken guidance, they meet each arising of thought or sensation in the ways languaged by the instructor. From a DST view, MBI instructions create the context for a new voice through which self-reification is challenged. Cushman's (1990) point was that psychotherapists unwittingly perpetuate a culturally conditioned reification of self, but MBI instructors intentionally use language to 'un-self' their participants.

Classroom inquiry dialogue

Beyond interviewees' talk and meditation instructions, the MBI voice can be seen explicitly in classroom discussions. The importance of the teachers' and participants' co-creation of an ethical space has been reviewed elsewhere, detailing MBI pedagogy and the unique micro-culture that emerges in each MBI classroom (McCown, 2013, 2017; McCown & Ahn, 2015). The inter-related concepts of *guidance* (i.e., meditation instructions) and *inquiry* (teacher-led discussions) frame how class discourse allows participants to relate to their experience in an open, non-evaluative and non-reifying way. Crane et al. (2015) conducted conversation analyses of MBI inquiry, which displayed this emergent culture. MBI discourse was seen to impact participants' self-construals and systematic analyses revealed

> how turn-taking happens and how the teacher reformulates participant contributions; particular participant competencies that are being trained through dialogue; and the atmosphere of affiliation that is created through the process of interaction in the group ... [as well as] the complexity of the interactional work that MB[I] teachers are engaged in when leading participatory dialogue.
>
> (Crane et al., 2015, p. 1113)

This nascent line of research examining MBI classroom dialogue displays how participants' discourse changes as this unique voice is taken up through practice. Here, the DST approach contributes to understanding empirically how the teacher's languaging serves as a promoter position to encourage de-reification of self. Whether attending to meditation instructions or engaging in post-meditation inquiry dialogues, MBI participants are afforded an opportunity to develop a new position that promotes non-self and recognizes fluidity of *I*-positions.

This embeddedness of the meditation practices and inquiry in the classroom context has been examined in depth by McCown and Reibel (2017), using Gergen's (2009) notion of *confluence*, a discursive community that creates an ethical space (McCown, 2013). To demonstrate, we provide a case example (McCown & Billington, 2017) that conveys how the confluence of the group enacts MBI pedagogy. Within class inquiry, participants are given space to approach and stay with aversive experiences. In the extract that follows, Jessica (pseudonym) and her MBSR instructor discuss her anxiety. Presenting only the two-person dialogue risks de-contextualizing their exchange from the larger ethical space in which it is embedded, however we reproduce portions of their interchange here to note that despite differing from psychotherapy, the interchange still facilitates what certainly appears to be a therapeutic moment. Jessica is encouraged to observe an aversive experience with curiosity and gentleness. The teacher's guided inquiry enables Jessica to articulate her experience without pathologizing, fixing, or reifying the *I*-position that is anxious.

T: So, Jessica, are you still noticing some anxiety?
J: Some, yeah.
T: If you bring attention to your body right now, can you feel where that anxiety is showing up? Just take your time and feel into it.

As might well occur within standard psychotherapies, this focusing on the aversive feeling is presumed to be locatable in the body as a sensation that can be observed and reported, from some distance, where the participant can dis-identify from it. As we saw in the body scan recording, personal pronouns are used primarily with regard to location within the body and the positioning of participant-observer, but they are not attached to anxiety (nor any psychological causes of it). Generic referents ("*some* anxiety," "*that* anxiety") are contrasted to her perspective ("are *you* noticing," "if *you bring* attention"), identifying anxiety as separate from the awareness noticing it. The suggestion to "take time" invites the valuing of *ma*, the space of not-knowing, encouraging a new way to relate to anxiety. The slow, patient, careful investigation of a scientist conveys that objectivity and a neutral curiosity can be brought to bear on this experience.

J: In my back. That's where it's been a lot recently. It sort of moves around.
T: Can you bring your attention there? And see what you find out about that feeling?
J: That's scary, but I'll try … [pause] ok, I am … I'm paying attention.
T: And what is the feeling like?
J: It's like, constricted … tight.
T: Do you know anything more? Like how big the area is, or, maybe, what shape it is?

Having readily identified a location in the body where the anxiety is apparent, Jessica is asked to explore subtle sensations even more precisely. Her statement "that's scary" goes unacknowledged as the instructor uses silence to convey patience, giving time and space for Jessica to observe and articulate physical sensations in detail.

J: It's a rectangle, about this big [raises fingers several inches apart], in the center of my back. It's really tight.

T: Ok, you're right there with it ... I wonder if you can find a way to give it a little room, to open some space around it? Maybe you can use your breath to soften around it ... [pause] Can your breath go to that part of your back when you breathe in? Do you know what I mean?

J: I think so ... Yeah.

T: So when you breathe in, letting some space open up around that rectangle ... and when you breathe out, letting it stay soft ... What more do you know about that spot now? Anything?

J: It's gotten smaller, much smaller ... It's like the size of my finger now.

T: So it changed ... You gave it space and it stopped taking up so much space in you.

Spatial language concretizes diffuse sensation while allowing Jessica to relate to it differently, enlarging *ma* rather than attempting to eradicate or interpret away her anxiety. Cognitivist MBI researchers would label Jessica's insight a moment of reperceiving. Dialogical theorists may frame it as her adopting the MBI voice provided during inquiry. Our example captures how a discursive approach enables us to better understand this voice in its inherently dialogical context.

Implications for psychotherapy and MBIs

As MBI teachers, it has been our goal to demonstrate how DST can help psychologists let go of outdated Western individualist self-constitutions, in order to recognize the relationality of mindfulness that undergirds the numerous benefits shown across diagnostic populations and institutional contexts. To articulate an MBI voice, we delineated three DST-based methodologies: (1) discursive analyses of mindfulness practitioners' talk, (2) examining the languaging of guided meditation instructions, and (3) classroom inquiry dialogue. We sought to show that MBIs reduce suffering and are therapeutic (i.e., enhance healing from physical or psychological distress) because a shared relational space is co-created in which practitioners' language their experience, moment to moment, thus de-reifying self. DST enabled us to articulate how the therapeutic benefits of mindfulness practice derive from dis-identifying with self in order to observe its arising – what MBI teachers would frame as gaining insight into *anatta*.

In contrast to traditional psychology, DST is uniquely suited to clarifying the therapeutic processes within the micro-culture of the MBI classroom. Through language selected to portray selfing as a flow of ever-changing experiences, MBI practitioners "re-mind" themselves and others to stay with the phenomenological flux, without judging, avoiding, or solidifying experience. MBIs provide a therapeutic space by instantiating openness, friendliness, and hospitality to each of the participants, particularly when they show little toward themselves. The MBI teacher, holding a promoter position that can be interiorized, exemplifies the potential to be with whatever arises, thus conveying the opportunity for liberation from old conditioned habits and the *I*-prison of over-identification with one's thoughts or emotional states.

Meta-positioning, parallel to mindful awareness, connotes the capacity to flexibly shift among a multiplicity of *I*-positions. This means observing one's reactivity without reifying the observing position. Both MBIs and DST assume healthy self-constitution is a complex process, marked by flexibility to take up and put down multiple perspectives (*I*-positions) without getting stuck (*I*-prison). Letting go of over-attachment to a single, simplified self-position is psychotherapy's implicit goal, whereas it can be seen more explicitly in the MBIs.[3] As psychotherapy process research continues to utilize DST (Cooper, 2004; Gonçalves, 2016; Gonçalves & Ribeiro, 2012; Martínez & Tomicic, Chapter 12 this volume), and as MBI pedagogy continues to examine the confluence of classroom culture (McCown, 2016), the relational-contextual nature of both psychotherapy and MBIs is becoming clearer.

If, indeed, psychotherapeutic benefits of MBIs derive from interactions that de-reify self and focus awareness on the de-positioning process, we suggest teachers be trained more explicitly in such dialogical development of an MBI voice. MBI instructors will benefit from seeing this voice as a *telos* toward which practice instructions and inquiry might fruitfully be aimed. A clear understanding of how MBIs convey mindfulness is needed to train teachers who are both confident and competent. Seeing these dialogical aspects of MBIs will facilitate assessment of competencies in would-be mindfulness teachers. Indeed, future research may show discursively observable markers that could distinguish skilled versus unskilled teachers-in-training. If MBI teachers are taught through a reductionist, overly cognitive, individualistic lens, they will struggle to understand how the group format and specific languaging allow for the ethical space to develop, let alone how it may shift self-portrayals. Without the contextual understanding of non-self, insufficiently trained teachers could inadvertently reduce mindfulness to simply sitting still on a cushion, calming the autonomic nervous system.

A second implication of our work, then, is that it be applied to MBI teacher training. The teacher's own mindfulness practice is not simply a matter of practicing what we preach: it is only through continual recognition of de-positioning, of shifting out of his own reifying discourse, that an instructor can adjust his language so as not to reify self in classroom dialogues. Only through cultivating compassion for her anger, will an MBI teacher be able to language for participants how they might be more hospitable to their own. A DST framework facilitates deepening MBI pedagogy by recognizing that teaching mindfulness cannot be decontextualized from the language and social interaction in which it occurs. We are only just beginning as a culture of academics, clinicians, and teachers to recognize the tectonic perspective shift involved in practicing mindfulness, let alone in bringing it into a culture with deeply held realist assumptions in which self is not only reified, but glorified. DST language shifts us out of the dualism of self and other in our scholarship, re-conceptualizing the MBI classroom as an incubator for detecting how we constitute otherness within ourselves and thus expanding our capacity to detect ourselves in others' experience.

Quantitative and physiological explorations of MBI outcomes will continue to have their place, but without updated conceptualizations of voice, self-as-process, and dialogical inquiry to propel its development, MBI pedagogy could stagnate. Bringing DST to MBI scholarship and pedagogy discards the misrepresentation that mindfulness resides in individual brains. The relational and discursive focus provides new ways to discuss how mindfulness is co-created via group interaction. By adopting a DST framework, future research will be able to take the structural and cultural features of MBIs into account, thus better highlighting how dialogue that de-reifies self sustains mindful awareness.

Notes

1 Mindfulness-based cognitive therapy (MBCT; Segal, Williams, & Teasdale, 2002/2013) is a notable exception: it was developed to prevent relapse in severely depressed clients, requires clinical training, and has been included in the UK National Health Service guidelines.
2 Throughout the rest of this chapter, we will primarily focus on MBIs as the overarching term, referring to the specific MBSR program, when relevant.
3 Additionally, just as DST enhances MBI conceptualization, dialogical theory may benefit from further examination of mindfulness. MBIs' emphasis on embodied experience at a micro-level allows us to examine the process of positioning and de-positioning, moment to moment.

References

Bertau, M.-C. (2007). On the notion of voice: An exploration from a psycholinguistic perspective with developmental implications. *International Journal for Dialogical Science, 2*(1), 133–161.

Bertau, M.-C. (2014). Introduction: The self within the space-time of language performance. *Theory and Psychology, 24*(4), 433–441.

Buber, M. (1958/1970). *I and Thou: A Translation with a prologue "I and You" and notes.* W. Kaufmann (Trans.). New York: Scribners.

Charmaz, K. (1995). Grounded Theory. In J. A. Smith, R. Harré, & L. van Langenhove's (Eds.), *Rethinking methods in psychology* (pp. 27–49). London: Sage.

Cooper, M. (2004). Encountering self-otherness: 'I-I' and 'I-Me' modes of self-relating. In H. J. M. Hermans & G. Dimaggio (Eds.), *The dialogical self in psychotherapy.* (pp. 60–73) New York: Brunner-Routledge University Press.

Crane, R., Stanley, S., Rooney, M., Bartley, T., Cooper, L. & Mardula, J. (2015). Disciplined improvisation: Characteristics of inquiry in mindfulness-based teaching. *Mindfulness, 6*(5), 1104–1114.

Cushman, P. (1990). Why the self is empty. *American Psychologist, 45*(5), 599–611.

Cushman, P. & Guilford, P. (2000). Will managed care change our way of being? *American Psychologist*, *55*(9), 985–996.

Dreeben, S., Mamberg, M. & Salmon, P. (2013). The MBSR body scan in clinical practice. *Mindfulness*, *4*(4), 394–401.

Edwards, D. & Potter, J. (1992). *Discursive psychology*. London: Sage.

Epstein, M. (1995). *Thoughts without a thinker*. New York: Basic Books.

Field, J., Mamberg, M. & Bassarear, T. (2014, October). Mindfulness-based stress reduction participants describe why they meditate. Poster presented at the New England Psychological Association Conference, Lewiston, Maine.

Frank, J. D. & Frank, J. B. (1991). *Persuasion and healing: A comparative study of psychotherapy* (3rd ed. Baltimore, MD: Johns Hopkins University Press.

Freeman, M. (2014). A theory for our time, size medium. *Theory and Psychology*, *24*(5), 728–730.

Fromm, E., Suzuki, D. T. & DeMartino, R. (1974). *Zen Buddhism & psychoanalysis*. New York: Harper & Row. (Original work published 1960)

Gergen, K. (2009). *Relational being: Beyond self and community*. New York: Oxford University Press.

Gonçalves, M. (2016). Innovative moments in psychotherapy: A dialogical research program. Paper presented at the Ninth International Conference on the Dialogical Self, John Paul II Catholic University, Lublin, Poland.

Gonçalves, M. & Ribeiro, A. (2012). Therapeutic change, innovative moments, and the reconceptualization of the self: A dialogical account. *International Journal for Dialogical Science*, *6*(1), 81–98.

Grossman, P. (2011). Defining mindfulness by how poorly I think I pay attention during everyday awareness and other intractable problems for psychology's (re)invention of mindfulness. *Psychological Assessment*, *23*(4), 1034–1040.

Gunaratana, H. (1996). *Mindfulness in plain English*. Somerville, MA: Wisdom Publications.

Harré, R. & Gillett, G. (1994). *The discursive mind*. Thousand Oaks, CA: Sage.

Hermans, H. J. M. (2004). The dialogical self: Between exchange and power. In H. J. M. Hermans & G. Dimaggio (Eds.), *The dialogical self in psychotherapy* (pp. 13–28). New York: Brunner-Routledge.

Hermans, H. J. M. (2011). The dialogical self: A process of positioning in space and time. S. Gallagher (Ed.) *Oxford handbook of the self* (pp. 654–680). Oxford: Oxford University Press.

Hermans, H. J. M., & Dimaggio, G. (2004). *The dialogical self in psychotherapy*. New York: Brunner-Routledge University Press.

Hermans, H. J. M., & Gieser, T. (2012). *Handbook of dialogical self theory*. Cambridge, UK: Cambridge University Press.

Hermans, H. J. M., & Hermans-Konopka, A. (2010). *Dialogical self theory: Positioning and counter-positioning in a globalizing society*. New York: Cambridge University Press.

Hermans, H. J. M., Kempen, H. & van Loon, R. (1992). The dialogical self: Beyond individualism and rationalism. *American Psychologist*, *47*(1), 23–33.

Hermans-Konopka, A. (2012). The de-positioning of the *I*: Emotional coaching in the context of transpersonal awareness. In H. J. M. Hermans & T. Gieser, *Handbook of dialogical self theory* (pp. 432–453). Cambridge, UK: Cambridge University Press.

Kabat-Zinn, J. (1990). *Full catastrophe living: Using the wisdom of your body and mind to face stress, pain, and illness*. New York: Dell.

Kabat-Zinn, J. (2003). Mindfulness-based interventions in context: Past, present and future. *Clinical Psychology, 10*(2), 144–156.

Kabat-Zinn, J. (2017). *Mindfulness-based stress reduction (MBSR) authorized curriculum guide.* Revised and edited by S. Santorelli, F. Meleo-Meyer, & L. Koerbel. Center for Mindfulness in Medicine, Health Care and Society. www.umassmed.edu/cfm/training/mbsr-curriculum. (Original work published 2009)

Linehan, M. (1987). Dialectical behavior therapy for borderline personality disorder: Theory and method. *Bulletin of the Menninger Clinic, 51*(3), 261–276.

Lutz, A., Slagter, H., Dunne, J. & Davidson, R. (2008). Attention regulation and monitoring in meditation. *Trends in Cognitive Sciences, 12*(4), 163–169.

McCown, D. (2013). *The ethical space of mindfulness in clinical practice: An exploratory essay.* Philadelphia, MA: Jessica Kingsley Publishers.

McCown, D. (2016). Stewardship: The deeper structures of the co-created group, in D. McCown, D. Reibel, & M. Micozzi (Eds.) *Resources for teaching mindfulness: An international handbook.* New York: Springer.

McCown, D. (2017). A new hope. In L. Monteiro, R. Musten, & J. Compson's (Eds.), *A practitioner's guide to ethics in mindfulness-based programs.* (pp. 1–20) New York: Springer.

McCown, D. & Ahn, H. (2015). Dialogical and Eastern perspectives on the self in practice: Teaching mindfulness-based stress reduction in Philadelphia and Seoul. *International Journal of Dialogical Science, 9*(1), 39–80.

McCown, D. & Billington, J. (2017). Correspondence: Sitting and reading as two routes to community. *Journal of Contemplative Inquiry, 4*(1), 165–185.

McCown, D. & Reibel, D. (2017). *Pedagogy in the MBIs: An international exploration.* Presented at the Third Conference of the Center for Mindfulness Research and Practice, Chester, UK.

McCown, D., Reibel, D. & Micozzi, M. (2010). *Teaching mindfulness: A practical guide for clinicians and educators.* New York: Springer.

Mamberg, M. & Bassarear, T. (2015). From reified self to being mindful: A dialogical analysis of the MBSR voice. *International Journal of Dialogical Science, 9*(1), 11–37.

Mamberg, M. & Bassarear, T. (2016). Voicing mindfulness-based stress reduction: A developmental-dialogical analysis. Paper presented at the International Conference on the Dialogical Self, John Paul II Catholic University, Lublin, Poland.

Mamberg, M., Bassarear, T. & Schubert, A. (2013, April). "So, how did you learn to practice mindfulness?": A qualitative interview study. Poster presented at the Eleventh Annual Scientific Conference of the Center for Mindfulness, Norwood, MA.

Mamberg, M., Dreeben, S. & Salmon, P. (2014, October). The languaging of MBSR's body scan: Cultivating self-as-process. Poster presented at the Mind and Life Institute's International Symposium for Contemplative Studies, Boston, MA.

Mamberg, M., Madonna, J., & Bassarear, T. (2017, October). Articulating an MBSR voice: A dialogical self theory analysis of re-perceiving in practitioners' interviews. Poster presented at the Fourth Biannual Psychology and the Other Conference, Cambridge, MA.

Morioka, M. (2015). How to create *ma* – the living pause – in the landscape of the mind: The wisdom of Noh theater. *International Journal of Dialogical Science, 9*(1), 81–95.

Neimeyer, R. & Buchanan-Arvay, M. (2004). Performing the self: Therapeutic enactment and the narrative integration of traumatic loss. In H. Hermans & G. Dimaggio (Eds.), *The dialogical self in psychotherapy* (pp. 173–189). New York: Brunner-Routledge.

Olendzki, A. (2010). *Unlimiting mind: The radically experiential psychology of Buddhism.* Somerville, MA: Wisdom.

Rogers, C. (1947). Some observations on the organization of personality. *American Psychologist, 2,* 358–368.

Salmon, P., Santorelli, S., Sephton, S. & Kabat-Zinn, J. (2009). Intervention elements promoting adherence to mindfulness-based stress reduction (MBSR) programs in a clinical behavioral medicine setting. In S. Shumaker, J. Ockene, & K. Riekert (Eds.), *The handbook of health behavior change* (3rd ed. (pp. 271–286). New York: Springer.

Salmon, P., Sephton, S., Weissbecker, I., Hoover, K., Ulmer, C. & Studts, J. (2004). Mindfulness meditation in clinical practice. *Cognitive and Behavioral Practice, 11,* 434–446.

Santorelli, S. (1999). *Healthy self: Lessons on mindfulness in medicine.* New York: Three Rivers Press.

Segal, Z., Williams, M. & Teasdale, J. (2013). *Mindfulness-based cognitive therapy for depression: A new approach to preventing relapse* (2nd ed. New York: Guilford Press. (Original work published 2002).

Shapiro, S., Carlson, L., Astin, J. & Freedman, B. (2006). Mechanisms of mindfulness. *Journal of Clinical Psychology, 62*(3), 373–386.

Stanley, S. (2008). From discourse to awareness: Rhetoric, mindfulness, and a psychology without foundations. *Theory and Psychology, 23*(1), 60–80.

Watts, A. (1961). *Psychotherapy East and West.* New York: Pantheon.

17 Epilogue
Looking back and forward

Hubert J. M. Hermans, Agnieszka Konopka, and Miguel M. Gonçalves

Arriving at the end of the rich variety of chapters, it is time to look back to what we have achieved in this book and look forward to some future perspectives as promising ways to go. With this purpose in mind, we will focus on three main questions: (a) What is the specific contribution of Dialogical Self Theory (DST) to the field of psychotherapy? (b) Which aspects of this theory make it particularly suitable to be applied in a variety of psychotherapeutic approaches? and (c) Are there neglected areas that deserve particular attention in future research and practice?

Specific contribution of DST

The best way to characterize DST is to qualify it as a 'bridging theory' that offers a new and broad conceptual platform on which different therapeutic schools and approaches from different cultural origins can meet and learn from each other, where they can discuss their commonalities and differences, and where they can explore new ideas.

In order to explicate what we mean by a 'bridging theory', it should be emphasized that DST is neither an integrative nor an eclectic approach (see Norcross & Goldfried, 2005; Palmer & Woolfe, 2013). Whereas integration suggests that the elements are part of one combined approach to theory and practice in which different approaches are synthesized, eclecticism draws ad hoc from several psychotherapeutic systems in the treatment of a particular case. DST is not integrative because it does not pretend to create one integrative theory in which the different approaches are components of a superordinate and synthesizing conceptual system. It is also not eclectic because, instead of bringing different theories and practices together on an ad hoc basis, it aims to connect different therapeutic traditions and schools in a theory-guided way. Instead of providing an integrative or eclectic psychotherapeutic framework, DST offers an original and specific system of concepts (e.g. *I*-position, meta-position, promoter position, centralizing, and decentralizing movements in the self) which function as conceptual bridges enabling practitioners and researchers to move to and fro between independent therapeutic schools or traditions and even stimulate a dialogue between their different perspectives. As the contributions in this book have demonstrated, DST concepts are broadly applicable beyond the boundaries of the presented approaches.

A bridging theory adds three main advantages. First, there is no necessity or desirability to 'force' different approaches into one integrative framework. Existing theories and practices are fully recognized and appreciated as autonomous systems of thought and there is no need of selecting parts of them as constituents of a new, superordinate theoretical system. Second, as a bridging theory, DST is able to link a larger diversity of therapeutic approaches than is usual. Here we touch a weakness of existing integrative approaches. It is our contention that, in a situation of growing diversity of psychotherapeutic schools, the Achilles heel of integrative approaches is their limited scope. For example, Anthony Ryle's (1996/2005) model of cognitive analytic therapy is an attempt to integrate ideas from psychoanalytic object relations theory and cognitive psychotherapy. Another example is Paul Wachtel's model of cyclical psychodynamics that integrates psychodynamic, behavioural, and family systems theories (Wachtel, Kruk, & McKinney, 2005). Typically, integrative systems integrate two or three approaches and, as a consequence, they have a limited theoretical and practical scope. DST doesn't aim to add another integration, but has the purpose to link a broader range of existing therapies by offering a meta-theoretical level where dialogical relationships between them can be established. In this way, DST creates communication channels between a larger diversity of existing therapies, including non-mainstream psychotherapeutic perspectives like Buddhist-inspired (Konopka & Van Beers, Chapter 13), indigenous (Mehl-Madrona & Mainguy, Chapter 15), and transpersonal (Rowan, Chapter 6) approaches. As these chapters exemplify, DST contributes to transcending existing cultural boundaries (see also Morioka, Chapter 14 on Japan and Martínez & Tomici, Chapter 12 on Chile). Third, as a broad-span theory, DST offers not only a link between a diversity of therapeutic schools of different cultural origins, it also bridges between psychotherapy as a field and other scientific disciplines and sub-disciplines, like cultural psychology, cultural anthropology, educational psychology, and psychopathology (see Hermans & Gieser, 2012). The broad-span perspective of DST as a bridging meta-theoretical perspective has the potential of creating conceptual linkages between therapy and other fields in psychology and outside. Research findings in these fields may broaden and enrich existing therapeutic practices and dialogues between established schools.

Which aspects of DST make it useful as a bridging theory?

The fact that the most central notion of DST, *I*-position, was applied in all chapters of the book underpins DST's bridging quality across therapeutic schools and cultures. What is the basis of its bridging capacity? An *I*-position is a spatial-relational act. It exists only in the context of other positions (e.g. I position myself as open in relation to a cooperative other and as closed towards an aggressive other). The act of *I*-positioning is placing oneself vis-à-vis somebody else and, at the same time, toward oneself in the metaphorical space of the self.

As a spatial-relational process it is taking a stance toward somebody, either physically or virtually, and it is a way of addressing the other and oneself via verbal or non-verbal orientations and communications. In the act of *I*-positioning there is always a 'here' and a 'there', both in the communication with the other and in the communication with oneself. Between this here and there, a field of tension is stretched in which one makes, physically or virtually, movements from the one to the other and back. When I take a stance towards, from, or against the other, this coexists with (or is followed by) a similar or dissimilar movement in the metaphorical space of my own self. I appreciate myself, when I had a productive talk with my colleague, and I criticize myself when I made a stupid remark during a conversation with my superior. Like between self and other, there are fields of tension between *I*-positions within the self. In both cases, continuous processes of positioning and counter-positioning are taking place and these processes are basically spatial and relational. As the different chapters of this book demonstrate, these processes are applicable across widely different therapeutic approaches: cognitive (Dimaggio, Ottavi, Popolo, & Salvatore, Chapter 10; Lysaker, Hamm, Leonhardt, & Lysaker, Chapter 7; Stiles, Chapter 5), psychoanalytic (Georgaca & Avdi, Chapter 11; Martínez & Tomicic, Chapter 12), narrative (Gonçalves et al., Chapter 9; Morioka, Chapter 14), Gestalt (Staemmler, Chapter 3), constructivist (Neimeyer & Konopka, Chapter 8), emotion-focused (Whelton & Elliott, Chapter 4), mindfulness (Mamberg & McCown, Chapter 16), Buddhist-inspired (Konopka & Beers, Chapter 13), indigenous (Mehl-Madrona & Mainguy, Chapter 15), and transpersonal (Rowan, Chapter 6). This variety illustrates the boundary-crossing nature of the *I*-position as an open, flexible, and non-specific concept.

The process of *I*-positioning is not only spatial but also temporal, as expressed by the dual concepts of positioning and repositioning. Positions are not to be conceived as stabilized, reified entities but as involved in a continuous process of transition and change from one position to another position, from open to closed and back, from sad to happy and back, from tense to relaxed and back. When such transitions are blocked and the self is not able to make a movement from a position associated with negative emotions to one with positive emotions, the *I*-position changes finally into an *I*-prison. An *I*-position has an entrance and an exit. When the self becomes locked up in an *I*-prison, there is an entrance but no exit. In an adaptive self, positions have entrances and exits open enough to permit a flexible process of positioning and repositioning. From the DST perspective, a dysfunctional self is maladaptive as the flexible process of positioning and repositioning is blocked. In a most general way, psychological dysfunctions can be described as problems in the organization of the position repertoire. Psychotherapy aims at transforming a maladaptive organization of the self into an adaptive one. As demonstrated in the chapters of this book, processes of positioning and repositioning are, like positioning and counter-positioning applicable across a diversity of psychotherapeutic approaches.

The organizational structure and dynamic nature of the dialogical self are further expressed by some other DST concepts that are widely applied in different chapters of the book. Meta-positions enable the self to take a helicopter view on the content and organization of a broader range of more specific positions so that adaptive and maladaptive patterns can be discerned, discussed, and changed. Promoter-positions can be implemented in the service of the integration of specific positions from past, present, and future, which gives direction to the development of the self as a whole. Of pivotal importance for psychotherapy is the distinction between centripetal and centrifugal movements in the self, the latter working in the direction of multiplicity and diversity and the former creating order and integration (for a more elaborate discussion of meta-positions, promoter positions, and centripetal and centrifugal movements, see Konopka, Hermans, & Gonçalves, Chapter 2).

The intrinsic social and relational nature of DST is further reflected in the distinction between internal and external positions in the self. Whereas internal positions refer to the inner domain of the self (e.g. I as trustful, I as humorous, I as pessimistic), external positions represent others-in-the self (e.g. my father, my children, my opponent). Such external positions refer not only to significant others in the client's social environment, but also to imagined or imaginary figures, like ancestors or mythological beings that populate one's experiential world (see Mehl-Madrona & Mainguy, Chapter 15). Many people have a relationship with invisible others, like gods, spirits, saints, or angels (see Rowan, Chapter 6). In the course of psychotherapy and even later, the psychotherapist may play his or her role as 'other-in-the self' in the self of the client and may even serve there as a promoter position. The other in the self is well in agreement with the general empirical finding in psychotherapy research that the quality of the relationship between client and psychotherapist is paramount.

Neglected areas and future directions

Overseeing the variegated landscape of chapters in this book, we nevertheless note that there are some 'neglected areas' that lead us to formulate some future directions in DST informed theories and practices. In this final section, we focus on three topics: (a) attention to the non-verbal aspects of the self; (b) taking into account recent developments in brain research; and (c) the need for acknowledging not only the maladaptive aspects of dysfunctions but also their adaptive features.

Attention to the non-verbal and embodied aspects of the self

In his preface of a special issue on self and dialogue, Stam (2010) proposed that future studies on self and dialogue devote attention not only to what is said but also to what is not said. This recommendation touches the well-known finding that in face-to-face communication, non-verbal cues, including body language, are even more influential than verbal aspects. However, the latter ones are in need of more attention, not only in this book, but in DST research in general (for notable exceptions, see the Compositionwork method by Konopka & Beers in Chapter 13 and Gieser's (2006), research on 'shape shifting').

From a theoretical point of view, the concept *I*-position potentially encompasses both conscious and less conscious aspects of the self, where the latter can gradually evolve from bodily experience that is not immediately verbalized or defined to more conscious and explicit levels. Accessing and expressing such unspeakable aspects of the self is crucial in psychotherapy as a source of possible new, transforming meanings (see Rowan, Chapter 6 on the unconscious, Neimeyer & Konopka, Chapter 8 on grief and Whelton & Elliot, Chapter 4 on emotions).

Closely related to non-verbal processes in psychotherapy is the well-known observation that there are clients who say that they want to change, but on a less conscious level resist this change at the same time. This observation challenges the seemingly self-evident assumption that the self is always involved in change and development. However, this assumption does not sufficiently take into account an important phenomenon that is generally discussed under the label 'resistance to change', In their book *Immunity to Change*, Kegan and Lahey (2009) demonstrate that resistance to change does not always reflect active opposition or passive inertia. Instead, even people who are sincerely committed to change on a conscious level, may unwittingly invest energy toward a hidden competing commitment that blocks the change that they consciously aspire. In DST terms, there are nonconscious *I*-positions that are not accessible because they are separated from conscious *I*-positions so that dialogical relationships between them are impeded. Insight in the dynamics of verbal and conscious *I*-positions on the one hand, and non-verbal and non-conscious *I*-positions on the other hand, is required to uncover hidden maladaptive patterns in the organization of the self. Basically, DST assumes that the self is spatialized, localized, and embodied. However, more research is required that permits access to non-verbal and bodily aspects of the self and more methods should be developed that stimulate dialogical relationship between its conscious and non-conscious domains.

Developments in brain research

Closely related to non-verbal and non-conscious processes in the self, are recent developments in brain research. The direct connection between neurological evidence and psychotherapy is particularly relevant to understanding what happens in the non-verbal domain. A recent example of this connection is Schore's (2012) research on the workings of the right hemisphere of the brain and its relevance to the communication between psychotherapist and client. He argues that the right hemisphere, more than the left, provides efficient cortical–subcortical and brain–body communication channels and is also heavily involved in self–other relationships. On the basis of collected evidence, he shows that empathy, humour, compassion, and morality are primarily mediated by the right hemisphere of the brain. In this context, he discusses the existence of 'right brain-to-right brain communication' (p. 7) that develops between therapist and client in those regions of their brain where knowledge operates in rapid, unconscious ways beneath levels of awareness. When such knowledge accumulates, it is spontaneously expressed in the form of intuition. This shifting emphasis into the direction of emotion, intuition, and unconscious knowing seems to be highly relevant to future DST research. The reason is that this shift coincides with a move from a classical one-brain neuroscience into the direction of a 'two-body approach' referring to processes taking place between two embodied participants involved in communication.

In his book *Society in the Self: A Theory of Identity in Democracy*, Hermans (2018) draws on recent developments in brain research in developing a model in which meta-positions function as 'meeting areas' where dialogical processes are taking place between self and other and between conscious and non-conscious *I*-positions.

Attention to adaptive aspects of dysfunctions

We recommend that future DST research pays attention to not only the maladaptive aspects of dysfunctions but also to its adaptive qualities. It is commonplace to notice that what is dysfunctional in a particular period of history is accepted as normality in another period. Dysfunctions can become identities. Homosexuality, originally considered to be a psychiatric disorder was finally accepted, at least in some countries in the world, as a normal identity. What was originally labelled as 'gender identity disorder' became later integrated in some societies as transgender identities. Apparently, dysfunctions are culturally relative and subjected to historical changes.

In psychiatric and psychotherapeutic circles we witness tendencies to give more attention to the adaptive aspects of dysfunctions originally considered as maladaptive aberrations from normality that just had to be cured or removed. Narcissism is a suitable example of research that has distinguished maladaptive and adaptive expressions. The narcissistic personality inventory (NPI; Raskin & Terry, 1988) includes scales of exploitativeness (e.g. 'I find it easy to manipulate people'), entitlement (e.g. 'I insist on getting the respect that is due me'), and exhibitionism (e.g. 'I get upset when people don't notice how I look when I go out in public'). These scales refer to maladaptive behaviour based on their associations with poor social adjustment. On the other hand, items from scales labelled authority (e.g. 'I see myself as a good leader') and self-sufficiency (e.g. 'I like to take responsibility for making decisions') have been considered relatively adaptive based on their shared relations with self-confidence and assertiveness (Barry, Frick, Adler, & Grafeman, 2007). A similar reasoning applies to other constructs, like perfectionism, see (Hewitt & Flett, 1991).

Another example of increased attention to the adaptive–maladaptive distinction can be found in research on autism. In his study on the relationship between autism and creativity, Fitzgerald (2004) notes that usually people with autism are characterized by communication problems, difficulties in social relationships, repetitive activities and routines, and an obsessive narrow range of interest. More unexpectedly, historical figures like Ludwig Wittgenstein, Lewis Carroll, Hans-Christian Anderson, William Butler Yeats, and many others, reveal classic autistic features that they apparently combine with excessive forms of creativity. People diagnosed as having an autism spectrum disorder often develop an intense interest in a particular subject and can display a strong attention to detail, focus, precision, and tenacity in working on a task that captures their interest.

The combination of adaptive and maladaptive features of dysfunctions is particularly significant to future DST research and practice. From a theoretical point of view this complex combination fits very well with the idea that a dysfunction can be considered as a dynamic multiplicity of *I*-positions in the self as a society of mind. The combination and integration of adaptive and maladaptive positions has the potential of inciting dialogical relationships between both types of positions so that they can learn from each other to their mutual benefit. Each position, considered to be dysfunctional, can be seen, from a DST perspective, as a dynamic process placed in a broader context of a socially and historically situated position repertoire, not as a separate or reified entity. The cultural relativity of dysfunctions and their change across historical periods underscore the self as a society of mind as it is, at the same time, participating in the society at large.

As editors of this book, we hope that our proposals will benefit not only future research and practice but also increase the awareness that psychotherapies (although their number and variety have increased dramatically in the past decades) have more in common than their underlying theoretical systems would suggest.

References

Barry, C. T., Frick, P. J., Adler, K. K., & Grafeman, S. J. (2007). The predictive utility of narcissism among children and adolescents: Evidence for a distinction between adaptive and maladaptive narcissism. *Journal of Child and Family Studies*, *16*, 508–521.

Fitzgerald, M. (2004). *Autism and creativity: Is there a link between autism in men and exceptional ability.* New York: Brunner & Routledge.

Gieser, T. (2006). How to transform into goddesses and elephants: Exploring the potentiality of the dialogical self. *Culture and Psychology*, *12*, 443–459.

Hermans, H. J. M. (2018). *Society in the self: A theory of identity in democracy.* New York: Oxford University Press.

Hermans, H. J. M., & Gieser, T. (2012). *Handbook of dialogical self theory.* Cambridge, UK: Cambridge University Press.

Hewitt, P. L., & Flett, G. L. (1991). Dimensions of perfectionism in unipolar depression. *Journal of Abnormal Psychology*, *100*, 98–101.

Kegan, R., & Lahey, L. L. (2009). *Immunity to change: How to overcome it and unlock potential in yourself and your organization.* Boston, MA: Harvard Business Press.

Norcross, J. C., & Goldfried, M. R. (Eds.) (2005). *Handbook of psychotherapy integration* (2nd ed.). New York: Oxford University Press.

Palmer, S., & Woolfe, R. (Eds.) (2013). *Integrative and eclectic counselling and psychotherapy.* London: Sage.

Raskin, R., & Terry, H. (1988). A principal-components analysis of the narcissistic personality inventory and further evidence of its construct validity. *Journal of Personality and Social Psychology*, *54*, 890–902.

Ryle, A. (2005). Cognitive-analytic therapy. In J. C. Norcross & M. R. Goldfried (Eds.), *Handbook of psychotherapy integration* (2nd ed., pp. 196–217). New York: Oxford University Press. (Original work published 1996.)

Schore, A. (2012). *The science of the art of psychotherapy.* New York: Norton.

Stam, H. (2010). Self and dialogue: Introduction. *Theory & Psychology, 20*, 299–304.

Wachtel, P. L., Kruk, J., & McKinney, M. (2005). Cyclical psychodynamics and integrative relational psychotherapy. In J. Norcross & M. Goldfried (Eds.), *Handbook of psychotherapy integration* (2nd ed., pp. 172–195). New York: Oxford University Press.

Index

For Product Safety Concerns and Information please contact our EU
representative GPSR@taylorandfrancis.com
Taylor & Francis Verlag GmbH, Kaufingerstraße 24, 80331 München, Germany